CRASH AND BEYOND

Crash and Beyond

Causes and Consequences of the
Global Financial Crisis

ANDREW FARLOW

OXFORD
UNIVERSITY PRESS

OXFORD
UNIVERSITY PRESS

Great Clarendon Street, Oxford, OX2 6DP,
United Kingdom

Oxford University Press is a department of the University of Oxford.
It furthers the University's objective of excellence in research, scholarship,
and education by publishing worldwide. Oxford is a registered trade mark of
Oxford University Press in the UK and in certain other countries

First Edition published in 2013

Impression: 1

British Library Cataloguing in Publication Data

Data available

ISBN 978-0-19-957801-6

Printed in Great Britain by
Clays Ltd, St Ives plc

In memory of my mother,
Margaret Jean Farlow,
and with gratitude to my father,
William Kenneth Farlow

PREFACE

Who would have believed it? By now we are accustomed to mid-crisis life—and yet, had this book been published just five or so years ago, its author would have been roundly condemned as completely and utterly mad. Its fanciful speculation about the future, and not its sober reflection on the past, would have been a danger to the banking system and to all those whose lives depend upon it. Back then, we were living in the best of times, the season of light. The consensus of educated opinion was that we were wise too. Never before had we had such sophisticated financial models to predict and, some said, to control the future. We had everything before us, even Heaven—which in those days, by recent convention, meant economic stability—itself. By day, gentle words of 'no more boom and bust' mesmerized and numbed our senses. By night we slept soundly, safe in the knowledge that never again would we be plunged into such frightening economic nightmares.

But the nightmares did not stay away. Slowly at first, then surely, they swept back in. One by one, our delusions were washed away. Millions watched on helplessly as their savings, and income from savings, sank, debts spiralled, and homes fell in value. Unemployment became the daily curse of many, austerity the grim reality of most. It gradually dawned that in our past we had squandered our future, and that in our future the reward of our every effort, and that of our descendants, would be eaten away by debt repayments and higher taxes as far as our eyes could see. Our hopes had turned to doom, our dreams had turned to dust. We had been willing participants not in an age of wisdom, but in an age of folly. We had sipped on lies and we had liked them. We had asked for more and we had been given it. Greed and credulity had been our bedfellows. And now we were going to pay.

President Obama seemed to understand this. In February 2009, in his first address to a joint session of Congress, he declared, 'We have lived through an era where too often, short-term gains were prized over long-term prosperity; where we failed to look beyond the next payment, the next quarter, or the next election. A surplus became an excuse to transfer wealth to the wealthy instead of an opportunity to invest in our future. Regulations were gutted for the sake of a quick profit at the expense of a healthy market. People bought homes they knew they couldn't afford from banks and lenders who pushed those bad loans anyway. And all the while, critical debates and difficult decisions were put off for some other time on some other day. Well that day of reckoning has arrived, and the time to take charge of our future is here.'[1] Then again, he could say such things; the past belonged to someone else.

In the United Kingdom, where the writing of this book was underway, the past belonged to those still in power—at least for a little bit longer. In mid-2010, in the midst of a general election campaign, according to focus-group evidence—for that is the way we do sound public policy these days—the average voter was not unlike a sick patient pondering through a dizzy haze three smartly suited surgeons in the hope that the illness would be less severe, and the cure less painful, if only the one with the nicest prognosis and the most reassuring smile could be picked. Astonishingly, with the country rapidly heading towards a government debt of a trillion, in the last televised debate before the election the three protagonists batted back and forth just six of those thousand billions. Nastier medicine was on the way, but talking about it now would only scare the patient.

By the middle of 2012, as the book went to press, the truth was out. It was not a pretty sight. In the United States, with a Presidential election fast approaching, the Tea Party, on flights of peculiar economic fantasy, had made inroads into Obama's vote. In the UK, a coalition government was engaging in the biggest ever experiment in UK peacetime austerity, and the economy was dipping its toes back into recession. Europe was tearing itself to pieces because of its seemingly irreconcilable economic and political contradictions. And China and a range of emerging economies were starting to wonder whether the next crash had some of their names scribbled all over it.

The causes and consequences of the recent crash are multi-dimensional, entangled like a ball of string, layered like an onion. Yet a book can only be written in a linear fashion. We have to prise the individual bits apart, stretch them out, pin them to the page—one after the other—and, sometimes with tears in our eyes, try to make sense of the blur. I have done this by separating material into three parts with a preface and some closing thoughts to seal the ends and keep the material from falling out.

Part I looks at the causes of the crash. Some go back forty years, others proliferated in less than ten. Of special interest are the interacting weaknesses in the financial and economic systems. For the crash was as much of economies as it was of banks.

Part II, no sadder than the first but hopefully just as informative, tells the story of the crash and of the efforts made to save the banking system.

Part III—half the book—looks at how policymakers set about rescuing their economies and the unemployed, dealing with collapsing housing markets, tackling long-term sovereign debt difficulties, handling the eurozone crash, managing global instabilities, and reforming monetary policy, financial regulation, and banking. It is both a chronicle and an analysis of the events and of the thinking of these years.

Throughout I strive to be critical but fair. Yet, since I know that there is nothing more irritating than a thoroughly balanced argument that is not the least bit opinionated, I will try to take a position as and when I feel the evidence supports it.

Of the many themes running through the book, one is an evaluation of President Obama's economic presidency. It would not be unfair to say that Obama arrived equipped for a very different kind of presidency to the one thrust upon him when the global banking system collapsed just weeks before his election. Arriving without the requisite economic and financial skills, how did he cope? Another is a necessary corrective to the account of the crash by former UK finance minister and prime minister Gordon Brown, published at the end of 2010, which glossed over the many failures that led to disaster for the UK. In contrast to Obama, for thirteen years Brown positioned himself as 'an expert renowned for his remarkable financial acumen . . . Long admired for his grasp of economic issues'.[2] Yet, in his account, Brown described the crash as a complete surprise to him, and even accused banks of tricking him. Surely, posterity will record that when it comes to financial acumen and the grasp of economic issues, Brown was not modest but had much to be modest about. Merkel, Sarkozy, Berlusconi, Cowen, Wen Jiabao, Papandreou and others will get their moments in the spotlight.

These days it is de rigueur for commentators to claim prescience of the events of the crash. It would be remiss of me to break from such an agreeable new tradition. To my advantage—and unlike some who threw themselves into the bright lights in their shiny new chameleon hues—a series of papers on which I base my own modest claim can be readily found online, placed there a few years before the crash.[3] In those papers I did not buy the story that we were living in the best of times, the season of some shimmering new economic light. In the first paper I tried to pick apart the explanations given for recent rapid rises in house prices, especially, but not exclusively, in the UK.[4] The prevailing justification was that the world was now so much more stable, real (i.e. adjusted for inflation) interest rates so much lower, and credit constraints so much reduced that a permanently higher level of house prices was the rational and decent way to go. I could not make the logic work and it worried me. In the second paper I argued that house buyers, and the banks supplying them with their credit, were pumping a bubble that one day would collapse.

It seems I was not alone. In 2010, out of the blue, and not requested by me, I was sent a small package, the result of a Freedom of Information request to the office of the British prime minister. It transpired that—by the deft hand of Martin Wolf of the *Financial Times*[5]—the logic of those papers had reached in and twanged a raw, if rather brow-beaten and somewhat sedated, economic nerve in the head of the British Prime Minister of the day, Tony Blair. As part of a power-sharing deal, Blair had long ago relinquished all but the tiniest crumbs of economic policy to his finance minister, Gordon Brown. Even Blair's 2010 autobiography does not deal with the economy until its postscript, written after the crash. There never had been a British prime minister so blissfully unengaged in the economic affairs of the nation. Or so it had seemed.

It turned out that Blair, breaking momentarily from habit, was sufficiently worried that he immediately sought advice from the UK Treasury. As a parable of the way economic decisions were made in the UK a few years before the crash, a substantial (by the standards of such things) briefing paper duly arrived at the door of Number 10,[6] and gently reassured the prime minister that all his fears were unfounded. As one journalist put it, '[I]t turns out Blair was rather more worried about the state of the economy than you might have thought . . . It underlines the simple fact that the Treasury under Gordon Brown was blind to the possibility that things could go horribly wrong—even within the confines of Downing Street. It turns out no-one was allowed to challenge the "end to boom and bust" trope—even Tony Blair himself.'[7] In the Irish parliament, the two papers triggered a question about the state of the Irish economy. Didn't this indicate that the Irish housing market and the Irish economy were heading for a crash? Irish prime minister Bertie Ahern, like Brown a self-styled economic visionary, had taken to labelling naysayers as 'cribbers and moaners', and he and his colleagues were having none of it. It is always nice to hear that people in high places get to hear one's views. It is a little less encouraging to know that it doesn't make the slightest jot of difference.

In 2005 I wrote a third paper in which I made a number of arguments that, according to various banking colleagues, economists, and journalists, turned out to be highly prescient in the light of what was to come. I was, as it were, one of the few to join up all the dots. To borrow an analogy from the music industry, the papers were an instant hit. The head of my department's IT unit expressed astonishment at the extremely high number of downloads in one year of just those three papers. The general public was interested. Wouldn't it be exciting to hear that Blair and others were too? Indeed, as Blair revealed for the first time in his autobiography, this was the time of greatest pressure from his supporters to sack Brown. He did not because in his view Brown 'was the best chancellor for the country', and having Brown 'inside and constrained was better than outside and let loose'.[8]

Just for the record, and to frame the thinking in this book, this seems the appropriate place to review the arguments I made a few years before the crash that attracted such interest. After all, this book gains some of its credibility from such a background. The reader can read the original papers for themselves; by agreement with the Oxford University Press, the content of this book is totally new so that those papers can stay available online. Having waited patiently for several years, I hope the reader will pardon me my little peccadillo. If nothing else, it might encourage the casual browser to make his or her purchase, an act that I can assure them will, in these straitened economic times, be very good for the economy.

Like many others, I identified the unsustainable imbalances in the global economy in the years before the crash, in particular between China and the US. I discussed the increasingly unbalanced nature of economies such as those of the US and the UK, as unsustainable levels of debt and property-based bubbles generated their apparent economic 'success' stories. I argued that extremely low interest rates and heavy banking competition had encouraged the rising indebtedness of banks, the 'chasing of yield', and the mispricing of risk on a global scale, with large levels of speculative investment in mortgage markets and housing, exploiting the belief that house prices could not fall. I argued that, on the contrary, property-market risk was being grossly underpriced. I also discussed the vulnerability of many US mortgages. Low interest rates could have encouraged productive investments, but I argued that all too often they had not.

I warned that house-price bubbles made financial firms' balance sheets look healthier than they truly were, falsely suggesting an ability to take on much more risk, while giving consumers an illusion of greater wealth than they really had, distorting their spending and saving decisions. I suggested that the effect of the implicit government guarantee of the US mortgage industry was being spread outside the borders of the US. I argued that holders of mortgage-backed securities (MBSs) needed to continuously roll over their positions, and that sooner or later this would not be possible. I discussed the various directions from which the crisis—essentially a bank run—might come, including from falling house prices, rising interest rates, and a reversal of bubble-generated low volatility. I explained how financial contagion would spread to the rest of the world via, in particular, mortgage bank and government balance sheets, and with it real economic contagion. Many were worrying about the imbalances between the US and China, but fewer had spotted that the real danger of a crisis was lurking in the US banking system. Indeed, it was not at the time by any means the conventional wisdom.

I described how, in response to the collapse of the equity-based bubble that expanded over the 1990s, policymakers had fed a debt-based bubble in the 2000s. I argued that debt-based bubbles are much more dangerous than equity-based bubbles, because of the underlying properties of debt. Eventually the burden would be shifted to sovereign (that is government) debt. I urged therefore a reduction in the government budget deficit[9] of economies such as those of the US and the UK to help give more of a cushion to deal with the impact when it came. I identified in particular the poor ability of UK public finances to withstand a crisis that was likely to be particularly severe in its impact on the UK (previously, I had written too about the long-term fiscal problems of the US).[10]

I contended that the past mispricing of assets and of risk would leave many households in countries such as the US and the UK with too much debt and too little saving, including savings in their pension funds. I noted that when the downswing came, the efforts of households to correct their 'balance sheet' mistakes by saving more and deleveraging (i.e. scaling down their debts relative to their asset worth) would coincide with governments finding themselves much more fiscally burdened by the shifting of the consequences of the collapsing bubble onto *their* shoulders and needing to support demand in their economies by running larger fiscal deficits. I argued that inflation had morphed from traditional measures based on goods and service prices into measures based on asset prices, in particular house prices, that when standard interest rate tools were unable to go below zero per cent unconventional monetary policy would be needed, and that recovery would be complicated by the knife-edge balance between inflation and deflation in a balance sheet recession. I concluded that failure to take early action was feeding imbalances that would become ever more difficult to unwind, and that policymakers were simply pushing off a 'day of reckoning' and by doing so making that day much worse.

A fourth and fifth paper were in the pipeline, about 80% complete, dealing with the risk and liquidity problems in global property and mortgage markets.[11] At that point I wondered why I should release these for free when the evidence suggested there would be good sales if all could be combined in a book. But 2006 was quite unlike 2007 and even less like 2008. The academic publisher I approached politely wondered if there would be a market for a book about a crash that had not happened, especially one involving such a prominent role for the US. The trade publisher proposed something 'hard-hitting' (could I 'do left-wing polemic'?) and thought it helpful to suggest that I write under a *nom de plume*. I did not have the standing to take the ridicule of academic colleagues or to be seen as a maverick, and a pseudonym would be the kiss of death in academia. The book went on hold.

My inbox filled up with invitations—they sit there still, polite witnesses to a more innocent era—Lehman Brothers, Credit Suisse First Boston, UBS, Goldman Sachs, the Bank of England, the Financial Services Authority (FSA), HM Treasury, and various US policy think tanks. There were hedge funds and others wondering if I might be interested in making a buck or two when the housing market crashed. However, I was getting increasingly involved in the field of 'global health'. Given my concerns about the state of the global economy, the recent financial flows into global health were vulnerable, and, it seemed to me, the efficiency and financial sustainability of global-health initiatives needed to be improved. Over just a few years I wrote about three-quarters of a million words on various areas of global-health policy and took a series of stands that, though often painful at the time, eventually started to bear some fruit.

In August 2008, a few weeks before the collapse of Lehman Brothers, the book shot up the agenda again. A group of investment bankers arranged a meeting with me in London in which they explained how the original papers had spread by word of mouth through their company following the financial collapse over 2007 and early 2008 along lines I had described. All summer long they had struggled without success to get the UK Treasury and the office of Prime Minister Brown to take the dangers seriously and recapitalize the banking system. In the US, a presidential election campaign had raged all year and there was no chance of action there. They urged me to get back to writing the book. With evidence at last that the exercise would be worth it, and thinking that the prescience of the prior papers would help sell a copy or two, the delegates of the Oxford University Press commissioned the book.

Usually, by the time historians pan the murky streams of time, at least some of the particles of evidence have settled to the bottom. When John Kenneth Galbraith produced his book on the 1929 crash, he had the good sense to wait 25 years.[12] Freidman and Schwartz published their analysis of the monetary policy mistakes that followed the crash of 1929 a thoroughly sensible 34 years after it.[13] Surely only a foolhardy person would write a book when events are still spinning? We live in a different era. These days the just-in-time media presence at the scene of the latest financial crash generates a veritable avalanche of instant data and analysis. Every dimpled, crumpled, jagged edge of the wreck gets gawped at, photographed, and written about, and then it's on to the next exciting story even before the full consequences of the last one have fully settled in. We will know a great deal more in five or ten years about exactly what happened and why. By then, econometricians will have processed the life out of every speck of data that passed through every ministry of finance in the world, through umpteen rounds of refinement that will have polished them into permanently stable lines and columns on a graph. But the time to learn the lessons and change direction is now.

I wish to extend my huge appreciation to colleagues and friends in Oxford and especially in Oriel College. I am enormously grateful too to all at the *Wissenschaftskolleg zu Berlin*, where I spent the academic year 2010–2011, for their generosity and kind hospitality. Maintaining my sanity while writing the book had much to do with being surrounded by a truly wonderful group of fellows, partners, and families. The OUP economics and production editors, in particular Sarah Carro, Adam Swallow, Aimee Wright and Kizzy Taylor-Richelieu, deserve very special thanks. They repeatedly, and graciously, went well beyond the call of duty. Every time they panicked that the crisis would be over long before I made any sales, I simply reassured them with the rather unprepossessing proposition that I knew enough about crashes, and this one in particular, to know that its consequences were going to drag out for years on end, and that—when I was being especially eloquent—watching and reflecting upon policy responses was a timely and even wise strategy.

All financial crashes have been compared to that of 1929. One suspects that in time this crash will take on some of the mantle of the 1929 crash. Maybe this will be for good reason—because policymakers handled it in some respects better than that one. But it might also be because this one turns out to be a great deal more intractable, and marks a turning point in our understanding of global capitalism. Or perhaps we will have done the usual, and forgotten the lessons until next time.

Oxford and Berlin   *June 2012*

CONTENTS

Part I

Before

Global Imbalances and the Rise of Debt

The Great Moderation Myth

On 4 December 1928, in his final State of the Union address, President Calvin Coolidge, looking back over 150 years, observed that 'No Congress of the United States ever assembled, on surveying the state of the Union, has met with a more pleasing prospect than that which appears at the present time. In the domestic field there is tranquillity and contentment...and the highest record of years of prosperity.' As Coolidge was speaking, the US stock market was approaching its zenith and, within a year, its nadir, the crash of 1929, and the economic infamy of the 'Great Depression'. The US economy would contract by nearly 30% from peak to trough. Unemployment would soar until one in four in the US was without work. Thousands of banks would collapse with little or no protection for tens of millions of savers. Up to three-quarters of all mortgage holders in the US would default. Monetary policy would be contractionary, as the US strapped itself tightly to the gold standard, and deflation would set in. Many countries would respond with trade protectionism; by 1933 US trade was 33% of its pre-crash level.[1] Taxes would be raised and government spending cut to balance the books, as the US economy dug itself into an even deeper hole. Before the crash, Coolidge had made a virtue out of inertia; as journalist Walter Lippmann observed in 1926, 'This active inactivity suits the mood and certain needs of the country admirably.'

On 16 March 2005, in his budget speech to Parliament, the UK's finance minister, and subsequent prime minister, Gordon Brown—not the sort ever knowingly undersold—declared, 'Britain is today experiencing the longest period of sustained economic growth since records began in the year seventeen hundred and one.'[2] He praised 'Britain and North America that have over the last eight years grown at twice the rate of most of our G7 competitors, our living standards also rising twice as fast'. He rebuked the French, Germans, and, for good measure, Americans for their lackadaisical employment records. He gallantly deflected the warnings of the International Monetary Fund (IMF), Bank for International settlements (BIS), and the Organization for Economic Cooperation and Development (OECD), and defied all who had made 'predictions of a recession—predictions wrong in 1997, wrong in 1998, wrong in 1999, wrong again in the years from 2000 to now'. Even as Brown was speaking, the banks of the global financial system were bulging ever closer to bursting point and a flood that would scour and transform the global financial landscape forever. Within a couple of years, like a dropped ball of string atop a very steep hill, the UK's economic 'success' story would be unravelling fast, with Brown chasing and struggling to catch it.

Perhaps presidents and prime ministers get a bit carried away at times? A touch hubristic perhaps? A hazard of the job maybe? A more useful observation is that both Coolidge and Brown *could* point to economic data to support their claims, if only with just the right angle of light and the occasional bit of torture to make the data confess—and their views were not out of line with the mood and certain needs of their times. We now know that there was something about the very fact that they *could* say such things that should have warned us that something was wrong. Many of the 'good' signs—vibrant stock markets, record rates of economic growth, and rapidly rising house prices—were themselves signs that risks were increasingly being stored up like energy in a spring. Truly, it was both the best of times and the worst of times. Fancy sat right next to fact, abundance to austerity, pleasure to pain.

In economic circles the justification for such high hopes was known as the 'Great Moderation', a phrase coined by Ben Bernanke in 2004[3] to describe the 'remarkable decline' of inflation and output volatility in the US and other developed economies (though not, by then, Japan) over the previous 20 years.[4] Bernanke argued that rather than structural change or 'luck'—by which he meant a pattern of shocks that had been unusually fortuitous but which would not last—'improvements in the execution of monetary policy can plausibly account for a significant part of the Great Moderation'. That is, policymakers should take the credit.

Lower inflation volatility improves the functioning of markets and makes economic planning more certain. Lower output volatility makes employment and income more stable, which reduces economic uncertainty to households. In a world of lower macroeconomic volatility, households and financial firms could feel more confident that interest rates, and therefore loan repayments, would be more stable, and the holding of debt less risky. They *could* increase the ratio of the stock of their debts to the stock of their assets—that is, more heavily leverage their balance sheets.[5] House prices *could* take a heady journey upwards, given a helping hand by financial innovations. Equity prices *could* surge on the back of rising productivity thanks to lower macroeconomic risk. The all-time one-off gains of the Great Moderation could be amortized in one giant leap in asset prices and a matching rise in the level of sustainable debts.

We notice straight away that even this 'rational' explanation implies only a transitional period, when rates of growth of asset prices and debt temporarily surge on the path to their new higher levels, and not that they climb vertiginously skywards for ever. Sadly, human nature is not very good at dealing with economic transitions. In experimental economics, supposedly rational human guinea pigs, who look as though they have come out of the cold attracted by no more than the promise of a cup of tea and the chance of a small financial reward, get caught up in the momentum of group psychology that takes them way beyond any rationally 'efficient' level. Besides, for those motivated to do so, there are rich pickings in convincing the more gullible, or simply the less well informed, that momentum will take them higher. Even if the Great Moderation was a true phenomenon, there was always the danger that humans would overreact.

There was also the danger of misinterpreting temporary flow-based phenomena as something far more permanent. The Soviet growth surge of the 1950s and 1960s worried the West into thinking that the USSR would 'overtake' it. It is popularly believed that this galvanized the US into going to the moon as a statement of political and economic virility. We now know that the surge in Soviet growth was almost entirely a statistical property of the mobilization of large flows of capital, including human capital (with a generous dose of exaggeration by officials). Because there were only so many workers who could be shifted from agriculture into factories and only 24 hours in a day, without a productivity breakthrough, growth would fall back when the mobilization ended. Similarly, a large proportion of the Asian economic 'miracle' of the early to mid-1990s was caused by the shifting of labour from the countryside into urban areas, including a huge increase in the average number of hours worked.[6] The phenomenon attracted much praise from international bodies, and investment banks flooded in to share the spoils. But the phenomenon inevitably passed. In the 2000s, in countries like the US and the UK, a range of flows—the shifting of consumption from future generations to the current generation, re-mortgaging into falling interest rates, and forms of borrowing based on property price rises—temporarily boosted measured performance, yet had their natural limits.

But had the business cycle really been tamed? Was lower macroeconomic volatility a true and permanent fixture of the new economic order? The problem was that rising debts, debt-fuelled asset price bubbles, and global imbalances that got ever more stretched, could for a while create the low volatility on which such suppositions of moderation were built. The first big global imbalance was in patterns of trade and current accounts (which measure the net *flows* over a period of time, usually a year, of the following: exports and imports; interest, profits, and dividends on holdings of assets; and transfers[7]). The US for years ran a persistent current account deficit (meaning that its debits exceeded its credits) that rose from a little over 3% of US GDP at the end of the 1990s to a peak of 6% of US GDP in 2006. Between the end of the Asian financial crisis of 1997–1998 and mid-2007, the cumulative current account deficit of the US totalled about $4.6 trillion. At its height, the US accounted for more than two-thirds of all the world's current account deficits. Since the balance of payments always balances, the current account deficits of the US were matched by changes in official reserve holdings of, and capital flows into the US from, surplus countries. The surplus countries included China, other emerging Asian economies, major manufacturing exporters such as Germany and Japan, and oil-exporting countries. By such munificence China and Asia ended up financing at least half of the US current account and budget deficits; but they were not the only ones.

Such flows were not a gift to the US. The US was able to consume, year after year, beyond its domestically-generated output only because others were amassing a stock of claims against it. Little did ordinary Americans seem to notice or even care, and their political leaders had little incentive to draw their attention to it. It is the stocks, and not the flows, that cause the headaches. First, if there is a sudden loss of investor confidence in a country with large outstanding stocks of claims against it, it is the total stock of claims that is at risk of being withdrawn. Second, if any assets that get purchased by the surplus country turn out to be of much poorer quality than first believed, losses on them will, like a nasty virus, spread and harm the surplus country too.

Instead of investing in real foreign assets, many of those running current account surpluses, especially China, invested in foreign currencies that they held in their central banks as foreign-exchange reserves. Remarkably, China was running both a current account surplus *and* a capital account surplus, by fixing the nominal exchange rate between its currency, the renminbi, and a basket of currencies linked to the US dollar. It soaked up any excess demand for renminbi (of those in the US and elsewhere buying China's goods and services who needed to exchange their currencies for renminbi to make their purchases) by having the People's Bank of China (PBOC) issue fresh renmimbi to buy the US dollars. The PBOC added the dollars to its already large pile of foreign-exchange reserves.

By the summer of 2007, total global foreign-exchange reserve holdings had gone from $1.6 trillion (dollar equivalent) at the time of the Asian crisis, to about $6 trillion, with US dollar reserves rising from about $800 billion to $2.5 trillion. Asia accounted for 80% of the increase and held about 70% of the total global stock of reserves.[8] In the pre-1971 Bretton Woods fixed-exchange-rate regime, global reserve holdings had never exceeded 2% of global GDP. Now it was 9%. Meanwhile, according to the US Treasury, the gross external debt of the US grew nearly fourfold over the nine years up to the end of 2007, hitting $13.4 trillion. By any metric, these were extraordinary numbers.

At the time, it was argued—and it needed to be, because otherwise policy would have to change—that there was a perfectly rational explanation for the persistent current-account deficits of the US. If a country has strongly favourable investment opportunities, the economically sensible thing is to allow its current residents to consume some of the future fruits of that investment *now* by borrowing from the rest of the world, investing in the new technologies, building up a stock of financial obligations to the rest of the world, and repaying those obligations later in the shape of real goods and services from the much higher output consequent on those highly productive investments. For the budding economists amongst the readers, let's just say that the decision as to how much to consume now is the product of two effects: a standard income effect (i.e. consume more in all periods, including now, consequent on the superior expected investment returns) and a substitution effect (i.e. consume less now and invest more so as to reap even more in future periods). Access to a flow of cheap capital enables more of an income effect and a surge in current consumption. It's pudding now, and pudding later—just the sort of thing most voters and politicians like. If the 'Great Moderation' had caused a surge in US productivity, a temporary surge in the growth of debt held by the US would be part of a transition phenomenon. If, as many argued, the superior productivity would last for decades, the effect on current account deficits could be very large and still be of little concern. Nevertheless, even if the favourable opportunities persisted, the level of the

stock of debt would reach a new steady state,[9] and so even this was not a story of
ever-spiralling debts.

Clearly, resources needed to be invested in the highly productive investments
on which such reasoning was based. Sadly, this was not so. Most of the inflow to
the US was used to finance public and private consumption, and wars. In 2005
I bluntly observed: '[The] grave suspicion must be that the US is simply "living
beyond its means", rather than consuming early from an inheritance that it is
actively creating. A consumption-bubble can only be sustained if the economy
can keep sucking finance in to cover it...a false sense of security has been
created.'[10]

The next big global imbalance, related to the first, was in patterns of savings
and consumption. Global gross savings as a percentage of global GDP rose from
about 21.5% in 2001 to about 24.5% in 2007.[11] Not that dramatic, it might seem.
However, on closer inspection, the increase is found to comprise a sharp drop in
the average savings rates of industrial economies (with the United States leading
the race into negative savings territory), and a surge in savings rates in emerging
economies. The US alone, representing only about 5% of the world's population,
accounted for about a third of the total increase in global consumption between
2000 and 2006, and it did it mostly by dis-saving. In the Middle East and in
China, savings rates were plus 50% and 58% respectively (a rise from about 34%
and 38% in 2001). Such rates get economic historians to sit bolt upright. Even
during the fabled 'Industrial Revolution', saving rates were only ever a fraction
of these. Contemporaneously, in a number of emerging Asian economies investment rates over the 2000s were below their peaks of the mid-1990s, and in other
countries investment rates rose but by nowhere near enough to match the rise in
their domestic savings. Something had to give.

The Long-term Forces at Work

These imbalances reflected forces at work over very long stretches of time. One
was the shift of global production towards countries with much lower labour
costs, with an ever-growing share of income going to the owners of capital.
Those being employed in places like China were being paid a small proportion
of the value of what they produced. The corporates that employed them were
saving a high proportion of what they were generating. Hence those being
employed were not contributing much to the global aggregate demand that
would absorb what they produced. Meanwhile, the shift in production also put
downward pressure on wages in richer countries, amongst those who might

ordinarily have been thought of as the source of demand for the output. In the US—and readers may find this utterly astonishing—real (i.e. inflation-adjusted) wages for many in the population stagnated for forty years. Wage stagnation was further reinforced by the downward pressure on wage bargaining power, the result of labour-market reforms and low inflation. As firms chased insufficient demand, it seemed that one solution was for them to cut costs even more and further shift their activities offshore. This, of course, intensified the underlying problem. Meanwhile, a range of oil-exporting countries was taking migrant workers, paying them less than the full social costs of their human capital, converting this into surpluses, and further squeezing global aggregate demand. In Russia and in the Middle East, the rise of oligarchs and crony capitalism was also fuelling the squeeze on global aggregate demand. Global supply was not creating its own demand as all the textbooks said it should. And something had to give.

Over 40 years, Western Europe and then Japan, and then China, Asia, and other emerging economies, upped their production and pushed down costs. The overcapacity pushed down the rate of profit of US manufacturers.[12] Indeed, the lowest annual profit rate in the US industrial sector of the 'long boom' of 1948–1973 was higher than the highest rate of profit in the 'long bust' during the Reagan and Clinton years.[13] US companies increased their scale of production to compensate, but reduced the number of workers. As a side effect, wages in the US for whole swathes of the population collapsed. It was not that US manufacturing was shrinking; it grew by nearly 4% per annum between 1997 and 2007. However, huge physical capital investments and developments in production methods improved US labour productivity by nearly 7% per year, and the US needed to add manufacturing capacity just for employment to stand still. This did not happen and the US lost nearly 6 million manufacturing jobs in about a decade. En route, the US became a nation of importers.

There were some troubling parallels with an earlier period about which, if one is not careful, one can become quite nostalgic. Back in the 1970s, oil-exporting countries were generating big balance of payments surpluses. These were 'recycled' through the global banking system to developing- and emerging-market borrowers, especially in Latin America. Before the Latin American debt crisis of the 1980s, this 'petro-dollar' recycling was praised by many of the key policymakers of the day for the way in which it fed countries that had supposedly high productivity and good growth prospects. In the 2000s, a similar recycling was underway. This time the flows were into the US, and petro-dollars were being supplemented by flows from a range of emerging economies running current account surpluses that had switched from borrowing to lending. This time the flow was into a capital-rich developed economy from a mix of oil-rich and high-income economies and what we would normally think of as capital-needy emerging economies. It was like an especially tasty honey and, although some of it flowed back out, quite a lot of it stuck. Because financial firms were sophisticated (or maybe just smart enough to work out on which side of the bread to layer the honey), a chunk of these flows ended up pumping mortgages. Thus, poorer segments of emerging economies—via those more privileged there, especially corporates—ended up funding the activities of relatively poorer and of some speculative groups in richer economies. In the debt-fuelled parts of the world (the US, Ireland, Spain, 'emerging' Europe, and parts of the Middle East in particular), the composition of investment shifted dramatically towards real-estate construction. This 'uphill' flow of capital was reminiscent of that of the 1920s into the US chasing a similar phony story of superior productivity. Then, as this time, much fed real-estate and other speculative investments.

And so it came to pass that credit- and property-related bubbles expanded to boost otherwise insufficient global aggregate demand and to enable econ-omies—especially richer importing economies—to continue to grow and con-sume when it was not achievable by more 'natural' means. The demand to borrow was created by the very same forces that created the supply of those willing to lend—the re-circulated dollars filling US and other banks. At first, the credit bubbles involved the middle classes and those with good credit histories. Eventually, by a sort of perverse trickle-down effect, the poor and those with poor credit histories were pulled in too. Supply was brought into equilibrium with demand, but at the cost of creating a long-term risk of instability.

Another long-term factor was the role of the US dollar. In 1971 the Bretton Woods international monetary system, based on the US dollar linked to gold, collapsed and was replaced with a system in which the dollar and other currencies floated against each other. The US dollar became the de facto global currency. This created a contradiction. The way for countries to get dollars was to run trade and payments surpluses while the US ran trade and payments deficits and used its power of 'seigniorage'[14] to create the necessary dollars. Eichengreen calls this the 'Exorbitant Privilege' of the dollar.[15] The first year in the twentieth century when the US imported more than it exported was 1971. Over the next 40 years, only in two recessions did the US balance of trade momentarily go positive. If the deficits and the supply of dollars got too large relative to the demand for them, it would risk a run on the dollar and a collapse of the global economy. This might not happen for decades.

Generations of US voters liked the arrangement because they benefited from the US sucking in spare global savings at an artificially-deflated cost. US banks liked it because they got to borrow short-term very cheaply and lend long-term at higher rates, and take the profits. Generations of US politicians liked it because they got to run huge budget deficits, ignore long-term fiscal challenges caused by US demographical changes and rapidly rising medical costs, and pursue military operations abroad without needing to raise taxes at home to pay for them. Not wanting to make their own exports uncompetitive by driving down the US dollar, first Japan and then China invested their surpluses in the US. Indeed, in the early 1980s, Japan, with its trade surplus peaking at about 40% of the US trade deficit, was viewed in a very similar way to China in the 2000s. For 30 years, the US managed the post-Bretton-Woods contradiction. Then the dot-com bubble burst at the end of the 1990s, and the US entered a decade of low growth. A housing bubble was a brilliant ruse to help hide what was going on, but it was only a temporary fix.

The Dance, and the Warnings Ignored

The relationship between the US and China over the 1990s and 2000s, after Japan had withered, is an important part of our story. For a decade or more China and the US were in a 'mutually self-reinforcing economic embrace'.[16] Sometimes they might swagger, and sometimes gracefully waltz. Sometimes they might tread on each others' toes, by accident or intent. But, at heart, they enjoyed the dance too much and—seeing no other partner ready to take the floor—danced on regardless. Increasingly it became clear that a range of countries, with the US in the lead, needed to cut domestic overconsumption, and China and other South-East Asian and oil-exporting countries needed to expand domestic consumption, and all needed to realign their patterns of economic activity. A similar dance was taking place between Germany and much of Europe, and a similar rebalancing was needed there. We shall explore this in Chapter 10.

Why did China—ranked below the hundredth in the world in terms of per capita income—come to run a current account surplus and capital account surplus uninterruptedly for two decades and lend heavily to the world's richest country? More bizarrely, why did China buy up piles of US Treasuries while becoming one of the world's biggest foreign direct investment (FDI) recipients, effectively lending money it had borrowed at a very high rate back to its creditors at a very low rate? The social rates of return from investing in health, education, transport, and housing must have been high in rural China, yet the Chinese authorities preferred to hold US Treasuries on which the rate of return was low. Indeed, the rate was pushed lower the more China pursued the policy. Even *more* bizarrely, to the extent that China had not pulled its positions in time (if it even could), a revaluation of the renminbi against the dollar by, say, 20% or 30% would wipe hundreds of billions, if not over a trillion, dollars off the value of China's holdings of US Treasuries and foreign-currency. For sure, China held a buffer that protected it from externally-driven shocks, the whims of capital markets, and the vagaries of the IMF and others, but it came at a very heavy cost to itself.

Of course, the lenders and borrowers were not the same. The outflow from China into US Treasuries and the increase in dollar reserves reflected China's statist economic model. The inflows of private capital into China reflected an open-door policy on the part of China towards foreign investors willing to exploit what could be got out of resources, especially human resources, in China. Both reflected the export-led growth model of the Chinese government, which hinged on holding down the value of the renminbi relative to other currencies to make Chinese goods more competitive in global markets. An undervalued exchange rate also reduced the value of Chinese household income by raising import prices. This acted as a kind of hidden consumption tax on imported goods, which transferred income from Chinese households to Chinese corporates, and further depressed global aggregate demand.

In China, household saving was high as a proportion of household income, but not unduly so. Household saving was not abnormal as a share of national income because household income was a small share of national income. The biggest component of the rise in China's savings came from its corporate sector. It was this that drove China's current account surplus from 2.8% of GDP in 2003 to 11% at its peak. This reflected (ironically, given what happened next) the undeveloped Chinese financial system. The only way ordinary Chinese people could save was via bank deposits, but the authorities controlled the banks. The PBOC set both a minimum lending rate, below which banks could not lend, and a maximum deposit rate, above which banks could not pay. By setting these rates well below the going market rate, the PBOC transferred huge amounts of wealth, around 5%–8% of China's GDP per year, from depositors to corporate borrowers. In the West, depositors would have walked away from such dire financial repression. But in China depositors were trapped. There were no bank competitors offering higher rates, and tight capital restrictions prevented ordinary people taking their capital out of the country. The ruling Communist Party guarded its power by controlling the banking system and aligning itself with state-owned enterprises to the neglect of the more general population. En route, by draining Chinese households of interest income, financial repression further drained the global economic system of aggregate demand.

The counterpart to China's external reserve accumulation was an internal imbalance in favour of the tradable sector, to the detriment of the non-tradable sector. This had happened in Japan throughout the 1980s, leading to stock market and real-estate bubbles that collapsed leaving Japan with overstretched balance sheets—the genesis of Japan's long deflation. Chinese manufacturing, with an emphasis on tradables, expanded to exploit a pool of low-skilled workers, especially from rural areas, and emphasized cutting costs and serving multinationals. However, by having a financial system that favoured capital over labour—labour was cheap, but capital was practically free—the PBOC encouraged manufacturing methods that under-used Chinese labour and skill and over-used physical capital. The profits were quite literally hoarded abroad.[17] Other Asian countries were conveyer belts to China, which was the last stage of assembly for products that got shipped especially to the US and Europe. At least until recently, it was not a model of development based on much technical innovation, and Chinese workers were achieving only about 12% of the productivity of US workers on the eve of the crash. The physical capital that embodied such innovations came from places like Germany and the US.

The effect was reinforced by uneven economic and political reform in China—in turn related to distorted political structures in the country. During the 1990s, China had removed the 'iron bowl' of social protection provided by state-owned firms that had virtually guaranteed jobs and welfare for life. While enterprises cut or stopped pension provision, free housing and free healthcare, a modern social welfare system was not put in its place. The financial demands on corporates to pay for social welfare—via the standard taxation mechanisms of developed economies—did not rise. The true costs of labour (which included all the associated human-capital maintenance) did not show up in the bottom line of Chinese corporates, who instead saw their profits and savings soar.

At the same time, the Chinese state enacted policies enforcing smaller families. This increased average dependency ratios. Individual households—not collectively via the state—had to save more to protect themselves against life-shocks, especially related to old age. In response, Chinese households over-saved. First, being risk-averse and unable to pool risks, they held more insurance than they would have held in a collectively-pooled mechanism. Second, the precautionary motive exaggerated this; that is, individuals were concerned about the consequences of extreme and not just average outcomes, and over-saved compared to what they would have done if only the average outcome mattered. Third, individuals did not have the 'shock absorber' of being able to borrow from future generations. Instead of re-circulating resources to rural areas through social programmes, China essentially privatized social welfare by attracting into its industrial regions workers who then sent their remittances back to rural areas. Something similar was going on in many oil-rich surplus countries, where migrant workers usually came from outside the borders of the host country, invariably from much poorer countries.

China was achieving annual rates of growth of 8%–10% (from a very low base). Its boom, and those of many other emerging and oil-rich economies, was partly the product of extremely lax US monetary policy that sent investors scurrying to seek higher yield elsewhere. Lax US monetary policy was in turn a function of China's economic policy. China was also able to run more negative real interest rates than the US and other more developed countries because of its heavy administrative controls. These controls distorted market signals and led to poor investment decisions and bubbles in China, including in its very own property markets.[18] Domestic inflation in China was pumped too. This was probably a reasonable price to pay for rapid rates of economic growth, and was anyway less of a worry than if it had been happening in the US where economic growth rates could never reach such high (catch-up) levels. Furthermore, it would have been difficult for China to raise interest rates to fight inflation without attracting yet more foreign capital.

In sum, the global imbalances on the eve of the crash reflected the awkward integration of China and a range of other emerging economies into the global economy, the inefficient social, political, and economic developments inside such countries, and distortions in the global economy related to the reserve-currency status of the US dollar. Incidentally, on this interpretation, the undervaluation of China's currency cannot explain all, and its revaluation would be no instant panacea. Even with revaluation, Chinese corporate savings would persist, at maybe a lower level, and still at the cost of China's poor.

According to JK Galbraith,[19] inequality, which peaked in 1928, was one of the four key drivers of the crash of 1929. Inequality peaked again in the 2000s, and both the IMF and the World Economic Forum identified this as a driving factor of the crash.[20] As global wealth and income became more skewed, economies became dependent on high levels of investment and luxury consumer spending, and there was insufficient global aggregate demand and deflationary pressures. Policymakers responded by pumping asset price bubbles and by relaxing regulation so as to feed credit bubbles and mortgages to boost aggregate demand. However, this 'coping' mechanism eventually led to instability and disaster.

Imbalancies in wealth and income were visible everywhere. In late 2010, the top 10% of the US population controlled over 70% of all of US private-sector wealth, and the bottom 90% shared the remaining 30%.[21] The top 1% controlled nearly half of the wealth of the top 10% and earned 24% of all income. Between 2002 and 2007, 65% of all US income growth went to just 1% of the population, which is why the median average income hardly budged. For many, incomes fell. Figures for household earnings hid the fact that households needed several incomes just to keep treading the same patch of water, and they then weighed themselves down with an additional burden of debt. Similarly, in the UK, real incomes barely grew for all but the richest. Between the general elections of 2001 and 2005, despite the Labour government's rhetoric of 'equality', the real income of the poorest 20% fell. The pattern was repeated in many emerging economies, such as China, and amongst oil-rich producers, as the share of global income going to the top 1% of the world's population rose from 10% in 1980 to 23% in 2008.

Interest Rates

Many blamed the crash on very low real long-term interest rates. These were the rates on which consumer spending and most house prices were based. Various explanations were offered, not all mutually exclusive. One, the 'savings glut' hypothesis, famously promoted by Bernanke,[22] argued that it was surplus nations, like China, that were in the driving seat; global real long-term interest rates had to fall to achieve global equilibrium between saving and investment. However, while there was indeed a large gap between saving and investment outside the US—which may be the source of Bernanke's phrase—it was offset by an equal-sized gap in the US such that there was little, if any, aggregate *global* savings glut.[23] Indeed, the average global savings rate was about 5% lower than in the 1970s.

Another possibility was that a range of emerging economies in Asia and the Middle East had the urge to build foreign-exchange reserve 'buffers'. An indication of this is that some of the biggest increases in reserve holdings were in countries that previously experienced 'sudden stops' in flows of capital (South Korea, Taiwan, and Mexico stand out). Some said the buffers were a response to the Asian crisis of the late 1990s and the realization of just how much damage could be done by sudden reversals of capital flows. Partly, they argued, this was linked to the weak and sometimes capricious provision of buffers by organizations such as the IMF, such that countries now wanted to 'self-insure'. Partly it was shaped by the limitations of the development of financial systems outside of the US.[24]

There was a story too about emerging economies adopting export-led growth strategies and trying to prevent current account surpluses from pushing up their exchange rates. There is evidence also that undervalued exchange rates are associated with rapid economic growth because they encourage manufacturing employment.[25] China seemed a prominent example of these phenomena. There was also the notion that this was a period of (relatively) poor investment opportunities worldwide. Was it simply easier for the US to generate self-justifying reasons to pull funds in, including for example via its 'more sophisticated' financial and property markets? At some point, China had more than enough reserves to use as a buffer, yet it still kept adding more. This suggests the export-led explanation is more likely to be the right one.

Although global imbalances made it more difficult to act on long-term interest rates, the Federal Reserve still had control over short-term interest rates. Adjustable-rate subprime mortgages were based on these, and it was these types of mortgages, and financial instruments based upon them, that turned out to be especially dangerous. The US Federal Reserve led the way, lowering the overnight federal funds target rate from 6.5% in late 2000 to 1.75% in December 2001, to 1% in June 2003, a new record low, where it stayed for a full year. The real interest rate stayed below 1% between mid-2001 and the end of 2005, and for much of that period it was negative. The pattern was repeated in many major industrial economies. The European Central Bank (ECB) kept real short-term interest rates below 1%, which helped to finance Germany's reunification. In Japan, rates were held between 0% and 1% for the best part of a decade. There was limited ability outside the US to fight the Fed's low rates. Many emerging economies followed for fear that their currencies would appreciate if they set their interest rates higher. Had the Bank of England not followed the US, hot money would have flowed into the UK to exploit the interest rate differential; the Bank of England was not as autonomous as some suggested at the time. The Federal funds rate was finally raised starting in June 2004, but only very slowly. After seventeen 0.25% increments, it reached 5.25% in June 2006. It was too late, and such a slow upward path may have created a false sense of security; the knowledge that there would be no big correction in rates might have encouraged excessive leverage.

Why were interest rates pushed so low? The main driving force seems to have been the fear of deflation in the wake of the dot-com bust. Deflation would cause the real burden of debt to rise and weaken the balance sheets of households and businesses—the dreaded 'debt deflation'.[26] The travails of Japan heavily influenced thinking.[27] Nobody had foreseen Japan's deflationary slump. Japanese policymakers had thus missed an opportunity to sustain growth and inflation before it became too difficult. The lesson others drew was that once inflation turned negative, monetary and fiscal stimulus should be pushed beyond the levels implied by current forecasts of future inflation and economic activity, i.e. that policy should pre-emptively stimulate the economy even if the evidence to support this was not yet fully in place; by the time the evidence existed, it would be too late.[28]

Rates were then kept low for the standard reason that growth was sluggish and unemployment rising—the equally dreaded 'jobless recovery'. Even with cuts in interest rates, US unemployment reached nearly 4 million. Indeed, such low interest rates may even help to explain the jobless recovery, since they effectively subsidized capital in a world already suffering a 'capital overhang' legacy (the more labour-saving the capital, the greater the subsidy).[29]

It has been argued that by holding rates too low for too long, the Fed encouraged bubbles in global credit markets and in asset prices. Evaluating culpability is complicated by what was said above about inadequate global aggregate demand and about the role of China and others; this would indicate that policymakers had few alternatives if they were to avoid deflation and unemployment spiralling. Indeed, deflation was already taking place across a large number of consumer goods sectors in countries like the US well before the stock market collapsed in the late 1990s, and perhaps as far back as 1995. The surge in the stock market in the late 1990s masked this for a while with a wealth effect.

Perhaps the pre-emptive strategy in the early to mid-2000s was more riddled with dilemmas than policymakers realized at the time. It now seems—and we have the benefit of hindsight on which to base our observations—that policymakers faced something of a Faustian trade-off. Either they kept interest rates higher and allowed unemployment to rise and risked deflation anyway, or they pushed rates lower, avoided immediate deflation but risked pumping bubbles that might later cause an even bigger deflation and a jobless recovery from an even deeper economic pit. And they had little to guide them as to how big the risks of deflation were. The dot-com collapse was much less of a credit event than that experienced by Japan after its housing and stock market bubbles burst: Dot-com 'losers' did not have debt weighing down their balance sheets, banks were not significantly exposed to the losses and the collapse raised no concerns about their solvency. So it seems that policymakers used ultra-low interest rates to rescue the economy in the early 2000s from a mildly deflationary scenario only to face a genuine credit event with a high risk of deflation at the end of the 2000s, consequent on the impact of those ultra-low interest rates.

It is clear that very low interest rates in the early to mid-2000s may take some blame for what happened, but they do not explain everything. Housing market surges were just as prevalent in many other countries that had experienced less credit easing than the US. Indeed, the housing boom of the 1920s was accompanied by rising, and not falling, interest rates, which suggests that poor regulation is at least as much to blame. The big mistake in the US in the mid-2000s was to hold interest rates too low for too long. It is also clear that the peculiar dynamics of the global macroeconomic imbalances, and a bag of policy instruments that was nearly empty but for the one interest rate instrument, curtailed the policy options severely. Nevertheless, policymakers could have done more to curb excessive risk-taking if they had had macroprudential tools at their disposal (and been willing to use them), or if they had simply been a bit tougher on the non-interest rate aspects of credit growth. We shall return to this in Chapters 8 and 12.

In the mid-2000s, Federal Reserve chairman Alan Greenspan, realizing that bubbles might be developing, and perhaps recollecting his famous 'irrational exuberance' statement at the height of the stock market boom of the 1990s, at first tried to dampen the market euphoria, but then stopped bothering.[30] This was partly because of political pressure. Partly it was because inflation seemed so low. Companies were holding wages down even as growth was high. New technology was replacing workers and boosting profits, and the stock market was booming again. Surely, anyone who worried about market euphoria was being a bit of a party pooper? The main reason however, was that Greenspan didn't believe that the market was behaving inefficiently; after all, the point of his famous 'irrational exuberance' statement was to cast aspersions on the practical usefulness of the notion of 'irrational exuberance': 'But how do we know when irrational exuberance has unduly escalated asset values...?'.

The Growth of Debt and the Underpricing of Risk

One consequence of low interest rates was the growth of the stock of debt relative to income. In the US, the annual rate of growth of real household debt went from an average of 4% in the 1990s to 7.5% over the period 2000–2006. In the UK, the rate was an astonishing 10% for the decade running up to the crash. It was not something that Gordon Brown talked much about in budget speeches of the time. In Ireland, in 2006 private-sector debt was growing at 30% per year; in a low inflation environment, this should have flagged danger. In nominal terms, the total stock of UK household debt went from £570 billion in the summer of 1997, a ratio of just over 100% of net disposable income, to a little over £1,500 billion, or about 175% of net disposable income, on the eve of the crash. The ratio also rose significantly in Spain, Ireland, Australia, and France, but fell in both Germany and Japan. In the US, despite the tag 'subprime' and frequent references to the poor, most of the growth of household debt was in middle-income households that were desperately trying to sustain their living standards. In Spain, in contrast, it was poorer households who especially tanked up on debt.

Not only households took on lots of debt. Government, non-financial businesses and the financial industry were also doing so across a wide range of countries. Aggregating all sources of debt together, the ratio of debt to GDP was just under 300% in the US, stretching up to 365% in Spain and 465% in the UK, while even further beyond lay Ireland at over 700% (with its financial sector accounting for 420%) and Iceland on 1,200% (with about half of that in the financial sector).[31] Germany and Japan were non-participants in the debt-fuelled binge (although, to nip any moralizing in the bud, it should be noted that German banks and politicians happily encouraged such behaviour in others). In the run-up to America's Great Depression of the 1930s and Japan's travails of the 1990s, most private-sector debt was in non-financial companies, such that when balance sheet deflation set in, it hit these companies hard. In the 2000s, the big increases in debt were in the financial and household sectors. Compared to non-financial companies, there was a relative lack of workable resolution mechanisms for big banks in financial trouble and for households in mortgage distress. This made for a crash that was inherently more challenging to handle.

Low real interest rates, *ceteris paribus*, increase the present discounted value of any stream of revenue that is generated by an asset. The flipside is that asset prices rise. Global equity markets rose 90% between 2003 and the eve of the crash in mid-2007. Compared to the early 2000s, real house prices increased by more than 60% in the US[32] and by more than 90% in the UK. Along with gains on other financial assets, households could post net wealth gains even after taking on higher debts. Furthermore, while in the UK private-sector borrowing from the rest of the world was matched by a build-up in foreign investments (such that the net financial balance of the non-financial private sector stayed roughly in balance),[33] in the US it was not, and in some eurozone countries, such as Greece and Portugal, it decidedly was not.

Very cheap money also encouraged 'risk-shifting' behaviour—the collective ignoring of downside risk because all that matters is the upside.[34] Many asset management companies, pension funds, and other bodies had entered into long-term contracts that committed them to relatively high nominal rates of return. With bond yields very low, this was proving difficult. Pension funds, for example, could only get about 1.5% real yield to maturity compared to the 3.5% they had got in the past. In a bid to meet their obligations, maintain profitability, and attract and retain clients, they increasingly engaged in a desperate 'search for yield'. Indeed, pension funds, and others in a similar predicament, may have had no choice but to take on more risk. If they stayed with low-return but safe investments they were almost certain to default on their commitments. If they took on higher-return but riskier investments they might last long enough to see rates rise and so survive.

At low interest rates, hedge fund managers—typically paid about 1% of funds under management and 20% of any excess return above a minimum nominal return—were also encouraged to take on more risk. At high risk-free returns, they were paid well even if they took little risk. As the risk-free return fell, the fund may not be able to meet even the minimum return if little risk was taken on. Low interest rates meant it was much easier too for banks to borrow, and so banks also began searching aggressively for new places to invest. Adding yield without adding much risk would have been good, but this is not what happened.[35] Very low interest rates encouraged 'catastrophe chasing' strategies, a theme to which we shall return later.

Of course, this 'search for yield' across so many different financial players at once relied on an enabling environment: a world in which credit ratings and other models were signalling that risk was low when, to the contrary, it was high; shareholders and regulators applying ever-decreasing levels of scrutiny when, if anything, the need for scrutiny was getting greater all the time; and politicians and policymakers declaring an end to boom and bust when this was no more than a convenient myth. For a while, investors got their precious yield.

Since debt was central to the crash, understanding the properties of debt will help us better understand the challenges of tackling the crash. Debt is a perfectly natural phenomenon, both for an individual and for society. Debt enables consumption to be distributed more optimally over a lifetime or across many generations. However, debt, unlike equity, can default. The default possibilities in a debt contract are disciplining devices in a world of costly monitoring and asymmetric information.[36] When a lender is unable to

monitor easily a borrower all the time, the debt contract requires the borrower to make periodic payments to the lender. So long as no payments are
missed, the lender keeps his or her nose out. Only when a payment is
missed—a sign of possible distress—does the lender investigate the borrower
more closely. This economises on monitoring costs. If the borrower defaults,
there are well-specified penalties including confiscating the asset used as
collateral for the loan and selling it to repay the debt. If the debt being
defaulted is a mortgage, the asset is usually the property bought with the loan.
Structuring the debt contract in this way also supposedly gives the borrower
incentives to invest wisely in the first place, and to put in higher effort and
thereby increase the probability of avoiding default. In contrast, equity is
traded on an open market and its price comes to embody the information
of the millions of participants in that market, and so fluctuates in response to
new pieces of information, but it does not suffer from 'default' states as debt
contracts do. Debt may also need to be rolled over in ways that equity does
not need to be.

When debt-based bubbles crash, the mess is much harder to clean up than
when equity-based bubbles crash. In 2005, I wrote: 'During a debt-backed
bubble, the default states in the contracts, in a sense, bite "less than they really
should" given the true underlying fundamentals. In particular, spreads tend to
be based on a false sense of security, since the bubble masks the real risks being
taken on. Post collapse, banks adjust upwards the true underlying risk of the
contracts they offer . . . and hence raise loan spreads . . . This can aggravate price
falls, but—in short—it is not unlike the crises that sometimes hit highly-
indebted countries: as spreads rise, the burden of debt rises which hits debt-
backed asset prices too, which makes the debt riskier, which increases the
spreads, and the burden of the debt rises, and so on. Failure to coordinate by
lenders compounds the crisis.'[37] When the stock market crashed in 1987, the
consequences turned out to be minimal, and when the dot-com bubble burst at
the end of the 1990s, policy responses were able to mitigate much, though clearly
not all, of the impact on the rest of the economy. This was because these were
equity-based collapses.

In spite of the default dangers inherent to debt, debt became highly favoured
in the run-up to the crash. For a start, it became much easier and cheaper to issue
debt than equity. Equity markets never really recovered to prior price-to-
earnings ratios after the 2000 stock market crash, whereas bond-market spreads
fell to historically low levels. Global imbalances, and responses to them,
therefore inadvertently helped promote the use of debt.

One heavily worked pump for debt was that manned by private equity funds, whose instrument of choice was the leveraged buyout (LBO). As a disciplining device, debt requires firms to meet regular payments, and this helps to enforce cost efficiency. Financial institutions like this. After 2002, about half of the rise in US corporate net debt came through leveraged buyouts. Assets under the management of private equity firms peaked at about $600 billion in early 2007, 250% of their 2000 level. The big providers of loans to fund leveraged buyouts were household names, the top three being, in order, JPMorgan Chase & Co., Bank of America, and Citigroup.

Debt was also heavily used to make companies bigger. For executives paid according to company size this had a certain appeal. Investment banks also made fees out of issuance and acquisition and had an incentive to recommend activities based on debt. Economic models based on 'agency' theories show that firms with stable cash flows (perhaps consequent on the 'Great Moderation'?) also issue more debt.[38] Finally, greater leverage was also used to push up pay and returns to equity owners (executives and shareholders); the return to equity is equal to the return on assets multiplied by the ratio of assets to equity, so the bigger this ratio the greater the return to those who own the little bit of equity.

By the mid-2000s there were all kinds of signs that risk was being tolerated and mispriced as a side-product of all this frenetic debt-based activity. The differences, the 'spreads', between the returns on risky assests and the returns on risk-free assets narrowed very significantly, indicating a willingness to take on higher-risk investments at any given previous rate of return. For example, by the middle of 2007, an investor in junk bonds was getting only about 3% per year more return than an investor in 'risk-free' Treasuries of similar maturity. The historical average was 5%, and the differential had been under that average since 2003. This shrinking 'spread' would normally be interpreted as meaning that the perceived riskiness of junk bonds had fallen. Meanwhile, across the eurozone, investors were happy to lend to one and all at rates only slightly higher than Germany.

Three novel features were at the heart of the crash. The first was the collapse of financial liquidity on an unprecedented global scale. History is littered with financial crises and crashes, but none before where the collapse of liquidity played such an extensive role.[39] With markets starved of liquidity, difficult-to-value assets (many based on underlying debt contracts vulnerable to default) took centre stage like never before. The second was the credit (as opposed to stock market) event nature of the crash, that made its fall-out especially difficult to manage. The third was the balance-sheet nature of the recession that followed. The balance sheets of a huge range of economic actors—corporates, financial firms, governments, and households—had got decidedly lopsided and fragile. Both the rescue of the financial system and economic stimulus would face the headwinds of mass deleveraging, especially of financial firms and households, because of the large amounts of debt and the preponderance of low-quality, high-risk activity favoured by debt in the years before the crash. We have come to think of the crash as about subprime, and subprime as being about only housing. In truth, lenders increasingly considered low-quality borrowers of all hues as fair game, not just those in mortgage markets. Even as they pursued them by all means fair or foul, lenders could still point to low measures of risk, just as naughty schoolboys might throw up their empty hands to suggest they are innocent of taking something they should not have.

Clouds Gathering

In the mid-2000s—I did not dare say it then, and I hardly dare say it now, except in the hope that the matter might be better addressed—the US was starting to look like the Roman Empire in about AD 200, according to one of the many interpretations of its demise. Under President Bush it was fighting, on various fronts, multi-trillion-dollar wars[40] that were funded by peoples abroad who would, under future presidents, have to be repaid in real goods and services that people in the US would have to produce. It was on a path of long-term decline, its problems temporarily papered over by a credit-fuelled property-pumped consumer-based binge and loose monetary and fiscal policy. Its people were living in denial but assured themselves that, as their political leaders often told them, they were owed what they were getting. To crown it all, Bush had no inkling of the impending crash, and so took no measures to forestall it. The only mitigating observation is that Bush was following in the footsteps of those who had gone before him. It was President Reagan who first over-sold to the US people the notion that they could live off ever-spiralling debt, especially government debt. President Clinton took the lesson and applied it to private debt, and presumed that rising housing and equity markets would make it sustainable.

There is a psychological element that economists sometimes miss. In the 25 years from 1982 until the crisis broke in the US in 2007, the US suffered only 16 months of recession, and these were much milder than in the decade or two before. Such a long period of steady, if not always spectacular, growth saw a whole baby-boomer generation go without experiencing a major economic downturn in their adult lives. This filled their minds with highly unrealistic expectations about returns, asset prices, and risks of all sorts.

When Gordon Brown condemned other countries in his budget speech of 2005, he forgot to mention that the UK's economic success story was also based on a string of unsustainable factors: soaring private-sector debt, growth in a public sector that employed 40% of the workforce, a bloated banking system, and heavily-pumped house prices. Under the Blair/Brown 'Third Way', the proceeds of the boom (totally misunderstood for what it really was) were siphoned off and showered on an expanding public sector, the cooperation of the middle classes was secured by a suite of highly agreeable benefits, and the City (and future generations of taxpayers) would pay. With the fortunes of the Labour Party depending on keeping the City happy, no awkward questions were asked about how the City made its huge profits. Macroeconomic policy should have been countercyclical against the credit boom in the private sector, but instead the UK government joined in, with a spending spree that was relentlessly procyclical. The government's (on-balance-sheet) budget deficit was pushed to 3% of GDP at the top of the cycle. In 2005, while Brown was touting 'record economic growth' and an 'end to boom and bust', those arguing that the UK should not be running high government deficits in a period of boom and low private-sector savings were simply ignored.

Not satisfied, Brown made sure that the UK government's financial cupboard was rattling with all manner of other skeletons. To the official government debt figures a generous sprinkling of off-balance-sheet liabilities was added: underfunded public pensions; student loans; the liabilities of quasi-public bodies; implicit guarantees (such as to bail out banks); and Private Finance Initiatives (PFIs), which were a way to borrow off-the-books, which got stretched to cover just about anything. Perhaps the reason Brown did not see the problems ballooning in the 'shadow banking system' was that so much of his own financial thinking was based on 'shadow' financial engineering that he could hardly tell the difference. Then there was a range of 'stealth taxes', such as the £100 billion taken from current and future pensioners by scrapping the tax relief on dividends paid by UK companies into pension funds, the proceeds of which did not find their way into any fiscal cushion. During the boom, and before the bust, in the UK nearly £400 billion went on welfare benefits, and still one in six UK households was without work, the UK was a highly unequal society, and child poverty was still for from eradicated. There was nothing magical about the UK's economic performance, and Brown and his advisors were no financial wizards, as they conjured up a present that had no future. The high renown on which the whole enterprise was based was mostly of the self-generated variety. In December 2010, Brown declared: '[E]conomic ortho-doxies for which people are feted today will quickly come to be seen as the great misjudgements of history.' As a result, there would be a 'decade of decline for the West'.[41] Brown proffered these as words of wisdom and, it seems, did not spot that they were an equally apt summary of his 13 years in charge of the UK's public finances.

And so, numerous economic imbalances gathered, like clouds warning of an impending storm. They fed the 'Great Moderation' myth and were in turn justified by it. Politicians scrambled to take credit, even though it was a global phenomenon and may not have been all that it seemed. They did not stop to wonder whether the 'Great Moderation' was true and the reaction efficient, true and the reaction excessive, or just plain false. To the extent that the 'Great Moderation' was only a temporary mirage, many in the population would stagger to its inviting edge only to discover later that they were saddled with excessively high levels of debt that they would need to offload, and with insufficient levels of savings that they would need to replenish if they wished to continue on their journey in any hope of physical or emotional comfort.

Many economists were worrying that these imbalances portended instability. Obstfeld and Rogoff repeatedly wrote of the dangers.[42] Charles Bean, deputy governor for monetary policy at the Bank of England, observed in November 2008: 'We knew they were unsustainable and worried that the unwinding might be disorderly.... However, nothing very much was done about these imbal-ances.'[43] The Governor of the Bank of England, Mervyn King, observed in March 2009: 'Year after year international meetings expressed surprise, and indeed concern, that the imbalances continued to accumulate, but in the absence of a correction the theme became a worn groove in discussions and interest waned.'[44]

'Moderation'—such a reassuring word. In the sunny pastures of the 'Great Moderation', policymakers could reminisce about the bad old days of the 1970s and other such immoderate times and count their blessings. All over the world, an age-old political morality play ran in an endless loop: the political elites—in China, oil-rich nations, Germany and the European periphery, the

US, and the UK—were more likely to be re-elected (or hold on for even longer) if they prolonged a boom than if they tried to tame a bubble. No politician was going to give up the badge of policy credibility by suggesting that the boom was based on imbalances and an unsustainable debt binge when they could declare it the result of policy reforms they had so bravely driven through. The imbalances benefited them all.

First, by supplying many developed economies with cheap goods, the export-led growth strategies of China and a range of other emerging economies helped hold down their inflation. The Federal Reserve calculated that imports from China to the US lowered US inflation by about 0.1%–0.3% per year, while another calculation reckoned that, once the effect of Chinese competition on other producers was taken fully into account, the downward effect was nearer to 1% per year.[45] It is a paradox that some in the US blamed US outsourcing to China for a 'jobless recovery' in the early 2000s, given that US consumers benefited so much from cheap goods. The problem was that the benefits were widely dispersed while the suffering was concentrated, especially in declining rust-belt regions and in some politically sensitive (i.e. swing) states. Second, by making consumers feel wealthier through lower goods prices and higher asset prices, including house prices,[46] it reduced pressures for higher wages, which further helped the anti-inflationary efforts of Western central banks. Third, the deal appears even better once one realizes that the actions of China and other Asian economies knocked between 0.5% and 1% off US bond yields.[47] Fourth, the downward pressure on yields fed through to lower US and global mortgage rates. Americans could borrow and consume beyond their means on the cheap. They liked that. Sometimes they seemed a tad ungrateful to the poor in China for providing such considerate welfare support. The electorate did not understand the dangers, and it wasn't the sort of issue that they would give politicians much credit for sorting out. Facing an intractable policy conundrum that would take longer to resolve than the horizon of most presidents or prime ministers, political elites everywhere took the time-honoured route. They looked the other way.

The Great Moderation vanished over 2007–2008, and the world entered a period of extremely volatile output. We were left wondering how real was the Great Moderation in the first place. As Minsky[48] had observed, a long period of stability encourages the very behaviour—the tanking up on debt and speculation—that one day turns it into instability. For once Greenspan was clear, and, it turns out, prescient: 'A decline in perceived risk is often self-reinforcing in that it encourages presumptions of prolonged stability and thus a willingness to reach over an ever-more-extended time period...Such developments apparently reflect not only market dynamics but also the all-too-evident alternating and infectious bouts of human euphoria and distress and the instability they engender.'[49] If only he had listened to himself.

2

Housing and Mortgage Market Excess

Housing Fantasies

The speculative excesses of the 1920s reached their glittering heights with the opening of the Empire State Building in New York in 1931. The new tallest building in the world—381 metres from tip to toe—it was a statement fit for its times. The opportunity was not lost to repeat the feat in 1998 when the Petronas Twin Towers in Kuala Lumpur topped out—at 452 metres—just as the Asian financial crisis was in full swing. In the 2000s it was the turn of Dubai. Between 2004 and 2009, tracking the rise and fall of the global property market with prescient perfection, the new tallest building ever built, the Burj Dubai, soared heavenwards. On the well-established principle that the height of the latest record-breaking building should be in strict mathematical proportion to the size of the crash with which it is associated, the Burj Dubai—at 828 metres—was well over twice the height of the Empire State Building and nearly twice the height of the Petronas Towers. It was a timely parable in other ways. To keep its inhabitants comfortable, the air-conditioning system alone used enough energy to freeze 5 million tons of ice a year—in a city that had the highest per capita carbon footprint in the world. The thousands of migrant workers drawn mostly from South Asia to haul the structure from the ground (for good measure marketed to the world's super-rich as no expense spared) occasionally rioted to protest at the conditions in which they were kept, their pay (a dollar for each sweat-filled hour), and at the numbers who died during its construction. The tower was part of a massive speculative overbuild that left Dubai up to its confectioneered neck in debt. But for a little bit of last-minute Middle East diplomacy, a multibillion-dollar bailout from Dubai's oil-rich next-door neighbour, and its abrupt renaming on the very day of its opening as the Burj Khalifa (in honour of the ruler of Abu Dhabi who now effectively owned it), the tower would have been an even more blunt exclamation mark at the end of an era of global debt-fuelled excess, the ultimate gilded trinket in memoriam to an age of capitalist bling.

Humankind did not just fantasize about money and easy celebrity in the early days of the new millennium; many were fixated with real estate too. As the economist Robert Shiller observed: 'The sobering truth is that the current world economic crisis was substantially caused by the collapse of speculative bubbles in real-estate (and stock) markets.'[1] The US Congressional Oversight Panel quickly got the drift: 'The global financial crisis that culminated in intervention by the United States and other industrialized countries to rescue their banking systems was largely the result of an asset bubble in housing.'[2]

In the UK the enthusiasm for housing goes back to the idea of an Englishman's home being his castle, in recent times nurtured by a myriad of TV home-improvement shows. The position of housing in US culture goes back to the years just after the Second World War when the average rate of private home ownership surged from 45% to around 65% in little over a decade. At the heart of this were innumerable small building and loan associations that diligently pumped a huge expansion in prime mortgages and established 30-year fixed-rate mortgages as the norm. Nevertheless, home-ownership gains were confined largely to the middle classes and, by the euphemism of 'redlining', excluded many minorities. The rates of home ownership stayed at 65% right through to the mid 1990s, when a mini-boom, which accelerated in the early years of the 2000s, took home-ownership rates to nearly 70%, one of the highest in the world. Social policy under both Clinton and G. W. Bush promoted home ownership like never before, including by incentivizing and, where necessary, cajoling mortgage companies to provide the finance to do it. Twelve million new homeowners were created in a decade, many of them low- and moderate-income households. Presidents and politicians of all persuasions took heart—and credit where they could—in the newly-elevated rates of home ownership, even as there were signs that it had come with some not inconsiderable side effects.

In the 1946 movie *It's a Wonderful Life* (frequently voted one of America's favourites[3]) George Bailey turns down the offer to take over the family building and loan association on his return from college, foreseeing in it only a life of scrimping and personal privation. In defending the importance of his 'shabby little office' for satisfying the 'fundamental urge' of many to save and buy their own home, Pop Bailey digs deep into the American property-owning psyche, with words of sacrifice and not of worldly gain. Sixty years on, and a couple of generations later, matters were somewhat different. As one commentator put it at the height of the boom, 'As everyone is now aware, *anyone* capable of fogging a mirror can essentially get a 100%-financed home.'[4] Indeed, some modern-day bankers were pocketing hundreds of millions of dollars by satisfying their own particular fundamental urges.

It wasn't just in the US. Multimillions were being made by mortgage brokers, investment bankers, and construction companies in many places in the world willing to take a punt on local and global property markets and create the financial scaffolding to hold them up despite the best efforts of economic gravity. Prices were shooting up as far afield as Australia, Argentina, Netherlands, Spain, Ireland, the UK, Poland, Israel, Lebanon, Canada, Greece, Bulgaria, Croatia, South Korea, Singapore, Ukraine, South Africa, the Baltic states, Norway, Sweden, France, Italy, New Zealand, Romania, and in parts of Russia, China, and India. Two especially conspicuous exceptions were Japan and Germany.

In parts of the Middle East they were dredging whole artificial islands and archipelagos into existence and getting 50% price growth per year on whatever was plonked on top. In Ireland, mega-developers criss-crossed the skies in squadrons of shiny new helicopters keeping watch over their precious new crop. Several emerging European economies, not satisfied with just pumping property bubbles, made sure that large portions of the debt to do it were denominated in foreign currencies, setting up a double economic whammy if ever it all went wrong—which, of course, they assured themselves would never be the case. It had the look and smell of a speculative bubble, and some commentators—*The Economist* made a regular habit of it[5]—took to referring to the world's first ever global house-price bubble, and, when they were feeling especially prophetic, to solemnly warning: 'The worldwide rise in house prices is the biggest bubble in history. Prepare for the economic pain when it pops.'[6] The BIS (Bank for International Settlements), the IMF, and the OECD all prognosticated on the dangers of overpriced housing and took stabs at how far prices might fall.

In the UK, people are quite used to house prices that go in booms and busts. Through thick and thin, they wear the 'This Time is Different' hat as a mark of national pride. For the US, this was something new. The US had experienced large regional house-price rises before, but none on quite such a nationwide scale. There had been real price booms in the 1970s and 1980s, which had collapsed, otherwise, average US house prices had a history of rising at about the same rate as inflation. In real terms, US house prices in

1997 were at the same level they had been in the late 1950s.[7] By the market's peak in mid-2006, the average nominal price of a US home had more than doubled in just 6.5 years, a rate of growth of nearly 12% per year.[8] In the UK, if house prices keep rising rapidly, it is usually attributed to restricted supply. Yet in many countries surging prices were matched by a strong surge in house building. In the US, the number of new privately-owned housing units peaked at an annual rate of 2.15 million in mid-2006.[9] Rich new seams of real estate ran through Nevada, Arizona, and the North East, and guiled[10] the ornamented shores of Florida, California, and Illinois. No crushing of rocks here to get at tiny nuggets of gold within; the stuff was scattered all over the surface, easy pickings, proliferating fast. In the mid-2000s, travelling through the deserts of Arizona, one could not help being awe-struck (I certainly was) at the site of block upon block of gleaming new housing (often empty, as if living in them was not the point), a modern-day version of the real-estate gold-rush of the 1920s, that proceeded the 1929 crash. In the 1920s, it was parcels of land in Florida that were the subject of rabid buying frenzies driven by no more than the fact—and sometimes just the rumour—that prices had risen rapidly in recent years, and even just in recent months. The logic, then as now, was simple: precisely because prices had risen a lot in a very short space of time, they were bound to rise a lot more. To leverage their bets, instead of buying the land, investors in the 1920s bought options to buy the land and traded those. Investors in the 2000s, lacking such vivid imagination, were less enamoured of swamps, and needed to see something more solid for their money. They bought bricks and mortar 'on margin' with debt.

In Australia, New Zealand, Canada, Spain, the Middle East, Iceland, large chunks of Eastern Europe, and downtown Beijing, the sparkling new outcrops, products of a global construction boom, were wearily familiar. In the UK, house-building is practically non-responsive to price signals.[11] In the US and in a range of other countries the problem was the opposite. At the peak of the boom about twice as many dwelling units per capita were started in the US than in the UK. In Spain it was 5.5 times as many, and for Ireland it was 6.5 times as many. Even with the supply response, in the ten years to 2007 real house prices rose by 180% in Spain and 240% in Ireland. The share of residential investment as a proportion of GDP peaked in 2005 in the US, at 6.2% (a 40-year high), and in 2007 in Spain and Ireland, at 9% and 12% respectively. In Ireland, with one in every eight euros of economic activity accounted for by house building, whole new towns sprouted in the middle of nowhere, like clumps of lucky shamrock, only to shrivel and die—ghost towns after the crash.[12] Expanding property-overhangs were another reason to criticize the Fed and the ECB for holding interest rates too low for too long and for not tightening up on credit, but they were also another reason not to put too much weight on stories of restricted housing supply causing price bubbles and crashes. It was easy credit and lax regulation, and not supply-side constraints, that drove the ensuing mess.

The growth of mortgage debt was in many places even more rapid than the rise in house prices. In the US, in the mid-1980s, the proportion of the total stock of housing wealth held by households was about 70%. By 2007 it was down at 50%. As financial institutions ratcheted up their level of mortgages, the proportion of total US housing wealth they held rose from 30% to about 50%. On such percentages one could easily conclude that a big enough fall in house prices and a big enough rise in defaults would swallow great chunks of the capital of banks. Few at the time were interested in such easy readings of the evidence.

As the one percentage, by falling steeply, met the other percentage, that was rising sharply, the staid old world of mortgage finance spun upon its head and a whole new breed of financial buccaneer—of decidedly dubious character—materialized in its place. In the US, huge new mortgage banks, like Ameriquest, Countrywide Financial Corporation, and New Century expanded voraciously. In the UK, politicians and regulators looked on, bemused and just occasionally worried, as banks like Northern Rock, HBOS, and RBS, gorged themselves on mortgages, and the ratio of total mortgage debt to GDP went from 50% to 80%. In Iceland, banks frolicked at the edges of the new financial thermals blithely unaware of the dangers simmering beneath. Many financial institutions that did not specialize in mortgage finance found themselves, by financial hook and crook, heavily exposed to it anyway. A housing bubble was shoring up the balance sheets of financial firms like never before—and probably never again.

Since price bubbles are just temporary but debt is for long-term keeps, promoting a heavy increase in mortgaging to turn the former into the latter was an altogether agreeable business model. Better still, the act of pumping easy debt in response to past house-price rises was like pumping air into a self-inflating balloon. House prices expanded further, which created yet more collateral to sustain yet more debt and pull even more customers in, and this pumped the balloon some more. It was child's play of a reassuringly profitable sort, or, in the logic of George Soros, the sign of an especially 'reflexive' market.[13] Despite record low interest rates, debt service relative to disposable income reached historic highs in the US because the size of loans grew so much bigger. In 1994, the median loan (that is, half of all loans were above and half of all loans were below) was $120,000 against a median income of borrowers of $73,000. In 2005 the median real income of borrowers was almost exactly the same ($74,000, in 1994 prices) but the average loan was $183,000.[14]

This was not a world of equals. If property prices fell, households would take the first losses. For those in the US holding the average amount of housing equity (50%), a 25% price fall would translate into a halving of their housing wealth. For those holding little housing equity—who tended to be those who were last to enter the market or who had tanked up a little too enthusiastically on mortgage debt—their little would become nothing or negative. In the US, mortgagees had a secret weapon up their sleeves. Defaulting on a loan is normally bad for the defaulter's credit history. In most countries, on the closeout of a mortgage loan any losses are still a liability of the borrower and, short of declaring bankruptcy, payable from any other assets the borrower has. This gives a decent enough incentive not to default, and may nudge borrowers towards renegotiating new terms even when a loan is in negative territory, so long as the borrower is able to make payments on the loan and the potential losses are not too large. In contrast, in many US states, lenders could not stake a claim to the other assets of those who defaulted on mortgages. Even if they could keep up repayment, borrowers had a heightened incentive to default when prices plummeted—on the not unreasonable financial principle of not throwing good money after bad. In the US, the widespread prevalence of this 'non-recourse' feature was a defence mechanism ready to spring into action: for any given stress on the real-estate market, default rates in the US were always going to be much higher than just about anywhere else in the world. The knowledge of this should have disciplined lenders. As we now know, it did not.

Housing and Consumption: The New Stop-Go

Like in most simple deceptions in life, so long as both sides got something out of it, each said nothing to upset the other. House buyers' nerves were calmed by the belief that ever-rising house prices had the potency to cure all financial ills. At the heart of the cure was the role of housing in sustaining consumption in economies like the US, the UK, Canada, and Australia, where 70% or more of economic activity depended upon consumption. Unfortunately, this particular economic medicine came with a range of potential side-effects, including balance-sheet headaches if used to excess and withdrawal symptoms if removed abruptly. Working out exactly how housing relates to consumption is more complicated than it might at first appear, and is the source of many an econometric headache in itself. Nonetheless, let's give it a go.

One of the difficulties is that housing produces a flow of services but is also an asset. As house prices rise, the costs of consuming housing services rise. Holding all else constant, for those at the bottom of the housing ladder (including those not yet born) and low in ownership of housing assets, rising house prices increase the cost per unit of housing services and make them worse off. For those at the top of the ladder, usually an older current generation, high in ownership of housing assets and not planning on boosting their consumption of housing services, rising house prices lead to wealth gains and make them better off; they can consume, in part, off the back of their housing wealth or, if necessary, from the proceeds of selling. For those part-way up the ladder, the rise in house prices involves a delicate balancing act: on the one hand, their borrowing ability is enhanced by the rising value of housing equity and they can consume more of everything else; on the other hand, higher housing costs reduce their lifetime wealth. The overall consumption response in the population is based on a complex pattern of gains and losses across the different groups.

In the US, the impact of housing wealth on consumption was especially high, with a marginal propensity to consume (MPC) for housing wealth (such that a higher MPC indicates a bigger impact) of about 0.07–0.09, i.e. each dollar of nominal housing wealth generated 0.7–0.9 cents of consumption per year.[15] This was more than twice what it was in the UK (at about 0.032[16]), Australia, and Canada, and much higher than in the eurozone, where home-ownership rates were lower and mortgage markets less developed,[17] and in Japan, where the absence of credit-market liberalization meant that housing was not so easily turned into consumption.[18] It was also a great deal higher than for stock market wealth. This helps to explain why the fall in US consumption after the collapse of the US stock market at the turn of the millennium was kept at bay by the rise in consumption caused by the rise in house prices over the early to mid-2000s.

Contrary to much popular opinion, little of the impact of housing wealth on consumption, in countries where housing wealth has important consumption effects, is a traditional wealth effect. The main effect comes through the credit channel because of the use of housing as collateral to support loans.[19] Indeed, Muellbauer and Murphy argue that the housing 'wealth effect' should, more accurately, be described as the housing 'collateral effect'.[20] In the US this effect was especially strong. First, the unlimited tax relief on mortgage interest encouraged US households to take out home-equity loans to fund consumption; in contrast, in places like the UK, tax relief had been phased out in the 1990s. Second, interest rate risk was lower in the US because the two publicly-traded government-chartered mortgage agencies, Fannie Mae and Freddie Mac, underwrote conforming loans, and cheap refinance options were available. Third, the non-recourse nature of US mortgages took away some of the risk of using loans for consumption. The collateral effect was also strong in the UK, weaker in much of Europe, and negative in Japan.[21]

In countries that had experienced lots of credit liberalization, such as the US and the UK, any given amount of housing wealth could more easily be used as collateral to support consumption (the exact linkage varied greatly according to institutional conditions, and hence across countries and time). On the one hand, it was worthwhile building up housing equity to take advantage of its role as collateral to support loans. On the other hand, if loans were becoming easier to get, it was less necessary to build up housing equity as collateral in the first place, and so the MPC from housing wealth increased in line with increased credit liberalization.[22] At high levels of credit liberalization, those not yet on the housing ladder also felt less need to save towards a deposit as house prices rose, because future borrowing would be less constrained by their lack of collateral. In Italy and Japan, where credit markets were more restrictive, when house prices rose, those not yet on the housing ladder saved more towards a deposit (or to cover higher future rents), and consumer spending fell.[23]

Greenspan and Kennedy[24] picked apart US mortgage-survey data from 1990 to 2006 (well, at least it kept Greenspan out of trouble for a while). They found that some 20% of the increase in home-mortgage debt was used to purchase a 'home' but that 80% was in the form of discretionary extraction of home equity. On average, some $590 billion of housing equity was released annually. After repayment of home-equity loans and non-mortgage debt, $175 billion was invested in assets and business investments, and about $70 billion went towards personal consumption expenditure (PCE). This was an average boost to PCE of about 1% per year. However, the annual boost was 0.6% over 1991–2000 and nearly 1.75% over 2001–2006. On a broader definition, including withdrawals used to repay non-mortgage debts, equity extraction financed $130 billion per year of PCE over the full period, an average boost of 1.8% of PCE. This comprised 1.1% over 1991–2000 and 3% over 2001 to 2006.

That 3%, in this context, is really rather a lot. In particular, it goes a long way towards explaining the plummeting savings rates in countries such as the US. It is an accounting thing. Rising house prices do not get registered in a country's GDP. So, as home equity is extracted and spent, consumption in the national income accounts rises but there is no matching increase in income. Thus the measured savings rate falls. In the UK the plummeting savings rate had an extra helping hand. At the height of the housing boom in 2006, UK mortgage providers were granting £10 billion in mortgages every month but taking in only about £5 billion from domestic savers. The rest came from abroad, via wholesale funding markets.

UK overseas debt mushroomed—to about $750 billion in 2006, about half of the UK's yearly GDP. And partly in response to that, the exchange rate rose and exports were clobbered.

At a time when the growth in average real take-home income was low, and negative for many, surging property prices were a key source of spending power for many. Only 'for many' because while some benefited from a consumption injection, others got little or nothing. The poor and those without housing equity had to rely on much more expensive forms of debt. Indeed, rising and falling house prices had ambiguous effects on the poor. More than half of all households in the bottom quarter of the US income distribution spent more than 50% of their income on housing costs.[25] As prices rose and low-income wages stagnated, affordability gaps opened up. Closing the gap by pumping debt into these groups set up house-price spirals that negated the affordability support. When house prices fell, foreclosure rates rose, but housing also became more affordable for the poor. House-price bubbles were a necessary corollary of inequality. In many places in the world, but especially in the US, house-price bubbles were a coping mechanism, a politically-sanctioned opiate to numb the economic pain of at least a portion of the masses. House-price bubbles were manna from financial heaven to those starving in the economic wilderness, and those who provided the mortgages to sustain the feast were appropriately revered.

Rising house prices had another boosting effect, but this time for governments. As Weale put it: 'There is rather a close analogy between the effects of rising house prices and the effects of government debt. The latter, like the former, imposes a burden on future generations while providing resources to those currently active. Rising house prices reduce the need for people to save to finance their retirement. Low taxes reduce the amount of consumption that they have to give up to finance their retirement, so the effect is similar.'[26] On the assumption that in the UK there had been an excess house-price appreciation of about 1.9% per year between 1987 and the market's peak in 2007, Weale calculated that the effect was about equivalent to a UK government deficit of about 4% per year. This was a welcome shot in the arm for a government bent on eating more of the national economic pie but embarrassed at the thought that its gluttony would be found out if it had to raise more taxes to pay for it. In the UK, housing became one of a long list of creative ways for the government to spend beyond its means.

Housing boosted the government's coffers in many other ways too. Rising house prices fed the slug of inheritance tax the government took each year. Tax from stamp duty rose about tenfold from the early 1990s. And taxation flowed in from all the hyperactive activity related to property-based financial instruments that channelled itself through London. Real estate, and the financial innovations that fed off it, were good business for the UK government.

At least higher explicit government debt might be used to pay for health and education, generating benefits for the wider population and maybe some longer-term growth potential. Redistribution of wealth via rising house prices, how-ever, was to the already-haves and away from the have-nots, and was more likely to show up in the consumption of the already-haves. By leading to a misallocation of both financial and human capital, long-term growth was harmed. House prices were a key part of the new economic stop-go cycle that had not gone away but been brightly repackaged for the 'new' era. The political trade-off was simple: a short-term spending boost from an extra hidden, impli-cit, 'deficit' and the ability to spend less on an aging population, but higher social exclusion and inequality and a surging government deficit when the truth was out. As Muellbauer and Murphy put it, in reference to the UK (but it can be applied to plenty of other places), 'The past 10 years have seen one of the greatest rises in social exclusion in post-war history.'[27] They added that the UK govern-ment 'has fallen for the easy but myopic politics of permissiveness towards rising house prices. The burden falls on the young, many too young to vote.'[28] The winners might give to some of the losers—a sort of intergenerational Ponzi scheme.[29] Indeed, over time, only those with pre-existing equity or family with such equity could hope to get on the 'property ladder'. Many losers even thought they were winners. They had put down 10% or 20% of the purchase price of a property and within a year they thought they had doubled their money. Or they thought of themselves as *potential* winners; they watched house prices rise and those tottering higher up the ladder gain, and thought that if only they could cling on, then like the lottery, one day it would be them. They failed to see the Ponzi nature of the scheme, and that they had lost because of the higher costs per unit of housing services and future government deficit obligations. The media and political spin was that rising house prices were always brilliant news for everyone and falling prices a tragedy; the economic reality was really rather different.

At the Heart of the Storm

If the global financial crash had a dark heart, it was pulsating in the mortgage market that lay beneath these surging property prices. The incen-tive to pump the mortgage market for financial and political gain (the two were highly agreeable accomplices) reached its apotheosis in the US, but the phenomenon was widespread. In the US an unholy combination of forces drove mortgage activity to unsustainable heights: excessively low interest rates, underwriting defects that would make a first-grader blush, contractual trickery that would shame the mafioso, and regulatory vigilance only just this side of comatose.

At the centre of it all sat subprime[30]—at the start so promising, now a crestfallen and sorry creature waiting for its comeuppance. Greenspan was for once unusually clear, and therefore more easily overlooked, when he declared, 'The roots of this crisis are global and geo-political... The actual trigger is securitized American subprime mortgages which became toxic and essentially proliferated around the world. However, if it were not that trigger, in other words if it were not the subprime, something else would have triggered it.'[31] There was a global financial iceberg, and subprime was its tip, but the financial sea was thick with other perilous hazards. Greenspan had a point. The role of subprime was much more subtle than most treatments have allowed.

If the marketing gurus had not been allowed to scrub it clean, 'subprime' would have been called 'superprime'. Even in a world of low interest rates and easy credit, many subprime mortgagees were paying interest rates into the double digits, fees were high, and hefty penalties for getting out of a loan early (prepayment fees) were the norm. The justification was that subprime customers posed a higher credit or prepayment risk.[32] However, so long as the housing market wasn't sinking, many of these risks did not crystallize, and subprime was highly lucrative business. To the political elite, subprime was a splendid new financial innovation for pulling (or pushing, depending on one's perspective) many over the ownership threshold. To investors, subprime was the next goldmine.

Subprime first took off in the mid-1990s, spurred by innovations that reduced, for lenders, the costs of assessing and pricing risk. With the growth of structured finance, subprime expanded even more rapidly in the 2000s. The rates of growth were impressive. Because of discrepancies and data anomalies, it is best not to rely on one measure.[33] According to the LP figures (calculated from LoanPerformance data), there were around 300,000 subprime originations in 1998, rising to 700,000 in 2002, peaking at 2,000,000 in 2005, and dropping to 1,500,000 in 2006. The HUD (United States Department of Housing and Urban Development) figures start at 750,000 in 1998, rise to 1,000,000 in 2002, peak at 2,200,000 in 2005 and then fall. That is, the LP figure shows a sevenfold increase and the HUD figure shows a threefold increase. The HMDA higher-priced measure (based on data gathered under the terms of the Home Mortgage Disclosure Act) gives the most comprehensive coverage, and shows nearly 3 million subprime mortgages in 2005, 800,000–900,000 more than the LP or HUD lender measures. All three measures show a marked acceleration in subprime origination from 2003 to the peak year of 2005, three years before the collapse of Lehman, before a falling off in 2006 and a collapse in 2007. The HMDA measure shows a near doubling between 2004 and 2005 alone (coinciding with the flattening of the yield curve). The proportion of subprime and Alt-A as a share of the US loan portfolio peaked around 2005 (Alt-A is short for 'Alternative A-paper', and refers to a type of mortgage that is considered more risky than 'prime', that is A-paper, but less risky than 'subprime'). If there was a time when risk was being locked in, it was between 2004 and 2005. Incidentally, it was in 2004–2005 that I published my first warnings about the rising dangers in the US mortgage market.

In a database covering half of all subprime loans originated in the period 2001–2006, the average loan size doubled.[34] In a world of low inflation and low real income growth, the individual loans were in real terms getting bigger. Like cuckoos in a nest, such mortgages would demand an ever-bigger chunk of the long-term resources of those who took them on. The subprime share of the flow of mortgage-market originations was about 5% in 1994 ($35 billion) and 20% ($625 billion) by 2006. This represents year-on-year growth of 26% over a decade. At its peak, the stock of subprime mortgages stood at an impressive 7% of the total outstanding stock of mortgages. Of course, this means that 93% of the stock was not subprime—a fact that is often overlooked. There was a huge increase in the volume of prime mortgage stock too; it is the percentage shift towards subprime that attracts all the attention.

Across all three measures of subprime originations, across all years, subprime mortgages were slightly more often used to refinance than to buy a home. This might surprise many readers, given the popular perception that subprime was all about helping the poor to buy homes. In the peak year of 2005 some 1.2 million subprime mortgages, or about 60% as measured by LP and HUD data or 50% measured by the HMDA data, were used for refinancing—almost all of it cash-out refinancing and not for first-time purchases. Compared to other types of loans, more subprime loans went on house purchases and fewer on consumption. Nevertheless, subprime was not just about buying homes. It was, like all mortgages, about funding consumption too.

While it was scattered, glittering, into innumerable neighbourhoods up and down the land, subprime was also much more unevenly spread geographically and socially than has often been acknowledged. This greatly complicates our attempts to understand its role and to derive appropriate policy responses in the event of a crash. It is true that US subprime originations were concentrated in more areas with moderate credit scores, including Black and Hispanic neighbourhoods, than were prime mortgages. Nonetheless subprime was also heavily concentrated (at two to three times the rates elsewhere per number of housing units) in fast-growing metropolitan states such as Florida, California, Arizona, and Nevada, where new construction was a high proportion of activity, and where house prices were growing above the US average and above prior averages for their regions.[35] As there was an excess of housing construction, some way had to be found to get people to buy the houses, and the causation was as likely to run from construction to subprime as the other way around. Besides, it was not a one-to-one correlation. In other areas with high house-price growth, such as parts of the North East, subprime growth was not strong, and there were large numbers of subprime originations in places such as Atlanta, Chicago, parts of Texas, and the Washington DC environs. Low income and high unemployment areas had more subprime than average, but the strength of association was weaker than many other associations. In depressed housing markets, few new home owners or investors were attracted in, and existing home owners had little, if any, house-price gain to extract via refinancing: in such markets subprime originations were low relative to housing units, but high relative to mortgage originations.

In summary; there were those who had been crushed in life but who, against all the socio-economic and discriminatory odds, finally owned their own roof and walls and fireplace because of subprime; there were those who used subprime as their only way to get credit while those richer than them got credit much more cheaply; there were those who speculated on rising property prices and pushed their spending beyond their means courtesy of subprime loans; there were those who were the victims of predatory behaviour, and others making 'consumption-smoothing' decisions. If and when the market turned, all would be lumped together. In truth, real estate had inestimably valuable dual roles. On the one hand, it was something socially valuable. On the other hand, it was something on which a keenly exploitable price bubble could be hung. The former would shield the latter from scrutiny, with subprime acting as the numbing cloak to enfold the two as one. This, we shall see later, is also why tackling the US foreclosure crisis turned out to be so very, very difficult.

There is some evidence that the expansion in the securitization of subprime loans—in the US, from 54% in 2001 to about 75% by 2006—contributed to house-price growth, but it is unclear to what degree subprime acting as lending itself was a cause or a consequence of the housing boom.[36] This might surprise some, given the constant assertion in much of the popular literature that subprime was causal. It is a critical issue. If subprime lending was more of a symptom, then the driving forces of bubbles in housing and mortgage markets need to be sought elsewhere. Housing-price bubbles were expanding and debt levels shooting up in many other countries where subprime and securitization were still undeveloped (and, indeed, in the commercial sector of the US prices were bubbling quite nicely without any subprime). If the property-price bubble was a global phenomenon, it becomes more difficult to blame securitization and subprime, and perhaps we should not blame the US property market as the sole source of all woes. We can for sure say that there was something peculiarly extreme about the way the US responded to the global pressures, and that the collateral role of housing played a very important role in the boom and the bust, but the causal role of subprime is less clear-cut.

It's the Incentives, Stupid

Bill Clinton once ran an entire presidential campaign (1992) on just the one slogan: 'It's the economy, stupid.' Taking a leaf out of his book, some economists successfully run their entire professional careers on the equally simple slogan 'It's the incentives, stupid.' Or, more precisely, 'It's the stupid incentives.' In the US mortgage sector, perverse incentives were everywhere, the bad drove out the good, and the industry populated itself with an especially rich mix of buffoons and financial stunt merchants armed with rods and lines to catch the unsuspecting and sometimes the perfectly willing.

It is difficult to make precise comparisons—the comparator is a composite index of many factors not all changing in the same direction[37]—but it seems that the greatest deterioration of mortgage standards was in the US. It was a worry at the time.[38] Even without lowering lending standards on any types of loan, the composition of the US mortgage book gradually tilted towards higher-risk mortgages and mortgages that contained features that made the overall portfolio of mortgages more risky. However, across a variety of dimensions, evidence also piled up that lending standards did deteriorate as the mortgage industry found ever more creative ways to milk the typical mortgage contract for all it was (and often was not) worth.[39]

Lenders slackened up on the documentation required to prove income and asset holdings. In 2001, about 30% of pools of securitized subprime loans were 'low-doc' (i.e. self-certified). By 2006, the proportion was well over half.[40] Astonishingly, by May 2008 matters had become so laid back that about 60% of fixed-rate mortgages of any sort lacked full documentation.

Then there were 'balloon' mortgage contracts that deliberately underpaid early, leaving a large repayment to the end, on the assumption that the borrower would be able to take out a new loan to pay off the previous one. In 2006, 25% of all US mortgages had a balloon built in. One wonders why they didn't just call them 'bubble' contracts, and be done with it. To the extent that the balloons never got repaid, they were a clever way to redistribute wealth from the taxpayer to the magicians who conjured them up but who had vanished long before they popped.

The loan-to-value (LTV) ratios on new mortgages rose too. According to one study, 18% of all new mortgages originated in 2006 were already in negative equity by the end of the year.[41] As Oscar Wilde might have put matters, to lose a few mortgages to negative equity within a year may be regarded as a misfortune; to lose nearly one in five looks like carelessness. Tha data therefore suggests that many mortgages started their lives equal or close to 100% LTV in the misplaced belief that property prices could only ever soar and the LTV shrink. In the UK and the Netherlands in particular, 100% LTVs became much more common, but they remained a relatively small proportion of all mortgages,[42] although Spain too got carried away with 100% LTV at the top of the market.

With the lowest Fed rates in decades, there was a large-scale shift to adjustable rate mortgages. In 2006, about 80% of subprime mortgages were adjustable rate. Even more illogical, by early 2007, nearly 35% of all securitized newly-originated US loans were interest-only, and a further 7% were negative amortization, a feature only really prevalent in the US.[43] With such mischief, the US saddled itself with higher LTVs that would also stay higher for longer.

Then there was the practice of 'piggybacking' a second mortgage on top of another. Thus many got 100% financing but without the irritating little inconvenience of having to pay the insurance to do it.[44] There was no 100% LTV piggyback lending in the UK, although in early 2008 six lenders were merrily offering 125% LTV mortgages, including the ill-fated Northern Rock. In 2006 in the US 40% of securitized Alt-A first mortgages and 25% of securitized subprime mortgages came with these 'silent second liens'; these had been no more than 1% at the end of the 1990s. This was largely unheard of anywhere else in the world. Often the first mortgage was not disclosed to the second mortgage grantor, and so the second mortgage was mispriced. For sophisticated financial players, this sounds a pretty dumb trap to fall into. Of course, many were complicit.

Then there were the low introductory 'teaser' rates that lured many to their financial ruin. In the US these were about 3%–4% below the rate at which the loan would eventually be reset. Nowhere else in the world was the tease so titillating. In the UK, teaser rates never went much below standard variable rates, and lenders were required to assess affordability on the basis of the full reversion rate, and not on the basis of the teaser rate. In Australia, the difference was, at most, 0.5% to 1.5%. In the US, the sort of people who in other countries were declined a mortgage were often breezily waved through right under the noses of the regulators. Many did not understand what they were signing up to or simply didn't care. When the introductory period ended and the truth was stripped bare, they would be in for a surprise. Worse, they might then try to clear the debt early only to face a clause, hidden, limpet like, deep within the small print on the bottom of some barely readable contract, stipulating stiff prepayment fees. Waves of subprime contracts rolled in like disorientated whales about to be beached, only to be rescued, at the last minute, by yet another low-rate deal—until, that is, there were no low-rate deals left. The largest wave of all, underwritten in 2004–2006, reached land in 2008–2009. Astonishingly, if house prices just stood still and the economy did not deteriorate and unemployment was unchanged, on one calculation, 12% of subprime loans would default on account of reset alone.[45]

Warren Buffett warned in his annual letter to shareholders in 2008: 'Beware the glib helper who fills your head with fantasies while he fills his pockets with fees.' This was never more applicable than to the mortgage market, where, under each layer of fees, like a Matryoshkan doll, unvariably lay another. The mortgage broker got 0.5%–3% of the value of the loan. The mortgage lender got 0.5% to 2.5% the moment the mortgage was sold. The bond issuer got 0.2% to 1.5% when the bond was issued. A rating agency got a fee from the bond issuer when the security was issued. Fees based on volume, not surprisingly, encouraged volume over quality. Within six to eight months of the original mortgage contract being signed, all had pocketed their fees and vanished. In stable times, the chance of any borrower defaulting by then was negligible. Mortgage originators generally retained little if any of the default risk. The only party with any real stake in how well a loan performed was the borrower.

Were Investment Banks Foolish or Knowing?

As lenders proudly laid their catch out, politicians were mightily pleased with themselves too. Yet, as a result of such trickery, on the eve of the crash the US was especially vulnerable to a messy economic unravelling. There was the high level of mortgage debt, the ultimate repayment of which was extraordinarily dependent on house prices not falling, an unusually large proportion of home owners with no or negative equity, who were vulnerable to large price falls but able to default more easily than just about anywhere else in the world, a sea of mortgage originators with hardly any skin left in the game, a huge construction boom and overhang of excess housing stock that would drag prices down when the market turned, an economy heavily dependent on housing because of its role as collateral to support borrowing, and an unusually high MPC out of housing wealth. Did financial firms know of the dangers or were they just plain foolish? The two are, of course, not mutually exclusive.

Signs of overhang were everywhere. In the US, the average house vacancy rate[46] had hovered around 1.5% for two decades, but had leapt to about 3% and was particularly high for houses built after 2000. A simple stock-adjustment relation (to determine how much construction was needed for housing stock to adjust to changes in fundamentals) indicated a required ratio of construction to GDP of about 3.8%.[47] The average over 2000–2006 was about 4.9%. Just as it might seem harmless to overeat by a small amount, so a bit of overbuild every year seems innocuous enough. But what if the gluttony goes on for years on end? There was a growing overhang in many other countries too, such as in Ireland and Spain, chunks of emerging Europe, the Middle East, and in a huge number of global housing hot spots, including in China and India. In July 2008, Moody's identified the UK, Spain, Ireland, Denmark, and the US as being at greatest risk from a negative economic shock related to their housing markets.[48] For the UK and Denmark the danger was the departure from house-price fundamentals and the high degree of vulnerability of heavily indebted households. For the US, Spain, and Ireland the danger was from a huge property overbuild.

When it came to other signs of danger, one had to be looking especially closely. Delinquency rates were low, but this should not have surprised anyone: property prices were rising sharply; borrowers who would otherwise be in trouble were able to take out new mortgages if the first one proved too tough; and the economy was not in recession. In the UK in the years just before the crash, mortgage banks reassured themselves that arrears and repossessions were at their lowest levels since 1989. Arrears were even lower on 'buy-to-let' (BTL) mortgages (those granted specifically to buy properties for letting out). Given a 25%–30% price rise in just a year or two and low levels of unemployment, this was not surprising. The clumsy notion was that the UK was safe from the consequences of a collapsing house-price bubble because it was experiencing a bubble. For those who work in the UK housing market, 1989 is a fabled year—the year that marked the start of the last housing market crash when arrears and repossessions were at their lowest level since, well, since the last lowest level on the eve of a crash.

One way to test the true level of risk was to adjust raw loan-level data on delinquency rates to take account of differences in loan and borrower characteristics and macroeconomic conditions. It was a 'simple statistical exercise' for those who did it.[49] Properly adjusted, the quality of US loans deteriorated each year in the six years running up to the crash. If the default risk of subprime mortgages was rising relative to safer mortgages, then the interest rate spread between subprime and prime mortgages should have been rising too. Instead, the spread (both adjusted and unadjusted for quality) fell, especially between 2001 and 2004; on a per-unit-of-risk basis, the subprime-to-prime spread fell even more than the level of the spread. It seems that although subprime rates were higher than on other types of mortgage, they were, over time, increasingly not fully pricing in the extra risk. Furthermore, even though the quality of mortgages deteriorated, the proportion of high LTV originations kept climbing. In 2007, even though the market had already peaked, nearly 20% of all US loans (and not just subprime) had an LTV greater than 97%. A decade earlier it had been a fraction of this. Meanwhile, mortgage rates became more sensitive to LTV, which suggested that lenders were aware that the quality of loans was deteriorating even as the frothy market masked this. In October 2010 the former boss of Countrywide, Angelo Mozilo, agreed to pay a record $67.5 million fine to settle US Securities and Exchange Commission (SEC) fraud charges. His crime essentially boiled down to knowing the dangers and hiding them from investors (of course, he was not sent to prison, and having made nearly half a billion dollars in the five years before the crash, the fine was not going to hurt him).

The US mortgage industry was facing a pincer movement. Long-term fixed-rate mortgage deals were so good that between 2001 and 2004 about half the outstanding mortgage stock switched to take advantage of them.[50] Mortgage holders saw large savings (some estimates put it at about 20% on average for loans refinanced through Freddie Mac[51]) while lenders saw large falls in their incomes. Meanwhile, while greater access to wholesale markets was driving down the price of credit to financial firms, more competition was driving the margins on property loans to ever-lower levels. If one lender did not cut its standards but others did, it would see its market share shrink. To keep the volumes up, lenders reduced their standards together and chased the apparently more profitable segments of the market, where the margins were higher—a 'cheat-cheat' race-to-the-bottom in a prisoner's dilemma game.

It is hard to believe that lenders, investment banks, and others with access to loan-level data and ever more sophisticated techniques for modelling risk could not have worked out that the underlying situation was getting ever more risky. Perhaps they knew but believed they were clever enough to get out in time and leave others to take the losses (and some of those involved clearly thought they were cleverer than most), or else they knew but believed the government would bail them out anyway if things went wrong, or else their risk-management systems simply failed to identify the risks. The last is not as silly as it sounds: when times are good, the incentives to do any analysis that might pour a little rain on the party are much reduced. Finally, the big banks had insurance (via credit default swaps (CDSs), which we shall discuss in Chapter 3), and this numbed their senses some more. An unusually large fraction of 2006 and 2007 vintage subprime loans were delinquent or even in foreclosure just a few months later.[52] It is tempting to speculate, and therefore I will, that since it was not going to make any difference to the already inevitable bailout, lenders reasoned that they might as well stuff as many subprime loans and other mortgages as they could into their already full mouths and take the fees before the season turned and hibernation set in.

Companies like Ameriquest, Countrywide, and New Century could not take deposits. They could never have survived but for the external injection of money from those who had access to such funds, usually investment banks based, in particular, in the US, the UK, Switzerland, and Germany. In a study of 7.2 million high-interest loans reported to the US government over the period 2005–2007, the top 25 originators originated two thirds, about a trillion dollars' worth of subprime mortgages.[53] By mid-2009 most were bankrupt. Of these 25, at least 21 were financed by banks that received bailout money. Most investment banks did not do subprime lending directly (they were not going to be *that* stupid!), but they got deeply involved by buying up the subprime loans of non-bank lenders, bundling them up, and selling them on as securities. Top of the list sat Lehman Brothers, which in the peak years of 2005–2006, underwrote about $106 billion of subprime loans, closely followed by RBS Greenwich Capital Investments (part of the Royal Bank of Scotland) with about $100 billion.[54] The others in the top ten were Morgan Stanley, Credit Suisse First Boston, Merrill Lynch, Bear Stearns, Goldman Sachs & Co., Wells Fargo & Co., and Deutsche Bank (alongside Countrywide Securities). Others in the top 25 included Citigroup, JPMorgan Chase & Co., and Bank of America. Keener than most, Wells Fargo & Co., JPMorgan Chase & Co., and Citigroup Inc. had their own subprime lending units. Not to be left out, the UK's HSBC, under chairman Sir John Bond, got in on the subprime act by acquiring Household International in March 2003—'the deal of the first decade of the 21st century', pronounced *The Banker*[55]—shortly after Household had been fined nearly half a billion dollars for predatory lending practices. The new division, HSBC Finance, became the second largest subprime lender in the US. 'It's an acquisition we wish we hadn't done, with the benefit of hindsight,' observed the next chairman of HSBC, Stephen Green, when the company finally sobered up.[56]

Even if some of these big-name investment banks had kept away from subprime, subprime mortgage lenders would have got their money instead from the others. This was high-volume, high-profit-margin business, and the demand from international investors at the top of the food chain was so overwhelming that the biggest concern of subprime lenders was of running out of enough customers at the bottom who would be willing to take out the mortgages that got bundled into the packages that the investors demanded. We focus on all the careless lending of banks; we too often overlook the careless lending *to* banks. Mortgage creators could not have behaved in the way they did had the ultimate financial investors into *them* been more discriminating and had regulators coordinated to stop them. Usually we think of higher rates as the compensation for taking higher risks. Instead, many subprime lenders and their backers fed off the higher rates and then parlayed the risks onto governments. As Citigroup chairman Richard Parsons put it, 'Everybody participated in pumping up this balloon and now that the balloon has deflated, everybody in reality has some part in the blame.'[57] Collectively, over the decade running up to the crash, the top 25 subprime lenders spent $370 million on lobbying Washington.[58] Perhaps they could have spent just a little of that on modelling the risks more accurately.

Government and Regulation

Many have given a central causal role to the US government's support for mortgage lending to households of lower credit quality.[59] Support showed especially in the shape of subsidies for 'affordable housing' via expansion of the two government-sponsored enterprises, Fannie Mae and Freddie Mac (sometimes called the 'agency sector' or 'conforming market' or simply the GSEs). The implicit guarantee to bail out the GSEs if ever they got into trouble, allowed the GSEs to issue debt at interest rates below those of competitors, and thus win market share. In the good years, the private shareholders in the GSEs profited. In the bad years, taxpayers took the pain. This conflict of interest was the source of a large indirect government subsidy to the US mortgage market that benefited GSE stockholders and home buyers.

After the crash, a raging bunfight broke out between the Democrats and Republicans regarding which party was to blame for the subprime mess. Naturally enough, they both were. Those who unthinkingly pushed the GSEs were at fault in that they did not spot the dangers. Barney Frank, the leading Democrat speaking on the issue, famously observed during the hearings investigating the solvency of Fannie Mae and Freddie Mac in 2003: 'These two entities—Fannie Mae and Freddie Mac—are not facing any kind of financial crisis ... The more people exaggerate these problems, the more pressure there is on these companies, the less we will see in terms of affordable housing.'[60] The critics must share the blame too because they used the various accounting and governance problems of the GSEs in the early 2000s as an excuse to promote something even riskier: pushing to limit the capacity of the GSEs via caps on their lending and encouraging non-conforming lending (especially subprime and Alt-A) to expand in the non-agency sector.[61] We see this clearly in the figures. In 2001, in the agency sector, banks originated about $1.4 trillion of conforming mortgage loans. $1.1 trillion of mortgage-backed securities was built upon this. In the non-agency sector the figures were quite a bit smaller, at just under $700 billion and $240 billion respectively. Subprime and Alt-A were just $250 billion (12%) of the total of $2.1 trillion origination. In the non-agency sector only $190 billion of origination and less than $90 billion of issuance was subprime and Alt-A respectively.[62] There followed, in 2003, a huge surge in origination and issuance across all classes of mortgages, related to the sharp reduction in long-term interest rates. Yet, while the agency sector peaked in about 2003, the non-agency sector kept on growing to the point that by 2006, non-agency origination was ahead of agency origination, at nearly $1.5 trillion versus a little over $1 trillion. If the GSEs were being risky, if they had ended up being a higher percent of the total system, the system would have ended up more risky—but they did not.

Policymakers were warned repeatedly that high-cost loans were a systemic risk.[63] Greenspan wrote in his memoirs: 'I was aware that the loosening of mortgage credit terms for subprime borrowers increased financial risk, but I believed then, as now, that the benefits of broadened home ownership are worth the risk.'[64] When, in 2001, Sheila C. Bair, then a senior Treasury official, tried to bring in a code of best practices for subprime lenders and outside monitoring, no lenders would agree that their compliance be monitored, and many rejected the code. Even those who adopted the practices soon let them slip. When seeking to blame the GSEs and policymakers, we should reflect too that there was a parallel commercial real-estate bubble in the US entirely driven by private interests with none of the distortions of state institutions, and that

Europe also had none of the government distortions found in the US, and yet property-price bubbles happily proliferated there.

Subsidies for 'affordable housing' were supposed to help individuals get on the property ladder. However, like all subsidies, they got amortized into market prices—that is, property prices were bid higher to include the value of the current and future expected subsidies—which offset the original purpose of the subsidies and meant that those who gained were those who owned property at the start and not necessarily those who wanted to buy at a later date. Such subsidies cannot therefore explain the run-up in prices in the 2000s, which must be caused by something else.

Wishful Thinking and Bubbles

A collective gamble that mass mortgage default would not happen was at the heart of the global financial system. This in turn rested on the notion that house prices could not fall. In 2005 Bernanke spoke for the consensus, declaring that US house prices 'largely reflect strong economic fundamentals'.[65] Similar wishful thinking filled the heads of policymakers from Sydney to Dublin and from Beijing to Dubai. Like all the best wishful thinking it was illogical too. The fundamentals pinning down house prices might have changed, but if so, an explanation ought to be at hand in terms of the new fundamentals. Income fundamentals could not do it, at least not in the US. Not only was the growth of US household income very low but expected future income growth, as picked up in household surveys, was also very low.

As we saw in Chapter 1, one leading 'non-bubble' explanation was of a global one-off upward adjustment in asset prices, including house prices, because of permanently lower inflation and output volatility, such that even if housing supply responded enthusiastically, house prices would still settle at a much higher level than before. We've already examined some of the dents in this explanation.

Another popular non-bubble explanation was that, consequent on the fall in inflation, lower nominal interest rates reduced the credit constraints faced by many households, that could thenceforth afford to take on bigger loans and bid house prices higher. I previously picked this explanation apart and argued that it was not strong enough to explain a large, rational, bidding-up of house prices for any given level of real income.[66] Financial liberalization in the 1980s and 1990s had long ago reduced the power of credit constraints in places like the US and UK. Indeed, those who worked a credit-conditions variable into their models of

UK house prices found that the negative nominal interest rate effect became weaker, and the negative real interest rate effect stronger, as financial market liberalization rose.[67] The credit-constraint-based explanation also implied changes in patterns of non-housing consumption that did not make economic sense.[68]

Under both leading non-bubble explanations, lenders would make large profits in the early years of adjustment. These would be eaten away by the entry and expansion of new and existing lenders until the profit per unit of bank capital would be 'back in equilibrium' at a higher level of mortgage debt than before. Certain categories of people who would not have got mortgage debt before would now be able to get it. Far from this being the sign of excessive lending, it would be the sign of efficiency and a rise in social welfare.

Was there, instead, a global house-price bubble? The problem was that policymakers everywhere faced a 'signal extraction' problem because the information regarding house price fundamentals was very noisy. How much of the rise in house prices was a reflection of efficient adjustment towards a new higher-price equilibrium, and how much was an inefficient 'bubble'? Different economists came to different conclusions on the relative probabilities of the two. Yet, since the natural resting state of most economists is denial of irrationality, not surprisingly the predominant position taken in the mid-2000s by economists ruled out bubbles. There is nothing quite as refreshing as a cold dose of reality to concentrate the mind, and after the crash many quickly shifted towards the possibility that there had been a price bubble. Indeed, henceforth no self-respecting congressional report was deemed complete without the obligatory reference to a house-price bubble from a suitably learned economist.

Testing for a house-price bubble is not straightforward. Simple measures, such as the ratio of house prices to incomes or rents, won't do, because they fail to take into account the impact of demography, house building, age composition, and changes in credit conditions and financial innovations that impact long-term trends in real interest rates and other asset prices.[69] The challenge is to model the key fundamentals that drive house prices, and then compare actual house prices with those estimated by the model using historical data. Deviations between the actual prices and the modelled prices indicate the presence of a bubble. The 'signal extraction' challenge is reflected in such tests, which are really tests of a joint hypothesis—of whether fundamentals have been correctly specified and of whether prices have deviated from the level dictated by those fundamentals. Find a 'bubble' and it could be that a more correct specification of fundamentals would see it disappear. For example, if it were the case that in 2005 the expansion in borrowing opportunities was a mirage based on global imbalances, a bubble test that did not filter this out would be less likely to generate the finding of a 'bubble'. Yet, it is incredibly difficult to distinguish temporary from truly permanent shifts in fundamentals until long after the event. Fundamentals should also incorporate expectations—yet expectations cannot be seen.

To get around these difficulties, one might think to draw up a list of 'plausible scenarios' for drivers of house prices, model these forward from a point in time using these drivers, and then look at the residuals. At least some of the psychological, and non-fundamental, patterns would get treated as positive residuals in a positive bubble and negative residuals in a negative bubble. The bottom line is that testing for a bubble in house prices is not easy. Sometimes it is just more useful to think of the inconsistent logic generated by bubbles as an indicator of their presence, which is largely the approach I took in the mid-2000s and that led to the conclusion that house prices were rushing ahead of fundamentals.[70]

If a bubble was taking place, what were its mechanics? The standard way to explain away the possibility of house-price bubbles is that economic agents are 'rational' and that backwards induction from the collapse of price bubbles stops bubbles from happening in the first place. In reality, there are multiple problems with this simple logic and there are many other possibilities in the case of house prices.[71] One possibility is a form of 'money illusion'.[72] When inflation falls and pulls nominal interest rates down, a typical loan-repayment schedule becomes less front-loaded and more rear-loaded (on a diagram with repayment per period of time on the vertical axis, and time on the horizontal axis, the loan-repayment schedule twists anti-clockwise and is flatter). If house buyers don't spot this, they take on bigger mortgages because of the eased repayments of the early years and push the new schedule outwards.[73] Over time, as a household works its way down the new repayment schedule, its total repayment is higher than it would have been before. If many suffer money illusion and bid house prices higher, many end up spending a higher proportion of their lifetime real income in order to get the same amount of housing services.[74] Teaser rates and super-low interest rates—such as those in 2003—were especially good ways of intensifying money illusion and feeding a bubble. Banks were complicit, but so were many borrowers.

The portfolio dynamics are interesting too. Increasing the number of those with loans based on loan-repayment schedules that have been shifted outwards generates a surge in profits for lenders and a cohort of customers locked into commitments to loan repayments much greater than before. However, eventually the growing burden on the finances of households will cause affordability to deteriorate and reduce the ability to trade up, and this will have a depressing effect on house prices and the flow of new loans.[75] At some point, there are no new customers to pull in and current customers cannot be encouraged to soak up more debt, the process naturally reaches its limits and collapses. It is lucrative for lenders while it lasts, but money illusion sews the seeds of its own destruction.

The second possibility is 'momentum' behaviour. Positive shocks cause price rises that feed into house-price expectations, and desire and momentum conspire to take prices even further beyond fundamentals.[76] The gains of early 'winners' incentivize others to enter and take on more debt.[77] Leverage exaggerates the apparent gains; a borrower puts down in cash just 5% or 10% in a rising housing market, and a year later the initial stake has doubled or trebled or maybe even more. Survey evidence shows a lively imagination on the part of house buyers, which feeds momentum. For example, Case and Shiller asked a random selection of home buyers in a range of US cities in which prices seemed to be in a bubble how much they thought the price of their home would rise per year on average over the next ten years.[78] The median answer was about 10%, or an increase by a factor of 2.5 in ten years, or, by the exponential wonders of compound interest, a more than thousand-fold increase in house prices over an average lifetime. However, 10%, never mind 15% or 20%, is clearly not a long-term sustainable rate of price growth and could only ever be temporary. Yet many think it reasonable that real-estate trees can grow to the moon.

If House-Price Bubbles are Hard to Correct, They Happen

Most arguments against the persistence of asset price bubbles rely on some notion of arbitrage, i.e. the ability to profitably bet against, and thereby correct, bubbles. The problem is that, as Keynes once remarked, 'Markets can remain irrational a lot longer than you and I can remain solvent.'[79] The modern version of this thinking combines asymmetric information (between 'principals' who provide funds and 'agents' who invest funds) and the limited resources of agents trying to profit from correcting a house-price bubble. If house-price bubbles are hard to correct, they happen.

Owing to asymmetric information, the principals cannot tell whether an investment position taken by an agent is fundamentally good or failing. If a position persistently goes against an agent (say, the market gets even more wildly overpriced), even if that position is ultimately correct, the principal will either reduce funds to the agent, or provide fresh funds only at a higher cost or on condition that the agent satisfies 'margin calls' (i.e. when a trading position has lost a lot of money, more money has to be posted as collateral to allow the position to continue). A resource-constrained agent who believes there is a house-price bubble (i.e. a 'pessimist') will rationally resist taking a position betting against the bubble if he or she fears that not enough others will adopt similar positions so that the bubble will be corrected within a time-frame sufficiently short to avoid losses caused by having to terminate the position prematurely. If the number of those pushing house prices higher (the 'optimists', sometimes called 'noise traders' in the literature) is large and they have a high level of wealth and high access to credit, the ability of pessimists to correct the bubble will be extremely limited.

If in the mid-2000s a bubble was taking place in house prices and a single lender tried on its own to correct the mispricing (say, by not lending), it would have seen its balance sheet, fees, and profits falling.[80] The problem was intensified by an increasing reliance on wholesale markets to fund mortgages and by the decline of branch networks (customers were much more mobile, and moved their deposits to banks paying higher rates even if they did not know why, and they priced in that their deposits were insured by governments). Conversely, if no other lender had fed the bubble, it would have been highly profitable for the one that did (especially if money illusion was being exploited). And so all were compelled to feed the bubble. If future industry profits were going to be squeezed anyway, the profit-maximizing strategy of an individual bank was to go along with the bubble and lock in the highest number of customers and profits immediately.

House buyers too might have wanted to coordinate between themselves not to push prices higher because this meant spending more over their lifetimes on housing services and less on all other consumption. However, if all other buyers did not overbid, it was the 'dominant strategy' for an individual to overbid. Unable to coordinate, all overbid.[81] Compared to stock markets, there was also limited ability to arbitrage the housing market by short selling.[82] Ordinary house buyers could only arbitrage the market by not buying and they had no way to leverage their 'not-buying' bets (whereas they could leverage their buying bets). In the absence of a complete set of derivative markets—which is typically the case in housing markets—even the arbitrage strategies of banks had to rely on simply refusing to lend. Besides, if it was believed that governments would panic and try to slow house-price corrections and that a crash would come with a bailout, this would further weaken the ex-ante ability to correct a house-price bubble.[83]

In sum, preventing house-price bubbles requires coordination across many layers—buyers of houses, mortgage brokers, mortgage companies, investment banks, and others—as well as within any particular layer. Failure at one layer (such as house buyers) to arbitrage against a bubble raises the difficulty and costs of arbitrage for those at other layers (e.g. mortgage lenders, investment banks, or shareholders).

Nevertheless, even if all the other layers failed, if long-term profitability was being fully and rationally incorporated into the share prices of investment banks, mortgage lenders, and real-estate agents, falling share prices would have forced up the cost of raising capital and so disciplined bad behaviour. Yet, in the mid-2000s the share prices of banks reached historic highs, the cost of wholesale funds became very low, and the rates being charged on CDSs indicated that financial institutions were very safe. This suggests that a bank-based bubble may itself have had stock market 'bubble' backing (and all the principal–agent arguments above apply in stock markets too). Bank shareholders faced a conflict of interest. Much of the upside went to them, while a crash would be shared with many others, and so bank shareholders disproportionately discounted the losses.

Furthermore, when it is not clear what fundamentals are, it is difficult to coordinate correction (i.e. there is no 'common knowledge' about how big a price bubble will get and when it will burst, so it is hard to do backwards induction on the collapse of a bubble). One of the biggest uncertainties in the 2000s was the relationship between global imbalances and credit expansion. Central banks have limited control over the amount of credit created in an economy, and this creates great uncertainty about the amount of credit expansion that will eventually take place. This uncertainty is especially great at times of financial liberalization. The expectation of credit expansion is factored into how much an investor wishes to borrow and pay for a risky asset, such as housing. In the 2000s investors understood that the financial flows shaped by global imbalances would persist for years, but they did now know for how many years, nor how big the imbalances would get. With asset prices at one date being determined by the expectation regarding aggregate credit at later dates, the possibility of credit expansion for very many years ahead created a great deal of uncertainty about how high a price bubble would go before collapsing. Large guaranteed profits now had much higher present discounted value (PDV) than uncertain future profits highly discounted on the basis of the highly uncertain path of global financial flows and house prices.[84] So long as aggregate credit kept going up, asset prices would be high and default would be avoided. When credit expansion was less than expected, or just fell short of the highest anticipated levels, investors struggled to repay their loans, asset prices were pulled down, and defaults started to occur. This sort of reasoning puts global imbalances at the heart of the story of global house price bubbles.

The lack of a convincing logic that house prices could not fall was not about to bother men and women of practical finance for whom exploiting the situation was a far more pressing concern than worrying about the consequences if prices did fall. As a result, by the mid-2000s large swathes of the global property market had turned into a trapeze act from which nobody ever seemed to fall. Politicians of every hue and stripe cheered at this most perilous of spectacles. Those clinging on, ordinary families and financial institutions, reassured themselves, and were regularly reassured, that house prices could not fall. To demonstrate their confidence, regulators, the ringmasters of this circus of grim hope over sober reality, were taking, in their view, a well-deserved nap. However, as anyone who has ever been to a circus knows, for even the bravest of high-wire acts it is usually only a matter of time.

3

Innovation and Excess in Banking

The Banking System Grows and Stretches

Global imbalances and low macroeconomic volatility encouraged financial innovation and risk-taking. In return, financial innovations helped global economic imbalances to go to levels they otherwise would not have. Having defied gravity in the boom years, in the bust many financial innovations shattered and sent their splinters shooting in all directions. Scrambling through the debris, one question repeatedly sticks to one's feet: were such innovations right in principle but wrong in practice, or just plain wrong? Can some of them be cleansed of the effects of misuse and poor regulation, rescued and rehabilitated back into useful roles for society? Or must they face life as outcasts in a desolate and broken financial wilderness?

It wasn't always this way. In 2005 Alan Greenspan declared: 'The use of a growing array of derivatives and the related application of more-sophisticated approaches to measuring and managing risk are key factors underpinning the greater resilience of our largest financial institutions.'[1] In June 2007, just months away from the collapse of the Northern Rock bank and with the rustling silhouettes of a global financial crash gathering on the horizon, Gordon Brown praised an audience of UK bankers for their 'remarkable achievements' over his years as Chancellor of the Exchequer, declared the City of London 'a new world leader', heralded 'an era that history will record as the beginning of a new golden age for the City of London', and prophesied that 'it will be said of this age, the first decades of the 21st century, that out of the greatest restructuring of the global economy, perhaps even greater than the industrial revolution, a new world order was created'.[2] He was right, in a way. After the crash, what Brown had praised so lavishly was characterised by the UK's City regulator, Adair Turner, as no more than 'an explosion of exotic socially useless product development'.[3]

The boom years before the crash showered riches beyond belief on those working in global finance. The total assets of the world's largest banks doubled between 2003 and 2008, and the 'value added' by finance to global GDP rose from about 4.5% in 2000 to about 7.5% in 2007.[4] This might have been efficient, and no new vulnerabilities were created. After all, as a society becomes wealthier, there is increased smoothing of consumption over typical life-cycles, which generates increased demand for both saving and borrowing products. As a bulging cohort of baby boomers works its way through their life-cycles, there is a surge in the use of financial instruments. And a more globalized economy entails the need for more, complex, financial instruments to help companies manage operational risks, including those caused by fluctuating interest rates, exchange rates, and commodity prices.

However, in the 2000s there were problems with this reasoning. Income growth for many was low. Supposedly, too, we were living through a period of unprecedented stability, which had reduced the profits to be made from volatility. Much recent financial innovation was complex, but complexity is not the same as efficiency. The growth in the use of financial instruments linked to surging property prices could just as easily have been part of a bubble. And what are we to make of the fact that lending became so skewed? For example, in the UK bank lending trebled in the ten years to 2007, yet lending to manufacturing companies fell, and most commercial lending was for real estate; by 2008, of £6 trillion of banking-system assets, only about £200 billion represented lending to businesses, about 3% of the total, and about £1 trillion was in mortgages. Many big financial firms were doing well serving the high-risk, high-return activity of global capital markets and pumping domestic housing markets.

In the ten or so years running up to the mid-1990s, in a selection of advanced economies, debt grew at roughly the same rate across households, non-financial corporates, and governments. Starting then, and accelerating from the early 2000s, the ratio of debt to GDP of the financial sector pulled away from all other sectors. Logically, on a consolidated basis, financial-sector assets and liabilities should grow in line with non-financial-sector liabilities and assets. There must therefore have been a huge increase in claims *between* financial firms, and a huge multiplication of the balance sheets of those involved in the financial intermediation process itself, because *internal* banking activities grew much more rapidly than *end* banking services for businesses and households. This multiplication process was matched by a huge increase in 'maturity transformation'. Maturity transformation is a key benefit of banking. Individuals prefer liquidity (i.e. difficult-to-predict but immediate access to their money). However, the most productive activities take time, and if they are unwound prematurely, the losses are great. By pooling the resources of many individuals, and allowing them to invest indirectly in more productive long-term projects, banks allow savers to share the greater rewards while still (barring a bank run[5]) having access to their money.

Deriving a figure for the total amount of 'maturity transformation' would require stripping out all the intra-financial system assets and liabilities to derive just the consolidated balance sheet of the whole system. The maturity transformation would be read from the mismatch between consolidated assets and consolidated liabilities. This is not easy to do, and nobody, as far as I am aware, has done it. We can, however, make a well-informed guess that the degree of maturity transformation rose significantly and that its pattern changed in ways to make the whole system more fragile. For example, there was a huge increase in the amount of long-term mortgage debt that was not matched by long-term assets held by the non-financial sector, and a huge expansion in very short-term lending on overnight repurchase agreements (repos), which in 2007 was three times the level it had been in 2001. The explosion in the use of repos was a warning whispering uncomfortable truths to those with an ear to listen. Mutual funds, especially in the US, were also doing large quantities of bank-like maturity transformation, holding long-term assets against liabilities that promised immediate redemption. Many firms too thought it smart to put spare cash in very short-term loans to investment banks and hedge funds.

Heading into the Shadows

It was an era when bank capital was spread ever more thinly. Banks fund themselves either by borrowing (including from those who deposit their savings, which is the equivalent of them lending to banks) or from issuing capital, such as ordinary shares. Unlike borrowing, a bank is not legally obliged to pay capital back. The total amount of capital in a bank is the value of everything it owns (its assets, including the loans it has made) minus all that it owes (its liabilities). When losses arise, they first eat into a bank's capital. If losses are large and wipe out a bank's capital, the bank will become insolvent. Just as a child learns not to touch a fire, banks should therefore learn to keep away from activities that risk great loss. To the extent that holding more capital makes a financial firm safer, its credit rating improves, and it finds it cheaper to raise funds.[6] One bank's holding of capital also benefits other banks by reducing the chances of systemic failure.

It seems mind-boggling now, but on the eve of the crash banks were able to show that, within the rules, they were well capitalized. It was misleading. In the US in 2007, the median leverage ratio of US commercial banks was about 35 and of US securities houses more like 50. In large European financial institutions it was 45. Major UK banks were at a slightly more sedate 30. Like all medians, these hid ranges—that stretched all the way to 55, over 100, 85, and 60 respectively. Some of the biggest names in US and European finance sat like sentinels atop these ranges, their eyes tightly shut.

To make their fall that bit more dramatic, regulators derived regulatory leverage ratios by comparing a 'risk-adjusted' measure of assets. The first was based on a measure of riskiness calibrated on the volatility data of the Great Moderation. The second was generously defined to include the value of intangibles such as goodwill and preferred shares and deferred tax credits, which were a function of future profitability and therefore vulnerable to collapse in a crash. A system called the Basel Accords, which guided the risk-weightings attached to different kinds of activity, provided a menu of possibilities to satisfy the appetites of those who could arbitrage their way around it. The incentive for a financial firm was to get as many assets as possible to be classified as low-risk weighted, so that balance sheets could be bigger and the return to capital higher. Residential mortgages, in particular, were treated as less risky and as needing less capital than many other kinds of loans.

Since the need to hold capital was a constraint on size, if financial firms could strip capital to zero, they could expand to infinity. Considering this marginally too risky, many did the next best thing and, through the 2000s, created a so-called 'shadow banking system'. Remarkably, in this parallel universe the normal laws of safe prudential finance did not hold. Hundreds of billions of dollars' worth of loans, and much profit, could be made without the need to raise anywhere near the levels of capital required in the 'real' banking universe. Just as astrophysicists have quarks, gluons, strings, black holes, and other esoteric phenomena, so the shadow banking universe had its own phantasmagorical creations—structured investment vehicles (SIVs), constant-proportion debt obligations (CPDOs), auction rate securities (ARS), and so on—that expanded like crystals in a jam-jar, around tiny grains of capital. Short-term asset-backed commercial paper, ABCP (with an average maturity of 90 days)[7] and medium-term notes (with an average maturity of a year) were sold, and the proceeds used to buy longer-term assets and bundles of assets, making profit from the difference between the yield paid and the yield earned. Magically, because they were technically not owned by their sponsoring banks, SIVs and other conduits for funds into this new world did not have to appear on their sponsoring banks' balance sheets, and so did not show up in their measured leverage. Even more magically, sponsoring banks could still take the profits. Anyone looking at the totality of what was going on might have worried that there was some sort of missing, off-balance-sheet, 'dark matter'. At its peak, this shadow system comprised 60% of the size of the whole US banking system.[8] Maybe that made the shadow banking universe the real banking universe.

The smooth functioning of shadow banking was based on 'liquidity through marketability', the idea that longer-term assets *could* be backed by short-term liabilities because, at a pinch, some of the assets could be sold quickly in liquid markets without affecting their prices. While reasonable at the individual level, the logic was dangerous at the collective level. The awe and wonder of operating in such a world overcame concerns about this tiny but critical flaw.

Just in case the SIVs and other off-balance-sheet funding vehicles had troubles rolling over, their sponsoring banks put in place 'liquidity backstops', credit lines that could be called upon in times of stress. Yet, this simply meant that the risks were still on the sponsoring banks' shoulders, even if their books showed nothing. This is what is known in the financial profession as a 'very clever wheeze'. The regulatory capital charge on a 'contractual' credit line was much lower than if the loans were held on a sponsoring bank's balance sheet. The capital charge on a 'reputational' credit line was zero ('reputational' since it was implicitly understood that a sponsoring bank would take problems back even if it was costly, so as not to harm its reputation and future business by dumping those that got into trouble now). To stop the system from self-imploding, the gravitational laws of this parallel banking universe relied on asset prices (especially housing) in the real universe continuing to rise, and on wholesale markets continuing to roll over short-term paper instruments. In 2005, I identified this as the key flaw of the whole enterprise.[9] The need to keep rolling over was a sort of perpetual-motion machine. The problem was that there was nothing inherently perpetual about it, and eventually there was not much motion either.

Critically, the 'shadow' banking system was not protected by any of the usual safety nets. These come at a price—the regulatory requirement to hold capital of particular kinds in particular proportions. This restricts and has a cost. Bankers don't like restrictions and they certainly don't like costs. So, under the noses of the dozing regulatory guards, they dragged and dropped activities over the perimeter fence into the shadow banking world. They outsourced risk just as a company might outsource manufacturing to a country with weaker employment laws. And for similar reasons: it was highly lucrative. The shadow banking system may have been in the shadows but it was still a banking system, with the potential for a huge bank run at its heart.

Just as one can't physically go into a parallel universe, so policymakers rarely ventured into this shadow banking system, and its goings-on largely escaped their attention. If perchance they did venture in, they invariably returned with glowing accounts of its wondrous beauty. One did not need a Hubble space telescope to spot what was going on, but regulators seemed to be peering in through the wrong end anyway. The instrument of regulatory choice—so-called Basel II—had been calibrated to ignore what was going on by putting zero risk-weighting on all the stand-by loan commitments with (rolling) maturities of under one year. With hindsight, it seems that this 'shadow' banking system both encouraged and hid a bubble in house prices and allowed financial firms (and governments) to extract profit from the bubble while it lasted.

Shadow banking activity was openly promoted by big-name banks at the very core of the regulated commercial banking system, who created, marketed, and invested in SIVs. Regulators equally openly applied capital requirements, even if woefully inadequate, to SIVs. There was nothing 'hidden' or 'secret' about it at all. Yet, in his account of the crash, Gordon Brown jumped on the linguistic possibilities of the word 'shadow', accusing banks of creating a hidden, secret banking system. Perhaps, he hoped, it would work as an invisibility cloak for himself too.

Structured Finance and Securitization

Side by side with the rise of leverage and expansion into the shadows, came the concept of structured finance,[10] the business of turning a pool of risky assets, such as mortgages, loans, bonds, and so forth into a prioritized capital structure of claims, known as tranches, against the pool. The top tranche had first rights to any cash generated by the pool and therefore had the lowest risk of default, and was given the highest rating of all, AAA. Bearing the lowest risk of all, it paid the least return of all. The next tranche down was rated AA, and so on all the way down to the equity, which wasn't rated. It might have been at the bottom, but the equity certainly was not lowly in return. The return was high to reflect the notion that it would be first in line to take losses. The issuing banks often held on to the equity tranche to give incentive, so it was said, to monitor the underlying loans. It is more likely that, not being the sorts to look a gift-horse in the mouth, they held on for the high returns. These lower tranches had another attractive property. They were not often traded, so were not frequently valued. Managers could, to some degree, choose when to value them and thus smooth their apparent returns as they saw fit.

Quite astutely, just as the manufacturers of meat products find clever ways to make the last extruded, and most unprepossessing, bits of offal taste quite palatable, the manufacturers of structured products worked closely with the credit rating agencies (CRAs) to make sure that the bits that got into each rating tranche just about made the grade. By such a ruse, structured products had on average more favourable ratings than corporate bonds. So long as plenty of buyers were prepared to take the financial products that oozed out of the end—often referred to as collateralized debt obligations (CDOs)—this was an ideal vehicle to pull in more funds to feed the creation and sale of yet more financial products. In the 1920s the investment vehicle of speculative choice was the securitized stock loan; in the 2000s it was the CDO based on mortgages. The AAA tranches were easy to sell to the hungry hordes at the investment-banking gates.

In Chapter 1, we saw how the potential default states in debt contracts work their disciplining spell over the whole probability distribution of possible outcomes. By cutting up debt contracts and redistributing ownership of the underlying risks, structured products also changed the distribution of those who did the monitoring. The incentives of the masses to monitor and discipline were reduced, and everyone trusted the few, especially the CRAs and regulators, to get it right. By chopping and slicing, dicing and juicing, new securities could be created that had—at least, it so appeared at the time—very little of the original default possibility left in them. Meanwhile, other new securities got created, which had much more of the original default possibility in them. So long as markets kept rising—and mortgage defaults were few and far between while the housing market rose—the bad bits were not that bad after all, and the new securities offered good returns. By the alchemy of structured finance, base financial metal got turned into slabs of pure gold, and the waste products somehow disposed of. Investors never asked awkward questions about the underlying collateral, as they eagerly threw their cash at hollow investments and hardly ever tapped them to see what they contained.

It was a very agreeable way to make money. Some say it was an excellent way to exploit gullible governments. Others say governments were not so gullible. While some investors made huge returns—supposedly reward for holding the riskier bits—but hardly ever had to take a loss, governments, especially in countries such as the US and the UK, pocketed plenty of short-term tax revenue based on all the profits and bonuses. When the defaults finally turned up en masse, investors would not get singled out and punished, and could, as it were, turn tail, scarper, and leave the government to foot the bill. Heads they had won; tails they would win. Governments and politicians could blame the bankers, look brave mounting a rescue, and pass the costs on to the next generation of taxpayers.

Especially in the US, there was a gradual shift away from the traditional model of banks holding loans to maturity on their balance sheets financed by deposits, towards the use of capital markets where loans got transformed into securities that could be traded—a process called 'securitization'—and towards the originate-to-distribute model of financial intermediation. The payment stream of the original loans supported the interest and principal payments on the new securities.[11] When the new securities were based on mortgages, the result was mortgage-backed securities (MBS) including residential mortage-backed securities (RMBS). When they were based on non-mortgage loans or assets with expected payment streams, the result was asset-backed securities (ABS). Securitization started at zero in about 1970, underwent gradual growth in the 1980s, and exploded in the 15 or so years before the crash. By mid-2009, about $9 trillion of assets worldwide were being funded by securitization. The beauty of securitization was that instead of waiting around for the payment stream and the principal to be paid back, the originator could receive the lump sum value of the lot up-front. The use of securitization in the subprime market has, it seems, become something of a legend in its own lifetime.

In a sense securitization was a natural financial innovation. By separating those who originate credit from those who bear the risk, a more efficient dispersion of 'credit risk'—which refers to the risk that counterparties will be unable to meet their obligations—could be achieved. Greater economic stability would follow. Applied to mortgages, a shock in one region, that might trigger a problem for a bank, could be diversified away, and the cost of credit would be lower. As the IMF cheerily remarked shortly before the crash: 'the dispersion of credit risk by banks to a broader and more diverse set of investors, rather than warehousing ["holding them" in layperson's language] such risk on their balance sheets, has helped make the banking and overall financial system more resilient', with the result that 'improved resilience may be seen in fewer bank failures and more consistent credit provision'.[12] Yet again, by the alchemy of financial innovation, banks and near-banks could extract more return for shareholders from any given lump of financial capital. Shareholders liked that sort of thing.

Securitization played to a form of 'comparative advantage'. Those along the securitization chain could specialize in those types of information-processing tasks that they had an advantage in performing. The more the efficiency gain, the more the downward pressure on the cost of credit. It was said that, with the eyeballs of thousands, and even millions, evaluating securities on a market, prices would adjust much more quickly and there would be better pricing of risk. It was also claimed that the risks of many forms of credit were, anyway, best assessed using quantitative scoring systems rather than individual bank judgments; turning loans into securities, the risk of which could be captured by credit ratings, would help to get a better handle on the relative chances of default, and allow the 'market' to better discipline behaviour.

Securitization also allowed big centralized lenders to enter mortgage and other markets, since no longer did they need to build branch networks and attract depositors. Pension funds and money market funds by regulatory *fiat* were only allowed to hold AAA-rated products; now they could get the AAA-tranche drawn off an otherwise less-than-AAA-rated set of securities once they had been passed through the securitization machine. Securitization created a vehicle to absorb and encourage large capital inflows from abroad and so enable local consumption to be high compared to local production. Securitization was milk and honey in a parched and bitter land of low yield.

If it had so many potential benefits, why did securitization become 'an unsupervised doomsday machine'[13] that 'made the economy more, not less, vulnerable to financial disruption'?[14] We often look for conspiratorial explanations when the merely prosaic will do. It seems that in the 2000s, with global demand for securitized products so intense, many less-well-qualified financial players were tempted into the market. The ultimate investors were fussy eaters demanding increasingly complex products, while in the kitchen—the trading room—the richly remunerated clot cooking things up was barely able to chop the vegetables without also chopping off a finger. The investors were in the dining room, with its glitzy drapings and fripperies, watching through a porthole the odd iceberg drifting by, munching on their tasty returns, and they didn't get to see the chaos in the kitchen.

In truth, the reference above to all the 'eyeballs' keeping an eye on things was an appeal to a rather simplistic, if highly reassuring, notion of market efficiency. Reality was a bit more complicated. At the micro-market level, securitization created a chain with a borrower at one end and final investors at the other, along which information travelled like an electrical or chemical signal through a string of nerve synapses. Incentives and good oversight were needed to monitor and police the information so that it reached its destination safely. Instead, those who monitored or performed due diligence at one link found that they got some private benefit, but they also created positive 'externality' benefits for those presiding at other links, the value of which they could not internalize to help cover their monitoring costs. Those at one link could not evaluate anyway the quality of monitoring and information at other links. Similarly, there were incentives to 'free ride', such that everyone under-monitored.

As securitized products became ever more complex and opaque, it also became ever more difficult to work out the relationship between the ultimate claims and the risks underlying such claims, and ever more difficult to expose each individual in the chain to the right amount and source of risk such that, collectively, over the whole chain, they acted as a joint-maximizer. Complexity, opacity, and the rapid growth of the market led to an over-reliance on the credit rating agencies. Yet, the understanding of the CRAs was not always good, was often bad, and was sometimes truly awful. The financial system was frothy and had bubble momentum, and only when the froth cleared, and sobriety returned, would the consequences of poor monitoring, inappropriate credit ratings, and the lack of due diligence come to light. The presence of an effective regulator might have increased the benefit of good monitoring. In spite of the dangers, many in these securitization chains believed that risk *had* been diversified away and simply got on with making money—and lots of it. In truth the typical buyer of the securitized credit product of one bank was the propriety trading desk of another bank, engaging in 'acquire and arbitrage' activities based on the fees and bonuses that could be gleaned. Like lemmings heading towards a cliff, they reasoned that since others were doing it, there was safety in numbers.

Bernanke identified three principles for successful mortgage securitization.[15] First, the credit quality of the underlying mortgages must be high and the originators of mortgages have an incentive to undertake stringent credit underwriting. Second, because risks (interest rate, prepayment, and credit risks) may be correlated within and between mortgage-loan pools, those who hold such pools must have the capacity to perform the necessary risk management. Third, because of the potential complexities, asset valuation systems must be transparent. In the early days, investors pretty much lived up to these three principles. The reader will not be entirely surprised to hear that, with time, the matter became somewhat more relaxed, and that a lot of very risky investment activities ended up being done with apparently safe mortgages and many apparently safe investment activities got done with very risky mortgages.

It turned out that many loans were 'warehoused' on bank and bank-like balance sheets.[16] In some cases—such as the UK's Northern Rock bank—the process of originate-to-distribute took time, and banks found themselves ware-housing the underlying mortgages or loans on their balance sheets until they had the time to package and distribute them on. Meanwhile they were vulnerable if liquidity dried up 'unexpectedly'. In another case, the CEO of Lehman Brothers, Richard Fuld, is reported to have said that Lehman was 'in the business of removal not storage',[17] but when Bank of America unravelled the accounts of Lehman ahead of a potential bid (that Bank of America did not make) the hole they found was in no small part because too much had been stored and not enough removed. It may have been that financial players got so convinced that the risks were so much lower than they really were (the 'Great Moderation' story helped on that front), and were so busy doing the apparently more profitable bit of creating yet more financial products, that they simply ware-housed much more than they should have. Having secured insurance through credit default swaps (described next), some simply did not feel the need to take full advantage of the 'selling on' bit of securitization.

Securitization was one case where the principle was probably right, but the application decidedly wonky. Had risk been transferred, as had so frequently been hailed, the losses would have been shared much more widely, and the fallout would not have affected the capital positions of banks as much as it did. This would have been bad news, but the impact on the credit mechanism would have been nowhere near the impact seen during the crash. Even then, it is not clear that the synchronized nature of global economic forces and the international correlation of house prices would not have undermined the supposed diversification benefits of securitization.

Derivatives and the (In)famous Credit Default Swaps

The 1990s and 2000s witnessed an explosion in the use of financial derivatives. To paraphrase Horace Judson, derivates were the DNA of finance. They were Midas's gold. And many who touched them went mad.[18] The payoffs of derivatives are derived from the payoffs of other financial instruments—hence the name. Often one reads stomach-churning figures of the nominal amount of derivatives outstanding. It is the stock-in-trade of some in the media to frighten the rest of us, and this is rather too juicy an opportunity to be missed. Nevertheless, although the figures sound huge, derivatives are in zero net supply[19] and most will never come to much.

In defence of derivatives (in the right hands and properly regulated) I need to be technical for a moment—a paragraph will do—for there is no other way to do it. To achieve an efficient allocation of risk, if markets were complete, there would be no need for derivatives. With a complete set of markets for 'contingent' commodities (commodities distinguished by their physical properties, by the date when they are delivered, and by the state of the world in which they are delivered), economic entities (that is, you and me, and everyone else for that matter) could sit down at the start of time and, constrained only by their budgets, trade once and for all and spend the rest of time making good on the obligations made in this start-of-time exercise. Because this would require potentially a massive number of contingent commodities and markets, a second approach, equivalent from an efficiency perspective, is to require goods and securities ('Arrow securities') to be traded on spot markets at each date. We do not live in either of these worlds. Derivatives can create some of the missing opportunities and, in principle, increase efficiency, mitigate risk, and improve social welfare. Incidentally, if derivatives markets were functioning efficiently, they would be one of the sure-fire ways to undermine the risky behaviour of bankers, by punishing those acting recklessly or simply not telling the truth. Because of the costs of creating a massive number of derivatives contracts, nevertheless only a small proportion of all possible derivative contracts exists. The key issue is to what degree, for all their benefits, derivatives repackage and hedge existing uncertainty, and to what degree they create new forms of uncertainty. In particular, how do defaults on 'derived' markets get to impact on the original markets and the economy?

To some, derivatives were the heroes of financial innovation, with some of the Wild West spirit about them, and should be allowed to push the financial frontiers forward; to suggest that they had limitations as well as possibilities was to limit their possibilities. They were the oil to lubricate the whirring circuits of the global financial system, and should be allowed to do their job. The problem was that many derivatives were opaque and traded direct with counterparties, such as other banks and insurance companies, and were not processed through an exchange such that the identities of the other side did not matter. Even a highly profitable trade could turn sour if the counterparty was no longer around to pay up.

Much has been said about one derivative in particular, the CDS. Who would have believed that the phrase 'credit default swap' would have quite so successfully entered the popular vernacular! It seems there is nothing quite like a good crash to push otherwise shy and retiring financial innovations into the public limelight. CDSs turned credit risk into its very own asset class so that it could be traded on a market. The first true CDS was carried out only in 1995. The twenty-to thirtyfold ballooning in their use started only in about 2000. At their peak in mid-2007 there was, by some estimates, about $55 trillion in gross notional outstanding CDSs. When the crash happened, if there was a focus for agitated finger-wagging and knotted eyebrows, it was in the hulking shape of CDSs.

A CDS is a form of insurance (to the *cognoscenti*, or perhaps for those who should just get out a bit more, the payoff structure is similar to a put option). Realizing that one might be subject to default on, say, an AAA-rated MBS, an investor could protect himself or herself by buying a CDS. Just like any insurance, the buyer would pay a regular premium to the writer of the CDS, in exchange for which the writer of the CDS would promise to pay a specified sum of money should the underlying security specified in the contract default. Thus, banks could make loans and transfer, via CDSs, the credit risk to others, usually insurance companies like the once-mighty AIG, or to foreign banks.

Why on earth, I hear some readers exclaim, would anybody do such a thing? If default states are disciplining devices in debt contracts, why amass a pile of securities based on debt contracts and then get someone else to pay up if they go wrong? Doesn't that weaken the incentive to take actions to stop them going wrong? The underlying rationale was that, being traded on a market, CDSs were exposed to the ruthless rational logic of that mythical creature, the 'efficient market'. Greenspan could not have put it more clearly than he did in a speech he made to a gathering of the great and the good, including Gordon Brown, in London in 2002: 'As the market for credit default swaps expands and deepens, the collective knowledge held by market participants is exactly reflected in the prices of these derivative instruments... and presumably in the process [CDSs] embody all relevant market prices of the financial instruments issued by potential borrowers.'[20] It was a statement of faith, and like all sensible statements of faith, there was, for good measure, an appropriately proportioned spoonful of agnosticism—'presumably'—in the final verse.

This contrasted with the view expressed by the IMF at the same time: 'More generally, the tendency for credit derivative spreads to be volatile and even decline below the spreads on the underlying bonds raises questions about whether participants in the credit derivative markets—especially those that have not traditionally managed credit risks—have yet learned how to price these contracts appropriately... If in fact credit derivative prices "overshoot" and are excessively volatile relative to the price of the underlying credit, this would distort signals about credit risks.'[21] No wonder Greenspan was cautious in his creedal statements.

The market for CDSs expanded beyond those who actually owned the underlying securities, with huge volumes of 'synthetic', or 'naked', CDS positions that did not insure any open default position in any underlying security.

Bank traders sold on the credit risk of a loan several times over, creating a multiple of credit risks for each initial loan. Then they created CDSs that did not even relate to loans on their books, but to indices of credit quality for this, that, and the other industry. Underlying loans thus ended up supporting nearly ten times their weight in outstanding CDSs. The Greenspan-style argument would be that this is all fine and hunky-dory. If markets are always 'efficient', speculating on the movement of CDS prices could only ever help make the world more stable in the face of shocks. The creators of even synthetic CDSs were just taking a cut of the rewards for bringing this about. The more the merrier.

However, we know that other financial markets can deviate from fundamentals and, at times, experience bubbles. What if CDS markets could suffer something similar, with prices on the CDS market driving behaviour in the underlying loan markets and not the other way around? What if irrational underpricing of credit risk via CDSs led to underpricing of on-balance sheet credit risk? Indeed, the crash demonstrated that CDS prices performed relatively well in indicating the relative risk of different financial institutions, but totally misled in terms of sector-wide credit risk until very late in the day. We know that even when stock markets get the relative value insights right, they can be miles off on the absolute insight, and it is the sudden revision of the absolute insight that is damaging. Perhaps the danger was even greater for CDSs markets? A sudden revision of CDS absolute insight would impact underlying debt-based markets; sudden revisions in debt-based markets are far more problematic than sudden revisions in equity-based markets. The best we can say is that in the summer of 2007 CDS prices got policymakers to act because they finally started to reveal the truth, but it was too late to avoid most of the damage.

We are not finished with CDSs. Even as all that trading in CDSs was supposed to be creating one kind of informational efficiency (via the prices of CDSs), another sort of information, namely regarding the balance sheets of the various parties involved, became less and less transparent. CDSs created a network of counterparty exposures, and yet it was virtually impossible to know who owned what or was obligated to what loss, and whether those who had promised to pay out could pay out. In a boom this hardly mattered, since counterparty obligations were rarely triggered.[22] If the default states in the loans underlying CDSs were triggered randomly, all would be well. However, if many defaults clustered together and triggered payments on many CDSs at once, it would wipe out the capital of the counterparties obligated to make good on the losses. If this forced them to sell from their portfolios, this would generate volatile and illiquid CDS markets that would then spill through the network and put pressure on bank liquidity. The consequences didn't bear thinking about. And so, it seems, nobody gave them a thought.

Just like other derivatives markets, CDSs allowed financial players to take a much bigger exposure, in this case to credit risk, with any given piece of capital than from holding the underlying securities. CDSs therefore appealed especially to hedge funds, pension funds, and insurance companies. Sadly, some of these non-traditional players were less obviously able and interested in pricing such instruments according to 'fundamentals' and had weak auditing practices. Maybe there was a bit of self-selection going on, too. In the Abraham Lincoln school of financial innovation, for those who liked that sort of thing, CDSs were the sort of thing they liked.[23]

As the CDSs market ballooned it became a source of great profits. How much of this was created by the 'value' of genuine financial hedging and how much was conjured from thin air (or, in the end, from taxpayers)? Rudimentary economic logic suggests that a market should expand until the marginal benefit equals the marginal cost of one more sale. Working backwards from the huge profits, one would think that the inefficiencies before the scale-up in CDSs must have been huge. This seems unlikely. The alternative possibility was that CDSs were a clever mechanism to constantly churn the market to generate fees, and were profitable because they helped suck profit out of an expanding bubble and were a great way to exploit the insurance (explicit or implicit) provided by the state.

In addition, the market for CDSs evolved to concentrate risk on a small number of very large insurers. One big player, American International Group Inc., AIG, the world's largest insurer, became the primary focus of much CDS activity. AIG had verily gorged itself selling credit protection in the shape of CDSs on CDOs, many linked to MBSs. Increasingly, AIG was taking a one-way bet on the market. Either AIG executives were collectively stupid (which allows for them to be individually smart but have a management system that generates a collectively stupid outcome, which, after all, is often the way), or they knew perfectly well what they were doing and had factored in that they were too-big-to-fail (TBTF). Or maybe it was a mix of the two. The owners of AIG got fat on the credit-insurance premiums from all the CDSs it sold even if it never paid out when it all went wrong. Meanwhile, there were insufficient checks and balances on AIG's behaviour, and dissenting voices were ignored. When all *did* go wrong, AIG was indeed TBTF. Had the risks not been concentrated in AIG, had there been better regulation, had mortgage markets been less euphoric, would the outcome of using CDSs been much better? Indeed, outside of AIG, the CDS market worked reasonably well. The practice was more faulty than the principle, but the principle was also somewhat oversold.

In the years before the crash, sheer complexity often passed for sophistication, and many ventured deep into the mathematical jungle to hunt for new kinds of derivatives, guided by elegant little pocket maps straight from the desks of half a dozen Chicago financial economists. Sadly for some, they were to find that the pages therein contained no more than 'bloody instructions, which, being taught, return to plague the inventor'.[24] Regulators, who needed to understand the mathematics of complex derivatives, also struggled, finding themselves at times as if navigating dark coastal waters in pre-sonar days, staring through brooding black shoals to see where the bottom was and trying to spot the flaw in the maths where they might be holed. Nevertheless, it would be utterly wrong to throw all derivatives out. Many derivatives played no role in the crash; some, such as interest rate derivatives, helped to mitigate its consequences. AIG aside, CDSs also had their uses. Here too, rehabilitation seems possible.

Interdependence and Illiquidity

Common to much of the above was the growing interdependence between bank-like activities and financial market-based activities, the consequences of which were grossly underestimated by both banks and regulators. Greenspan yet again had an excuse: '[U]nregulated and less heavily regulated entities generally are subject to more effective market discipline than banks...In essence, prudential regulation is supplied by the market through counterparty evaluation and monitoring rather than by authorities...Except where market discipline is undermined by moral hazard, for example, because of federal guarantees of private debt, private regulation generally has proved far better at constraining excessive risk-taking than has government regulation.'[25] It is worth reading this a few times to more fully appreciate the exquisite philosophical logic behind 'light-touch' regulation. Greenspan and others all too often looked on the sunny side of arguments in favour of financial innovations (and there were usually some) and ignored micro-market details of how such instruments would work in practice, as if 'efficient-market' reasoning worked its magic all the way through whatever layers of 'players' and informational problems were present. In Greenspan's worldview, the more 'nodes' added, the more diversification and spreading of risk there would be. The failure of one or a few would be ironed out by some sort of law of large numbers, and the system would be naturally more robust.

To the contrary, a modern global financial system is more akin to a very complex adaptive network comprising a large number of players. Each performs a small bit of the credit intermediation and maturity transformation process, yet is often individually too big to fail without causing contagion effects. Each has a leveraged balance sheet and a small amount of capital, and interacts with many other counterparties over different products, markets, and horizons. All inhabit a world where markets and institutions are highly interdependent and end up sharing the same capital base. The financial innovations used to link together the bits of financial fabric are sometimes complex and opaque, such that the more interconnected an individual player is, the harder it is to predict the impact of that player's failure on the whole system.[26] We have a poor understanding of how networks work, but we know that they can crash, and that even a network that starts out with apparently heterogeneous behaviour can switch to homogeneous behaviour. In such a world, as some apples go bad, they are more likely to spoil the whole financial barrel, and there are natural limits on how much of the risk of this can be diversified away.

Perhaps the biggest interdependency showed up in 'liquidity'. It is helpful to visualize two kinds of liquidity problem. 'Market' liquidity is excessively low if it becomes too costly to transfer an asset with its entire future cash flow by selling it (for example if forced sales are pushing asset prices excessively low). 'Funding' liquidity is excessively low if it becomes too expensive to replenish funds by borrowing against the cash flow of an asset or a trading strategy (for example if the collateral value of the asset has fallen).[27] The two liquidity problems can feed each other—illiquid markets harm the ability of banks to fund their operations, and stressed banks harm the ability of financial markets to function.[28] Many financial players seemed to believe that both 'market' and 'funding' liquidity would always be there. The shadow banking system was a key part of this illusion. As a result, on the eve of the crash, London clearing banks held about 1% of their assets in short-term liquid instruments. In 1970 it had been 30%.

Critically, what matters is the change in liquidity demand relative to the supply of liquidity. Even a small change in demand for liquidity can have a big impact if the supply of liquidity is low.[29] When there is plenty of market liquidity, asset prices behave as normal and reflect the expected future payoffs; individual liquidity trades are absorbed with no impact on prices. When there is a shortage of market liquidity, prices are determined by the ratio of the amount of the asset sold to the amount of liquidity, i.e. there is 'cash in the market' pricing, and prices are lower than they would have been.

When a financial market crashes, financial institutions would like to have more liquidity. However, they had to make a decision ex ante that would dictate the amount of liquidity they would have available in a crash. In the mid-2000s, the incentive to hold a portfolio that would generate the needed liquidity was low for numerous reasons, including the following: low market volatility (after all, it is asset price volatility that generates opportunities for profit); high returns on 'long' illiquid assets compared to 'short' liquid assets (the yield curve was upward-sloping) such that small reductions in liquidity could be leveraged into large gains in expected returns; the expectation that shocks were mostly non-synchronized; the apparently low expectation that the market would crash and hence the low expectation that cash-in-the-market pricing would materialize; the overexaggerated expectation that individuals could use the market to get the liquidity they needed; and the expectation that governments would anyway pump liquidity in if shocks were ever synchronized. Throw in a dollop of misjudgement, and the result was too little ability in the private sector to generate liquidity in times of stress.

A month before the interbank market crashed in the summer of 2007, the chief executive of Citigroup, Charles O. Prince, famously observed: 'When the music stops, in terms of liquidity, things will be complicated. But as long as the music is playing, you've got to get up and dance. We're still dancing. The depth of the pools of liquidity is so much larger than it used to be that a disruptive event now needs to be much more disruptive than it used to be. At some point, the disruptive event will be so significant that instead of liquidity filling in, the liquidity will go the other way. I don't think we're at that point.'[30] Many quote just the famous 'dance' part of this, which misses the jaw-dropping admission of knowing culpability regarding liquidity. Perhaps such complacency is why Citigroup ended up 36% owned by the US government. Incidentally, the liquidity problem that hit the whole financial system was reminiscent of one of the big mistakes made by Long Term Capital Management, LTCM, in the run up to its failure in 1998, applied en masse: namely, getting into huge, illiquid (this time at the collective level) leveraged trades with no hope of an exit strategy, and no ability to absorb losses.[31] Bankers might be clever, but sometimes they have the memory of a goldfish.

Rewards Hidden in the Tails

There has always been a layer of management between investors and their investments, and the challenge has always been how to align the incentives of the layer of managers with the wishes of investors. Over the 1990s and 2000s there was a shift (especially in the Anglo-Saxon model of financial intermediation) away from traditional banks and long-term relationships towards a more arm's-length approach involving financial institutions such as hedge funds, mutual funds, insurance companies, pension funds, private equity, and venture capital funds acting via markets. This structural shift changed the nature of incentives and risk-taking, generating problems that were understood well before the crash.[32]

In the past, rewards came mostly from fixed salaries, which were limited on the upside. Risk-taking was disciplined via bank-capital structure (i.e. depositors and investors might run if risk-taking was excessive). Bank shareholders were happy; limited competition created pricing power, which enabled them to extract profit nevertheless. In came the need to incentivize investment managers to seek out 'good' investments, and rewards that increasingly came in the form of short-term cash bonuses based on volume and mark-to-market profits, and not on the basis of long-term profitability. The movement of foot-free investors strengthened the link between returns and investment managers' rewards.

One side effect was the increased value of risk-shifting, as first touched on in Chapter 1, and the taking of risks the natures of which were hidden. The easiest risks of all to hide were 'tail' risks, gambles that with very small probability generate a very big negative outcome (a 'tail' outcome because they are in the 'tail' of the probability distribution over all possible outcomes) but that most of the time generate a high return. If payment is based on short horizons, creating and exploiting tail risk is the way to secure higher rewards. Take for example two investments with the following simple payoff structures. The first investment has more safe payoffs in general. The second has a big loss in one tail, but pays out more in non-tail outcomes to compensate. If both investments have equal expected payoff, a risk-neutral investor will be indifferent between the two. Eventually, investors in the second investment will make a big loss because of the tail outcome (unless the government takes the loss for them). Until then the second investment enhances the wealth of those who invest in it. If rewards are based on short horizons, the second investment comes to crowd out the first investment in the affections of investment managers.

What happens if the second investment has a lower expected payoff than the first investment? Should it be avoided? What if the lower expected payoff is because of the tail outcome, but, so long as the tail outcome is avoided, the second investment pays much more than the first investment? If investment managers are paid over short horizons, they have an incentive to promote the second investment even though it has the lower expected payoff. Now imagine a world where investments are much more complex than this, few investors really understand the probability distributions such that it is hard to tell that the second investment has the worst expected payoff, credit ratings are based on very short horizons, and governments bail out investors when really big losses materialize. Now we are in the real world where bad investments crowd out good investments.

Investment managers also increasingly 'herded', copying in very large numbers, the same investment strategy.[33] In particular, they tended to push asset prices. Those who herded shared the upside and were protected on the downside, which often just meant they did not get a bonus or the bonus was smaller than usual. As Keynes put it: 'A sound banker, alas, is not one who foresees danger and avoids it, but one who, when he is ruined, is ruined in a conventional way along with his fellows, so that no one can really blame him.'[34]

In other areas of banking, workers were paid according to the volume of instruments they originated and sold and according to how much risk they shifted off their balance sheets and onto the balance sheets of investment managers. When tail outcomes materialized, would those in these other areas of banking be capable of providing the liquidity that investment managers needed to unwind their financial positions and to allocate losses efficiently without causing a huge negative impact on the economy? With banks increasingly relying on the liquidity of the market to hedge their risks and make their balance sheets more sound, their ability to provide this 'backstop' deteriorated.

One particular tail risk was very valuable. It came, often for free, courtesy of government insurance of the financial sector, via a variety of safety nets. In a crash (i.e. a really bad 'tail' outcome) governments would make payouts in the form of compensation to retail depositors (deposit insurance), liquidity support (liquidity insurance), and equity injections (capital insurance).[35] Often the payout would be triggered because banks were deemed TBTF and could not be allowed a disorderly failure. The TBTF banks knew this, and were not about to pay a fee for the service.

Safety nets have good economic logic. Many high-risk high-payoff investments fail, but the value of the few that succeed will more than outweigh the ones that fail. If investment managers face limitless liability, their fears about the failures will hold back the successes, and economic growth and society's welfare will be lower. The problem is that, once a safety net is in place, investment managers face limited liability and so they risk bigger and more mistakes.[36] Applied to banks, the upside gains to shareholders and investment managers, paid with bonuses, is potentially unlimited, but in the bad states (especially in systemic bad states) the loss to shareholders and investment managers is limited to the loss of their ownership stake. Beyond that, losses fall onto other parts of the capital structure of banks (to the extent that governments allow it since, as we saw in the crash and in the eurozone crisis, policymakers often do not allow it), or onto governments. In the years before the crash, banks, under strong pressure from their shareholders, adopted six strategies to boost profits by increasing tail risks and exploiting the limited liability of bank shareholders and investment managers; the once-in-a-blue-moon payout, courtesy of the taxpayer-funded safety net, was what made the distortion so profitable.[37]

First, they increased their leverage, which made the banking system's balance sheet more fragile. This harvested more upside for private interests and exported more downside to taxpayers. Regulated banks were able to do this, even while keeping within the capital rules, by exploiting shadow banking, and funding themselves increasingly from wholesale markets and not deposits. By strapping more debt to their equity, on the eve of the crash, bank owners were making 30% return on their equity, which was several times what it had been up to the 1970s.[38] In corporate finance there is a concept called the Modigliani–Miller theorem, which shows that in the optimal capital structure of a firm (the mix of equity and debt that constitutes the way a firm is owned), debt is slightly favoured when interest rates are tax-deductible and dividends are not.[39] Nevertheless, after a point, too much debt in a firm's ownership structure makes a firm too risky, and its risk-adjusted cost of raising capital increases; that 30% looked good, but a large portion of it ultimately came courtesy of the rest of society and taxpayers.[40]

Second, they increased the proportion of their assets held on their trading books, and decreased the proportion held on their banking books. Trading-book assets are mark-to-market and so are sensitive to aggregate market fluctuations. Mark-to-market leverage is strongly procyclical.[41] In the years before the crash, mark-to-market gains on banks' trading assets greatly boosted profitability and hence returns to bank equity.[42] As Haldane put it: 'As long as asset prices rose, this created an Alice in Wonderland world in which everybody had won and all had prizes.'[43] At the time of the crash, when banks complained bitterly about mark-to-market losses, it was easy to forget just how much they had used mark-to-market in the years before the crash to boost their profits and bonuses and how the losses were an inevitable part of that strategy.

Third, they increased their levels of business-line diversification. For individual banks this reduced idiosyncratic risk, but it increased the similarity of the asset portfolios of banks, which increased systemic risk. Because systemic gain is privatized but systemic failure is socialized, being more systemic is better for bank owners.

Fourth, more assets were originated that had asymmetric returns. High-risk loans, with high payoffs in good states and big losses bunched in a tail, were an especially good way to exploit the taxpayer-funded safety net.

Fifth, the writing of deep out-of-the-money options replicated high-risk lending. CDSs had this by the bucketful. The 'good' returns, most of the time, came to the writers of protection (like AIG and those who invested in AIG) in the form of a steady flow of insurance premium income, which supposedly compensated for the rare catastrophe that would wipe out all the good returns—but in case of catastrophe, the government, and taxpayers, would bail them out and take the loss instead.

Sixth, they pumped asset prices. In corporate finance, debt-financed firms risk-shift by investing in projects that have negative net present value (NPV). Asset price bubbles have negative NPV once the collapse of the bubble is factored in. The bigger the price bubble, the bigger the negative NPV, and the bigger the expected return from risk-shifting. With so much debt finance in the early to mid-2000s, the asset bubble of choice for risk-shifting purposes was housing. The more uncertain the payoff of a risky asset, the more ability there is to shift risk, and the higher will prices be bid compared to fundamentals.[44] Because of global macroeconomic imbalances and highly uncertain credit expansion, the path of true house-price fundamentals was particularly hard to establish and the payoffs to housing unusually uncertain. And so the opportunity to risk-shift via housing markets, to exploit government insurance, was especially high.

Financial firms pushed tail risks higher as a way to exhaust the available resources of the government, i.e. taxpayers.[45] US banks were constrained from expanding their balance sheets by a regulatory leverage ratio, and so they tended to push their asset pools towards riskier and mark-to-market assets to take advantage of government insurance. European banks, in contrast, had no regulatory leverage ratios imposed upon them, and so tended to rely more on leverage to boost equity returns and to take advantage of government insurance. Thus, on the eve of the crash, US banks had generally lower leverage but higher risk per unit of leverage, and European banks (including those in the UK) relied more on higher leverage. When the crash came, this would show up early in the US as difficulties with high-default risky assets, and later in Europe as large drawn-out losses based on leverage. Europe was following in the footsteps of the US. By the collective behaviour of all, and because of modern developments in finance, a procyclical financial sector emerged that raised welfare (and especially of those in the financial sector) most of the time, at the cost of a catastrophic meltdown some of the time, at which point taxpayers would pay up.

Failures in Risk Management

Just when we thought our sorry tale could get no sorrier, failures in risk management were taking place at all levels: in the internal risk assessments that financial firms used to guide investment decisions; in the accounting companies that audited and validated the accounts of financial firms, sometimes pushing accounting rules to their limits; in the CRAs; and amongst the regulators overseeing the lot. It would not be impolite to say that there was collective regulatory amnesia, and that, sometimes, not seeing was believing.

The job of the CRAs was to offset the asymmetric information problems inherent in debt finance by providing an independent evaluation of whether or not a borrower was likely to default. The views of CRAs therefore became increasingly important as debt-based activities exploded. While there was much talk of relying on 'the market', often the 'market' relied on the 'non-market' CRAs. The ratings of the CRAs were key to investment, risk-management, and regulatory decision-making processes. Since lower credit ratings force an increase in the amount of capital needed to back a particular kind of activity or financial institution, in principle a poor credit rating would persuade financial firms to reduce the amount of their risky activities and redeploy their capital elsewhere. Unfortunately, the key risk models employed by the CRAs, and many others too, downplayed the amount of risk in the system, and so did not push the system away from danger. Worse, since capital regulation targeted individual bank risk but not systemic risk, financial institutions took on huge aggregate risk even when they were abiding by individual risk requirements.

A heavily used measure of risk was 'value at risk' (VaR). An example is best, since otherwise matters quickly get complicated. If a financial portfolio has a one-day 5% VaR of $10 million, this means that there is a 5% probability that the portfolio will lose more than $10 million of its value over a one day period, assuming markets are normal and there is no trading.

The problems with VaR had long been identified, but ignored.[46] First, VaR typically relied on limited and short-run series of historical data for deriving probability distributions over future patterns of price movements. In housing markets, which are highly cyclical over durations much longer than those used in rating mortgages, key statistical properties were lost.[47] Periods of low measured risk generated good credit ratings, a signal of low future risk. This encouraged capital to enter, which pumped house prices, which made low measured risk self-fulfilling. Thus credit ratings made credit and asset price behaviour even more procyclical.

Second, VaR presumed normal probability distributions over possible outcomes from which regulators and investment managers drew supposed random samples of price movements to guide their advice. Yet, price movements were anything but 'normal'. Series of price movements materalised each of which, according to the models, had a probability that was so infinitesimally small as to be highly improbable. David Viniar, Goldman Sachs's chief financial officer, observed in August 2007: 'We were seeing things that were 25-standard deviation moves, several days in a row.'[48] This was the financial equivalent of asking how many monkeys randomly beating out letters on typewriters it takes for at least one of them to produce a perfect copy of a play by Shakespeare. It was an Alice in Wonderland world where half a dozen or more impossible price movements had to be believed every day before breakfast. The probability model was wrong.

Third, VaR was an idiosyncratic and not a systemic measure of risk.[50] One of the more memorable features of the crash (and, let's not forget, of previous crashes) was the sudden coordination of the masses towards very similar behaviour, and the way covariances seemed to appear out of nowhere. Idiosyncratic-based models are hopeless at capturing such phenomena. We have known for a long time that financial market price movements demonstrate 'fat-tail' properties and not normal distribution properties.[51] This suggests that systemic risk, and not just idiosyncratic risk, is at work, and this needs frameworks totally different from VaR.[52]

These three modelling faults came back to bite in all sorts of uncomfortable places. However, many have argued that as well as 'running the wrong models', the rating agencies also faced conflicts of interest. Ratings are expensive to produce and, once produced, they are public goods (everybody gets to see them for free). Hence, rating agencies charged issuers a fee (the ratings information is then 'free' for everyone else, but paid for already) and competed against each other for business. Rating agencies even got higher fees on structured products than on corporate bonds.

As ever, Greenspan had a quote fitting to the moment. This time, coming after the crash, it was somewhat more penitent than usual: 'This modern risk management paradigm held sway for decades. The whole intellectual edifice, however, collapsed in the summer of last year because the data inputted into the risk management models generally covered only the past two decades, a period of euphoria. Had instead the models been fitted more appropriately to historic periods of stress, capital requirements would have been much higher and the financial world would be in far better shape today, in my judgment.'[53] A pity, perhaps, that the most powerful man in global finance said nothing about this fundamental error during all the years it was being committed.

One particularly crazy example came in early 2007. Moody's got it into its head to give Icelandic banks a Triple-A rating. Having well performed the charm, it sat back and watched as Iceland's banks promptly collapsed. Although it now looks absurd, Moody's conditioned its ratings on the ability for Iceland's banks to be bailed out. The rating was more a comment on the creditworthiness of the Icelandic authorities than the banks. The rating was neverthless wrong. The CRAs were not alone. Seeming truth easily ensnared even the wisest. A high-profile report in 2006 concluded: 'Although the [Icelandic] banks' reliance on external financing poses the biggest risk to the financial system right now, the probability of a credit event occurring is low...although Iceland's economy does have some imbalances that will eventually be reversed, financial fragility is currently not a problem, and the likelihood of a financial meltdown is low.'[54]

Just a Huge Financial 'Bezzle'?

Would better models have made a difference if nobody was looking? Picking over the financial detritus of the 2000s, a horrible suspicion dawns. Was the whole thing just one giant act of financial embezzlement that built up over the 1990s and 2000s and then collapsed? As the US Treasury Secretary Tim Geithner put it: 'The rising market hid Ponzi schemes and other flagrant abuses that should have been detected and eliminated.'[55] Too right, if a bit late.

We shall finish this chapter and Part I of the book—if only to lighten the load of the reader, who has worked hard to get to this point and deserves some sort of respite—by looking at the most flagrant example, our number one pin-up model in the rogues gallery of financial-crash superstars, pillar of New York high society, permanent fixture in the more exclusive echelons of the Palm Beach social circuit, and prominent philanthropist, Bernard Madoff. Madoff ran the largest Ponzi scheme in history, at $65 billion (Robert Allen Stanford gave him a run for his money with an $7 billion Ponzi scheme, but Stanford was a fly-by-night amateur in comparison).

A Ponzi scheme is simple. Advertise a market-beating rate of return to sparkle and attract. The praise of early investors for your financial wizardry will draw in yet more investors. Regarding those who don't move their money, don't bother to pay them anything; just credit their accounts every year, completely fictitiously of course. Use the injections of new investors to pay those who leave. So happy will most investors be, many may even keep their money with you for years and years. Meanwhile, cream a generous slice off the top to fund a luxurious lifestyle for yourself. The only thing you need to worry about is that financial regulators will one day turn up, pull back the curtain, and expose your trickery. In the climate of the 1990s and 2000s, as Madoff cranked away on his levers, it seems there was not much chance of that.

Madoff claimed that while he operated his scheme, for twenty years or more,[56] he made no genuine investments. A remarkable achievement in the circumstances. Of course, since no returns were actually being generated, it was, all along, a house of cards. So long as the market kept rising, and more punters were pulled in than left, the scheme kept working. But all such schemes eventually collapse. The trigger in the Madoff case was a demand from clients in late 2008 for $7 billion to be returned, which Madoff naturally did not have. It is easy to blame Madoff. However, once someone has slipped into this behaviour, at some point—and in the case of Madoff, that point was probably many years ago—it simply becomes impossible to go back to normal investment methods. The unreal returns of the early years can never be made good in any honest way. The only way to stop the total size of the scam reaching into the tens of billions of dollars is the prompt intervention of a regulator. Astonishingly, Madoff would still be free and active today had the global financial system not beaten him by imploding first.

What secret investment alchemy, what goose laying golden eggs, had Madoff stumbled upon that allowed him to make market-beating investment returns that, through recessionary thick and thin, were consistently less volatile than those of anyone else? There were many on Wall Street who had their doubts.

Madoff's lack of negative monthly returns suggested that he could time the market brilliantly; a bit too brilliantly perhaps. And how could a sophisticated market-beating investment strategy, pulling in crowds of new customers over more than two decades, be serviced from an accounting and audit firm of just three people, including just one accountant? Why was a scheme that now looks so obviously like a scam not exposed long ago?

It was not for want of trying. For a decade the US Securities and Exchange Commission (SEC) received a string of warnings. Most prominent of all, in 1999 an independent financial fraud investigator, Harry Markopolos, first raised his concerns. He could not see how mathematically and legally Madoff could possibly be making the returns he reported. Over the years, Markopolos several times raised his concerns with the SEC. A review in 2004 by a lawyer in the SEC's Office of Compliance Inspections and Examinations found numerous inconsistencies, a veritable smoking gun. Yet the SEC, a sheep at the wheel, wound the investigation up in 2005.

Frustrated with the SEC's handling of the case, and short of attached to the leg of a grand piano, dropping it from a very great height onto the head of the SEC, Markopolos—in scenes reminiscent of the best crime capers of a John le Carré novel—anonymously delivered a batch of evidence in a brown paper envelope to the SEC. It showed that Madoff was running 'the world's largest Ponzi scheme'. Markopolos claimed that just five minutes looking at Madoff's SEC filings was enough for the SEC to know that something was wrong. Whatever more pressing issues the SEC spent those spare five minutes on— and we are assured that there were many—they were the most expensive five minutes in the whole of financial history.

The US economist John Kenneth Galbraith used the term 'bezzle' for just such scams in his book *The Great Crash: 1929*. He argued that there is always a certain amount of embezzlement going on in an economy. It goes up and down with the economic (and financial) cycle, being especially high in the run-up to crashes. It is highest when it is least observable, and lowest when it is most observable. For a time, this creates a sort of double-counting of wealth. The embezzler has substantial resources under his or her control that he or she has siphoned off from the victims. Those whose wealth has been embezzled think they have all this wealth too, since they have yet to discover that it has been embezzled. The total 'bezzle' in an economy at any time is the amount by which the economy is apparently better off until the scam has been discovered. According to Galbraith, the collapse of a bezzle was a prominent feature of the 1929 crash.

In modern times a booming real-estate market was fertile ground for Ponzi schemes and bezzles. Real estate made apparent wealth gains look 'real'.

Mortgages involved the mortgagees making a commitment to spend a long stream of their income on a lender. Securitization allowed lenders to go from holding these streams on their books, as loans held to maturity, to offloading them in a single transaction at a single point in time, and trousering a large profit now. Money illusion in a low-inflation environment was ideal for getting the bezzle going. By the time the high-burden parts of all the mortgage-repayment schedules arrived, the original sellers, their fees and bonuses, would be long gone. CDSs provided a comfort blanket to those who skipped around the real-estate playground, reassuring them that the big bad risks had been nicely locked away. Housing was a highly democratic bezzle too; those involved could run into the millions and even tens or hundreds of millions. Many housing borrowers were less financially sophisticated than professional stock pickers. Better still, taking part was socially very acceptable.

Another way to exploit bezzles involves exploiting accounting rules.[57] Most commercial activity takes place over time and the profits from it are reported every year. Where exactly the profits are during the life of a contract would not matter for the terms of the contract were it not for uncertainty about cash flows. In the past, accountants would recognize cash only when it had been received or legally committed to be paid. Only profit that was certain could be counted. Modern mark-to-market accountancy, driven by key reforms in the mid-2000s, is different. It is based on the notion that financial markets are always efficient, have dealt with all uncertainty, and have discovered all information. With assets and liabilities mark-to-market, the potential profit of a project is constantly being re-estimated by financial market participants. One very nice side-effect that mark-to-market accounting has for investment managers is that they can take the anticipated profit from an idea the moment they have it by putting it to the market; they don't need to hang around until maturity (either of the asset or of themselves). If they can get leverage, this is a powerful way to exploit a bezzle.

Smart investors can favour themselves even more by marking profits to market but leaving losses until later, treating them according to 'fundamental value'. If accountants quibble about this, one way around it is to trade profitable assets and simply hold on to the unprofitable ones. Add in the odd bit of asset price volatility and a valuation error or two and there is even more opportunity to trade the profitable over the unprofitable. If there is a financial bubble, instead of fighting it—that's for wimps—extract as much value now by dealing in assets with high mark-to-market prices. Madoff was just the most extreme case of a widespread phenomenon. Instead of great skill at investment, all too often the biggest rewards went to those most skilled at getting around (that is 'arbitraging') regulation, working out how to shift risk onto others, and exploiting bubbles and financial bezzles of one sort or another. The ultimate victim of the bezzle was the taxpayer.

And so, one by one, the seeds of the financial crash were sewn. In truth, many of the financial innovations at the heart of the crash were really just fancy ways to bend the financial rules, just as time is bent around a black hole. Many were taking a punt on ever-expanding prices of notoriously illiquid real estate, which was bound to go wrong. The new financial innovations only ever got tested under fair-weather conditions, neither too wet nor too dry, neither too cold nor too hot. Like Icarus, many in the financial sector strapped the innovations on and soared ever higher towards the sun—that is, until the heat became too much, the laws of physics took control, and gravity was their fate.

Part II

Crash and Rescue

4

Crash

The Spikes Come Out

Major turning points in history are often associated with dates referring to especially notable events: 4 July 1776, the day that the US Congress approved the wording of the Declaration of Independence, is regarded as the birth date of the US; 1 September 1939, Germany's invasion of Poland, is taken as the start of the Second World War; 9 November 1989, the fall of the Berlin Wall, marks the collapse of the Soviet Empire. However, as any historian will tell you, while dates are useful organizing devices, major events are usually the result of numerous smaller, individually unmemorable, but collectively momentous, occasions. Usually it is only the sheer size of a particular event that gets it identified in the public's imagination as the 'start' of something new.

One way to date key events in financial markets is by looking at 'spreads' of various sorts. For example, the TED spread is the difference between LIBOR (the London Interbank Offered Rate, which is the short-term interest rate at which banks lend to each other) and the interest rate on US Treasuries of the same term. The spread gives the market's view of the current state of credit-market risk relative to a risk-free benchmark (presuming a US government default is ruled out and the LIBOR rate is not manipulated). In times of financial stress, LIBOR rises because banks charge higher rates for unsecured loans to each other (to compensate for the chance of not getting repaid). Banks also look for better collateral, and so their demand for Treasuries rises, which tends to push the risk-free rate lower. The spread between the two rates widens, or, if it is measured on a graph with zero at the bottom, the spread rises. There are also spreads based on the rates on CDSs compared to the risk-free rate, and LIBOR versus the overnight index swap (OIS) rate, which measures the costs of extremely short-term borrowing by financial institutions; a rising spread shows that market participants are increasingly worrying that counterparties may not deliver on their obligations.[1] The uninitiated reader only really needs to remember that when spreads rise, the market is saying that the financial system has got more risky.

According to spreads, just before the crash the global financial system was very safe indeed. At only 30–40 basis points, or about 0.3%–0.4%, the TED spread was extremely low, and the LIBOR–OIS spread was only about 10 basis points, or 0.1%. The spreads also displayed another interesting statistical property: they were flat—like traces on a seismograph in a time of tectonic calm. Stretching the 2002 to 2012 sheet before us, we see a long period of low and flat, then a spike in August 2007 and another towards the end of 2007, a spike in the middle of March 2008 and an even bigger one in September and early October 2008 (something big must have happened then). The TED spread and the LIBOR–OIS spread hit nearly 460 and 355 basis points respectively. The spreads then fall and steady off in mid-2009 with just the occasional twitch of an aftershock. If we are looking for clues as to where to find key crash 'events', the spreads have left a trail for us to follow. If we date the crash from the moment it became inevitable, that would take us well back into 2007, probably into 2006, and maybe even earlier. If instead, we look for moments of maximum turmoil, we would choose August 2007, March 2008, and, most spectacular of all, September and especially early October 2008.

In this chapter I shall confine myself to key events during the lead-up to the crash and around the times when spreads spiked. I will also describe the key amplification mechanisms at work, which kept ganging up together in new disguises as they moved restlessly from markets to banks to whole countries and back again, wreaking their own peculiar kinds of havoc. When they were done with the US, they moved on to Europe, the subject of Chapter 10. In this chapter I shall only mention rescue efforts when it helps to keep the narrative flowing, even though at times it will feel like describing a house burning down and only incidentally mentioning that the fire brigade turned up, or that sometimes those at the scene used just buckets of water. Chapters 5 and 6 will evaluate the rescue efforts to breathe life back into the banking system.

The spreads don't tell us everything. Many risks were being locked in between 2005 and 2007. Yet the annual cost (taken from an index of CDSs) of insurance against default of large financial firms bottomed out at only 30 basis points (0.3%) in February 2007; on the eve of the crash, the market (that is the collective wisdom of smart investors) said that large financial firms were extremely safe. We now know that such measures were only as safe as . . . houses. So, spreads are like seismographs in other respects; they might be good at telling us when an earthquake is in full swing—at which time, frankly, we hardly need a seismograph—but they are pretty hopeless at warning that an earthquake is approaching (CDS spreads gave some warning, but it was very late in the day). We might look back at them to see how serious the quake had been. The spreads tell us that the crash was high on the financial Richter scale.

As we follow the trail, we need to tread carefully. Because of the way contagion pulls all financial and economic vessels down together, those firms and individuals that played more innocently will often find themselves tarred by the same brush of shame as those who played more wickedly. Good public policy requires we don't treat all of them the same. What will be the point of being a good banker in the future, if all get pilloried today? Besides, there are crooks and clowns aplenty, so we do not need to go after the innocents too.

The Housing Market Turns Nasty

In the US, the first signs of trouble came in 2006 when average US house prices started to fall. It was only 3% in the first year.[2] It doesn't sound like much, but it was a swing from a record rise of 14% in 2005. In the heady atmosphere of the time, it was enough to create the sound of a bubble popping. Subprime borrowers in particular started to miss mortgage repayments. Many relied on the ability to refinance before being hit by a higher interest rate and had little or no equity. Lenders started to worry that borrowers might default and so refused to refinance or refinanced only on much more expensive terms—which, of course, increased the chances of default. Investors into mortgage lenders also demanded higher returns to compensate for the risks. Financial intermediaries that had relied on being able to sell the loans they had originated into a robust secondary market (perhaps bundled up into some ever-so-clever-looking package with an expensive credit-rating ribbon tied around it), started to struggle as losses on subprime MBSs began to mount. With many investors having little or no information about the value of collateral backing their MBSs, all MBSs became suspect. Many had long accepted MBSs in all their rich finery at face value. Now, word began to spread that perhaps they were not so finely enrobed after all. In truth, by 2006 it would have been very difficult to avoid the approaching mess. By the spring of 2007 it was too late. A pity perhaps, that in the summer of 2006 the Federal Deposit Insurance Corporation (FDIC) noted that 'more than 99% of all insured institutions met or exceeded the requirements of the highest regulatory capital standards', and that in April 2007, according to the IMF, global economic risks had fallen over the previous six months.[3]

Even in mid-2007 it was widely presumed that losses would be contained within a small part of the financial system, and that all might yet end well. Bernanke summed up the thinking: '[G]iven the fundamental factors in place that should support the demand for housing, we believe the effect of the troubles in the subprime sector on the broader housing market will likely be limited, and we do not expect significant spillovers from the subprime market to the rest of the economy or to the financial system'.[4] If Bernanke—a world expert on the Great Depression—could not spot the signs of disaster at such close range, it says something about the difficulties lesser economic mortals must have been having. And on the subject of happy endings—bailing out the reckless and the down-right corrupt in the mortgage market, which had ballooned under Bush, and making demands on prudent taxpayers, was hardly an appealing platform for a presidential valediction. In the cooling embers of the Bush administration, difficult decisions were put off for some other time on some other day. It would be the market, not politicians, that would force action.

A series of events in the summer of 2007 signalled that this day was fast approaching. In early May, the Swiss bank UBS closed its fund for handling subprime-related activity and put its fingers in a bucket of iced water. In late May, Moody's issued a 'downgrade review', signalling the likelihood that a range of subprime-related tranches would be downgraded. On 1 June at the 'Beyond Belief' exhibition at the White Cube gallery in London, the artist Damien Hirst unveiled a diamond-encrusted skull, *For the Love of God*, with a price tag of £50 million—a timely reflection on the corruption of values in the years before the crash. In mid-June, the US investment bank Bear Stearns was forced to inject $3.2 billion into two hedge funds facing margin calls. In the multi-trillion-dollar scheme of things this was going to be nothing, but it seemed like a big deal at the time. On 20 June Gordon Brown declared that the UK was 'a world leader in stability, and we will entrench that stability'.[5] To the bitter end, the death of stability seemed a physical impossibility in the minds of some.

In July a small bank in Germany, IKB, found that it could not make good on the credit line it had promised to its conduit for ABCP. A mix of public and private entities pulled a rescue package together; the private sector was already showing itself more than willing to let the public sector help it out of a spot of self-inflicted bother. On 24 July Countrywide Financial Corporation, the world's most aggressively expanding mortgage-making machine, bloated on

$500 billion of home loans, once its gargantuan appetite had finally got the better of it, announced an earnings fall. In the cathedral of mortgage finance, brilliant acoustics and all, it was the equivalent of a very loud burp. Within days, and right on cue, the National Association of Home Builders announced a year-on-year fall of 6.6% in new US home sales. In June and July, Moody's, Standard & Poor's (S&P), and Fitch, bolstered by such a confluence of bad news, made ratings downgrades. On 6 August American Home Mortgage Investment Corporation declared bankruptcy and became one of the first and biggest mortgage lenders to enter the subprime graveyard. The stage was set for the dénouement of more than a decade of financial folly.

Liquidity Crashes

In New York and even in London, 9 August 2007 was a sunny day. But it was a bleak day for those trying to roll over their ABCP, as problems in mortgage markets finally washed over into the interbank market. Unable to value outstanding holdings of ABCP, large investment funds froze investor redemptions until problems would be resolved. The LIBOR–OIS spread jumped tenfold to about 100 basis points (it would spend the next year flinging itself around like an out-of-control firework in a range of 50 to 100 basis points, before finally taking off in September and October 2008). France's largest bank, BNP Paribas, suspended three of its funds until, it hoped, liquidity returned. Thus, the perpetual-motion machine that had driven years of mortgage expansion fell silent. The shadow banking system was suffering a 'run'. Instead of depositors running as in all the classic 'retail' bank runs of the nineteenth and twentieth century, this time it was financial firms running on other financial firms, by not renewing repo agreements or by increasing repo margins.

With shrugs that barely concealed red-faced guilt, those in the shadow banking system, with empty pockets stretched out, turned to their sponsoring banks like teenagers turning to their parents after the party the night before had been just a little too good. Their need for capital surged as billions of dollars of securities held in SIVs were forced back onto sponsoring banks' balance sheets and suddenly required 4%–8% of capital support. The normal banking system did not have enough capital for that. Therefore, from the middle of 2007, there was already a growing need for recapitalization. Nothing would be done about this for well over a year, until a full-blown crash had first taken place. Until then, all the attention was on liquidity. Leveraged-loan originations also collapsed in the summer of 2007. These had been running at over $60 billion per month in the first half of 2007. By August, they were down to a tenth of this. Many financial institutions were left holding large volumes of loans on their books, having failed to complete previously agreed leveraged-buyout deals.

The collapse of liquidity was to become a recurring theme, and was at the heart of the first amplification mechanism.[6] The market for ABCP froze because of problems with 'funding liquidity'. Self-fulfilling 'liquidity spirals' set in: banks forced to sell their assets in very illiquid markets drove down the current market prices of similar assets on the books of other banks, which made all balance sheets worse, which forced others to sell some assets, which further turned the loss spiral. Most firms and regulators simply under-estimated the difficulties the whole financial system would have trying to price complex, structured products in less than fully liquid markets. Some-times it takes a bit of real-world experience to temper our more extreme assumptions.

Those that found themselves with low capital then faced 'funding liquidity' problems.[7] Because of their lack of collateral, they struggled to acquire enough funding even to continue as going concerns. They looked as if they might be insolvent, and why would anyone lend to them in such a state? Non-linear feedback loops spun themselves back and forth between illiquid asset markets and illiquid funding markets.

The preference for holding longer-dated assets was greatly reduced because of the risk of owners being forced to liquidate early at a loss in highly illiquid markets. This fed a race towards shorter maturities (they might get lower returns, but those on shorter maturities could more easily get out before firms went bust).[8] Those holding longer-term maturities needed higher compensation to hold on (something similar happened when the eurozone crashed).

The drying up of liquidity can be usefully framed as a case of rising infor-mational friction hindering optimal risk-sharing and the flow of funds from the less well informed to the better informed (i.e. 'expert investors' and arbitrageurs who usually employ such funds).[9] If risk cannot be shared optimally because the lubricant that enables the machine to work has dried up, many will find themselves bearing risks that they had expected not to face, and at a greatly elevated cost. On the other hand, those who would ordinarily bear such risks, for profit, will be unable to do so.

The difficulties were greatly aggravated by 'lemons' problems.[10] Often we work on the simplistic notion that financial prices will adjust to clear markets. Under severe stress, the pricing mechanism did not work like this. With buyers suspecting that those who were selling assets would hold on to the good ones but sell the bad ones (i.e. the 'lemons'), the expected quality of what was offered in the market fell. This reduced the average price that anyone was prepared to pay. Sellers responded by further holding back their better-quality assets. Buyers reasoned that anyone selling must have been absolutely desperate—which was reason enough to give them a wide birth. Thus, quality in the market and price chased each other downwards. Eventually the market imploded, and there was nothing left.

Similarly, because of 'lemons' problems, a rise in interest rates could not be used to bring supply into line with demand in wholesale and interbank markets. When interest rates rose, less risky borrowers exited the market as their projects could not meet higher interest payments. The proportion of riskier borrowers in the market increased. In normal times, banks could, to some degree, work out which were the more risky and the less risky borrowers, and price accordingly. However, with a major recession in the offing, risks all around were rising, and many banks reasoned it better to ration at any given interest rates than to try to raise interest rates to 'clear' the market. This is effectively what happened when the interbank and wholesale credit markets crashed in August 2007. At first interbank rates rose as the market began to price in the risks of subprime loans. At some point, however, it became clear that any borrowers that were prepared to pay 'over the odds' were signalling that they might have a liquidity problem, maybe even a solvency problem. In classic self-fulfilling fashion, this made matters worse by starving all of cash, even those who were of low risk. This sent asset prices falling. This fed back to make portfolios more risky, which fuelled the original problem.

Standard financial models suggest that at such times financial arbitrageurs enter markets to buy up underpriced assets and make a profit. As they bid against each other, this drives prices back to efficient levels. However, some investors, such as hedge funds, were in as much trouble as everyone else. Others were financially very constrained, and faced a very high internal cost of capital. All worried that markets would overshoot downwards; with performance evaluated on mark-to-market measures, they would register losses and be punished.

To make matters worse, it was becoming clear that losses were starting to stretch their way up to investors holding supposedly safe AAA-rated CDO tranches. To the extent that the valuation of these had been based on a period of calm, and had—by the short-sightedness of ratings models—ignored the possibility of positive correlation, investors in these tranches did not believe they were vulnerable to loss, and were taken by surprise or simply suffered the consequences of their own gullibility. As the financial sea went out, it revealed those who were less investment guru, more emperor swimming naked. And the beaches were very crowded.

A second amplification mechanism was precautionary hoarding. The logic of the interbank market is to allow liquidity to flow freely from those with a surplus of liquidity to those with a deficit of liquidity. However, even if a bank does not need its own liquidity right away, when there is great uncertainty about future liquidity shocks,[11] and being 'caught out' with insufficient liquidity is expensive (for example if it might destroy a company), then a bank is incentivized to hoard an excessive amount of liquidity now even if it means forsaking apparently profitable opportunities.[12] Many reasoned this way and the system got locked into a very strong hoarding equilibrium. Banks refused to risk their capital by lending to other banks that might go bust.[13] It was like a game of musical chairs: but when the music stopped, each had taken as many chairs as it could. The notion that the chairs could be shared around, to minimize the disappointment, was met with about as much enthusiasm as it would at a particularly competitive five-year-old's birthday party. This triggered a generalized collapse in lending, and tears all round. The surge in demand for liquidity in August 2007 sent LIBOR shooting up and spreads rising. LIBOR remained elevated for months, damaging many prime as well as subprime borrowers because the interest rates on many prime business loans and adjustable-rate mortgages were indexed to LIBOR. Because of liquidity and hoarding problems, for most of 2007 and 2008, banks could only borrow very short term.

Subprime has become a convenient cipher for understanding all that went wrong. However, even as late as October 2008, the estimated write-down across all US mortgage types was 'only' about $170 billion, and by April 2009 the figure had risen to 'only' $430 billion, a cumulative loss of 8.4% on the stock of all US mortgages. The figure is large, but even several hundred billion dollars of losses is less than a per cent of yearly global GDP, and easy to absorb in a well-diversified global financial system. Subprime was the squeaky wheel that demanded all the early oil.

The squeak was loud. As expected defaults rose, securitized loans revealed the problem sooner than those loans that impaired over time, that nonchalantly sat on banks' books and then unceremoniously defaulted and dumped their losses. Those financial systems that were heavily securitized and had non-recourse mortgage lending, such as the US, naturally showed their losses early. This created, at least in part, a sort of statistical fluke, but a convenient one nevertheless. It gave everyone else a way to assuage their guilt by offloading most of the blame onto the US, usefully deflecting attention from their own complicity and the way in which they had speculated and stuffed as much risk as possible into their own bloated banking systems. After the crash, in a state of abject denial (and wriggling out of a question about the imprudence of Northern Rock offering 125% mortgages), Prime Minister Brown pleaded: 'What caused it was not something that happened in Britain...I think everybody understands, even the Americans now say, this is a global problem that started in America'.[14] For political convenience, the myth was created that something went wrong only in America and spread—and not that the UK and many others in Europe had just as firmly built their castles (and two-ups and two-downs) in the financial clouds.

Smashing the Rock

In the UK, the Northern Rock bank was turning out to be a little less solid than its name might have implied.[15] Northern Rock had adopted a strategy of stretching its loan book well beyond the level of its deposits, and relying on short-term wholesale funding to fill the gap. It was not alone. By 2007, some £800 billion of external financing had flooded into UK banks courtesy of global imbalances. British banks Bradford and Bingley, Alliance & Leicester, and HBOS were also heavily reliant on wholesale funding, as were a stack of banks in particular in Ireland, Spain, Portugal, and Iceland. In Germany, Hypo Real Estate would be brought to its knees by a subsidiary exploiting short-term money markets. Shareholders did not see this as dangerous, and even punished those who stuck to the traditional route of funding their activities by boring old deposits.

In the US, banks' problems were caused by the low quality of borrowers and subprime. In the UK, and elsewhere in Europe, the key problem was the dependency of mortgage banks on wholesale markets. As wholesale markets dried up, Northern Rock and others found themselves struggling to fund their operations. In the UK, the strains proved too much, and in mid-September 2007, the UK suffered its first bank run since 1866. Matters had not reached the critical 300-year threshold by which UK economic performance is measured these days, but they had come close enough. The Northern Rock's demise was even a bit like that of Overend, Gurney, & Co. that made its losses in the 1860s from a speculative boom in part fuelled by banks reducing their liquidity ratios to dangerously low levels. Of both banks, one could truly say that they behaved 'in a manner so reckless and so foolish, that one would think a child who had lent money in the City of London would have lent it better'.[16] The collapse of Northern Rock signalled the global nature of the crash.

This being Britain, Northern Rock's customers formed orderly queues to withdraw their money. As a form of personal and collective catharsis that the British do especially well—and also to make sure that nobody could mistake this very British orderliness for yellow-bellied cowardice—they collared any TV reporter who happened to be passing by to give him or her a jolly good piece of their mind. Some even accused the media of triggering the run. However, a subsequent careful analysis of Northern Rock's balance sheet revealed that it was the withdrawal of short-term wholesale funding and not the run by depositors or securitization that did the Rock in.[17] The queues made for sensational media coverage in a way that could never have been achieved by the numerous quiet clicks in offices from New York to Frankfurt withdrawing the odd $100 million here and there.

If the fall of the Rock was not to ripple out and cause a generalized run on all UK retail banks, something needed to be done quickly. The UK's Chancellor Brown was forced to temporarily guarantee deposits in all UK retail banks, and subsequently the Rock was nationalized.[18] Northern Rock's Chief Executive Adam Applegarth didn't have to queue. He quit a few months before Northern Rock was nationalized and was given £63,000 a month as redundancy pay until he could find himself another job; those who became unemployed because of Applegarth's recklessness would have quite liked a year or two of that. By all accounts, Applegarth suffered his deprivations with commendable fortitude.

Even when they are solvent, the maturity transformation role of banks makes them vulnerable to self-fulfilling runs, the third amplification mechanism. In a deposit-based bank run, panicking depositors making premature withdrawals force banks to liquidate long-term investments at a loss, making it likely that there will not be enough to pay those who do not withdraw early. With bank capital evaporating in the heat of panic, *all* rush for the doors. When a bank is fundamentally solvent and when the returns promised to both early and late withdrawers are based on the expectation of the returns from long-term investments, all are made worse off. This is a classic 'prisoner's dilemma'; if only everybody could resist the temptation to run, all would be better off, but they cannot coordinate their individual actions to bring about this happy outcome. As a coordinating device to take away their incentive to run, financial regulators have instigated various deposit-guarantee programmes that reassure non-panickers that their deposits will be safe. This, naturally enough, carries a new risk, that of moral hazard. However, financial intermediation, like life itself, is a delicate balancing of many different risks. If one never leaves the house, one might be safer, but it makes for a very dull life, and insanity carries a new set of dangers. Likewise, a world without maturity transformation, even if therefore without the possibility of bank runs, would be an impoverished and unhappy place. The problem was that in the 2000s many of the activities that were vulnerable to runs were not deposit-based and so not protected by (explicit) guarantees. Whilst markets rose, this did not show, and the incentive to run was offset by a heavy return for those who did not run. Once the tide turned, the lack of a guarantee across large swathes of the financial system made for a much bigger run component than normal. Of course, without a guarantee in place, behaviour should have been less reckless. Yet, banks *had* been reckless anyway, and so the lack of a guarantee made the consequences much worse.

In early December 2007, concerned about renewed pressure on the money markets, five key central banks mounted a coordinated injection of liquidity, including the establishment of new currency swap lines. After all their hard work, for a while policymakers enjoyed some welcome respite. Spotting an apparent buying opportunity, and perhaps misunderstanding the dangers, between November 2007 and mid-January 2008 a number of sovereign wealth funds invested about $38 billion in the equity of large US banks. This was very public spirited, since one feature of equity is that it is first to be wiped out in a financial crash. There was also, however, a growing concern that for all the cuts in central-bank interest rates, there was no significant impact on those caught in the mouth of the credit crunch.

In late 2007 and early 2008, rating agencies started to worry about the solvency of a number of US 'monolines'. These were bond insurers narrowly focussing (hence their name) on writing insurance cover on municipal bonds who had branched out in a new line of business in subprime mortgages via CDSs. The profits had proved just a little too tempting. It was increasingly unclear whether the monolines would be able to meet their obligations if called upon to do so. Astonishingly, a downgrade of monolines would have lowered the rating on $2.4 trillion of financial instruments. On 19 January 2008, the rating agency Fitch stepped up to the plate and downgraded one of the monolines, Ambac. With share prices all over the world falling, the Fed announced a 0.75% cut in the Fed funds rate, down to 3.5%, and cut it by another 0.5% at the end of January.

The Bear Growls

Bear Stearns, a global investment bank and securities trading and brokerage firm, had been a pioneer at the giddy heights of mortgage-backed securitization. Its assets had more than doubled from $185 billion in 2003 to $400 billion in early 2008. Sadly, the first principle of structural financial engineering—when in a deep hole, stop digging—didn't seem to apply at Bear Stearns. As losses mounted over 2006 and 2007, instead of reducing its exposure, showing consummate self-assurance and no small amount of stupidity, Bear Stearns dug itself in even deeper. What had once seemed so cutting-edge, and then a mere foible, was rapidly coming to be seen as just a downright vice. Maybe Bear Stearns saw some sort of buying opportunity. Maybe its executives were maximizing on the basis of an expected bailout. Maybe they just miscalculated. Whichever the case, Bear Stearns was now in trouble. After two of its hedge funds had blown up in June 2007, Bear Stearns had become increasingly reliant on short-term funding. In early March 2008, several institutions decided to stop doing repos with Bear Stearns.

When markets are febrile, little details start to matter. After trading hours on 11 March, a hedge fund sent Goldman Sachs an email requesting that it enter a contractual relationship with it, which would have increased Goldman Sachs's direct exposure to Bear Stearns. It was too late to be dealt with that day and Goldman Sachs only 'cleared' the contract on the morning of 12 March. The media, at first, interpreted this as a refusal. Bear Stearns's hedge fund clients were unnerved, and some say this contributed to the run on Bear Stearns. What little liquidity Bear Stearns had was being handed to customers to support the appearance of solvency. On 13 March 2008, with its liquidity down to zero, Bear Stearns was at a sickening low and just one day away from filing for bankruptcy. The bank was effectively suffering a run on repos. Bear Stearns had fallen a long way very quickly; in 2007, *Fortune* magazine had declared it the second 'most admired' securities firm in its 'America's Most Admired Companies' survey (Lehman was first).[19]

On the one hand, it was felt that a disorganized collapse of Bear Stearns would ripple through its network of counterparties, hit confidence in financial markets, and lead to reduced credit to the US economy. On the other hand, Bear Stearns was not a deposit-taking bank, and therefore not covered by the protections such banks got. The logic was that if investors take a risk in order to make a higher return than they would get in a protected bank, they should monitor the investment bank in which they place their money and make sure it does not take excessive risks. If the bank goes bust, they lose their money—a decent enough incentive to keep an eye on it. Investors in a protected bank accept a lower return because such banks have stricter requirements on holding capital buffers, and the investors do not expect to have an obligation to keep their eyes quite so beadily on it. The investors are safer, but the capital buffers have a cost, and the investors absorb that cost via the lower return they agree to accept. It was not supposed to be possible to take the higher, but more risky, return of investing in Bear Stearns and still expect to get the same protection as those who had paid for it. Allowing this would create yet more of the famed moral hazard. Worse, if it became known that this was so, it would increase the incentive to deposit and invest in higher-risk financial institutions and this would crowd out lower-risk financial institutions—a sort of adverse selection that would reinforce the moral hazard problem. Although no explicit fee had changed hands, those investing in a protected bank had, in effect, paid an implicit insurance fee. Those investing in banks like Bear Stearns had not. Bear Stearns should not get protection.

There was a problem acting out this long-held piece of logic. Bear Stearns nestled in the middle of a great big web of derivative contracts woven together over many years, some 150 million trades with 5,000 other firms, including 750,000 contracts with an aggregate notional value of $14.2 trillion (in investment banking, by 2008, the trillion was the new billion). It was feared that if Bear Stearns was taken out, the whole tightly-strung structure would tear apart. The authorities had no desire to come along later, gingerly stepping amongst the tangled mess to unstick the numerous smaller players caught within it. Fearful of the systemic consequences of letting Bear Stearns collapse, regardless of the niceties as to which financial institution should or should not get government protection, and although Bear Stearns was not key to the payments system, a rescue mission was mounted. On 16 March 2008, the New York Fed facilitated, with a loan of $30 billion, the takeover of Bear Stearns by JPMorgan Chase at a fire-sale price (JPMorgan eventually paid $10 per share compared to the $133.20 the shares had peaked at only a year before, demonstrating yet again the consummate ability of investment banks to time the market perfectly). Bear Stearns had spent its life devouring others. Now it was its turn.

Perhaps Bear Stearns was big and ugly, but what really bothered policymarkes was its 'too interconnected to fail' nature. This was an example of a fourth amplification mechanism: the way in which counterparty risks created network effects. In the crash, not only was the network of financial institutions less complete than many had thought (especially because of the failure to fully exploit the diversification benefits of securitization), but even where the network was more complete, the pattern of claims may still have facilitated contagion.[20] With financial institutions acting simultaneously as both borrowers and lenders, there were gridlocks such that individual institutions were unable to cancel their offsetting positions because of worries (and disputes, actual and potential) about counterparty risk. With the ventricular system locked in confusion, the financial heart stopped pumping.

Bear Stearns executives had made good money for their run. Between 2000 and 2008, the top five individuals in the firm had pocketed, just between themselves, a staggering $1.4 billion in cash bonuses and equity sales.[21] 'Performance-based remuneration' they called it. A money-making machine on a grandiose scale at the expense of everyone else, more like it. Bear Stearns executives had done their utmost to try to prove that the best way to rob a bank was to run a bank.[22] In the panic, policymakers did not bother to ask any of them to pay any of it back.

The period after the near-death experience of Bear Stearns, was in retrospect, one of relative calm. Maybe success at averting a disaster strengthens the markets' belief that disasters can always be averted. Although the interbank market was moribund, for a while asset prices even rose—a sort of financial Indian summer but in the spring of 2008. In June, Moody's and S&P dampened expectations by taking negative rating actions against two monolines, MBIA and Ambac. As night follows day, this reinforced worry about possible losses amongst monolines, especially because of their CDSs. In mid-July 2008, the SEC issued an order restricting 'naked' short sellers from venturing forth into the financial waters. Nevertheless, outside of the US, financial markets seemed to regard this as by and large a US problem. Emerging economies grew quite healthily. Bond yields and the monetary-policy stances of developed economies did not give any hint that problems might run much wider than the US. Not only were politicians in denial, but—it is striking to reflect in hindsight—so were the markets, it seems. Where were the efficient markets of the 'efficient markets theorem' at their hour of greatest need? Again, the respite did not last.

Fannie Mae and Freddie Mac and Problems in the Derivatives Larder

By mid-2008 falling house prices were weighing heavily on the fortunes of Fannie Mae and Freddie Mac, whose capitalization had become so thin that one could shine a torch straight through it. In one week in early July 2008 they lost almost half their market value. Since they owned or guaranteed nearly half of the US's $12 trillion mortgage market, and had outstanding more than $5 trillion in MBSs and debt, this was, to say the least, problematic. As the US

Treasury put it: 'Investors have purchased securities of these government sponsored enterprises in part because the ambiguities in their Congressional charters created a perception of government backing...Because the US government created these ambiguities, we have a responsibility to both avert and ultimately address the systemic risk now posed by the scale and breadth of the holdings of GSE debt and mortgage backed securities'.[23] The promise of government backing had never been explicitly charged for. Yet, so long as such as guarantee implicitly existed, allowing the rug to be pulled out from under Fannie Mae and Freddie Mac would be construed as a form of reneging, even default, by the US government. As everyone knows, it is utter folly to even hint that the US government might default, and so, on 7 July, the FDIC intervened in the IndyMac Bank and, on 13 July, US authorities announced backstop measures, which included purchasing some of the GSE's stock. The backstop at least made the implicit guarantee explicit (although there was still no charge for it). In what the reader will by now recognize as a familiar refrain, it was not enough. Being publicly traded, the stock prices of these two financial monoliths continued to slide.

On 7 September, Fannie Mae and Freddie Mac were taken into government conservatorship. In all but name this was nationalization. The US Treasury agreed to purchase up to $100 billion of preferred stock in each GSE. The Treasury and Fed eventually bought $1.6 trillion of the debt and MBSs issued by the GSEs. Given the political sensitivities in the US surrounding the word nationalization, the 'all but name' bit is really quite a crucial desideratum.

By now it was becoming clear that CDSs were the mice in the financial larder; there were tell-tale footprints all over the balance sheets of many financial institutions. Like so many things that went wrong in the crash, all seemed fine so long as the good times rolled. When the level of defaults was very low, financial players banked the profits and didn't worry too much about the losses. A 10% loss on $55 trillion of gross notional outstanding CDSs would equate to $5.5 trillion of losses. There would be offsetting profits in a system of derivatives that in theory balanced out, so that most of this loss should never materialize. However, as the default rates rose, one by one, it became clear that real losses would mount, and that somebody, somewhere, would have to make good on the losses. En route, one by one those who had offered credit protection would be picked off, unable to pay as their capital was wiped out by earlier claims, leaving their counterparties—who had thought they were insured—facing a sudden loss. But who were whose counterparties? Because of the way the market was set up, each firm knew its obligations, but not much about the obligations of its counterparties—nor of the counterparties of its counterparties, nor the counterparties of the counterparties of its counterparties, and so on. The CDS market was a hall of broken mirrors. To add to the uncertainty, it was not clear what regulators and policymakers would do in such a situation. Like a car crash seen in slow motion, defaults would appear first for the underlying borrowers, then for those who had bought the CDSs, then for those who bought instruments based on the original CDSs, and so on. Some hedge funds found they carelessly offered credit protection way beyond the capital they held, and they had no hope of paying. The lines between insolvency and illiquidity got blurred as confidence between counterparties collapsed, and the chances of panic runs increased. Just as some companies had burnt their fingers overselling subprime because it was just too easy to do and too hard to resist, so also was it becoming clear that some companies had oversold CDSs for much the same reason.

The Lehman Boat Sinks

The next protagonist in our sad tale is Lehman Brothers, the fourth-largest US securities firm. Like Bear Stearns before it, Lehman had been a top underwriter of MBSs and CDOs. Not satisfied with its recklessness, Lehman had added over $80 billion of commercial and residential mortgages on top, much of which had turned sour. Lehman was counterparty on over $700 billion in derivatives contracts, of which about $400 billion were CDSs. This was a high-risk high-growth strategy that had taken Lehman's assets from $354 billion in 2003 to $814 billion in 2007. Towards the end, Lehman was funding about half of this through overnight, or other short-term, loans.

One could write a whole book about the collapse of Lehman. Indeed, some have. Some accounts are entertaining, even comical—for there is quite a lot of comic material here. Some read like a veritable Shakespearian tragedy, since there is much of that too. Some mix the two to stunning effect. I have a few spare paragraphs and will return in Chapter 5 to analyse how Lehman was handled. Lehman had just about managed to stay afloat after the collapse of Bear Stearns. Now, it was slowly and painfully sinking, with only the screeching sound of its CEO, Richard Severin (from the Latin *severus*, severe, stern, strict) Fuld, Jr, who, having slipped from his burnished throne, was now sliding, by his fingernails, down the side of the vessel he had once commanded. If Lehman sank, the fear was that its CDS contracts would be mostly worthless, and this would ripple through a network of counterparties. By the weekend of 13–14 September, Lehman's customers and lenders were fleeing like rats from a sinking ship, grabbing whatever they could as they lept, fearful that they would not get paid. Like Bear Stearns before it, Lehman was suffering a repo-based run. And it was insolvent. Bust. Kaput. Dead.

Right up to the moment of its demise, all the main CRAs maintained the fiction of an investment-grade rating for Lehman, as they had with Bear Stearns. Just months before Lehman's collapse, Moody's and S&P issued reports declaring its liquidity profile 'solid' and 'very strong'. Lehman had, just a few weeks before, estimated its tier-one capital ratio at 11% (tier-one capital consists primarily of common equity and other equity-like instruments and so is regarded as capital of the highest quality). This was more than the regulator's minimum ratio, and Lehman declared itself safe. Maybe no CRA wanted to be the proximate cause of such a large and powerful investment bank's demise, but, with hindsight, it was a glaring example of the inadequacies of the CRAs. No wonder then that as Lehman listed onto its side, the back offices of every major bank in New York were crammed to bursting point with staff frantically trying to work out their institution's counterparty risk to Lehman.

Even those who prided themselves at being at the helm of global financial policy failed to see what was coming. In his account, Brown admitted just how out of touch he was with the growing dangers: 'In September 2008, like almost everyone else [except that, unlike everyone else, he was the UK's Chancellor of the Exchequer for ten years, and architect of its new regulatory system], I was surprised by the news of Lehman's problems and the rapid sequence of events that followed.'[24] Maybe also he didn't know that the top five executives at Lehman had cashed out, just between themselves, $1 billion in cash bonuses and equity sales between 2000 and 2008.[25] Television news footage showed Fuld being chased down the street by former employees and shareholders demanding he pay some of his back. Nobody else had. He was not about to. The success of Bear Stearns and Lehman executives in cashing out before the crash was not shared across the industry;[26] perhaps they were more aware of the reckless risks they were running than they let on at the time.

The US Treasury spent a weekend desperately trying to pull together a private-sector rescue. We are now told that the Treasury doubted its legal authority to step into the breach and lend to Lehman without adequate collateral. Others say that top officials, already weary of the view that they were the easy suckers who would pick up the pieces when all went wrong ('moral hazard' was the technical jargon they used), wanted to send a clear message, to all who might have formed such an unfortunate impression, that no such arrangement existed. Lehman was also international, and there were political constraints to worry about, such as what would happen if, Heaven forbid, chunks of bailout money benefited, at US taxpayer expense, those who lived abroad; there was no system for dealing with such delicate niceties. Others simply felt that Fuld had made such a monumental cock-up, and been so deluded in his belief about his firm's God-given right to survive, that he should be allowed to sink as a cautionary tale to others. It irked some that Fuld failed to prepare his firm for the inevitable liquidity shortage, no doubt thinking that it would have been a waste of his precious energies given that the government would surely see the light and stump up (after all, it had with Bear Stearns). For a while, it seemed that Bank of America or Barclays might be interested, but laying down their bodies for Lehman to trample across to its salvation, did not especially appeal. The potential saviours would need a guarantee. The US Treasury said no. Barclays was too fragile to swallow Lehman whole (although, once Lehman had gone into bankruptcy, Barclays was able to snap up Lehman's North American investment banking and trading operations at a knock-down price, which was palatable enough). Some say Lehman was jilted at the altar, when Merrill Lynch, perhaps realizing that there was not going to be enough room in the fractious government lifeboat, sold itself to Bank of America for $50 million on the night of the 14 September. Whatever the reasoning, on 15 September 2008, Lehman Brothers Inc., one of the world's leading investment banks, filed for Chapter 11 bankruptcy protection, the largest bankruptcy in history. Lehman had always striven to be first and biggest at everything. Yet again it was.

With Herbert Lehman turning, and no doubt tut-tutting, in his grave ('Grabbing and greed can go on for just so long, but the breaking point is bound to come sometime'[27]) the collapse of Lehman sent the signal—for a fleeting moment at least—that no bank was too big not to be allowed to fail. Within days, problems were crashing down on the global financial system like waves gnawing away a crumbling cliff-face. In an interview in *Newsweek*, Nobel-prize-winning economist Paul Krugman observed: 'Letting Lehman fail basically brought the entire world capital market down.'[28] Lehman was a kind of psychological tipping point. Like drunk drivers who had pushed the survivability envelope, for a moment other investment banks, at last sobering up, wondered whether, perhaps, after all, they were not as invincible as they had thought. Within days, a crisis of confidence spread like wildfire across financial institutions, markets, and countries. In Chapter 5 we shall explore how much of this was a consequence of Lehman's collapse, how much was 'stored up' in the system already, and how much was the fault of policymakers. Shocked by market reactions over the coming weeks, central bankers and politicians, like guilt-stricken parents who now regretted denying their children special treats, vowed to never again be so beastly. Lehman was to become a very rare exhibit, a dead investment bank, stuffed and in a glass viewing cabinet for all the world to gawp at, the word 'shame' printed across the top. It was one of a kind, a dodo of sorts. What had started as a liquidity crisis had over time revealed itself as a deeper, and much more pernicious, asset quality problem. In truth it had always been so. Policymakers just didn't want to accept the fact until it stared them in the face. The collapse of Lehman made it clear that there was a systemic problem, and that liquidity support would not be enough.

Some Procyclical Hardwiring

During the crash, market-value accounting standards and capital adequacy regulations (CARs) based on credit ratings interacted in self-defeating fashion—the fifth amplification mechanism. Ratings downgrades led to the need for more capital just at the time when profit was low and it was hard to raise new capital. This generated downward spirals of asset price falls, further deleveraging, more asset price falls, and so on in feedback loops of ever greater perversity. As a consequence of increased securitization, many more investors relied on credit ratings. Many institutions also had investment rules to guide their portfolio management—such as only to hold instruments with a rating of AAA. Thus, when ratings fell, many institutions were legally obliged to cast the offending components out. This exacerbated the impact of forced selling.

Neither did it help that many ratings did not capture risk well; as soon as it became clear that ratings were wrong, those instruments to which the ratings were attached got an unceremonious chop, regardless of the knock-on consequences. The use of market-value or rating-based 'triggers' was supposed to protect investors, especially the more senior ones, by guaranteeing that if asset values fell below predefined levels, the SIVs holding them would be wound up before the senior creditors faced losses. This had some innate logic in the individual case, but it was, to say the least, inane logic when applied to many SIVs all at once, triggering spasms of forced selling that drove prices even lower. This was similar to the selling triggers that automatically forced sales and magnified the stock market crash of 1987. It seems that 20 years is about the average time for such practices to move in and out of vogue.

Paradoxically, CARs rendered more vulnerable the banks that were supposedly safer because they held lots of AAA-rated securities.[29] Capital is held against *unexpected* losses. *Expected* losses are covered by charging a higher interest rate, so BBB securities already pay more to compensate for higher expected losses. Ratings reflect the expected probability of default. Two banks holding the same risk-weighted capital ratio, the same capital buffer above the requirement, and the same risk of downgrade for both AAA and BBB assets, will fare differently according to the proportions they hold of AAA and BBB. The bank holding more AAA carries more systemic risk for three reasons. First, AAA assets are systemic: they only lose value in a systemic crash. BBB assets have more idiosyncratic, and therefore diversifiable, risk. Second, the mark-to-market decline in value is greater for the same downward migration in rating. Third, an equivalent downward migration in ratings leads to a greater proportional need for extra capital for AAA -than for BBB-rated securities (i.e. the relationship between ratings and the capital adequacy requirement is curved). Thus, for the same ratings migration and for the same initial capital buffer, the AAA bank faces greater difficulties than the BBB bank. Ratings are all about incentivizing banks to be individually prudent; they are not about anything systemic, so when problems are systemic, the ratings, in a sense, backfire and harm those that are supposedly safer. This, of course, means that many triple-A-rated tranches based on mortgage-backed securities of CDOs never deserved their triple-A-ratings in the first place. As a result, over 2004–2007, there had been a huge explosion in potential systemic risk, because banks had held on to such a large proportion of the AAA-tranches, especially those tied to real estate, in what turned out to be a $2–3 trillion one-way bet on the economy.

AIG and Others Quickly Follow

The next scary monster in our tale is AIG. AIG had operations across 70 US insurance companies and 130 countries. It was not a financial holding company and so was not regulated by the Fed. AIG had been one of only eight US companies rated triple-A by those reliable judges of financial character, the credit rating agencies. AIG's shares had been generously priced in the market partly because investors were off-guard owing to AIG's top-notch credit rating. On 16 September, after AIG's credit rating had been downgraded below AA, the US Fed—no doubt reasoning that when traversing Hell the best thing to do is to keep going, and, whatever you do, not to look down—stepped in with an $85 billion loan and a package of measures to save AIG, in return for which the government got a 79.9% stake in the company. Congressional Reports indicate that the decision to do this was made quite literally overnight. The reason for AIG's hunger was revealed in the summer of 2008. AIG had exploited a gaping hole in the regulatory system, by hosting a shadow financial-products creature, lodged deep within its guts (actually, based in its London offices) which had pumped way beyond its means the level of credit risk insured by its host. AIG was a sort of super sugar daddy to companies, ready to pay up in times of their distress, even if their distress was self-inflicted; except that it was now in distress itself, and was hardly in a fit state to rescue others.

As with Lehman, what you saw with AIG was not what you got. All other banks and hedge funds bought and sold CDSs, so when defaults happened something had to be paid out, but something also had to be paid back; what mattered was the net position. In contrast, AIG treated CDSs as just another form of insurance. That's fine, and profitable, when risks are not correlated— one person's death does not trigger another person's death, and one house burning down does not set a whole city ablaze. AIG only sold CDS protection, amassing a tidy little pile of contracts totalling about $440 billion. Supposedly, AIG was insuring banks on the safest parts of their CDOs linked to MBSs, and AIG would only lose when all others had been wiped out first. But this meant it was sitting on the mother of all one-way bets. This situation had been 'allowed to build up without any adult supervision', complained Geithner.[30] When the US housing market collapsed, and mortgage defaults started to appear like rows of burning dominoes, the CDOs protected by the CDSs created by AIG succumbed to ratings downgrades. Counterparties to the CDSs increased their demands on collateral. AIG suffered a bank run of sorts, based on margins.[31] By September 2008, AIG had had to post $30 billion in fresh collateral. With the MBS market illiquid, AIG could not sell MBSs and raise the cash it needed to post any more collateral. AIG was in a death spiral.

As AIG's losses mounted, the AIG rescue package was, over the ensuing months, restructured and expanded dramatically, with another $37 billion in October and $40 billion in November. The main benefit of such bounty to the counterparties of AIG, it was argued, was to avoid an otherwise very disorderly unwinding of AIG and the losses on its CDSs being rushed quickly onto clients' balance sheets where they would inflict further damage. For any bank that had staggered thus far without default, the price of CDSs on it rocketed.[32]

Also on 16 September, the $60 billion Reserve Primary Fund, one of the biggest, and the oldest, US money market mutual funds, 'broke the buck'—i.e. it was unable to redeem its investors' shares at a net asset value of $1 per share—because its shares fell to 97 cents after writing off debt issued by Lehman Brothers.[33] As the reader can probably guess, it is very bad form to 'break the buck'. Many Americans have investments in mutual funds, and when they panicked, there was a flood of fund redemptions. This raised concerns that there might be a run on many other firms in the $3.6 trillion money market industry. A few days later, the US Treasury announced that it would temporarily guarantee money market funds, which stopped the run.

On 18 September, $160 billion of new or expanded swap lines were announced in a coordinated move by central banks. The UK authorities, ordering the sea to turn back, placed a ban on the short selling of financial shares. It was hoped that this would be a sort of financial market circuit-breaker. Shorting financial firms' shares might discipline bad firms, but—policymakers reasoned—those who engaged in shorting tended to be a tad too enthusiastic at the time of a crash when it was a bit too easy to create self-fulfilling bets that sent the solvent as well as the insolvent to the wall. In its worst form, 'bear raids' involved shorting a struggling bank and then circulating bad rumours to prompt its demise. The SEC, not to be left out, placed a ban on the short selling of financial shares.

Other mating rituals were in the offing, some more surreptitious than the others. By now, banks were being chaperoned by Treasury and Fed officials, and some were engaging in their own *Liaisons dangereuses*. Attempts were made to achieve the mergers of Citigroup with Goldman Sachs (now, that would have been interesting!), of Citigroup with Morgan Stanley, of Citigroup with Wachovia, of Wachovia with Goldman Sachs, of Wachovia with Morgan Stanley, and of JPMorgan Chase with Morgan Stanley. They looked each other up and down, and with none finding any of the others particularly attractive (or, more likely, thinking there were better fish in the sea and a more favourable government rescue deal around the next corner), there were to be no wedding bells.

Investment banks were hit hard in this period. Brimful with clever people (we know they are clever because why else would they get paid so much?), many had managed to stuff their portfolios with remarkably stupid investments. Their business models were built, on the one hand, on the throughput of increasing volumes of transactions that would generate growing revenue and, on the other hand, on cheap short-term credit to fund high levels of leverage. Smart it might have appeared once upon a time. Now it did not look so clever. Both pillars of the business model had toppled and, in the third quarter of 2008, the net revenue of the largest investment banks was over 90% down on the year before. Presenting themselves to the Fed in the most parlous light possible, on 21 September Goldman Sachs and Morgan Stanley were cleared to become insured bank holding companies, a sure sign that the pair would not be allowed to die. Given that they had never paid any insurance fees for years and years, this was very decent charity on the part of the government. Neither of them had further need of a marriage contract nor for all the compromises that married life would bring. Not without good reason did JK Galbraith punctuate the title of Chapter 4 of his classic book about the 1929 crash, 'In Goldman, Sachs We Trust'. Eighty years on, Goldman Sachs was proving yet again that it was a master of self-preservation and of the art of financial escapology.

Later there were some happy nuptials. Wachovia ('Wachovia. Uncommon Wisdom' went their marketing slogan) had demonstrated such uncommon lack of wisdom that it ended up being acquired by Wells Fargo ('The Next Stage in Banking', or at least it was for Wachovia). Morgan Stanley got a capital infusion from Japanese bank Mitsubishi UFJ Financial Group. If someone had written that over six months all major stand-alone investment banks would be gone— having changed their charters to become banks so that they could avail themselves of the safety nets afforded to banks, or having been absorbed by larger banking institutions—nobody would have believed it. Even the most prescient would be hard-pressed to prove they had entertained such dark and demented thoughts. But, by September 2008, in the land of the mad, only the truly lunatic were sane.

On 25 September, Washington Mutual, the largest thrift institution in the US with just over $300 billion of assets, and now effectively suffering from a bank run, was put into receivership by the US authorities. Later it would be absorbed into JPMorgan Chase. It says something of the extremes of the time that, if politely cross-examined in the street, most Americans would not know that this was the largest US bank failure in history. Washington Mutual became no more than an interesting footnote—or, if luck was in, a paragraph—in the story of the fall of Lehman.

Britain's Shame

Bad behaviour was not confined to the US. Many firms had taken an extremely cavalier attitude towards risk management. As a case study—and as a sad example to add to the likes of Lehman and Madoff to help balance the ledger of disgrace— the UK had HBOS plc, a bank created by the merger of Halifax plc and Bank of Scotland in 2001. All countries have their HBOSs; in Ireland it was Anglo Irish

Bank, in Belgium it was Fortis (an insurance company), in Germany it was Hypo Real Estate, in Spain it was the regional savings banks the cajas, and in Iceland it was Landisbank. In the 2000s HBOS had aggressively sought to wrestle market share from the 'big four' UK retail banks, Barclays, HSBC, Lloyds TSB, and NatWest/Royal Bank of Scotland—for market share was everything in those days. HBOS's strategy involved de-emphasizing risk management and deposit growth and emphasizing the expansion of its loan book by all means possible. By September 2008, HBOS was sitting on a huge and dodgy loan portfolio built on bloated commercial-sector lending, and it was starting to hurt.

The bank was particularly lax at dealing with impaired and high-risk assets, bad debts, and provisioning. By clever accounting techniques, bad debt did not get registered as a loss, while the interest payments continued to be booked as profits. Selling on risk through some of the new-fangled financial innovations helped the illusion. Some insiders said that, towards the end, HBOS continued to lend to companies that would have been treated as technically insolvent by other banks, with elements of a gamble for resurrection. The larger loan book meant bigger bonuses to the bank's executives. The British newspaper *The Guardian*, showing reckless disregard for a new form of moral hazard, granted the bank's former chief executives Sir James Crosby and Andy Hornby a place in their list of the top 25 people who caused the crash.[34] Eventually, put before the Treasury Select Committee of the UK House of Commons, like a pair of startled rabbits caught in headlights, Crosby and Hornby admitted to having no banking qualifications. In the medical or legal professions this would have got them struck off. But 'bankers' in their positions in the 2000s were largely snake-oil salesmen and confidence merchants, and they did not feel the need to be up-to-date on the finer points of safe prudential banking. We tend to think of Madoff when we think of Ponzi schemes, but HBOS had about it elements of a Ponzi scheme or perhaps of an accountancy-bezzle. As in the case of Madoff before them, it was not eagle-eyed regulators who caught and snapped up Crosby and Hornby. It was the global financial deluge that had washed from beneath them their feet of clay. Not only did the risk-management and credit-checking functions of HBOS fail to keep pace with the growth of the loan book, but in the benign environment of the mid 2000s, instead of being punished, HBOS was rewarded by the stock market. So much, yet again, for the 'efficient-market hypothesis'.

When the money market froze, a number of UK banks were exposed. A run of depositors at HBOS might have concatenated into runs at other banks, including Bradford and Bingley, Alliance and Leicester, RBS, and Barclays. If deposits in, and loans to, non-insolvent banks were pulled, such banks too would face liquidity problems, which would raise their cost of funds, which would increase the risks of them becoming insolvent. This would hit especially hard those with a large maturity mismatch between their assets and their liabilities. In the vain hope that the government would not have to pay anything, the new British prime minister Gordon Brown personally (over cocktails, we are told) sweet-talked a healthy Lloyds TSB Bank into saving the sickly HBOS. Lloyds TSB had made profits of $1 billion in 2008 and was deemed a sound bank, which seemed to make it a good partner for HBOS. To ease the merger through, annoying little inconveniences such as European competition law were dispensed with by the silver-tongued Lord Mandelson, advisor to the matchmaker of the marriage. The prize to Lloyds TSB, its eyes far bigger than its belly, was a slug of that precious elixir, greater market share. It would also get a hidden subsidy courtesy of higher prices due to greater market power (the merged company would sit on a third of the UK mortgage market). 'The bank that likes to say yes' was not about to say no to that.

Unfortunately, this *marriage à la mode* was not a happy one. HBOS had not been entirely forthcoming regarding its prior financial promiscuity. And nobody seemed to have bothered to do the full background checks, or, if they had, they were not telling (in November 2009 it was revealed that the Bank of England had given HBOS a lifeline under the Bank's Emergency Liquidity Assistance scheme, starting on 1 October 2008 and peaking at £25.4 billion on 13 November 2008 before being repaid by mid-January 2009, which suggests that the risks were known to the Bank of England). Showing neither grace nor gratitude, HBOS promptly passed its infected loans on and sank the hapless Lloyds. The share price of Lloyds Banking Group, LBG (the new amalgamation), plummeted by over 90%. To protect all concerned from the full consequences of their haste, not least Prime Minister Brown, the previously healthy LBG ended up being over 43% government owned. The political fallout was to give many a British newspaper editor more material to fill column inches than they could ever have hoped for. The story had incompetence, hubris, greed, and opportunism of every hue and spot slapped all over it, and newspaper editors took great delight in pouring scorn and disapprobation on in equal measure. At a time when the British public was baying for a target on which to vent its spleen (the media was full of stories about British MPs' expense scandals), Prime Minister Brown—red-faced, broken-arrowed Cupid amongst the ruins—had at last delivered.

Another banker offering his punch-bag services was the fabled Sir (now, plain Mr) Fred Goodwin of the Royal Bank of Scotland (RBS). According to its 2008 accounts, RBS had assets of £2.4 trillion, nearly twice the size of the UK's GDP. RBS had adopted an especially aggressive growth strategy based on high-risk lending, much of it to property companies and large borrowers, and highly vulnerable in a downturn. In 2007, Goodwin had led RBS, with insufficient due diligence, in an ill-fated acquisition of the bulk of the giant Dutch bank ABN Amro and of the US-based Charter One. This misadventure watered down, to all of 2%, the capital RBS held as a buffer against losses when its exposure to subprime backfired, and left the new bank over-reliant on wholesale markets. There was regulatory failure too, since the FSA had cleared the deal. As markets turned in 2007, RBS was slow to respond, and its corporate division even increased the size, complexity, and risk of its transactions. During 2008 RBS made £7–8 billion pre-exceptional losses, with a further £15–20 billion write-downs on the acquisitions that had gone sour. Instead of allowing an ignominious collapse, the UK government took a 70% stake (which later rose to 83%). The government also injected a secret £36.6 billion loan on 17 October 2008 that the bank repaid in December.

Grainy photos—generously sprinkled across the British tabloid press like snaps from CC-TV footage, to enhance the surreptitiousness of the moment—showed the shamed Goodwin being driven away, having first secured for himself a just-about-adequate, to his sensibilities at least, £12.3 million pension pot (a one-off lump-sum of £2.7 million, and a pension of £650,000 every year for life). It was a nice little earner, courtesy of the British taxpayer. There was one little snag. He hadn't earned it. Had RBS not been rescued and instead been put into insolvency as Goodwin had left it, he would have got what the pension protection fund would have allowed him, £28,000 a year at age 65 (which in the upper echelons of the banking world was the equivalent of nothing). Even though their own shambolic incompetence had allowed Goodwin to become, in the words of *The Economist*, an 'accidental multimillionaire',[35] for the politicians involved this was just too much of a juicy tale of personal greed to resist a few moralizing punches to deflect attention from their own conduct.

The Waves Come Crashing in

In the UK the mortgage bank Bradford and Bingley was also nationalized; in Germany commercial property lender Hypo Real Estate was thrown a government-facilitated credit line (and eventually nationalized); in Belgium the insurance company Fortis had capital injected by three European governments; and the Russian government injected billions into its banking system. A large number of countries, such as Australia and the Netherlands, banned short selling. At the end of September 2008, Ireland's government guaranteed, with a €400 billion scheme, all deposits, covered bonds, and senior and subordinated debt of six of its largest banks. For a country of just 4.6 million people, it was easy to do the terrifying sums. Many worried that, as their banks collapsed, higher interest rates and credit restrictions would weaken their economies, which would increase the chances of default, lead to more asset-price declines, and further pressure to deleverage and raise credit rates. This was the last amplification mechanism, this time involving whole economies.

In late September and early October, the Icelandic banking system fizzled and popped like a melting glacier atop a sizzling volcano, as Iceland's three internationally active banks, Glitnir, Landsbanki, and Kaupthing, and its local currency, all came under speculative attack. Even if its banks were fundamentally solvent (i.e. if their assets held to maturity would cover their obligations), Iceland was vulnerable to a bank run because of four inconsistencies: it was a small country; it had a large internationally-exposed banking sector; it had its own small currency; and it had very limited fiscal capacity relative to the size of its banking sector—which meant that it had no effective lender of last resort or market maker of last resort, and certainly none of the liquidity facilities available to those in the US and the eurozone. During October 2008, the Icelandic government nationalized all three banks before they had entirely melted away, and requested a $2 billion loan from the IMF and a $4 billion loan from Iceland's four Nordic neighbours. Iceland's bank failures were the highest of any country in the crash, at 90% of total bank assets. The Icelandic banking system was much bigger than the Icelandic economy. One particularly inciteful cartoon pictured a glum-looking Icelandic couple peering into a box of Icelandic Monopoly to find it completely and utterly bare. September and October 2008 had been busy months at the helm of global finance. A boiling sea of financial trouble had finally washed in. Its foam had swept its victims into the uttermost rims of the rocks—and the rescue was only just beginning.

5

Saving the Gods

The Challenges of Evaluating the Rescue

Before the crash, those working in global finance made enormous profits. With equal spectacle, many failed to deliver to society a chunk of the value upon which those profits were premised. They failed to allocate savings and capital efficiently across people, time, and geography. They eased the flow of credit; then they blocked it. They fed a global property price bubble; then they starved it. They mesmorised with spell-binding song. Now, while their victims were perishing on the rocks beneath, it was the financial sirens who demanded to be saved! A deep irony will mark these years—how those at the pinnacle of the modern capitalist system became so utterly reliant upon governments, and taxpayers, for their own survival. Many a developing country had, over the years, felt the disapproving slap across its fiscal wrists and been forced to squeeze the poor dry to satisfy the harsh discipline of financial markets. How different things were going to be when the disciplinarians got into trouble themselves. Free-market principles would be suspended on a gargantuan scale to protect the institutions that, more than any others, had touted the virtues of free-market principles.

I can't deny that while wading through the dense forest of literature on the bank rescue, in gloomy moments it crossed my mind that a fraction of the effort expended upon its production would have been more fruitfully employed five or so years before. Sadly, human nature being what it is, emergency surgery is much more exciting than boring preventative stuff, and detective work far more fun than crime prevention.

As a way to break down such a colossal subject into more digestible pieces, we shall look at broad categories of rescue through an economic lens. This chapter tracks the early realization of the growing dangers, the plethora of liquidity measures, the *ad hoc* institution-by-institution interventions, and the first attempts at a system-wide rescue—including purchase programmes for 'toxic assets' (securities and loans gone wrong), recapitalization, and nationalization. Chapter 6 will dig deeper into guarantees, stress tests linked to further recapitalization, yet more efforts to buy toxic assets, and some of the alternatives that were little used. It will finish by asking how well the rescue worked.

It is not easy to judge the actions of rescuers as they struggled through the wreckage, bruised and dazed. We seek a fair—not an idealized—counterfactual against which to evaluate their actions. They faced a range of daunting constraints. Let us look at a few of the main ones.

First, the biggest costs of banking crashes are not the bailouts but the lost economic output. Just a few months of economic dislocation in early 2009 created losses equivalent to all subprime losses, and the improving economic prospects in early 2010 removed about the same amount of losses. Acting quickly but imperfectly and preventing self-fulfilling feedback between a collapsing financial system and a collapsing economy may be much less costly than being slow but perfect.

Second, an insolvent bank is prone to 'gamble for resurrection' strategies. These have a small probability of generating a big win that will flip a bank from insolvent to solvent but will, on average, leave taxpayers with an even bigger loss. This is no mere curiosity. The losses from the US Savings and Loan (S&L) crisis of the 1980s got much worse because banks tried to gamble their way out of their mess while policymakers dithered. This time, the early reluctance to act allowed risky activities and leveraged lending to keep growing, which made the crash even worse.

Third, accounting practices shape choice and speed. In the Nordic banking crisis of the late 1980s and early 1990s (affecting Finland, Norway, and Sweden),[1] which also had a collapsing housing bubble at its heart, losses were recorded on a hold-to-maturity basis, and appeared only when defaults took place. This time, the greater prevalence of mark-to-market assets constructed from loans meant that, when expectations of mortgage defaults rose, the prices of such assets immediately fell and inflicted losses. This was a double-edged sword. Hold-to-maturity allows greater control in cleaning up balance sheets, but might encourage delay. Mark-to-market prompts a quicker response, but might encourage hasty and inappropriate policies.

Fourth, policymakers face a standard 'collective action' problem. Rescue involves large wealth redistributions. A small number of very large parties stand to gain a lot. A diffuse mass of small parties, mostly taxpayers, each face a small loss that collectively amounts to a much bigger loss than what the larger parties gain. Quick action needs good information that only financial firms possess, which enables the few to extract the better deal from the many. At the heart of the crash were innumerable contracts that had gone wrong. Many of the parties to such contracts concluded that they could not have been in their right minds when they signed them in the first place. With no 'sanity' clause to ease them of their pain, the rescue became a mad scramble to divide the losses, and redistribute wealth, between lenders (and their insurers), borrowers, and taxpayers.

Fifth, some apparently good rescue schemes may be difficult to enact in a timely fashion if legal frameworks have to be changed to turn otherwise illegal breaches of contract into legal acts. In particular, some actions might be an improvement for society on average but, with no pre-set clauses to renege on contracts in specific circumstances, the rights of individual contractees will have precedence.

Sixth, the performance of one set of policymakers depends on the performance of others. As Henry Paulson, then US Treasury Secretary, put it in September 2008: 'I'm playing the hand that was dealt me...I'm dealing with the consequences of things that were done, often many years ago.'[2] Willem Buiter added: 'Panic moves at the speed of light and even well-intentioned, cooperatively-minded parties will find it hard to engage in synchronized swimming while piranhas and sharks lurch at their tender extremities.'[3]

Finally, success or failure depends on ideas making it from one end of the political tightrope to the other. A 'better' rescue might register a bigger cost, of which a high proportion gets repaid. On the other hand, a rescue that avoids a government budget line might, however, end up costing more because of hidden subsidies, moral hazard, and drawn-out, economic damage.

As we go, a motley crowd of economic concepts will be our constant travel companions. First comes moral hazard. The costs of fighting moral hazard are now, but the consequences of moral hazard fall on the watch of future politicians. Then comes time inconsistency. To persuade a bank to take, or to refrain from taking, an action, policymakers may threaten punishment (such as not to rescue). But when a crash comes, punishment is not credible because it may trigger financial contagion, or the loss of positive NPV projects,[4] or have a political cost. Policymakers are not believed in the first place. Finally, blessed with hindsight, we must take care not to judge harshly those who had no choice but to act quickly on the basis of incomplete and asymmetric information. What were the best responses that policymakers could have taken, given the information they could reasonably have possessed at the time rather than the information that we now possess? In particular, since the self-fulfilling nature of runs can make otherwise solvent institutions look insolvent, a key part of the task of rescue is to work out which banks are irrefutably dead and which ones only suffering debilitating runs that only make them look dead, and adjusting the rescue effort accordingly.

Early Action and Procrastination

At the end of 2010, under new disclosure rules stipulated in the 'Dodd–Frank Wall Street Reform and Consumer Protection Act', the Fed released details on 21,000 of its crash-related transactions (henceforth, the 'Dodd–Frank' data). Bernanke subsequently pointed out that, contrary to much media coverage, the magnitude and manner of such lending had never been secret.[5] Names of recipients were withheld so as not to undermine the whole point of emergency lending, but the data were regularly released to Congress and made it clear that large financial firms were in trouble long before Lehman collapsed.

Since financial exposure outside the US was a key propagation mechanism,[6] much of the Fed's early lending was to non-US banks, including some large UK banks. The Fed's focus then shifted overwhelmingly to US banks. The Fed was not alone. In August 2007, the Eurosystem (i.e. the ECB and the central banks of the member states of the eurozone) launched a series of liquidity operations that ultimately totalled about €200 billion. In September 2007 came the Northern Rock liquidity facility. The Fed's first central bank liquidity swap (effectively a 13-month loan for $10 billion to the ECB) was in December 2007. By the end of 2007 the Fed, Bank of England, ECB, PBOC, Swiss National Bank (SNB), and Eurosystem were all actively pumping liquidity into the global banking system. Early initiatives allowed banks to swap illiquid private assets for liquid government securities which, being of much higher verified quality, could be used as collateral to back borrowing on the interbank market. Terms were loosened (for example the ECB guaranteed unlimited funds for up to six months rather than the usual one week) and facilities already in place were opened up to many more institutions than normal. Since solvent financial firms would avoid seeking help to tackle temporary liquidity problems if it might signal that they were insolvent, the Fed set up the Term Auction Facility (TAF) in December 2007 to allow anonymous borrowing. In March 2008, the IMF published a $1.2 trillion estimate of the US financial sector's potential losses.[7] Deutsche Bank and

Goldman Sachs came up with bank-by-bank estimates. These were being worked on in late 2007 and early 2008 and must have been available to regulators whose actions were nevertheless very restrained.

Two errors were made during the March 2008 rescue of Bear Stearns that would come back to haunt policymakers. The first was to save all unsecured creditors. This conditioned creditors of other financial institutions, like hungry Pavlovian dogs, to expect this treatment next time round, and created a media and political backlash that constrained what politicians could do later. The second was to not start creating a Special Resolution Regime (SRR) with Prompt Corrective Action (PCA) for investment banks facing similar problems in the future, though it was clear that many were heading in that direction. Granted, it is doubtful how useful such a regime would have been for financial firms deemed TBTF, it should have been set up years before, and fear of triggering panic held policymakers back.

Liquidity measures now moved up a gear. The Fed launched its $200 billion Term Securities Lending Facility (TSLF) on 11 March and announced its Primary Dealer Credit Facility (PDCF) on 17 March. The Bank of England launched its Special Liquidity Scheme on 21 April. Over its lifetime, the PDCF made 1,300 loans to broker-dealers outside the Fed's usual discount window (reserved for deposit-taking commercial banks), a sign of how vulnerable the system had become. By now the Fed was lending directly to US investment banks. Bear Stearns, before it collapsed, got $28 billion. Lehman, Goldman Sachs, and Morgan Stanley got loans too. Nothing like this had happened since the 1930s.

At the end of March 2008, UBS separated securities linked to US mortgages, on which it had suffered heavy losses, into a new subsidiary. At 300% of its GDP, Switzerland had by far and away the biggest cross-border banking exposure to the US.[8] Making sure to miss April Fools' day by a good full day, the UK's *Financial Times* revealed on 2 April that a range of Wall Street banks—including Citigroup, Morgan Stanley, Merrill Lynch, and Lehman Brothers—no doubt recognizing a smart move when they saw one, were working on similar plans to UBS.[9] US and European lenders were even in discussions with regulators about creating a common fund to buy up troubled assets, in the hope that outside investors would buy stakes and end the pressure to recognize mark-to-market losses. Thus the concept of a 'bad bank', a separate legal entity into which financial toxic waste could be dumped, entered the popular vernacular—if only fleetingly. Unfortunately, the investment banks could not agree on the terms of the fund, and there was nobody to gently bang the necessary heads together.

According to a fly-on-the wall account by Philip Swagel (an aide to Paulson between December 2006 and January 2009), US officials started their crisis-management plans in March 2008 in response to the collapse of Bear Stearns.

However, the US Treasury did not act, because if felt the electorate was not yet convinced of the dangers.[10] Discussions regarding the use of public money to avert a disaster came with visions of flying pigs. As Bernanke observed in October 2008: 'If Lehman hadn't failed, the public would not have seen the resulting damage, and the storyline would have been that such extraordinary intervention was unnecessary.'[11] Just as policymakers in the late 1920s worried that if they pricked a stock market bubble they would get blamed by those who lost, so, in mid-2008, policymakers feared being blamed for triggering big losses rather than being praised for mounting a rescue. From such base dilemmas are political incentives fashioned. According to Swagel, in the US it took the failure of Lehman Brothers in September 2008 to make it politically feasible to ask for serious levels of public funds to tackle the underlying solvency problems.

In the UK, Mervyn King knew about the damage to market sentiment that would be done if he was seen to be too readily at odds with his chancellors and prime ministers, and he had long ago learnt to bite his tongue (and cross his fingers). In October 2008, he observed: 'It would be a mistake, however, to think that had Lehman Brothers not failed, a crisis would have been averted. The underlying cause of inadequate capital would eventually have provoked a crisis of one kind or another somewhere else.'[12] He added: '[I]t took a crisis caused by the failure of Lehman Brothers to trigger the coordinated government plan to recapitalize the system.' One learns to read between the lines; throughout 2008, procrastination was playing itself out in London too. Given what we know about the intensity of liquidity efforts, it is all the more surprising that Gordon Brown describes the events of September 2008 as coming as a surprise, and that he makes no mention of UK crisis-management plans being developed over 2008. Either he was unaware of the frantic liquidity efforts, or he knew but preferred a narrative of an 'out-of-the-blue' surprise to absolve himself of blame. It is not clear which is worse. Since there are many more blockages in the path of a US president than of a UK prime minister, Brown could have led on this. Had the creation of 'good' and 'bad' banks and recapitalization taken place in the spring or summer of 2008, some of the more cataclysmic elements might have been avoided. It was not to be.

With banks unable to agree on a strategy for disaster-prevention, politicians dithering, and central banks prioritizing other goals, especially inflation, it is no wonder that Tim Geithner, Paulson's replacement as Treasury Secretary, gamely admitted that 'we went in without instruments',[13] just as a general might say that he and his soldiers had been sent over the top without rifles. In spite of more than a year of build-up, instead of having a system-wide approach ready to go and the resources to back it, policymakers found themselves condemned to an *ad hoc*, institution-by-institution, rescue mode, acting as 'an extraordinarily vigorous dealmaker',[14] responding with 'a series of improvisations',[15] and engaged in 'behind-the-scenes political dealmaking which tends to benefit well-connected but not necessarily deserving entities'.[16] Like all improvisation, it had occasional rhyme and sometimes reason, but rarely any consistency.

The Collapse of Lehman

The popular narrative is that what triggered the crash was the failure to come up with a rescue package for Lehman Brothers over the fateful weekend of 13–14 September 2008. Causality is less clear-cut. Mervyn King summed up the 'two fundamental causes' of the crash as 'the big imbalances in the world economy' and the 'fact that the banks were allowed to build up their balance sheets to levels where they were ready to topple over'.[17] This suggested that the crash was only a matter of time and the subtle dynamics of grains of sand being added to an already unstable heap, and that Lehman was nothing special—except that it was first—in a crash that was inevitable. Bernanke told the Financial Crisis Inquiry Commission (FCIC), '[O]ut of maybe the 13 most important financial institutions in the United States, 12 were at risk of failure within a period of a week or two.'[18]

In an event study, Taylor points out that on the day Lehman filed for bankruptcy, the three-month LIBOR–OIS spread rose slightly, to about 1%.[19] When AIG was rescued, it went up a bit more, and then kept rising over the rest of the week. However, this was not out of line with anything seen over the previous year. It was only after Bernanke and Paulson were grilled on 23 September by the Senate Banking Committee about their proposed Troubled Asset Relief Program (TARP) that the three-month LIBOR–OIS spread started its relentless upwards trajectory, topping out at over 3.5% about three weeks later. Taylor is quite emphatic: '[I]dentifying the decisions over the weekend of 13 and 14 September as the cause of the increased severity of the crisis is questionable. It was not until more than a week later that conditions deteriorated. Moreover, it is plausible that events around 23 September actually drove the market, including the realization by the public that the intervention plan had not been fully thought through and that conditions were much worse than many had been led to believe.'[20]

Whatever they subsequently said about the lack of an SRR, this is not what officials emphasized at the time. More important was their aversion to the idea of a bailout, having been stung by criticisms over the rescue of Bear Stearns. The

FCIC published e-mails reflecting the mood, such as the one from Treasury Chief of Staff Jim Wilkinson, just days before Lehman's demise, saying that he couldn't 'stomach us bailing out Lehman. Will be horrible in the press.'[21] Many central bankers were also voicing their concerns about the moral hazard implications of all the easy liquidity. Days after Lehman's collapse, Paulson testified: 'I never once considered that it was appropriate to put taxpayer money on the line in resolving Lehman Brothers.'[22] Bernanke added: 'The failure of Lehman posed risks. But the troubles at Lehman had been well known for some time, and investors clearly recognized—as evidenced, for example, by the high cost of insuring Lehman's debt in the market for credit default swaps—that the failure of the firm was a significant possibility. Thus, we judged that investors and counterparties had had time to take precautionary measures.'[23] Indeed, while policymakers justified their inability to lend to Lehman with section 13(3) of the Federal Reserve Act, they could have lent to Barclays or any other financial firm interested in buying Lehman just as they had lent to JPMorgan in the case of Bear Stearns. It was not that they could not intervene; they did not want to.

Protecting the unsecured creditors of Bear Stearns was the sort of act that policymakers fearful of triggering a systemic collapse would do, and in exchange for this they would tolerate moral hazard. Yet, just months later, in the case of Lehman, they put the emphasis the other way around. Perhaps they felt that liquidity measures were working and sufficient, and that focusing on moral hazard was now in order. Perhaps they thought the systemic dangers were lower. Indeed many traders thought that Lehman was at risk but that it was not systemic. Judging market reaction is complicated by the near-simultaneous panic-driven bailout of AIG. As Bernanke added, '*While perhaps manageable in itself*, Lehman's default was combined with the unexpectedly rapid collapse of AIG' (italics added).

A big concern at the time was that settling Lehman-referencing CDSs would wreak havoc. The fear turned out to be largely unjustified. Many of the contracts to which Lehman was a counterparty were marked-to-market daily with collateral adjusted to reflect changes in market price, and losses were kept low. Large dealers and hedge funds had both bought and sold protection, and took gains as well as losses on Lehman's default. The concerted efforts of the International Swap Dealers Association ensured that positions were closed out without major ramifications in late October 2008. The total net settlement on $400 billion of Lehman-referencing CDS was only about $5.2 billion, lower than anyone dared speculate at the time,[24] and well within reasonable bounds for the risk-reward decisions investors had made.

The problem was not so much that Lehman was too big to fail; it was primarily that it was too opaque to fail. Lehman hid its true state of financial health using so-called 'Repo 105s'. Apparently legal, as all the best tricks are, these involved temporarily removing loans from Lehman's balance sheet for short periods of time and booking them as sales; while the balls were up in the air, they didn't count.[25] At the end of the first and second quarters of 2008, Lehman carried out $50 billion of Repo 105 transactions. This pulled its reported net leverage lower, and was critical to keeping the rating agencies and counterparties happy. However, with its back to the wall, it was nearly impossible to know how much capital Lehman needed.

Another problem was that Lehman had been managed as an integrated entity with centralized information technology and financial management, yet it comprised many separate legal entities—433 subsidiaries in 20 countries.[26] This made sense as the way to run a going concern, but was a total nightmare to process through multiple national-level bankruptcy procedures. Worse, US authorities focused on Lehman Brothers (US), casting Lehman's subsidiaries in Europe and Asia adrift. Many thousands of trades placed with Lehman's broker-dealer did not settle, and ended up in legal proceedings because, when the bankruptcy petition was filed, most subsidiaries had not been funded that day, and the cash was tied up in court proceedings in the US. One of the most important channels for contagion was through the exposure of unsecured creditors to Lehman's outstanding debt. It was the need to write off $785 million of short- and medium-term notes which propelled the Reserve Primary Fund into becoming the first money market mutual fund to 'break the buck' in 14 years.

It is impossible to argue that, but for the collapse of Lehman, there would not have been a crash. More likely, policymakers underestimated the nature of the problems brewing outside of Lehman, were overly confident that liquidity measures were working, and so emphasized the dangers of moral hazard in the case of Lehman. It was the extreme fragility of all other parts of the financial system, combined with the lack of sufficient legal procedures to unwind Lehman, that made Lehman so very hard to handle. If so, attention might more usefully concentrate on the quality of policy-making and preparation for the crash, and more blame should be apportioned to those who failed to act in advance than to those who acted at the time. If we could run historical experiments, in another parallel universe AIG would be the trigger (AIG was due huge losses come what may), in another Citibank the trigger, in yet another Bank of America, and, at a push, in yet another, Europe, but slightly later. It is better to blame the collapse on the structure of the pile, than on the one grain.

One sometimes got the impression that the public wanted to see the corpses of more investment banks than just Lehman Brothers pinned inside a display cabinet for future posterity; not because they thought such specimens especially beautiful, but because it might have hurt. However, it quickly became clear that no systemically important bank, nor many others besides, would be allowed to fail, and that the word 'systemic' would be stretched to catch others tightly within its sympathetic embrace. By such acts were the teeth of the moral-hazard beast sharpened.

Maximizing Moral Hazard the AIG Way

The other particularly scorching moment came with the rescue of AIG, with a bailout package that, like Pinocchio's nose (and on a fairly similar principle), grew and grew to reach about $181 billion at its peak.[27] Like Lehman before it, the rescue of AIG came with the accompanying loud sounds of barn doors being hastily scraped shut, and the odd scream or two, as a policymaker's finger or toe got caught in the process. 'If there is a single episode in this entire 18 months that has made me more angry, I can't think of one,'[28] exclaimed Bernanke, taking his pick from a generous assortment of possibilities. Geithner and Bernanke argued that they lacked legal authority to seize such a complex and systemically important non-bank, that no private-sector alternative was possible, and that AIG could not be put into conservatorship or receivership and, in such state of suspended animation, like a huge and extinct woolly mammoth, slowly thawed and chopped up with haircuts for shareholders and unsecured creditors.

There was a sting in the tale of AIG. Instead of allowing AIG's counterparties to take their losses, the Fed thought it best to pay a slew of them off at full face value. By early November 2008, some $72.2 billion of taxpayer money had been handed over to about a dozen counterparties, the fact quickly surfacing (as many juicy secrets do) in confidential documents in December 2008. On the principle that a bit of naming and shaming is good for incentives, perhaps the beneficiaries of such largesse should be named? Sometimes one wonders to what degree any one of them was guilty of manipulating the outcome, and to what degree they were just lucky (and to what degree their embarrassment now will make the slightest bit of difference). Nevertheless, just for good measure, the biggest beneficiaries were Goldman Sachs Group ($12.9 billion), Société Générale SA ($11.9 billion), Deutsche Bank AG ($11.8 billion), Barclays ($7.9 billion), Merrill Lynch & Co. ($6,8 billion), Bank of America ($5.2 billion), UBS ($5.0 billion), BNP Paribas ($4.9 billion), HSBC ($3.5 billion),[29] and Crédit

Agricole SA's Calyon investment-banking unit ($1.8 billion). The FCIC identi-
fied Goldman Sachs as the largest single beneficiary because it had made the
heaviest use of AIG and had also received a decent portion of what was paid to
Société Générale and possibly also to Calyon because these bought CDSs from
AIG on behalf of Goldman Sachs. Treasury Secretary Paulson was a former
Goldman chief executive—which made for some lively conspiracy theories.

The only possible arguments in favour of such acts of wanton generosity
would be that a major default in the CDS market on top of the collapse of
Lehman might have been the straw to break the financial system's back, and
that if the counterparties were not bailed out via AIG, they would anyway have
sought more direct bailouts later. Neither argument is entirely satisfactory. Had
AIG's counterparties taken their losses, at least taxpayers would have got more
for their investment (such as ownership rights and a chance to take some
upside). Political constraints were also likely to limit the resources available to
mount a system rescue, so it was careless to waste limited financial ammunition
quite so enthusiastically. Above all, by shielding those who had failed to exercise
proper due diligence when they did business with AIG from the negative
consequences, the Fed nourished the moral-hazard beast some more. Hauled
before the Senate Banking Committee to explain the handling of AIG, Don
Kohn, Vice Chairman of the Federal Reserve Board, pleaded: 'I'm worried
about the knock-on effects in the financial markets. Would other people be
willing to do business with other US financial institutions . . . if they thought, in a
crisis like this, they might have to take some losses?'[30] Kohn's statement should
be read for all its Freudian worth; policymakers sacrificed future financial
stability to protect US financial institutions from losing business.

The average voter couldn't tell an SRR from their elbow (but, then again,
why should they?), but they understood a bonus when they saw one. So when,
in March 2009, AIG executives indelicately dipped their grubby paws into
the trough to scoop out $165 million in bonuses, Obama understood the
public's need for outrage.[31] Yet, in the background, in broad daylight, the
doors of AIG had been blown clean off, $70 billion and more was gone, and
the public hardly noticed (at least for now). The Treasury and the Fed failed
to renegotiate AIG's bonus plans as a condition of Federal assistance, which
suggests the bailout was on terms that were far too easy on AIG. The need for
speed was no excuse.

Even if an SRR had existed, would it have been used in the case of AIG? Such
an SRR existed for FDIC-insured banks. One would have thought that, with
limited resources to recapitalize and guarantee, there would have been more
desire to clear the system of large failed FDIC-insured banks so that safer banks

could prosper and get financial intermediation going again. However, the US, the UK, and other authorities seemed peculiarly resistant to the SRR-style wind-down of big-name financial firms, while accepting the principle much more readily when it came to smaller banks. This does not encourage us to believe that an SRR, even if it had been available, would have been used in the much more complicated case of AIG. One suspects that AIG's 'interconnected' and 'system-ically significant' nature and severe time constraints would still have been used as the overwhelming justification to intervene in a similar way to what we saw. The proof of the pudding, as they say, is in the eating, but, alas, this is not a pudding that we are ever going to taste.

The Liquidity Taps Are Fully Opened

By now the liquidity taps were set at full. The use of the PDCF peaked in September 2008 at $156 billion. Many non-financial firms and some foreign banks turned to it for support,[32] including Royal Bank of Scotland, BNP Paribas Securities, Daiwa Securities America, Deutsche Bank Securities, Mizuho Secur-ities US, Dresdner Kleinwort Securities, and UBS Securities LLC. The UK's Barclays Bank, more fragile than it let on at the time, tapped the facility 49 times in loans that ranged from $300 million to $15 billion. In late September, the Fed launched the 'Asset-Backed Commercial Paper Money Market Mutual Fund Liquidity Facility'. Fearing that this might be a bit of a mouthful, and having nearly exhausted its box of financial-rescue Scrabble letters, the Fed threw ABCP and MMMF together with LF, closed the lid, shook the box, and by such strange chemistry, out popped AMLF. At the end of October, the Fed launched yet another liquidity facility, the Commercial Paper Funding Facility (CPFF) that purchased ABCP in an effort to improve liquidity in short-term funding markets. Across its liquidity programmes, over about 14 months (March 2008 to May 2009), the Fed extended nearly $15 trillion of loans. Many were revolving such that the outstanding amount was always a fraction of this, peaking at about $1.5 trillion in December 2008.[33] Morgan Stanley was the biggest borrower in terms of peak borrowing, followed by Citigroup and Bank of America. Merrill Lynch (subsequently part of Bank of America) and Bear Stearns were also heavy users, followed by Goldman Sachs, JPMorgan Chase, and Wells Fargo.

Goldman Sachs always argued that it had plenty of cash, but the Dodd–Frank data showed that it turned to the Fed 84 times and had been the sixth highest user. Citigroup was still borrowing from the Fed in late April 2009, and Bank of America took out its last loan in May 2009. About $71 billion of loans went to non-bank institutions, including many hedge funds. For example, a loan of $1.7 billion went to One William Street Capital Management, run by the former head of mortgage securitization at Lehman Brothers. Having ridden the roller-coaster up, some knew only too well how to cling on for the ride back down. By early 2009, the size of the balance sheets of the Bank of England, the US Federal Reserve, and ECB had roughly doubled relative to GDP. Adjusting for the falling quality of eligible collateral, the effective scale of liquidity support was even greater.

In defending the Fed against accusations that it had provided funds at below-market rates that boosted financial firms' profits,[34] Bernanke argued that the Fed's emergency lending was 'priced at a penalty over normal market rates so that borrowers had economic incentives to exit the facilities as market conditions normalized',[35] had generated $20 billion interest for the US Treasury, and that all loans were repaid. Nevertheless, even if the Fed charged 'over normal market rates', this was still less than what financial institutions would have charged for loans at a time of great stress, and so, properly risk-adjusted, the loans were subsidized. Yet, was this so objectionable if it prevented even more collapse? The more serious problem was that the biggest subsidy went to those who had taken the biggest previous risks.

We also need to factor in the risks that the Fed took on to make its return. To minimize moral hazard, access to government-subsidized liquidity should be: at punitive terms; only to illiquid but otherwise solvent financial institutions; and only against assets with a viable future in the absence of official intervention. The Dodd–Franks data revealed that only 1% of the collateral pledged for overnight funding under the PDCF was Treasury bonds which, in non-stressed times, would be the norm, that about 36% was equity or bonds below investment grade, and that 17% was unrated or loans. One of the reasons that bonuses were such an egregious issue after the crash (although this was rarely the reason given at the time) was that they followed immediately after much of the risk had been foisted onto governments. Mounting losses would jeopardize the operational independence of central banks, but the bonuses would be long gone. Liquidity support was much broader than the TARP and Quantitative Easing programmes, but stirred little media attention because the full risk-adjusted costs, unlike the costs of other programmes, did not enter a government budget line.

Liquidity support proved critical to creating confidence amongst banks that they would get repaid, and this stopped them from panicking. Yet it also added considerably to the future legacy of moral hazard: If those who would ordinarily bet against very risky practices know that liquidity will be pumped in just at the moment when their rewards were due to appear, their incentive to correct risky behaviour is weakened. Moral hazard is further reinforced by the effect that the potential for liquidity support has on the probability distribution over types of financial firms. As a thought experiment, imagine the following. One set of banks, the 'risky' banks, invests almost entirely in long assets, and relies on the market for its liquidity. Another set of banks, the 'safe' banks, holds mostly short assets and provides for the liquidity needs of the 'risky' banks by purchasing, at depressed prices, the long assets of the 'risky' banks when the 'risky' banks are in trouble, and holds the assets to maturity (or to a point when they can be sold based on their maturity value), pocketing the difference. If governments indiscriminately provide liquidity, the profitability of this strategy is undermined. If the 'safe' banks understand this in advance, their numbers shrink, and the overall system is less safe. In a crash, policymakers may want to avoid creating moral hazard, but refusal to inject liquidity is not time consistent because this will make the crash worse. Even Germany pumped €500 billion of liquidity support into its banks as the crisis spread in 2008. Creating moral hazard via liquidity activities is simply one of the prices to be paid for calming financial markets, and the only way to avoid it is to design a system to minimize the need for liquidity injections *ex ante*.

When You Haven't Got a Clue ... Come Up with a Very Big Plan That Won't Work

It did not help that when all financial hell broke loose, the US was in the throes of a presidential election. Just-in-time crash management isn't well-suited to politicians distracted trying to squeeze themselves through the eye of the next voting needle. President Bush had no interest in benefiting either of his potential replacements. There was bad blood between him and McCain. And Obama was a Democrat. Besides, Bush seemed even more than usually out of his depth, declaring at the height of the crash: 'Anyone engaging in illegal financial transactions will be caught and persecuted.'[36] Bankers were learning to be grateful for small mercies.

Just to rub chaos into the wounds, McCain—not wishing to waste the opportunity of a jolly good financial crash to embarrass political opponents—suspended his campaign and called an emergency meeting of Bush, Obama, and himself. Obama's advisors wanted none of it, but knew that refusal to attend would invite accusations of not taking the crash seriously. Surely, the clue was in the word 'emergency'? Policymakers were forced to put actions on hold for several days. Then McCain had nothing especially urgent to say, and, for the benefit of the massed media ranks, squeezed it into as few words as possible.

The sorry gathering, showing all three ill at ease and without three clues to rub together to make a conclusion, did more harm than good—a case, if ever there was one, of 'I see nothing, I hear nothing, and I say nothing.'

President Obama took a lot of criticism for his actions; in a number of cases, rightly so. However, far more criticism should be heaped on his predecessor, who presided over the reckless build-up to the crash, did little as the signs of systemic dangers proliferated in 2007 and 2008, and was in charge until January 2009. An outgoing president can take measures that no competing potential incomer could ever risk. Are we to believe that in late 2007 and the spring and summer of 2008 nobody talked Bush through the dangers? Or did he simply 'misunderstimate' what was needed?[37] By the time Obama arrived in office, his chalice was well and truly poisoned.

It was time for a plan, a very big plan, the 'Paulson Plan'. And so, on 19 September 2008, the US government announced a $700 billion rescue package followed by a two-and-a-half-page proposal on 20 September (it's amazing how succinct officials can be, especially if leaving out trifling little details like how to spend $700 billion and what the oversight arrangements will be). The $700 billion was a little under 5%, or the equivalent of about two and half weeks', of US GDP. It was a lot of money, but modest compared to past financial rescues.

Early rescue efforts had stopped the out-and-out collapse of the financial system, but made little impact on the depressed prices of toxic assets, the detritus of five to ten years of mis-selling of one sort or another. Prices were heavily depressed because of forced sales, illiquidity, and uncertainty (regarding the future trajectory of the economy and the impact of financial-rescue approaches). This, it was felt, was exaggerating losses and creating great uncertainty about the true financial health of banks. It was decided to deal with the offending assets directly rather than via the structure of ownership of the firms in which they sat. Thus 'bad assets' ended up taking the lion's share of early attention. And that, of course, was why they had been so very naughty in the first place.

Since euphemisms are the essential syrup for easing unpalatable ideas through fractious political processes, toxic assets were labelled 'troubled' and deemed in need of sympathetic 'relief'—the 'Troubled Asset Relief Program'. The phrases 'bad', 'very bad', 'terrible', and 'What on earth were they thinking?' seemed a tad too judgmental. It did not exactly reassure that Paulson exuded the air of an overly-enthusiastic school prefect clenching a fragile little piggy bank. Section 8 of the plan, a 32-word sentence with just a comma to break the pain, declared that once he'd smashed it open, 'Decisions by the Secretary pursuant to the authority of this Act are non-reviewable and committed to agency discretion, and may not be reviewed by any court of law or any administrative agency.' To some, this seemed a warm cloak allowing special pleading and moral hazard to snuggle up next to each other, with nobody to pull it away to expose the nefarious truth. Congress voted the bill down on 29 September. The revised bill left the TARP essentially unchanged, added a variety of measures that had absolutely nothing to do with banks, and so was duly approved by Congress on 3 October. Paulson, in a state of deeply concealed surprise, found himself able to buy any financial instrument he deemed 'necessary to promote financial market stability', a catch-all, if not exactly catchy, phrase. It did not convince the markets. The following week the US stock market suffered a drop of 18%, its worst week ever.

It gradually became clear that, in all the rush, nobody had a clue as to how such a programme might work. Economic blogs filled with the lexical equivalent of a very energetic head scratch. Surely, a modicum of efficiency, or at least the absence of rank inefficiency, is not a luxury even in a crash? Wouldn't an inefficient scheme leave a legacy of moral hazard? Again, the choice of words was important. As the Paulson Plan had bobbed its way through Congress and the Senate, it had deftly avoided using the words 'government', 'clever', 'big', 'buy', and 'scheme' in the same sentence. The US Treasury, by proposing only the purchase of pre-existing toxic assets and not the support of new 'clean' assets, seemed intent on taking a shotgun and aiming it squarely at the taxpayer's foot.[38]

Even with such a programme, asset prices would still have settled well below prior levels. It might have been tempting to allow overpayment as a way to indirectly recapitalize loss-making banks. That would have been a very bad idea. First, more hidden subsidy would have gone to those banks whose portfolios had been most distorted in the direction of toxic assets; the moral hazard consequences are obvious. Second, wealth would have been transferred from taxpayers to bank owners, leaving taxpayers with no ownership rights. Third, if banking needed restructuring towards smaller financial institutions with profit-making strategies different from those of the past, this would have achieved the opposite. Fourth, media stories about overpayment would have made it politically difficult to pull in further rounds of rescue money (and, as in the US S&L crisis, overpayment *would* eventually be uncovered). A core principle of any bank bailout is that the less blatantly obvious the subsidy, the more politically acceptable it is.

One way—eventually—proposed for pricing toxic assets was via auctions. However, a simple reverse auction would have overpaid: if the government had bought all assets offered up at a market-clearing price of, say, 60 cents on the dollar of the original assets, it would have ended up holding assets with true values distributed between zero and 60 cents, with an average below, probably well below, 60 cents. Then there was the usual problem of adverse selection. Maybe, to avoid this, sellers could have been required to sell whole portfolios of assets with no opportunity to cherry-pick, but that would have involved compulsion.

The most important determinant of whether or not prices are efficient in an auction is how competitive the auction is.[39] Because of the innate complexity of some assests and asymmetric information problems, there were few potential owners of the types of assets (usually securities) causing the worst problems. One solution might have been to purchase toxic assets and run an auction later when markets had recovered. If assets sold in the auction at lower prices (after adjusting for inflation), the original holder would owe the Treasury the difference plus interest (and vice versa if they sold later at higher prices).

Whether or not an auction was used, selling loans at any price below their carrying value would have registered as a depletion of bank capital and would have required banks to raise new capital. Some banks would have argued that if illiquidity and uncertainty were not fully removed by the programme, they would risk being underpaid. So why should they be forced to sell? But if participation was voluntary, and many banks kept out, the mechanism would have failed in self-fulfilling fashion anyway.

No politician would want to be seen promoting a scheme to help investors buy synthetic, 'speculative', assets with no collateral (such as underlying mortgages) to back them, and it is not clear that investors would have been interested in buying such assets either. Some CDOs were based on reference pools of mortgage loans, and the underlying collateral was just too complicated for investors to figure out; these also were not likely to be purchased via such programmes, even though this was a key asset category to sort out.

This created a paradox. Even if a toxic asset purchase programme could have been made to work efficiently, it would have had little impact on dealing with 'legacy loans'—the value of which could have been worked out and would not have needed such a programme. Meanwhile, if the programme was supposed to deal with 'legacy securities', it would have been limited to CDOs backed by mortgages, and the most problematic bundles of trouble would have stayed out of the programme in large numbers. A lot of effort would have gone into setting up a programme that would have generated little benefit, and some other approach would have been needed anyway.

It was also not wise to use limited public resources purchasing toxic assets from firms that were already well-capitalized, and since there would be no requirement regarding what to do with the proceeds of 'toxic asset' sales, officials could also only hope that lending would improve. Finally, the programme might have been captured anyway by those in banking, especially given the short time-frames and intense political pressure to act.

An alternative approach that left value to be determined at a later date, when the market had stabilized, was less open to capture and to a taxpayer loss. For sure, there were costs of leaving toxic assets on banks' balance sheets. Monitoring the risks would use up precious management time. Banks that were close to insolvency might engage in 'gamble for resurrection' behaviour. And there was a risk that the 'walking wounded' would distort the incentives of healthy banks and create a credit crunch.[40] But all such costs could be greatly reduced if banks were well-capitalized, which suggests that recapitalization ought to be a higher priority. As Japan's experience in the 1990s indicated, if the intention was not to overpay for toxic assets and to anyway leave them on banks' balance sheets, there was a need for recapitalization of some sort anyway.

The original Paulson Plan illustrated the limitations of much made-on-the-hoof policy. Once thought through, it became clear that it was just too complex and risky to be workable and not likely to clean up the worst of the mess. Focussing on a plan that, in the end, was not used gobbled up valuable Treasury and Fed staff time, and managed to create great uncertainty and confusion. Some countries later managed some sort of toxic asset scheme—notably Switzerland, where the Swiss National Bank (SNB) did eventually buy mortgage-related assets from UBS and put them in a special investment vehicle, such that the SNB bore risk but also shared on the upside. En route, UBS made massive write-downs and announced the biggest-ever Swiss banking loss. It will not be lost on the reader that the one bank and the one country that seemed to make most progress on this approach was the one thinking of doing so already in early 2008.

At the end of 2007, US and European banks had been capitalized to the tune of about $3.6 trillion; by April 2009 this had fallen to about $1.6 trillion.[41] There had been some capital infusions into banks, totalling about $700 billion, but nowhere near enough. US and European insurers had seen their capital fall from about $1.7 trillion to just under $1 trillion, with a much smaller capital infusion. A race was on. Capital was needed to cover growing write-downs and also to help get leverage down. Calculations of how much capital was needed hinged on assumptions about the trajectory for economic growth and for earnings of financial institutions. It also hinged on capital requirements, not only as officially stipulated, but also as dictated by the market which—being especially jittery—required higher capital cushions. Calculations were highly uncertain and regularly revised, but the IMF showed that even if bank earnings covered losses, they would not be enough to reduce leverage.[42]

Another Plan Was Hatched: Recapitalization

Whilst US policymakers were getting nowhere quickly, in the UK policy had moved in a different direction, towards recapitalizing the more direct route. Recapitalization has a long pedigree. In the Great Depression, the Reconstruction Finance Corporation played a key role in recapitalizing US banks by injections of preferred stock. Recapitalization was used to resolve banking crises in Scandinavia, Japan, Asia, and Latin America, and, on a much smaller scale, during the UK's secondary banking crisis of the 1970s and again in the UK in the early 1990s. A British US embassy cable released by Wikileaks in late 2010 showed that in March 2008, the Governor of the Bank of England Mervyn King had been pressing for significant bank recapitalization involving the US, the UK, Switzerland, and perhaps Japan.[43] He pushed the idea again on 28 March, this time entirely openly, in the Treasury Select Committee. Recapitalization was also proposed in the Bank of England's April 2008 Financial Stability Report. Brown mentions none of this in his account of the crash. Recapitalization before September 2008 might have been more ordered and effective, but it would have required admitting to mistakes that had brought on the need for it in the first place. A crash would be needed first.

On the first page of his account, Brown does describe—in capital letters—the moment that recapitalizing UK banks finally reached the top of his 'to do' list, eleven days after the collapse of Lehman Brothers, halfway over the Atlantic Ocean while flying back from Washington. In Brown's own words, the UK was just 'days away from complete banking collapse'. One next expected to read that he got off the plane and walked the rest of the way home. Action was still slow. Two weeks later, on 6 October 2008, the FTSE 100 suffered its biggest one-day fall since the crash of 1987; nearly 8%. Developments that day in Ireland—where UK banks were exposed to the tune of about €224 billion—raised the prospect of UK banks failing if recapitalization and guarantees were not put in place pronto. Through the night of 7 October, UK officials worked away, and details of the multi-pronged plan were finalized at dawn on the 8 October, more than three weeks after the collapse of Lehman, eleven days after the mid-Atlantic revelation, and on the very day that, in Brown's words: '[T]wo of our banks, then amongst the biggest in the world, became our biggest banking casualties ever'.[44] Never was an admission of procrastination and failure proclaimed with such an air of triumph.

The package comprised £200 billion in a special liquidity programme, £250 billion in guarantees to encourage interbank lending, and a 'Bank Recapitalization Fund' of up to £50 billion for UK-incorporated banks.[45] Recapitalization was voluntary to the extent that if a bank could prove that it had privately raised the capital it needed, it did not need to take from the fund. During October and November, the Treasury injected £37 billion into RBS and LBG and the government took stakes of 83% and 43.4%[46] respectively, on top of its 100% stakes in Northern Rock and Bradford and Bingley. HSBC launched a £12.5 billion cash call in March 2009 and avoided government capital. Barclays took $7 billion of capital from Middle Eastern investors, giving them a 30% stake in the bank on generous terms.[47] Only a very vulnerable bank keen to avoid government scrutiny would have tolerated such an arrangement. Barclays got its government support in the shape of guarantees on £25 billion of bonds (issued before strings were attached to such guarantees in April 2009) and courtesy of the implicit guarantee of being TBTF. The German government injected €10 billion of capital into Hypo Real Estate alongside €145 billion in liquidity guarantees.

With suitably appropriate fanfare, Prime Minister Brown took to arguing that, like some great military strategist who had led the Bank of England and US Treasury to a great victory, he had saved the banks, and even 'saved the world'.[48] Brown was no Hannibal. The only thing elephantine was the scale of exaggeration. He did not consider recapitalization in the months before the crash because, by his own admission, the crash came as a surprise. He talked and wrote of recapitalization as, for him, a post-crash revelation. Even then, in a position to be early and resolute, he was, as usual, late.

The thinking dovetailed with the voices of leading economists in the US, such as Paul Krugman; from his perch as a columnist at the *New York Times*, he had concluded that it was better to take ownership stakes in banks than to try to buy their toxic detritus (lost like ships in fog, politicians seemed more than usually willing to be guided by the piercing beams of economic columns). Not even a week after driving doggedly off in one direction, Paulson pulled on the brake and spun off in a new, and—he must have hoped—sunnier direction. On 14 October, the US announced its own equity investment programme, the Capital Purchase Program (CPP), which within weeks had injected $145 billion into nine large US banks.[49] Recapitalization was nothing if not quick. The US government took its equity stake in AIG via the even quicker Systemically Significant Failing Institutions (SSFI) Program, specially created for those who were failing but systemic and significant, something so rarefied that the US Treasury eventually renamed it the 'AIG Investment Program'. Then there was the smaller Targeted Investment Program (TIP) for those deemed critical to the functioning of the financial system, but, perhaps, not significant or failing enough. It was reported that, between Obama's election and inauguration, much effort went into planning for an 'aggregator bank' (a 'bad bank'?) to buy up toxic assets. However, within days of Obama's inauguration, the US Treasury announced that the original idea of buying toxic assets was on hold—indefinitely.

Although the title, TARP, stuck, Congress and the Senate had voted for a plan pitched to them as all about purchasing toxic assets, but that had ended up doing nothing of the sort. Nevertheless, in our tale of twists and turns, where one mirror is angled to reflect in yet another and then another to bounce the feeble ray of light all the way to the end of the tunnel, with the odd wisp of smoke wafted in to achieve the full effect, this does not mean that toxic assets were not purchased. The original plan was partially implemented, indirectly and at taxpayer expense, by the Treasury, through its bailout of Fannie Mae and Freddie Mac, and by the Fed through its policy of quantative easing (QE). The UK and Switzerland were the other two countries that made significant asset purchases.

Ownership Structure Is Everything

When thinking of recapitalization, ownership structure—the 'capital structure'—of a bank is everything. It is a time-honoured principle (if not always strictly followed to the letter) of a capitalist system that when firms mess up it is the owners who take the losses. The 'capital structure' of a bank is a pecking order across those who own equity in the bank and those who own debt issued by the bank (comprising bondholders or 'creditors', ordered by 'seniority' from senior to junior or subordinated). The equity capital is the stock of wealth built up from previously accumulated profits and from selling shares that entitle owners to a share of a bank's future profits. When losses occur, they eat their way through this pecking order: first the equity holders, and then the bondholders according to their seniority in the ownership queue. In the good times, the common equity owners made the highest returns, because they strapped onto themselves more debt in the ownership structure. They also got to vote on the positions of senior bankers, their pay, and how financial firms were run. It was not unreasonable that when the strategies of bankers backfired, the owners of the common equity should be first in the queue to absorb losses and even to have their stakes wiped out.

In normal times, when losses are idiosyncratic, one year of losses is more than offset by other years of gain. The problems only really get out of hand when the losses stretch for years on end, and getting anyone to inject fresh private capital requires them to take temporary leave of their sanity. In the economics literature, the problem is called the 'debt overhang' or 'co-insurance' effect.[50] Existing senior creditors in a bank have claims to some of the profits of new projects supported by new capital, and so the net present value (NPV) of such projects to those who inject new capital is lower, and may even become negative. Why should new investors inject capital if all they are doing is securing with more collateral the claims of more senior creditors, who were around when all the risks built up?[51] New investors also worry they will overpay because of all the buried toxic assets. Furthermore, when one bank on its own makes a rights offering to existing shareholders, it suffers from a negative-inference problem; the bigger the offering, the bigger the possible signal of problems. So as to remove the signal, the infusion of private capital needs to be coordinated across banks and mandated, but this is difficult. The private sector's willingness to own places in the ownership queue also depends on the expected size of future government capital injections, and the government's treatment of non-government owners. As a first principle of recapitalization, government should not drip-feed capital into financial institutions but make it large enough and early enough to protect investors from future policy risk. As a second general principle, and a corollary of the first, if (temporary) nationalization is likely to happen anyway, it is better to get it over and done with than to drag out a phase of denial and have to do it anyway.

Undercapitalized banks hold back on lending. If they lend and a worst-case economic scenario materializes, capital will be needed to absorb the losses. If all banks hold back, a self-fulfilling economic contraction justifies the initial decisions not to lend.[52] Policymakers hoped that if government capital injections created incentives to lend, the recession would be less deep and total economic losses lower. The challenge was to find a way to inject government capital so that it was available to take losses and not just offset the loss-taking responsibilities of current owners. This turned out to be difficult, in part because of the time constraints, in part because of the lack of ex ante legal wherewithal to do it, and in part because of the collective-action problem that gave to bank owners greater say than to taxpayers in a decision that would involve many billions of dollars/pounds/euro of wealth transfer between the two groups.

Government capital injectors faced another difficult trade-off. In an effort to mitigate moral hazard, it might have seemed desirable to remove current failed managers and wipe out shareholders and unsecured creditors, by seniority, up to the level of losses made by the financial institution they owned. But if government was tough in the case of one bank, it would make it difficult for similar banks to raise fresh capital and survive. To avoid this, action to wipe out bondholders needed to be coordinated across many banks at once. Once again, this turned out to be difficult to achieve in practice.

A string of economists urged a variety of approaches to stop government injections of capital from turning into large wealth transfers from taxpayers to bank owners.[53] The priority was for current equity to absorb losses. If losses were low enough, some of the value of the equity would survive. If not, the equity would be wiped out and losses would start to chew their way into the next layer of bank owners, longer-term bondholders.

Perhaps governments could buy off bondholders at prevailing market prices, so that taxpayers would obtain the positive 'externality' benefit that current bond holdings would otherwise get from government capital injections? However, like the 'hold-out' problem common in takeovers, current bondholders would not want to sell. As in the case of takeovers, one way to prevent this is to have in place a rule that forces the purchase of all bond holdings at the current market price if the majority of bondholders have agreed to sell. However, to be credible, the government must commit to letting financial institutions go bankrupt if bondholders do not agree to sell. During standard Chapter 11 insolvencies, bondholders in solid underlying businesses, facing a take-it-or-leave-it offer, take the offer; otherwise, if they hold out, the business will be closed and they will get less and possibly nothing. But, could governments credibly commit to go through with such a threat in the case of systemically important banks? Policy-makers were also frequently frustrated by the fact that senior bondholders had rights equal to insured depositors, which made it difficult to punish bondholders without also punishing depositors.

Bondholders in financial firms did not make the high level of return made by equity holders, and so were not first in the queue to take losses. Nevertheless, they had made good returns on the back of risky management strategies. Their high returns reflected the risk of loss, and it was perfectly reasonable for them to face actual loss now; in future, bank bondholders would charge a higher premium to high-risk banks, which would create an incentive for such banks to take less risk and lower their leverage, which would reduce the chance of crashes. To refrain from forcing losses on bank bondholders would feed moral hazard later. Banks, insurance companies, and pension funds lobbied hard against such logic, sprinkling policymakers' paths with gratuitous scare stories about how the economy would suffer if they were punished. Besides, it was argued, bank bondholders would respond by shifting towards shorter-duration bond holdings to give greater ability to get out before being wiped out. As the proportion of short-term bond holdings rose, the risk of loss to those still holding long-term bonds would rise, incentivizing them also to shift to short-term bond holdings. If part of the initial problem was an ownership structure with not enough long-term owners, matters would get worse.

Supposedly, the choice was between contagion now and greater risks of crashes later because of increased future moral hazard. Perhaps unsurprisingly, governments tended to go in the direction of the latter. Many big-bank share-holders saw big losses, but they were not wiped out, and many bondholders were not forced to face standard take-it-or-leave-it offers. As of early 2012, only Iceland and Denmark had actually written down the debt of senior bank creditors. Iceland had no other option. Denmark started to have second thoughts. Ireland continued to argue that it would not write down senior bank creditors even as it sought to re-finance the senior obligations of its now mostly publicly-owned banks.

Paulson had argued that the CPP 'is an investment, not an expenditure, and there is no reason to expect this program will cost taxpayers anything'.[54] However, in the closing months of 2008, for every $100 the US Treasury injected via the CPP it got about $66 of value, which, for the top ten TARP recipients, translated into $78 billion redistributed from taxpayers to banks.[55] In its haste, the US Treasury used one-size-fits-all documentation, and there was a lack of rigorous audits and inspections. Thus, the likes of Citigroup got capital on the same terms as institutions that were in much healthier financial shape. The reported losses would have been even bigger had they been compared to what other investors got for their capital injections: Mitsubishi got $102 for every $100 it invested in Morgan Stanley; Berkshire Hathaway $110 for every $100 in Goldman Sachs; and Qatar Holding and Abu Dhabi $123 for every $100 in Barclays. In exchange for large public subsidy there was no insistence that increased lending and nonpayment of dividends should be the *quid pro quo*. There were also few restrictions on bank compensation. Once again, we are struck by how lenient the US rescue programme was on its recipients, especially those who had been the most reckless. Given that private investors, facing similar time constraints, did so much better than the Treasury, this suggests that the need for speed was no excuse.

The US Treasury furthermore claimed that recapitalization via the CPP was limited to viable, solvent, banks. Here again the evidence made uncomfortable reading. First, failures started to rack up amongst CCP recipients, and several dozen missed their dividend payments in an effort to conserve capital. Then, Citigroup needed more injections via the TIP programme only weeks after receiving its CPP infusion. Indeed, even though the US Treasury had put $45 billion into Citigroup ($25 billion via CPP and $20 billion via TIP), by late February 2009 the market valued Citigroup at about only $11 billion. If there was a bank that was insolvent at the time of its recapitalization, it was Citigroup. Instead, courtesy of US taxpayers, the lame duck waddled its way into 2009 and beyond. Once more we see that rescue was too easy on its biggest, and previously most reckless, recipients.

Keeping Government Out

The US government took its ownership stakes in the shape of preference shares that could be converted into equity to absorb losses if a bank became insolvent. The logic was that just the knowledge that conversion was possible would help prevent panics. The US government's stake also had the potential for capital gain because it included ten-year warrants that gave the option to buy common shares at a specified price in the future. This meant that taxpayers could benefit from any rise in the share prices of financial institutions the government had invested in. Meanwhile, preference shares paid dividends, which was like being paid interest. Although preference shares were classified as tier-one capital, they were more like debt. Thus, the US government recapitalized in a way that risked its capital less. This had a downside. Existing bondholders knew that they would face losses before the government's preference shares would ever get converted into equity, and so the government's capital injection did not solve the 'debt overhang' problem. Private capital was also deterred by uncertainty caused by an intervention that might need to be topped up later, at terms that were not yet clear, and that might also still lead to nationalization if the economy deteriorated.

US authorities chose preference shares for at least four reasons. First, the level of overall rescue funds was unclear, and a portion could not be risked on absorbing big losses. Second, preference shares carried no voting rights. There were political risks associated with being involved in the management of banks, especially that of being accused of 'socialism'. Fannie Mae and Freddie Mac were exceptions because they had long been part of the apparatus of the state, and AIG was a 'basket case' whose fate was already sealed. Restrictions on executive pay and bonuses, when laid down as conditions of rescue, often came to little because the government, lacked the votes to enforce its demands, didn't have the support of bank boards, or simply didn't have the will to act. Third, if the government was a major shareholder, this would raise the chance of greater scrutiny of banks' balance sheets. If banks were close to being insolvent, or even already insolvent, there was risk that, at some point, there would be full government ownership, orderly restructuring, and liquidation. The heavy engagement of the government during the S&L crisis had seen more than a thousand banking executives jailed for corruption, compared to hardly any this time. Fourth, the prior experience in the US of one-off localized banking crises favoured the logic of preference shares, even though in a systemic banking crisis they made much less sense. When President Obama found himself in 2009 and 2010 shaking a big stick at the banks, it was largely because the US government had injected its capital in a form that kept him firmly on the outside.

In contrast, the UK government took its ownership stakes in common shares. This must be one of the few instances when a government being willing to absorb a loss is a good thing. By improving capital's overall quality (defined as ability to take loss), a lower capital buffer would on average be needed. It would be easier to pull private capital into financial institutions, and the prospects for lending would improve. Before we get carried away with praise for the prescience of this, the original intent had been to purchase preference shares, but the 12% per year charge to banks proved too high, and UK policymakers gravitated towards common shares. Common shares entailed government ownership— and strings. Thus the UK government ended up disproportionately in the news for trying to influence bank lending and bonus policy, although, oddly enough, it did not meet with much success.

If a government's capital injection is big enough to give it a majority holding (or if it might become so if the economy deteriorates), banks may have an incentive not to lend, so as to acquire private-sector capital more quickly, exit the government programme, and avoid scrutiny and restrictions.[56] To mitigate this, some governments attached lending targets to their capital injections, but many (the US being a prominent example) did not. However, if rescue schemes to which lending targets are attached are voluntary, the incentive of individual firms to wriggle out might undermine the targets. Yet, compulsory schemes are a balancing act too: if many customers are only surviving because of low interest rates, and banks judge the optimal level of lending to be lower than the government target, they might stay away from recapitalization schemes that force them to lend even if membership of such schemes is socially beneficial.

Insolvent Banks and Nationalization

Recapitalization should be limited to undercapitalized but otherwise solvent banks. If a bank is insolvent, policymakers have two options. The first option is to let it die as a warning to deter others from making such silly mistakes, and to allow its replacement with new banks that use capital to back only new loans. The new financial firms can be crafted out of parts of the old firms and, indeed, contain many of the employees of the old firms; the key is to liquidate all previous bank ownership contracts. The second option, if policymakers are terrified of the systemic consequences of death, is to rescue even an insolvent bank, reasoning that the social benefits of preserving systemic stability outweigh the losses, including those losses caused by future moral hazard. In all cases of saved, insolvent, systemic banks, their shareholders should be wiped out, and their CEOs should not walk off with multimillion pension pots and golden handshakes (that is, they should face the same financial consequences that they would have faced if the institution had not been rescued by the government). In order to get the full value of any new equity they inject, governments would have to temporarily nationalize these large, insolvent, systemic, banks. Nationalization carries the dangers of distorting markets, but the goal in all cases would be to exit nationalization as quickly as possible. Even Greenspan took to arguing for temporary nationalization, followed by clean-up and resale.[57] When such a way of thinking broke out in that particular economic quarter, it was a sign that the world really had moved into a new financial era.

Significant nationalizations were made in Austria, Belgium, Denmark, Germany, Iceland, Ireland, Latvia, Luxembourg, Mongolia, Netherlands, Ukraine, the UK, the US, and eventually, in 2012, Spain. Of as much note are some of those that avoided significant nationalizations, including France, Greece, Hungary, Portugal, Russia, Slovenia, Sweden, and Switzerland. It is difficult to interpret what we saw. Governments took over a range of insolvent institutions for sure, but it happened usually only when it was hard to avoid. Court injunctions were used to nationalize key parts of the Bradford and Bingley bank in the UK and Fortis (as part of its breakup) in the Benelux countries. Regulatory takeover was used in the cases of Fannie Mae and Freddie Mac in the US and the Icelandic banks. Acquisition of a majority shareholding (and hence voting rights) was the case of RBS in the UK, AIG in the US, and Hypo Real Estate in Germany (Germany's first nationalization since the 1930s).

But we saw resistance too. By February 2009, as the recession worsened and housing losses mounted, Citigroup struggled to persuade its investors that it was adequately capitalized, and turned to the US government for more capital. According to the FCIC, had Citigroup's assets been properly accounted for, in 2007 its ratio of assets to capital would have been 48 and not the 21 it reported. Citigroup had a long history of misbehaviour. It had aided and abetted Enron and WorldCom when they were tricking the financial system, and had been fined more than any other financial institution in the late 1990s and 2000s. Its financial alchemy had blown up in its face three times in less than three decades—in 1982 from bad loans to emerging economies, in the late 1980s from US commercial real estate, and now from subprime mortgages. To put it out of its misery, the US administration could have bought a controlling stake, removed managers, and made the long-term bondholders bear their richly-deserved losses. A successful nationalization, resolution, and turnaround might even have taken away fears that, if other banks failed, Lehman-style disasters would follow. The US administration chose, instead, to keep its stake at 36% (later falling to 29%), and put in place a toxic asset guarantee. No management in Citigroup was removed. By the time nationalization of Citigroup was being considered in Washington, the Obama administration had already ditched any notion of nationalizing the whole banking system because the financial needs of doing so would have had to go through Congress, and it was clear that Congress would not agree. Resistance to the nationalization and break-up of insolvent financial firms ultimately led to bank owners and bank executives getting off far too lightly. One of the great paradoxes of the bailout is that Obama got the blame for this although it was Congress and his Republican opponents whose actions did more to protect big failed banks.

In the UK, the merger between HBOS and Lloyds TSB in September 2008 was also an attempt to avoid nationalization. When, as we saw, the plan went horribly wrong, Prime Minister Brown publicly stated his intent not to nation-alize LBG. After all, it was he who had so very publicly pushed for a merger, torn up European competition law to get it through, and sought to take full credit. The government ended up taking its 43.3% ownership stake in LBG. HBOS was a hopelessly failed bank that could have been wound down. Instead, by early 2010, some £23 billion of public money had been pumped into LBG/HBOS, which became reliant on some £157 billion of public loans and guarantees. The UK government paid 74 pence per share. By September 2011, the shares were trading at less than half of this. By then, the combined losses on the £65 billion invested by the British government in LBG/HBOS and RBS stood at £38 billion.

Recapitalizing banks just because they are insolvent, without any systemic justification, is wrong-headed. So, it must have been that HBOS and RBS were saved with little penalty imposed because they were a systemic danger. It is difficult to evaluate this. The secret loans to both HBOS and RBS (at that time secret to their shareholders) suggest that UK policymakers believed there were systemic risks. Yet, policymakers also knew that the costs of avoiding moral hazard were in the present and the consequences of moral hazard in the future. Whichever way we look at it, the debacle of HBOS and RBS, at huge expense to taxpayers, was either half-baked industrial policy dressed up as systemic rescue or the result of prior regulatory and political failures. It is not clear which is worse.

Ideally, nationalization should entail a clear plan to break up failed banks and create leaner and more competitive banking systems with reduced pricing power. As a result, a government's shareholding may never recover in value, and criticism should be heaped on those who caused such a sorry state of affairs in the first place. Yet, once governments are major shareholders in some of their domestic banks, they face a dilemma. A break-up would be good for taxpayers in their capacity as borrowers, but the lower pricing power would reduce the value of governments' shareholdings, making the initial decision to rescue banks look less justified. New banks that might replace old failed banks are not saddled with commitments to the government, such that, paradoxically, keeping them out of the market is good for increasing government returns. The process of creative destruction says that old failed banks should be allowed to die. Instead, governments might be tempted to avoid the death of some of the beasts they had so painstakingly preserved.

6

Healing the Sick
and Raising the Dead

The Guarantees Roll Out

Once panic subsided, policymakers settled down to making the biggest commitment of taxpayers' money to any single group in society since the Second World War. The guarantee—a promise to stand behind another's obligation to a third party—was a popular way to do it. Guarantees have the endearing property of not showing up as government spending, and they quickly surfaced in many guises.

More than 40 countries stretched their existing deposit-insurance schemes that guaranteed depositors up to specified limits. In the US, the limit per depositor went from $100,000 to $250,000.[1] Some countries temporarily removed limits entirely: Australia, Austria, Germany, Hungary, Iceland, Ireland, Mongolia, and Slovenia.[2] Others, such as the UK, removed limits implicitly (in the case of Northern Rock and Bradford & Bingley, the guarantee on deposits was unlimited, and it is hard to believe that this would not have applied to other UK banks in distress). The argument against extending limits is the usual one of moral hazard. Yet it would have been very risky not to have allowed limits to increase if the crash intensified: In the 1930s there was no deposit insurance, and, by 1933, 10,000 (about 40%) of all US banks had collapsed, and loan books had fallen by 50% peak to trough. Besides, it was bank owners, who had been getting much higher rewards than depositors, who needed to be first in line for losses. If the mere presence of deposit guarantees prevents bank runs at otherwise solvent banks, the cost to governments is low.

Many governments extended guarantees on other bank liabilities. The French employed €320 billion in guarantees alongside €40 billion in capital injections.

In October 2008, the UK guaranteed up to £250 billion of short- and medium-term lending, for up to three years, in return for an annual fee. In the US, the FDIC offered a guarantee to all new issues of unsecured bank debt until June 2009 for three years. In Germany, the Bad Bank Act (Deutsche Bad Bank-Gesetzgebung), passed in July 2009, allowed private banks to transfer assets to a special entity, in exchange for government-guaranteed bonds; the direct fiscal costs were a bit over 1% of German GDP for guarantees totalling about 6% of German GDP.

In the US, guarantees were used to help kick-start securitization. The Term Asset-Backed Securities Loan Facility, TALF, announced in November 2008 and launched on 3 March 2009, was authorized to provide up to $200 billion to support issuers of ABSs who would post the securities as collateral for the loans. The loans were non-recourse, and the Fed had no right to any of the issuers' other assets if the securities defaulted. With all the downside risk on the shoulders of government, it might seem that there would be a good return to those using TALF, and securitization would be revived. By the time the scheme closed in July 2010, the total loaned came to just over $70 billion. The maximum outstanding at any one time was $49 billion.[3] Over 2,000 loans were made under the TALF, supporting about three million car-finance loans, a million student loans, nearly 900,000 loans to small businesses, 150,000 other business loans, and millions of credit-card loans. Car-finance lenders that funded their operations in part with ABSs supported by the TALF reported that they found it cheaper to do so and could extend lending,[4] while student-loan and credit-card issuers found it cheaper to use other sources of funds. The US Treasury argued that low take-up illustrated TALF's success in reopening the ABS markets. The risk premiums on ABSs shrank and the levels of issuance went up a little, but it was hard to disentangle the role played by TALF. Since the loans were ultimately secured by TARP funds, it seems that some TALF recipients worried that the sort of conditions imposed on TARP recipients might be imposed on them.

The biggest guarantee schemes of all were to cap the 'toxic asset' losses of financial firms. At the end of November 2008, the US launched the Asset Guarantee Program (AGP) and, in January 2009, the UK announced its own Asset Protection Scheme (APS). Some in the UK Treasury dubbed it 'Operation Broom'.[5] All losses on a portfolio of assets up to a predetermined threshold would be borne by the financial institution, like the excess on an insurance contract. Above this, for a fee—the 'insurance premium'—a government would promise to make good most losses. The 'ring-fenced' assets could sit on the balance sheet of a financial institution without the need to be priced in illiquid markets or in an artificial 'market' that might not work. With the size of potential losses capped, the 'quality' of a bank's capital would improve, new private capital enter, and lending revive. Or so it was reasoned. Such 'contingent capital' would reduce the actual capital needed ('contingent' because if the economy deteriorated, the government would make good most of the lost capital). If economies were suffering because banks were not lending out of fear that other banks were not lending, a guarantee would help prevent economic collapse and prevent loss of bank capital; i.e. 'toxic asset' guarantees had 'public-good' properties.

Presuming that such schemes were not used to save banks that were insolvent,[6] governments (the monopoly suppliers of the insurance) would even have been able to make a profit by charging fees on the basis of the high risks of loss that banks would face without such schemes in place. Governments would have been able to share some of the profit with banks by charging them lower fees in return for promises of increased lending. If all banks faced a collective take-it-or-leave-it offer to have or not to have such guarantees, and were charged fees no higher than their (risk-adjusted expected) losses without such guarantees, it would have been in their interests to have the guarantees. But would governments make a profit from providing 'toxic asset' guarantees and would banks value the guarantees? We need to think through some principles and look at what actually happened.

First, what if a bank is insolvent even with all the 'public-good' benefits of an asset guarantee? The guarantee becomes an expected subsidy transferring wealth from taxpayers to bank owners. Taxpayers' interests might be better served by temporary nationalization and restructuring, and the *only* justification for not doing this would be the dangers of 'systemic' risk.

Second, 'insurance' fees need to vary according to the riskiness of the asset portfolios being guaranteed. However, governments face an asymmetric information problem very typical for insurance contracts: those being insured know more than the insurers about their past risky behaviour—locked up in their asset portfolios. Adverse selection problems reappear as banks self-select bad assets into guarantee schemes and leave the good ones out.

Third, *ex post* guaranteeing the investment decisions and capital structures of those who have generated failed portfolios leads to moral hazard. In a bankruptcy, unsecured bondholders face losses and might even be wiped out. If this efficient punishment is removed by a guarantee, it reduces the ability of market signals to incentivize banks to allocate capital efficiently in future. Worse, since the fee is charged to the whole bank, the part of the fee paid by unsecured bondholders is not in proportion to the losses they avoid.

Fourth, just because 'toxic' assets are not sold, it does not mean that judgments about their value are avoided. The fee and the first loss rest on knowledge of the potential losses under a range of macroeconomic scenarios. For banks, the value of managing insured assets efficiently is reduced if the first loss is set too low.

Fifth, if an asset guarantee generates systemic benefits, like any public good it will suffer 'free rider' problems: those who keep out will pick up systemic advantage without paying. Such schemes may have to be compulsory.

Sixth, guarantees work because the cost to bear 'toxic asset' risk is lower for solvent governments than for banks. However, if economies deteriorate and guarantees are triggered, a heavy fiscal burden falls on the shoulders of governments just as they are struggling fiscally. If the macroeconomic outcome being insured against turns out unfavourable, but not so unfavourable that it causes sovereign default, guarantees might work. If the outcome is sufficiently unfavourable that it causes sovereign default, even actuarially-fair guarantees would be a disaster. 'Toxic asset' guarantees would be risky for heavily-indebted developed economies (Iceland, Greece, Spain, and Ireland stand out) and could not be entered into by poor countries.

Seventh, if guarantees protect the current generation of politicians at the expense of future generations, they become part of 'gamble for resurrection' behaviour. Governments take positions that, in the expected sense, are worse than alternatives that have more obvious cost, but that will be low-cost if the disastrous tail outcome is avoided.

So, what happened? In the US, the AGP was voluntary. Only two banks—the saddest specimens of all—lined up to enter. Systemic benefits were therefore low. Citigroup proposed a $301 billion pool of assets, including nearly 80% of its residential real-estate loan portfolio. Bank of America proposed a $118 billion pool. Citigroup would take the first $39.5 billion of losses, beyond which taxpayers would swallow 90% of losses. The fee was low, just over $7 billion or a little over 2% of the portfolio's value, and, better still for Citigroup, paid for with preferred stock and warrants. Far from the government exploiting its position to make a profit from big failed banks, the logic was to be generous to avoid Citigroup inflicting systemic damage on others. Recognizing Citigroup's weakened incentives to monitor, after $27 billion of losses the US government could seize management of failing assets. In December 2009, Citigroup terminated the agreement early, and paid a bargain $2.2 billion to exit. Bank of America signed an agreement in January 2009, but it was never implemented and the program was cancelled in September 2009. Having derived implicit protection for most of 2009, it paid $425 million in fees. By the end of 2009, the flagship AGP was dead and buried.

In the UK too, only two banks lined up to enter the APS. RBS agreed in principle in February 2009, with a £325 billion pool of assets, and managed to wriggle its 'first loss' down to £19.5 billion (6%), for a fee of just £6.5 billion (2%) payable over seven years. RBS, in exchange for a low fee (paid by issuing B shares that pay dividends but have no voting rights), faced a legally-binding agreement to expand lending to UK homeowners and borrowers over two years by £50 billion. Vince Cable (soon to become the UK's Secretary of State for Business, Innovation, and Skills) described the terms as 'fraud at the taxpayer's expense'. Mind you, since UK taxpayers already owned most of RBS, they were robbing themselves to pay themselves, a crime perhaps more easily overlooked.

LBG followed in March 2009, with about a £260 billion pool of assets. After no small amount of argy-bargy, LBG pulled out in November 2009 without signing, raised private capital, and paid an exit fee of £2.5 billion to cover the implicit guarantee it had had for most of 2009. The rate of return charged was well below what investors would have demanded in early 2009, when LBG derived great benefit from the scheme. Instead of exploiting its monopoly position to make profit, the UK Treasury was keen for LBG to pass its stress test and raise private capital, and so subsidized LBG's exit fee by about £500 million to £2 billion (based on 20%–30% cost of equity). LBG had repeatedly balked at the notion of a binding agreement on lending. Now, it would not have to enter one.

In the UK's toxic asset guarantee hall of shame, RBS stood alone. It did not like it one little bit, and vowed to exit as soon as possible. By the time RBS signed in December 2009, its pool of insured assets had fallen to £282 billion and the first loss had risen to £60 billion, beyond which taxpayers would take 90% of losses. So that RBS could absorb as much of the loss as possible itself, the UK Treasury injected another £25.5 billion of capital and promised a further £8 billion in contingent capital. Instead of an upfront payment, there was an annual fee—£700 million in 2009, dropping to £500 million in 2012. RBS also had generous flexibility to exit the APS early.

By September 2010, the loss on the RBS portfolio already stood at £37 billion, meaning that, at the originally proposed terms, RBS would have had no incentive to improve performance on its insured assets. Vince Cable was right after all. How irritating for some. Thank goodness too for the Asset Protection Agency (APA). The National Audit Office found that the revised £60 billion first loss had been based on as much information on the underlying assets as was available at the time, and on a robust assessment of the likely incentives. The head of the APA observed that the only reason that the RBS losses were not even greater was because of super-low interest rates;[7] RBS was being saved by huge transfers of wealth from savers to itself. To keep within EU rules on state aid, the European Competition Commission insisted that RBS wind down or sell by 2013 some £250 billion of non-core assets and £50 billion of core business. All banks but the truly desperate would have found a way to avoid such a scheme. Asset guarantees were billed as a 'central part of the government's efforts to stabilize the financial sector and promote the flow of credit in the economy'.[8] In the end, only the truly desperate went anywhere near such guarantees, which reduced their collective public-good benefits. Others kept out to avoid restrictions on lending, pay, and bonuses.

In both the US and the UK, a lot of time and energy went into creating toxic asset guarantee schemes that were not much used. This does not mean they did not have a use. Citigroup and RBS were dead banks, but able to use such schemes both as a form of contingent capital and for their option value (if all went wrong they could go ahead with the schemes, but they did not have to). The first, especially in the case of Citigroup, reduced the amount of government capital injection needed from other programs, which kept government at bay. The second meant that more radical, and, for bank owners, terminal solutions were avoided.

Stress Tests and More Equity Injections

In February 2009, the US Treasury launched its Capital Assistance Program (CAP). This time, government capital injections would follow stress tests. European regulators got the stress test bug and followed in 2010, putting 91 banks under the microscope. They were a rag-tag bunch of specimens. And the banks were not much prettier.

Readers may be reminded of the famous Monty Python 'Dead Parrot' sketch, in which the pet shop owner insists on denying that the parrot he sold is—permanently, irrefutably, definitively, and beyond any shadow of a doubt—dead. First, he ventures the bird is only sleeping. Then, he praises the beauty of the bird ('Remarkable bird the Norwegian Blue, idn'it?, ay? Beautiful plumage!'). In desperation, the man who bought the parrot stress tests the bird by banging it on the counter (the sketch did not use a real bird of course). Prior to the crash, some in the world of high finance had preened themselves a bit like Norwegian Blues— fabulous, plumped up, highly-strung demanding, little creatures, it was a wonder they hadn't keeled over long ago with the worry of it all. Now, it seemed, some had. Unfortunately, it wasn't clear which ones. Those that had stretched their balance sheets till their bones came out of their sockets were in that strange limbo-land between earth and heaven, not sure whether they were dead or just thought they might be. In principle, a stress test would tell them.

Only for the 19 largest US bank holding companies, those with over $100 billion in assets, was a test compulsory. This consisted in taking their starting levels of capital, adding projected profits over the coming two years under various macroeconomic scenarios, subtracting expected losses, having a big argument over the results, changing the results, seeing if capital at the end was above the benchmark at the start, and then deciding what the benchmark at the start should have been anyway. Those that failed would get six months to raise capital privately before having to accept government capital in the shape of non-voting, convertible, preferred stock. Banks would fall into three categories: those deemed solvent without need of a CAP injection; those that would be dragged from death (insolvency) to life (solvency) thanks to the confidence trick of CAP injections, such that the CAP injections would be repaid; and those that were insolvent regardless, such that CAP funds would on average not be repaid. The last—those at death's door—could be put out of their misery and restructured, or revived and kept on life support through CAP injections if death was deemed too systemically damaging. They might not be dead, in the strictest definition of the word, but they might find themselves with a majority government shareholding. From all the squawks, one would think that the two were near enough equivalent.

So, once again, what happened? The release of the US stress-test results in May 2009 was preceded by two weeks of haggling between banks and the Fed, at the end of which the capital holes in Bank of America and Citigroup had, miraculously, fallen from $50 billion to $34 billion and from $35 billion to $5.5 billion respectively. The $35 billion easily swamped Citigroup's market value of $10–$15 billion (depending on where its volatile share price was on any given day). But $5.5 billion, thankfully, did not. So eloquent were the arguments down at Wells Fargo that its capital hole shrank from $17.3 billion to $13.7 billion. It quickly became clear that no real banks were going to be harmed by the tests, and so, in the week the results were out, US bank share prices soared, on average, by about 10%. At Bank of America it was 17%, while down at Fifth Third Bank, it wasn't bones but champagne corks that could be heard popping—60% in a week. The biggest 19 US banks were told they faced $600 billion of losses over two years, and ten were instructed to boost their capital buffers by a combined $75 billion. This they did comfortably over the following year, raising $140 billion in equity capital and $60 billion in non-guaranteed secured debt.

In November 2009, the CAP closed without spending a cent of public money. To reflect this happy, if unexpected, turn of events, US Treasury literature morphed from emphasizing 'capital assistance' to emphasizing the tests as some sort of magic potion, the drinking of which so swelled investor confidence in the health of big failed banks that government capital was no longer needed.

This is hard to believe. Since no insolvent bank could rely entirely on the private market for its capital needs, the stress tests must have been so powerful that not even the most sickly-looking bank was actually dead. Yet, surely, even the most brilliantly-executed stress test could not turn a dead bank into a live bank?

The results of the tests were not all they seemed. Solvency was partly down to discretion. Herein was a critical bit of wiggle room. The natural inclination of any financial firm facing a little bit of wiggle room is to make like an octopus and squeeze into it. By the time the results were out, the US economy was already reflecting the worse-case economic scenario used in the tests—10% unemployment in 2010 and a 27% fall in house prices over 2009 and 2010. Gloom-monger Geithner turned cheerleader, and argued that many banks were sufficiently capitalized, even though his own Treasury said the government's growth forecast was optimistic. The tests also had not factored in any deterioration in Europe and they covered only two years, and so missed losses at longer horizons.

Nor was it clear how banks should account for assets whose market values had fallen below those reported on their balance sheets. The Treasury reasoned that many assets were greatly underpriced because of illiquidity, and so it allowed fair-value accounting rules to be relaxed and prices to be backed out from banks' own models. For sure, there was a tension between a quick piecemeal reassessment and a slower, more comprehensive fundamental reassessment and due process that might take so long that financial firms would collapse before the accounting standards got adjusted. Yet, banks were not averse to having their cake and eating it, happy to have assets on their balance sheets when prices were rising, and off their balance sheets—and priced how they saw fit—when prices were falling. The tests also relied heavily on private bank information that was hard to verify, and were complicated by the lack of regulatory structures for dealing with border-straggling banks. Cooperation would be difficult to achieve if it was known that a sizable number of those being tested were going to be failed. Firms also faced a prisoner's dilemma: if other financial firms were exaggerating their state of health, it was rational to do so too.

Many financial firms argued they could replenish capital through earnings if given enough time. Yet profits were being boosted by policy responses to the crash, such as low interest rates, liquidity injections, and one-off boosts to revenues such as fees from managing government-backed debt issues, high bid-ask spreads and margins in 'flow' business such as fixed income, currencies, and commodities (FICC) because of greater pricing power. It seemed odd to allow earnings boosts consequent on the crash to help banks pass their tests—but such it seems are the surrealities of modern-day banking crashes.

The stress tests relied heavily on tier-one common capital and not on tangible common equity (TCE). TCE is the equity of a bank minus its preferred shares, goodwill, and intangible assets, and so refers to the purest and most flexible form of capital able to bear the 'first loss'. By now, large chunks of tier-one capital came in the form of preference stock and was not truly loss-bearing (for example dividends on government preference shares could be deferred but not cancelled). Had TCE been used in the stress tests, the amount of capital that needed to be raised would have been much higher.

To make matters worse, the US government took a long time to spell out what its desired tier-one ratio was—as if it wanted to see how bad things were first. And then it imposed a low ratio. For example, in spite of huge government capital investments, Citigroup was still the worst capitalized of the lot (on less than 2% TCE and on 2.3% tier-one common capital ratios). If the US government had taken a tough line, it would have ended up being a majority shareholder in Citigroup and Bank of America, and a big minority shareholder in PNC Financial Services, US Bancorp, and Wells Fargo. Clearly the stress tests boosted confidence, but not in the way policymakers intimated. Instead, the signal was sent that no matter how large a bank was, or how much it had misbehaved, it would not be allowed to fail. Bank share prices did wonderfully on such happy news. As one blogger enthused: 'I'm telling my broker today to invest everything in Citigroup. Sky's the limit!'

In this topsy-turvy world, the ability to raise capital privately was in inverse proportion to the severity of the tests; surging share prices, caused by soft stress tests, could be spun as positive news by politicians hungry to demonstrate the wisdom of their ways. Avoiding moral hazard required the worst banks to be liquidated and for government capital to be targeted at others. If some banks really were dead but injections of moral hazard were making them solvent, then the costs of past failures would be socialized, but not directly through CAP capital injections as some had feared at the start, but in the shape of moral hazard.

If the US stress tests were soft on financial firms, the EU-wide stress tests were an unmitigated disaster, the sort that only the EU could pull off with cool aplomb. In July 2010, their folly and delusion finally having caught up with them, seven of 91 banks failed the European Banking Authority tests: five Spanish banks (Diada, Espiga, Banca Civica, Unnim, and Cajasur); one German bank (Hypo Real Estate); and one Greek bank (the presciently named ATEBank). Even then the new capital stipulated was a paltry €3.5 billion. And Anglo

Irish alone, it shortly transpired, had a gaping capital hole of €70 billion and still got through with flying colours. National regulators were in charge of the tests and many seemed more concerned about the competitiveness of their own banks. The stress tests were also based on historical exogenous shocks (and not the sort of endogenous shocks that had recently been witnessed), excluded potential liquidity shocks, and did not even include the possibility of a default by a eurozone government.

Not only did no US banks take any government capital from the CAP but, by the end of 2009, about 50 had managed to pay back their CPP capital investments and about 30 had repurchased their CPP warrants. Supposedly a key reason for requiring banks to hold more capital was because of the positive externality benefit onto other banks of that capital. If so, then allowing stronger banks to repay early would leave weaker banks exposed. Just three—Goldman Sachs, JPMorgan Chase, and Morgan Stanley—accounted for nearly 60% of all repayments. Goldman Sachs was especially clever at exploiting the interactions of rescue schemes. It took $12.9 billion from the rescue of AIG and then purchased back the $10 billion preference stock it had issued to the government (paying $1.1 billion to repurchase its warrants) and, in so doing, cut the strings tied to government capital injections regarding bonuses and hiring practices. Goldman Sachs claimed that it only took the $10 billion in the first place to 'show solidarity' with other banks (Goldman Sachs' philanthropic attitude to its competitors is, after all, legendary). Goldman Sachs still got to take advantage of the debt-guarantee scheme.

The rush to dispose of government investments as quickly as possible—apparently spearheaded by President Obama—meant that the government was exiting before it had a chance to maximize the returns for taxpayers (in contrast, 30% of the equity injected into Japan's financial institutions in 1997 was still held by the Japanese government at the end of 2008). The US Treasury also found itself bound to a specific negotiating process for banks trying to buy back their warrants—and not an open, market-based process. This had been agreed to when the banks gave the Treasury the warrants in the first place, and was now being used to drive discounts and buy back government stakes on the cheap. As this became known, public pressure seems to have encouraged the Treasury to achieve valuations that gave it a fairer return. This was yet another case of the terms of rescue being soft on banks. In negotiations over the details, banks had been far cleverer than the Treasury.

Losses on the horizon were still set to overwhelm some banks. Even if banks used earnings to cover their losses, these would still have to come from the rest of a society already in the grip of recession. Banks, with the full cooperation of the government, were playing a game of hide-and-seek, hiding the dangers, cutting strings that bound their behaviour, yet still hoping to wrangle a second bailout later if the economy deteriorated.

Squeezing the PPIP Until It Squeaked

In late March 2009, Geithner revived the idea of buying up toxic assets.[9] Not averse to making himself a hostage to fortune, he boldly laid down his logic in the *Wall Street Journal* (in an article entitled 'My Plan for Bad Bank Assets'): 'By providing a market for these assets that does not now exist, this programme will help improve asset values, increase lending capacity by banks, and reduce uncertainty about the scale of losses on bank balance sheets. The ability to sell assets to this fund will make it easier for banks to raise private capital, which will accelerate their ability to replace the capital investments provided by the Treasury.'[10] He also worked to the time-honoured principle that when one is flogging a dead donkey, one should dangle a more juicy carrot. This time, the carrot came with a large PPIP (Public-Private Investment Program) in its middle. Nicely finessed as an 'Investment Programme', the PPIP was not deemed government spending because it was based on government loans. To make it more palatable, the word 'toxic' was out and the word 'legacy' was in. Let's look at the theory of the PPIP and—after a period of suitable suspense and incredulity—at the practice. As we have seen, the two are usually not the same.

Initially, the idea was to 'leverage' (a polite way of saying to 'lend' or 'guarantee lending') $75–100 billion of TARP capital into about $500 billion of 'legacy-asset' purchases, perhaps rising to $1 trillion. The PPIP came in two flavours: the Legacy Loans Program, for the purchase of distressed loans, to be administered and guaranteed by the FDIC; and the Legacy Securities Program, for the purchase of mostly ABSs, to be administered through the Treasury. Given the constrained finances of the FDIC, both were in effect backed by a Treasury guarantee.

As anyone who works in public policy knows, the best way to improve the credentials of a dubious government programme is to masquerade it as 'market-based', even though poorly designed artificial markets usually deviate in significant ways from real markets. The Treasury proposed that it would match every $1 put into the Legacy Loans Program by private investors, and the FDIC would lend up to $12 for every dollar invested to help private investors buy 'legacy loans'. Any future upside would be shared 50:50 between private investors and taxpayers. Thus, taxpayers would risk $13 for the same potential upside as private investors risking $1. The Legacy Securities Program was less generous. For every $1 of private equity raised by the Public-Private Investment Funds (PPIFs) the Treasury would add $1 co-equity and lend up to a further $2. Investors would get the same potential upside for every dollar they put in as taxpayers would get for putting $3 at risk.

The PPIP was an old idea—a guarantee—in a new skin. Instead of guaranteeing banks on their portfolios of toxic assets, the investors in the PPIP would get a de facto guarantee against losses. If losses materialized, investors would walk away from the government loans. If gains materialized, investors would share them with taxpayers. This created a sour taste in many an economist's mouth. The consensus quickly developed that investors would price in the non-recourse nature of the loans and overbid, leading to the transfer of hundreds of billions of dollars of public money to bank owners. *The Economist* magazine quickly sussed it out, describing the PPIP as capitalism of the 'heads I win, tails you lose' variety.[11]

To understand the concern, let's start with a nice big pile of toxic assets with a face value of $1 trillion (jump the next two paragraphs if you wish to avoid the maths). Let's keep it simple and imagine the assets have only a 20% chance of the good state, of fully paying back, and an 80% chance of the bad state, of repaying only $200 billion. How much would risk-neutral well-diversified investors who do not have access to non-recourse loans pay for the pile? The answer is a little over one-third of its face value (0.2 times $1 trillion plus 0.8 times $200 billion, equals $360 billion).

However, if we presume competition between risk-neutral investors, with access to non-recourse loans, investors would bid the price up to $636 billion, the present discounted value of the investment once all losses are shifted to taxpayers. The overbid amount ($276 billion) would go to owners of banks and into the bonuses of those who run them. As bank share prices priced the largesse in, politicians could claim that they were 'reviving the banks'. The Treasury and private investors would each put in just over $45 billion (their portions of the $636 billion spent on the assets), and the FDIC would loan the rest, $546 billion. In the good state of the world, when the assets paid out the full $1 trillion, there would be profit of $454 billion above and beyond repaying the loan. The profit would get split between private investors and the Treasury, at $227 billion apiece. But this is breakeven: 20% of the time private investors would get $227 billion, and 80% of the time they would get nothing—about $45 billion on average, which is what they invested. On average, bank shareholders would get $276 billion. In the good state, the FDIC would get repaid. In the bad state of the world the FDIC would get to hold on to bad assets worth just $200 billion, a loss of $346 billion on the $546 billion it loaned to pay for them. This would happen 80% of the time. So, the FDIC on average (over good and bad states) would take a $276 billion loss, which is on average what the bank owners would gain. The PPIP would be an elaborate hidden subsidy for the banking industry. Even those who did not follow the maths will have spotted the dud deal for taxpayers.

Curiously, in this simple scenario, the investors sandwiched in the middle would not make any excess profits, and would just be the patsies for boosting the wealth of bank owners. In a real-world scenario, investors would pick up a return from risk-taking and information gathering. Rules quickly had to be added to avoid banks gaming the PPIP through affiliates or partnerships, investing in themselves, writing off their toxic assets, and staying solvent courtesy of massive taxpayer loss. On reflection, though, such scams were also dangerous: imagine if they got found out!

Many of the same problems that existed for the original asset guarantee programs resurfaced. The 'lemons'—adverse selection—problem did not go away. While there would be some disclosure requirements, banks would still know more about their own toxic assets. Those buying would have to reduce their bid prices to reflect the chances of picking up low-quality assets (the non-recourse loans would partly offset this). Private investors too would encourage adverse selections. The bidding process would allow them to 'see the goods' first, and this would allow them some opportunity to choose what to buy in a PPIP and what to buy outside. As an extreme case, if financially-unconstrained investors were 100% sure of there being *only* upside to a particular portfolio (clearly the logic works when they are simply very sure), they would rather buy the portfolio outright than bid for it inside a scheme that would require them to share the upside 50:50. Financially-constrained investors might share an opportunity with a government, using the cheap government loan to leverage their buying power. Those firms that bid within the scheme would also get a competitive advantage over those who might seek to buy the same assets outside the scheme, because of the ability to pay a higher price factoring in the non-recourse subsidy. To complicate matters, banks with the biggest piles of bad assets—Citigroup and Bank of America—had already secured guarantees (even if they might turn out to be only temporary). Yet again, policymakers risked being caught in the interaction of two rescue schemes. Moral hazard came back by the spadeful too: if there was overpayment for toxic assets, most of the subsidy would go to those with the most toxic assets.

'Investors reacted ecstatically' with a 'thundering response', reported the *New York Times* on the day the details of the PPIP were released.[12] By the end of that day the Dow Jones Industrial Average was up nearly 7%. Bank share prices did especially well. There was not much reaction in credit-market indices. By now, the stock market was becoming a convenient barometer of bad public policy, and it quickly understood the PPIP as a subsidy from taxpayers to banks, with zero impact on bank lending. The latter was a bit unfortunate, since the need to stimulate lending was the purpose for bothering with such hare-brained schemes in the first place. As Willem Buiter put it: 'If there were a stock market for taxpayer equity, it would have tanked by a commensurate amount.'[13] Some were heard to mutter that investors who were not smart enough to keep the global financial system out of a mess in the first place were now deemed smart enough to sort the mess out and, in recognition of their smartness, were to be given big juicy non-recourse loans to do it.

So, once again, what happened? In spite of the overpayment logic and of much huffing and puffing in the economics blogosphere, the incentive to sell 'legacy' assets was not that great. Many banks were holding assets on their books at prices well above current market prices. If prices were not bid high enough even with the subsidy, banks would still prefer not to sell, so as to avoid a write-down that would force them to take government capital with all its strings, or to raise more private capital. At the end of 2008, the ten biggest US banks had about $3.6 trillion of 'legacy' loans (about one-third of their assets), and the carrying value of the loan books of these top ten US banks was only about 3% above market price. If even such a small loss was realized, about $110 billion, it would destroy about a quarter of the common equity of these banks.

After absorbing much energy of the US Treasury and others, by 2010 the legacy loan part of the PPIP had been abandoned. The legacy securities PPIP did fly and was even allowed to go to the top of its proposed 'leverage' scale, but the amounts were scaled back drastically. By the end of June 2010, the PPIFs had raised about $7.4 billion of private equity capital. Matched 100% by the Treasury, this resulted in about $14.7 billion of total equity capital to invest. This was matched with $14.7 billion in loans from the US Treasury. Thus the total purchasing power of the legacy-securities PPIP reached only $29.4 billion, a fraction of what was originally envisaged. Of this, about $16 billion had been invested in eligible assets and cash equivalents, pending investment. Of this, about $13.5 billion had gone into non-agency RMBSs. However, only 11% of this was subprime, 45% was Alt-A, and 38% was prime. The median prices paid as a proportion of face value were about 55%, 63%, and 80% respectively. The US Treasury reported rates of return of the eight funds ranging from 9% to 66% per year.[14] Clearly, private investors were not dumb, kept well away from most of the really toxic stuff, charged a decent haircut on what they did buy, and made a good profit. What a true trillion-dollar scheme would have done is not clear (the above figures are based on a marginal program able to pick off the best deals for the few investors).

The Obama administration had backed itself into a corner. It had made it abundantly clear that government-supervised bankruptcy, i.e. receivership, of any big risky insolvent bank was ruled out. Instead of a judgment day when the good and the bad in banking finally got separated, the administration faced a perpetual groundhog day. Instead of breaking banks up and leaving the valuation of toxic assets until later (and not overpaying) it faced an endless struggle to price toxic assets (risking overpayment). Then the administration so alienated voters that it was forced into proposing a scheme that did not require the approval of Congress, but that ended up offering big subsidies in the shape of cheap loans and long-term high profits to persuade investors—hedge funds and private equity firms—to buy toxic assets and to encourage banks to be willing to sell. This would have become political dynamite as the public cottoned on, and so even this scheme was eventually ruled out politically. Again, the US Treasury took to claiming that the mere announcement of the PPIP so reassured investors that the prices of certain MBSs increased, and that banks were raising capital privately and making such schemes less necessary anyway.

The premise of the PPIP was that the underlying problem was illiquidity. However, if property markets had experienced a price bubble that had collapsed bringing MBS prices down with it, the issue was solvency, and a very different strategy to that of the PPIP would be needed. Meanwhile—and as another example of the opportunities being generated by the interactions across schemes, this time benefiting governments—the lax stress tests and the enthusiasm of the private sector for bank shares because of all the moral hazard, relieved the pressure to sell assets. In return, at least for a while, the PPIP pumped bank-stock prices which improved stress test results.

The Good Bank/Bad Bank model

Dismayed at what was going on, a number of economists argued that policy-makers should stop trying to value toxic assets, and instead reorganize the ownership claims of banks. As Bulow and Klemperer put it: 'Re-establishing a healthy banking system is crucial, but doing so through the purchase of toxic assets is costly, inefficient, and risky.'[15]

A range of ways was proposed for breaking old failed banks into 'good' and 'bad' new banks. Just setting up a 'bad bank' was no panacea. In Germany, a

€200 billion 'bad bank' plan was delayed because of political difficulties. The German government did not want to transfer the risk of losses to taxpayers without first punishing shareholders, but this conflicted with a desire not to nationalize any more German banks by wiping out the equity owners. Just two German banks offloaded toxic assets into 'bad banks' in 2010, at only a small discount to book value. In February 2010, the EU approved Ireland's 'bad bank' scheme, so that five Irish financial institutions could offload about €80 billion of loans linked to property to its 'National Asset Management Agency', NAMA. Anglo Irish alone transferred €23 billion of loans at an average discount of 43%. The hit to Anglo Irish's capital was topped up by Irish taxpayers. The UK set up something akin to a bad bank in the shape of UK Asset Resolution (UKAR) to wind down the toxic assets of Northern Rock and Bradford & Bingley. In late 2011 there was talk of a Spanish bad bank, but stronger Spanish banks were against it. Some had already formed their own bad-bank divisions and argued it would make it harder to take over failed banks and shrink the banking sector. The Spanish government would also have to be tapped for funds at a time when it was struggling with sovereign debt difficulties.

More interesting proposals linked the structure of ownership across a new 'good bank' and a new 'bad bank', both derived from an old failed bank, to leave more of the loss on the shoulders of the original owners.[16] The trick was to give to creditors in the new bad bank any equity of the new good bank. The new good bank would have a decent cushion of capital, while the new bad bank would have the same amount of capital, and be as solvent, as the original failed bank—no more, no less.

The new bad bank would get all the original debt claims of the old bank and all the toxic assets; there would be no need to purchase or guarantee toxic assets, and unsecured bank creditors would not get a government guarantee. The new bad bank would not be able to lend or buy any new assets. Its job would simply be to manage down its portfolio, extracting as much value as possible for the new bad bank's owners, at a pace to minimize systemic risk.

The new good bank would get all the insured bank deposits and the non-toxic assets of the old failed bank. Only the new good bank could raise new capital from the market or from the government, or be allowed government guarantees of new borrowing or lending. If a government wished to protect categories of unsecured bank creditors (arguing financial stability or fairness), the government could top up an undercapitalized new bank with more government equity, raising the value of the claims of old creditors at the point of insolvency, or the government could simply make a cash payment to the old bank. Apart from these two possible injections of cash, the new good bank/bad bank would be a low-cost solution.

If, subsequently, the toxic assets fell in value or never recovered, the new bad bank would be allowed to enter standard bankruptcy procedures. Its shareholders and unsecured creditors would have the value of their holdings wiped out. Depositors, now sitting in the well-capitalized good bank, would not feel the urge to run. Via their equity stake, the holders of the old bank's liabilities would be fully compensated for the liquidation value of their claims. To put it more plainly, if the old bank were simply liquidated, what would the non-guaranteed creditors be entitled to in law? It was fair and equitable that they got this amount—no more, no less. The original shareholders—of, say, Bank of America, Citigroup, Anglo Irish, and a wide range of others—would be wiped out, but that was the situation they would have faced anyway had such banks stayed as integrated wholes and their governments refused to save them.

The only reason that owners of failed banks were not getting their just deserts was because of worries that the whole banking system would be taken down if they were singled out and punished. The new bank/old bank idea was about getting rid of this unfair bargaining position. And it had other advantages too. Instead of elaborate and easily-lobbied judgments about the value of toxic assets, these assets could be wound down later at values closer to their fundamental values. The problems with guarantees would be removed too, especially the weakened incentive to monitor and extract value from toxic assets, since the new bad banks, no longer protected on the downside, would have an incentive to maximize value of toxic assets. Moral hazard would be reduced, because in the future investors would monitor and discipline much more rigorously than in the past and allocate capital more carefully. The new good bank would be left with a clean balance sheet. The uncertainty of dealing with the new good bank would be much lower than dealing with an unstructured original bank. With the *stocks* of existing bank assets and liabilities decoupled from the *flows* of new lending and borrowing, good banks would have an incentive to lend.

Whether or not a good bank/bad bank approach would have been better than what we saw we will never know. Perhaps the more interesting question is why some rescue approaches were promoted, sometimes over and over again, even though they were getting nowhere, and others were not even brought under the public spotlight. There are four main reasons why good bank/bad bank thinking got nowhere, even in policy discussion.

First, was the problem of capture. Killing off the unsecured bank creditors, especially in the US, in favour of taxpayers was never on the political cards. The US administration seemed to have particular difficulty with the notion that one could save banking without saving a particular group of bankers and bank owners. As early as possible, large organized unsecured bank creditors pulled rescue thinking off in the direction of schemes that were more generous to themselves. The losers—taxpayers—were dispersed. Early disorganization also made the US administration vulnerable to capture.

Second, legal issues might have made some parts of the good-bank/bad-bank solution less workable than the theory suggests. In particular, some of the key legal requirements would have to be in place in advance (investors could otherwise argue that they invested on the basis of a contract that was now being *ex post* renegotiated). Such things are easier to do in a calm period than in a crash.

Third, there was path dependency in policy-making. What was possible depended in part on what rescue measures had already taken place. Could the benefits derived from early rescue programmes be removed from the liquidation values of banks being closed down to leave only what the liquidation values would have been without such programmes? Could shareholders (including taxpayers) have their stakes in banks wiped out?

Fourth, international coordination was needed. After the US bailed out unsecured bank creditors, the eurozone struggled to get its unsecured bank creditors punished because of the fear that it would trigger panic. Punishing unsecured creditors had to be done all at once globally, not bank by bank, country by country.

So, Did the Bank Rescue Work and How Did It Work?

In order to evaluate the effectiveness of the bank rescue, we need appropriate counterfactuals. If the only counterfactual is a financial system collapse, anything looks good against that. The Congressional Oversight Panel spelt the logic out: 'Evaluating the wisdom and success of these efforts requires a broader understanding of the basic choices available to policymakers during this crisis.'[17] Yet, by the end of 2009, it had concluded: 'Failure to articulate clear goals or to provide specific measures of success of the program, make it hard to reach an overall evaluation.'[18] The lack of clear goals and *ex ante* metrics had a certain logic. By 2012, goals could be articulated in ways that were closer to what had actually happened, avoiding reference to clearing bad assets off balance sheets (a goal that the administration would have made key in early 2009, and on which it would have failed) and emphasizing the role of private capital (which would never have been articulated in early 2009 but on which a modicum of success could later be attributed).

One way to measure success is by looking at credit and risk spreads. From its record high of 364 basis points in October 2008, the LIBOR–OIS spread fell to about 100 basis points in early 2009 and to just 13 basis points by mid-November 2009 (in mid-2012 it was revealed that this had, in part, been manipulated). The TED spread fell back to pre-crisis levels too. For many borrowers, excessive spreads took the cost of funding above their return on capital and also generated adverse selection problems. Getting the spreads down was therefore vital to both reviving credit and allocating it efficiently. Financing constraints were one, but not the only, factor driving high spreads, so reviving funding markets was critical. On such metrics, policymakers succeeded. Yet, what did falling spreads mean? If the spreads on the CDSs of major banks fell because investors believed that these banks were not going to be allowed to fail, stability was being purchased at the cost of future moral hazard. A banking system registered itself as 'healthier' in the short run only because it was riskier in the long run.

What about success as judged by lending? This is problematic because it is difficult to separate the failure to supply credit from the collapse in the demand for credit. A paradoxical attitude to banks set in. Because of mass deleveraging, loan delinquency rates had risen dramatically, many balance sheets had collapsed, and the number of potential borrowers had fallen. If banks leant, they risked weakening further their own balance sheets. Moreover, even if banks expanded credit, they faced high levels of customer payback, which pulled the credit figures down anyway. Much rescue effort also got absorbed in ways that did not impact lending. A chunk of recapitalization made good the wealth of owners of failed banks, notably unsecured bondholders, and *ex post* insurance of old lending that had gone wrong was a blunt way to encourage new lending. Financial firms used earnings to improve their balance sheets and not to lend. A desire to pay back government support and escape government strictures also made banks unwilling to lend.

Small and medium-sized businesses—critical to economic recovery in past recessions (because they tend to employ more people relative to their turnover than big firms)—were hit especially hard because of their greater reliance on borrowing from banks. Large businesses generate internally most of the cash they need to invest, and so they were relatively well-cushioned from disruptions in banking. They also benefited from QE. In the US, only about 5% of the TARP money targeted small businesses and consumer lending. In the UK, the government injected capital and liquidity far more than was needed to fund bank lending to real businesses. Yet in late 2011 banks were failing to hit the few lending targets they had been set for small and medium-sized firms. For example, under the terms of the UK's APS, LBG and RBS agreed on lending targets. The temporary 'recovery' in house prices in early 2010 helped to reach the mortgage target, but this hardly suggested success. The business investment target proved more difficult to hit, and the two banks fell short by about a combined £30 billion. A scheme called 'Merlin', mutually agreed between UK banks and the government, was meant to ease government pressure on bank bonuses in exchange for more lending. The banks got more of what they wanted, but in terms of lending, whereas HSBC hit its target for UK businesses, others did not. This suggests that it would have made more sense to give loan guarantees directly to small and medium-sized enterprises (SMEs) and perhaps even a subsidy. As it took majority stakes, or complete ownership, of a number of huge failed banks, the UK government should have announced plans to break them into smaller and more manageable units, but it missed the opportunity.

Another way to think of success or failure of rescue is to look at its costs. According to the IMF, at its peak in May 2009, $11 trillion of financing had been made available to support financial firms, comprising a little over $9 trillion of central-bank and government support in the US, the UK, and the eurozone (about half of it in the US), and $1.6 trillion in emerging economies. Globally, about $1.2 trillion had been provided in capital injections, $2.5 trillion had been provided in the form of liquidity provision, $1.9 trillion had been set aside for asset purchase schemes, and $4.6 trillion was in the form of guarantees. It was all too easy to portray these large figures as 'costs' to taxpayers.[19] Yet such figures represented maximum possible exposures. Many guarantees would never be called upon, most liquidity facilities would be reversed, a proportion of loans would be repaid, and a proportion lost, and governments would pick up fees on their guarantees and make gains and losses on their capital injections. Even larger figures appeared in the media based on the multiple-counting of government loans that were on a revolving basis.

Rescue costs are usually minor in comparison to the costs of crash-induced recessions. For example, if we take the difference between the actual path of output and some estimate of what that path would have been without the crash (usually the trend rate of growth),[20] the crash was associated with about $4 trillion of lost global output in 2009 alone. This was way beyond any official measures of the real resource costs of the bank rescue. Even an apparently expensive rescue might save a lot more, in terms of otherwise irrecoverably lost economic activity, than it might eventually cost. To complicate matters, if the US and other major economies were already in recession at the end of 2007 and heading towards big economic losses anyway, it is difficult to decipher from casual observation how much of the total real economic loss was a result of economic failures before the crash, 'caused' by the crash, or consequent on failures of policymakers in their handling of the crash. No doubt, apportioning the relative blame will give many an economic historian much to chew on in years to come.

The top three most costly bailouts over 2007–2009, in terms of direct fiscal costs as a percentage of GDP, were Iceland (13%), the Netherlands (12.5%), and the UK (9%).[21] At about 5%, the US came about halfway down the list of countries in trouble. A large proportion of such costs constituted transfers, which were not the same as the direct using up of real resources (both have an impact, but in very different ways). The measured costs for countries like the US were kept lower than in many past financial crises because of: a much greater ability to support financial systems indirectly through expansionary monetary and fiscal policy; the direct purchase of assets to support asset prices; and the ability to take huge contingent liabilities onto government balance sheets. However, all these indirect costs mounted up and significantly increased the burden of public sector debt and contingent liabilities. Early estimates suggest, as a percentage of yearly GDP, an increase in the public sector debt over 2007–2011 of about 80% in Iceland, 50% in Ireland and Latvia, 30% in Denmark, and about 25% in the US and in the UK.[22]

This still does not capture all the costs. Huge risks were also shouldered by taxpayers in all kinds of hidden ways. The Federal Reserve and the FDIC ended up exposed to potentially much higher losses than the US Treasury ever was through the TARP. The loans of the US Treasury, Federal Reserve, and the FDIC were the out-of-thin-air equivalents of the shadow banking system, with the Fed itself becoming a bit like a (low-return) hedge fund. The Fed got small positive returns in exchange for the occasional massive loss that would transmogrify into burden for taxpayers. Even if huge losses did not materialize, this did not make the returns reasonable. Enumerating—as Obama, Geithner, and others did—the fees paid and the capital returned without mentioning potential losses was the equivalent of an insurance company listing its income and conveniently forgetting to mention the hundreds of billions, if not trillions, of losses it would incur if things went wrong. If the banks did not quickly crash again, Obama, Geithner, and others would look good however poor the quality of the rescue. If disaster was avoided only because of newly injected moral hazard, the returns are even less reasonable.

Why did the US Treasury feel obliged to put its balance sheet and those of the Fed and of the FDIC at the service of financial institutions like never before? One reason was the lack of financial firepower. By the spring of 2009, of the $700 billion put aside to rescue banks, no more than about $100 billion to $150 billion was still available (subsequently, the funds that were repaid to TARP boosted what was available, but this was not known about in early 2009). This tight financial constraint on what was possible was, to some extent, caused by the early parts of the bailout, especially the failings over AIG, which had left the US electorate feeling jittery over what they saw as the bailout of profligate bankers. However, it was mainly caused by the lack of willingness of Congress to make the rescue pot any bigger in the first place. If Congress did not want to stump up enough to support a more thorough and radical financial rescue, the only option left was to 'leverage' what was available. The expected cost of the risk that the US government was taking on was huge, but it was hard to measure, and it was difficult for the media to get worked up about something that they could not see. Critically, the Treasury and Federal Reserve did not need the clearance of Congress to create loans and loan guarantees and expand their balance sheets.

In principle we tax the rich and redistribute to the poor. In financial crises we do the opposite. All bank bailouts involve huge wealth redistributions from taxpayers and those who prudently saved and invested to those who took excessive risks. The economist Luigi Zingales was more forthright than most, describing the US bailout as 'the largest welfare program for corporations and their investors ever created in the history of humankind', and the huge redistributions of wealth it rested upon as 'a premeditated pillage of defenceless taxpayers by powerful lobbies'[23]—by which, presumably, he was referring to all the super-low interest rates that redistributed wealth from sober savers to recovering lenders, capital injections that made bank owners whole, the QE that boosted the value of assets, moral hazard that sparked new life into a string of zombie banks, and the numerous instances of overly generous payment.

Many of the costs went unrecorded on government accounts. For example, in the US, the net interest margin on the loans made by stress-tested banks went from about 2.1% in 2006 to 3.0% (even allowing for rising nonaccruals); when the Fed slashed its rates, the rates banks had to pay to fund their activities fell further than the rates they charged. A difference of nearly 1% was enough to generate an extra $70 billion of income per year from mortgage customers. In the UK, when wholesale rates fell by about 1%, RBS trimmed its mortgage rates by about half of this, such that its mortgage profit margin rose from 2.54% in early 2009 to 3.02% in early 2010, or about £900 on a £200,000 mortgage.[24] By being able to borrow very cheaply from government, banks did not have to pay more in order to borrow from the public.

Over its life, the CPP disbursed $205 billion in capital to just over 700 financial institutions, including over 300 small and community banks. However, the top 20 recipients under CPP, TIP, and SSFI took 89% of the $319.5 billion that such programmes disbursed.[25] For those that were big and 'systemically significant' and, best of all, failing, their luck was in. Thus the capital programs fed slugs of public subsidy to the biggest prior offenders, reinforced the notion of 'Too Big To Fail', stoked moral hazard, and increased the risk of crashes later. To escape rebuke, the obvious excuse was that by 2011 many of the banks that had been such a poor deal for taxpayers in late 2008 were now turning out a 'good', or at least better, deal. This does not wash. First, it does not alter the loss that the US government made relative to what it could have paid. Second, many of those now turning a profit were doing so on the back of high levels of moral hazard, super-low interest rates, GSE purchases, and QE. Third, the counter-factual is the healthier set of banks that would have expanded to replace the likes of Citigroup or Bank of America if those had been less generously treated. Fourth, many banks were still not lending.

One of the more curious phenomena boosting banks' profits was the Treasury rescue of Fannie Mae and Freddie Mac, estimated to cost the US taxpayer approximately $291 billion up to fiscal year 2009[26] and $389 billion up to fiscal year 2019.[27] This big loss to taxpayers meant that other financial institutions did not have to take toxic asset losses themselves. Even better, those who had previously written down their MBSs, could book an accounting gain. In effect, losses under one programme (the rescue of the GSEs) were being booked as a gain on another programme (TARP). Thus, when the US Treasury announced the return of $68 billion of TARP money by ten banks on 9 June 2009, it allowed Obama to announce: 'As this money is returned, we'll see our national debt lessened by $68 billion—billions of dollars that this generation will not have to borrow and future generations will not have to repay.'[28] Yet government funds had simply gone on a round trip from the US Treasury to Fannie Mae and Freddie Mac, to TARP recipients, and back to the Treasury via TARP repayments.[29]

In March 2009, the Congressional Budget Office estimated the lifetime cost of the headline TARP at about $356 billion. By January 2010, it had revised this down to about $99 billion. A few months later, it was estimating that the US Treasury would about break even on the loans to banks but lose on the housing and car-finance components. At perhaps 0.5% of US GDP, the cost of TARP was much lower than the cost of the bailout of the S&L crisis in the 1980s. In contrast, according to an IMF study of 40 financial crises, the average costs of resolving past financial crises in industrial countries was 15% of GDP, split roughly 50:50 between the costs of recapitalizing banks and the cost of asset purchases and debt-relief programmes.[30] As a percentage of GDP this was many times the final registered cost of the TARP. Previous crisis management had cost Finland, Japan, South Korea, Mexico, and Turkey multiples of TARP costs (up to 32% of GDP in the case of Turkey). Norway and Sweden had managed to keep the taxpayer costs of mending their banking messes in the 1990s to 3% and 4% of GDP respectively.[31] The low measured cost of the TARP sits incongruously next to a financial system stuffed full with large failed banks facing the biggest global financial crisis since at least the 1930s. The IMF's estimated bank write-downs from the start of the crisis through to 2010 peaked at $2.8 trillion.[32] With the improving economy in early 2010, this was reduced to $2.3 trillion by April 2010.[33] But this still meant that there was a large loss that somebody had to absorb. If the TARP had not absorbed it, what, and who, had?

In the US, financial firms became the source of much-celebrated dividend- and warrant-related income for the government, and banks paid back their capital injections early and returned to making good profit and to paying big bonuses. Yet lending was collapsing and unemployment rising. Were financial markets and bank shareholders rationally pricing in the eventual macroeco- nomic recovery—since financial markets usually 'turn first'—such that surging bank share values were a sign that was good for all? Or were they simply responding to the fact that big banks had come out of the financial fray far less touched by the policymaker's scalpel than they could have believed possible in the darkest moments of the crash? Indeed, whilst the big banks were taking the plaudits, it was small- and medium-sized banks that were toppling; no US bank failed in 2005 and 2006 and only three did in 2007, but the numbers jumped to 25 in 2008 and 140 in 2009. Other than in September and October 2008, these were mostly smaller banks.[34]

In the US, most of the apparent improvement was because of bank share prices rising because banks had driven a soft deal out of the government. The TARP, for all the angst it engendered at the time, turned out to be favourable for the administration because it ended up being structured, in large part, as bank equity investments. It was not that political wisdom led to the establish- ment of the TARP that saved the banking system. Rather, it was the saving of banks by moral hazard and other means that revived the value of bank equity which, in turn, made the TARP look like the product of wise political thinking. And here was the source of another bundle of ironies. On the TARP's own terms, the cost of the most high-profile part of the US rescue machine was very low. Indeed, by April 2012, the US Treasury was claiming that the TARP had realized a $19 billion profit. Yet, the Congressional Oversight Panel concluded that the TARP became so unpopular that: '[T]he greatest conse- quence of the TARP may be that the government has lost some of its ability to respond to financial crises.'[35] Yet the public's distaste for the TARP had nothing to do with its true failings—its legacy of hidden moral hazard. And the public's distaste hardly ever stretched to the much bigger costs that did not show up on the government's balance sheet.

A major factor in reviving profitability was the free or heavily subsidized government insurance at the heart of the banking system—the central bank acting as lender of last resort, and the Treasury acting as market maker of last resort and as recapitalizer of last resort. We can get some idea of the value of this by comparing the credit ratings of banks with and without support.[36] After the US stress tests, the CRAs boosted credit ratings because government had signalled its willingness to be the implicit guarantor that no big banks would be allowed to fail. In February 2009, Moody's argued: 'In this environment, the senior debt and deposit ratings of systemically important banks are naturally less sensitive than they would otherwise be to changes in their intrinsic financial strength.'[37] On the basis of 'a very high probability of systemic support' Moody's upgraded the deposits and senior debt issued by the six largest US banks relative to their unsupported, or 'stand-alone', ratings by: five notches for Bank of America; four notches for Citibank; one notch for Goldman Sachs; two notches for JPMorgan Chase; two notches for Morgan Stanley; and four notches for Wells Fargo. S&P upgraded Bank of America, Citigroup, Goldman Sachs, and Morgan Stanley by three, four, two, and three notches respectively. In 2007, at the global level the difference between supported and stand-alone ratings was 1.68 notches. By 2009, the difference was 2.89 notches.[38] Not only did CRAs factor in government support, but the implied support increased significantly over the period of the crash.

If we map ratings onto yields paid on banks' bonds, this translates into a 'global' implied bank subsidy of $37 billion in 2007, rising to $220 billion in 2008, and to $250 billion in 2009.[39] Incidentally, this is far higher than the cost of sorting out the eurozone crisis, where the very same banks were forcing up the cost of borrowing for troubled countries that were getting the total opposite credit-rating treatment. Some even went as far as to describe this as an ongoing world financial plague.[40] The UK case was even more plagued than most: the credit rating difference in the UK went from 1.56 notches in 2007 to 4.00 notches in 2009, and the implied fiscal subsidy from £11 billion in 2007 to £59 billion in 2008 and £107 billion in 2009 (falling back to under £50 billion in 2011). The value of government protection was greater than banks' annual profits, which approximated just under £50 billion before the crash; without government bankrolling the banking system, it would have been broke.

In the UK, the average ratings difference was 3.5 notches for small banks and up to nearly 5 notches for big banks. No wonder then that in the UK, 90% of the implied subsidy went to just five banks. As Haldane put it: 'On these metrics, the too-big-to-fail problem results in a real and on-going cost to the taxpayer and a real and on-going windfall for the banks.'[41] This was happening even as savers with these banks were being paid peanuts, and millions were facing harsh austerity measures and job losses. Governments had breathed new life into moribund, and sometimes even dead banks. In return, big banks went straight back to business as usual, extracting much of the value of the state support in bonuses. *The Economist* described it as 'part of the monstrous bargain the bankers have extracted from the state'.[42]

For all the limitations of rescue efforts, a massive disaster would have ensued without this monstrous bargain. The trade-off was a huge economic depression now or greater risks from moral hazard later. The disaster averted hardly registers in the imagination of the electorate. Or perhaps we should give the electorate more credit for understanding, intuitively, that a rescue should not just be judged according to the disaster averted but according to its quality relative to a baseline of how a rescue could have been done and the benefits big banks extracted from governments.

With policy conditioned on denying the fundamental insolvency of several big banks, there was a 'gamble-for-resurrection' and 'beggar-thy-neighbour' quality to much US rescue thinking. If all went well, the electorate would not notice the huge risks taken on by the government. If all went badly, and some of the risks crystallized as losses, the Fed would have to seek rescue from the US Treasury. If, as likely, such help was not forthcoming, the Fed would have no option but to expand the monetary base to avoid its own insolvency. That would lead to inflation. The ultimate payers of today's rescue would be future taxpayers, the jobless, those who lost on account of spending-programme cuts, and the holders of nominally-denominated liabilities of the US government (including monetary liabilities of the Fed and US Treasury bills and bonds) as inflation ate their wealth away. But that was all off in the future. Meanwhile, a 'soft' rescue allowed US banks to survive by taking, or holding onto, market share they would otherwise have lost to banks based in tougher jurisdictions. A race to the regulatory bottom between the US and other countries had characterized the years before the crash. The US bank bailout was cut from the same piece of beggar-thy-neighbour cloth. Injections of moral hazard and a barrage of rescue efforts that transferred wealth from taxpayers and savers to banks helped banks survive.

Japan's 'two lost decades' demonstrate that it is not a good idea to live in denial that banks are fundamentally insolvent.[43] Japan's recapitalization needed to be at least two and a half times bigger than it actually was in 1999.[44] Ironically, Japan's deposit-insurance fund contained untapped capacity sufficient to do the job had political backlash not prevented it. The Japanese government denied the scale of Japan's problems for a decade. Similarly, the resolution of the Nordic banking crisis—often thought of as best practice—required first the complete recognition of losses, the write-down of equity, public ownership and strict conditionality, and the contraction of balance sheets and branch networks; the only capital injection was in Finland. Similarly, the lesson of the S&L crisis was that to get private capital to return, an early and aggressive write-down of the value of the assets held by the government was needed.

It was only after Japan did a thorough independent audit, acknowledged the losses, and published estimates of the level of capital needed, that its financial system started to recover. Until then, allowing wild speculation about what was going on was worse than just coming clean. The Japanese took the—wrong— view that free market pressures would force banks to come clean. Early on in the crisis, the US seemed about to repeat the same mistake, with no effort to conduct an audit, and the notion that the problems had been contained. That changed with the stress tests. The only problem was that the stress tests were designed (if that is not too strong a word) not to allow any significant banks to fail. Liquidity disguised the true loss of wealth. Just like in Japan, politicians seemed more concerned about preventing bank collapses than in building a vibrant credit supply. The latter might have meant more radical structural changes that would have led to much bigger losses for bank owners.

In the long run, it is sustained economic recovery that helps banks to recapitalize. In both the Japanese and the Nordic[45] banking crises, export growth drove the macroeconomic growth that eventually helped to recapitalize the banks. Japan had the benefit of large and growing economies (notably China and the US in the mid-2000s) to help pull its recovery—and recapitalization— out the bag. By 2011, the US and the UK, and Ireland and Spain and others, were much more dependent than Japan had been on domestic economic growth to revive bank profitability, yet many politicians seemed happy enough to kill off domestic growth.

The way the bank rescue was done, especially in the US, but also in a range of other countries including the UK, removed the only natural predator of banks—the market. Moral hazard was not a side-effect of the bank rescue, it was central to the way the rescue had worked. A victory of sorts had been won, but the using up of all moral hazard possibilities could be done just the once. As the Greek general Pyrrhus once put it after a famous but costly victory: 'If we win one more battle . . . we shall be totally destroyed.'[46]

Part III
Beyond

Return from Slump, and the Jobless and Joyless Recovery

Recession and Economic Damage

Many traps lay in wait on the labyrinthine path back to stability. Some were left there long ago, others had been more recently laid. It took a touch of madness to gaze into the future and to predict how the journey might end. It was even more foolhardy, perhaps, to commit to paper words that, in years to come, will be held up to pity, stretched out, and prodded by hindsight—that most painful of human tormentors. The days ahead will be far wiser judges and probably not the kindest. Nevertheless, I was inspired, perhaps made overconfident, and certainly reckless, by the likes of Kenneth Rogoff, who quickly got to the point: 'All the major regions remain trapped in post-crisis macroeconomic strategies that are either inconsistent, incoherent, or both.'[1] Others were blunter still: A 'breath-taking mixture of suicidal irresponsibility and farcical incoherence'[2] was one of the more candid assessments of European policy-making. The next six chapters look at how policy-makers responded in the aftermath of the crash. We start with the economic slump and attempts to revive economies. As we proceed, we will compare and contrast the recession with previous crash-related recessions, especially that of the 1930s.

The Great Disenchantment didn't start with a bang, but with a whimper. The US economy turned its back on excess and pointed its nose towards recession in late 2005. Housing and construction went first. Other sectors followed quickly. By December 2007 the whole US economy was in recession. A range of industrial countries were next. By mid-2008—before the collapse of Lehman Brothers—most leading forecasters were predicting that global output would shrink by up to 2% in 2009, the first time such a thing had happened since the Second World War. Even without a banking crash, there was going to be a really nasty recession. And if there was a nasty recession, given the fragility of the banking system, there would be a banking crash.

As a sign of just how desperate things must have been, at the end of August 2008 the UK's new finance minister, Alistair Darling, broke cover and warned that matters were 'arguably the worst they've been in 60 years' and, for good measure, 'it's going to be more profound and long-lasting than people thought'.[3] There are few instances in politics when prescience gets its due reward, and this was not about to be one of them. Darling was stung from behind, anonymously, from within the prime minister's office. In the finest traditions of political damage-limitation exercises, the act got nearly as much media coverage as Darling's initial utterances—which, of course, drew even more attention to them.

After the crash, it quickly became conventional wisdom that the banking system had pulled the global economy down. It was also the other way around. A long string of debt-fuelled excesses had run their course, turned and gone into reverse. The unwinding of enormous imbalances on the balance sheets of the private sector was anyway going to suck the economic lifeblood out of whole economies, destroy swathes of banking capital, inflict fiscal calamity on some, and generate a slow and painful economic recovery for many. Politicians heaped blame on bankers. They had to. The alternative involved taking responsibility for their own acts of folly. They were not about to do that.

Many worried that the global economy was about to repeat the experience of the early 1930s. The fears were well-founded. When Reinhart and Reinhart— surely the most emotionally drained academic household in the land—gathered big piles of their data into a composite 'crisis index' of banking, currency, sovereign debt, inflation, and stock market crises and crashes, and weighted each pile for every year by its share of world income in that year, they found that in late 2008 the world had indeed experienced by far and away the biggest financial collapse since the Second World War.[4]

The decline in global industrial production, at first, tracked that of the Great Depression, with collapses in every region of the world. By the spring of 2009 it was 13% below its recent peak.[5] In the last quarter of 2008, industrial production fell by 7% in Germany, 12% in Japan and an astonishing 22% in Taiwan. The decline in the volume of world trade replicated in less than a year what had taken two years in the early 1930s. This time (and probably that time too, but overlooked because of all the talk of protectionism) it was the fragility of global production lines that drove this. Trade finance (on which 90% of world trade depended[6]) dried up in ways that mirrored the banking-system crash: goods sat in ports as payment chains froze because of fears about counterparties; interest rates required to secure trade-related letters of credit rose precipitously; and the ability to insure flows of goods evaporated.[7] At its trough, the volume of world trade was down 20%.[8] Between the last quarter of 2008 and the first quarter of 2009, the collapse of global trade accounted for 75% and 60% of the fall in output in Japan and the eurozone respectively. In the third quarter of 2009, the GDP of Japan, in nominal terms, fell below what it had been in 1992. In China, by the start of 2009, with Christmas comfortably out of the way, half of all toy exporters were bust—a cautionary warning to the children of the world that the pain of austerity was going to be shared by them.

In 2007, net private-capital inflows into emerging economies had peaked at nearly $1.3 trillion, their highest ever. In 2008, such countries were no longer the number-one twinkle in the eyes of their financial beholders, and the flows had shrunk to a little over $600 billion. The falls were concentrated in Latin America and emerging economies in non-China Asia. Net capital flows to China hardly changed, suggesting a degree of protection because of China's hefty reserve cushions; other countries hastily scribbled a note for next time. In 2009, it was the turn of emerging Europe and the Middle East to see the biggest falls in net capital inflows. Grasping the importance of finance for flows of international trade, urgent measures were taken at the G20 summit in April 2009 to boost the supply of trade finance by some $250 billion.[9] We think of the crash of 1929 as a stock market crash and the recent crash as a banking crash. Yet, in the year to March 2009, world equity markets lost more than half their value, a much greater fall than in the early 1930s. No wonder that Eichengreen and O'Rourke observed: 'Globally we are tracking or doing even worse than the Great Depression . . . This is a Depression-sized event.'[10]

Unemployment soared. In the month Obama was inaugurated, January 2009, US job losses peaked at 800,000. By July 2009 the US had lost 6.5 million jobs since the recession began. This was on top of about 2 million extra jobs needed just to keep pace with US population growth. The total deficiency of 8.5 million jobs far exceeded the 3.5 million jobs that President Obama said his first stimulus plan would create by late 2010, itself a generous interpretation of the facts. The official estimate of US unemployment was 10%, not far short of the post-1945 peak of 10.8%. It had been 4.6% just two years before. The widest measure of labour-market underutilization—those who do not have a full-time job because of economic conditions, and not because they are sick, old, or in training—was registering 17%, one in six. The collapse of building activity in Spain and Ireland quickly pushed official unemployment rates there well into double digits. In China, 20 million migrant workers were laid off overnight. The numbers gave but a hint of the human misery beneath the statistical surface.

In the US, the paths of various categories of spending were similar in shape, although not so extreme in texture, as those experienced into and through the

Great Depression. In the mid-1920s, growing overcapacity in the automotive and other industries pushed investment into speculative investments, such that in 1927 housing investment peaked at 60% above its 1929 level. It swung to 90% below by 1933. This time, housing investment peaked in the last quarter of 2005 50% above the level when the recession began in the last quarter of 2007, and collapsed to about 40% below by mid-2009. In the mid-1920s, all forms of expenditure grew until their 1929 peaks. This time, consumer-durable expenditure was nearly flat and non-durable consumption and non-residential fixed investment were still rising. In both crashes, housing investment fell the most, followed, in order, by non-residential fixed investment, consumer durables and consumption. In both cases a financial crash was on top of a slowing economy.

The most recent comparable *global* economic contraction was during the oil crisis of the 1970s when the doubling and then doubling again of oil prices effectively wiped out a large chunk of physical capital, too energy-intensive to be economically viable at much higher energy prices—a big supply-side shock—while simultaneously transferring huge amounts of wealth from oil-dependent to oil-rich regions of the world. This time, the collapse of a global debt and property bubble was the source of loss for those who lost, and of wealth redistribution, but much of this was wealth that had only ever really existed in the imaginations of millions and, it seems, in the heads of their bankers.

In the thirst for clues as to how bad things might become, past crises became a welcome source of morbid refreshment. Reinhart and Rogoff[11] found that, on average, after past systemic banking crises, before recovering, GDP per capita fell by about 9% over about two years, unemployment rose by about 7% over about four years (that is, unemployment kept rising after the real output consequences had ended), real house prices declined by about 35% over about six years, and stock markets lost 55% of their real value over about three-and-a-half years. The IMF compared 122 past recessions in developed economies since 1960, and found that those that followed a financial bust were longer and deeper than other crises, that private investment fell even after the economy had reached a trough, and that private consumption grew more slowly than in other types of recoveries.[12] After globally-synchronized recessions, recovery took 50% longer.

Others urged caution. The current turmoil stood out as unique, and this suggested that past crises might not be such helpful guides. Averages might deceive. Cluster analysis of 28 systemic crises since 1980[13] showed that similar-looking past crises had markedly different impacts, and revealed a number of lessons.[14] First, that systemic banking crisis tended to be associated with longer and deeper contractions when accompanied by a currency crisis or when growth was low before; in the US and UK the first did not apply but the latter, correctly measured, arguably did.

Second, that systemic banking crises were *less* costly when accompanied by a sovereign debt default, usually because the debt was held by foreigners and default exported pain to them; it was difficult to imagine the US or the UK defaulting on their sovereign debt (other than by inflation), and a large portion of their sovereign debt was held domestically. Greece, Ireland, Portugal, and others ignored such scholarly insight for the time being. Third, and somewhat more tentatively, that the more global nature of the current crisis would not obviously slow recovery relative to a typical crisis in a single country; just as there was peril in numbers going in, so there might be safety in numbers coming out (so long as policymakers didn't do anything to harm recovery).

The Policy Adventure Begins

And so the great economic policy adventure began. Over the next few years, policymakers would find themselves paddling up miles of uncharted waters, with no obvious sign that a safe harbour was within reach, and with no more than hope and some lofty rhetoric to sustain them on their way. At least they knew what not to do. In the 1930s, according to President Herbert Hoover, the delirious, yet entirely conventional, advice of US Treasury Secretary Andrew Mellon had been to: 'Liquidate labor, liquidate stocks, liquidate farmers, liquidate real estate . . . it will purge the rottenness out of the system. High costs of living and high living will come down. People will work harder, live a more moral life. Values will be adjusted, and enterprising people will pick up from less competent people'.[15] A crash is nothing if not a jolly good time to moralize about those less fortunate than oneself. Back in the 1930s, according to accounts of the time, now buried by hindsight, it was 18 months before policymakers—even Keynes and Fisher—fully understood that the global economy was slipping into a deep recession. This time, many were aware of the dangers much sooner and were better primed to use fiscal and monetary policy.

In late 2008 and early 2009, in the midst of growing panic and confusion, policymakers thumbed, until their fingers were numb, any horoscope that passed itself off as an economic forecast and chose their lucky numbers. In the US the number was 787, the billions of dollars of 'discretionary' federal stimulus in the American Recovery and Reinvestment Act, ARRA, signed into law by Obama on 19 February 2009. In the early 1930s, the weighted average annual government budget deficit of two dozen or so core economies stayed below 4% of GDP; in the US, in 2009, it rose to about 13%, and other countries followed suit (in 2011, the US budget deficit was still over 10% of GDP).

However, although the combined US government budget deficit for 2009 and 2010 was about $2.5 trillion, the package of 'discretionary' measures was less than a quarter of this. Even this exaggerates. Just under $300 billion of the $787 billion was for tax breaks; only if that got spent, and not saved, would it have a stimulus effect. Then 30% was classified as spending on health and other social expenditures that countries like the UK, Germany, France, and Canada routinely spend. Finally, much of the federal stimulus was absorbed just offsetting the squeeze caused by US states balancing their budgets. In one study that properly adjusted for the declining fiscal expenditure of the 50 US states, in 2009 the aggregated federal and state pure fiscal stimulus—which includes government consumption and government gross investment but, unlike the published 'total' government expenditure figures, does not include transfers to the financial sector and automatic stabilizers such as higher unemployment benefit[16]— was close to zero. Of 29 OECD countries, the US came in the bottom third in terms of the rate of expansion of its aggregate pure fiscal expenditure.[17] With not much aggregate pure fiscal expenditure at work, there was not much of a standard Keynesian fiscal multiplier at work in the US.

Under severe duress the US had stretched its fiscal sinews; yet natural economic stabilizers—many not available in the 1930s—and the collapse of tax revenues, played by far a greater role than discretionary fiscal policy. As a corollary, the increase in the US budget deficit had more to do with the economic mistakes of those who went before Obama than with anything 'discretionary' he ever did. But for the ARRA, the US would have been in an even worse economic mess, but the discretionary stimulus was quickly over, and so had little lasting impact on unemployment.

Similarly, when in April 2009 the G20 calculated that the total global fiscal 'stimulus' by 2020 would be $5 trillion, most of this was a reflection of how much public finances would deteriorate as economies collapsed. To rub the point in: as a percentage of GDP, the *discretionary* fiscal stimuli of Germany and Canada were bigger than that of the UK. In the UK, the finance and the property sector accounted for half of the increase in UK tax receipts between 2002–2003 and 2007–2008, and so the fiscal position of the UK government suffered proportionally much greater damage than that of countries with a smaller financial sector. As the UK's deficit soared for all the wrong reasons, Prime Minister Brown took to claiming that the UK 'led the world' on fiscal stimulus. The truth was a little more damning. Meanwhile, China unleashed a stimulus package equal to about 15% of its GDP; as we will see in Chapter 11, neither was this all that it seemed.

Why was the US discretionary stimulus so small and slanted towards tax cuts, which, for each dollar of extra deficit they created, had less impact on the economy than spending programmes? Perhaps, if Obama could have proven that the bank rescue would cost so little (at least up-front and ignoring moral hazard), he could have asked for more. But the information on the bailout was not yet in. It probably would have made no difference. All requests for money had to go through Congress, where baying Republican voices—'liquidate, liquidate, liquidate'—were against even the initial modest stimulus. If Obama had demonstrated convincingly that a recession caused by a financial crash was likely to be much worse than the forecasts in late 2008 were predicting, Congress still would not have authorized a bigger stimulus or a smaller tax-cut component. Instead of saying that the discretionary stimulus was too small and blaming it on his Republican opponents, inexplicably Obama declared that it was big enough and that the economy was on track when it decidedly was not. When a supposedly large stimulus failed to revive the economy, Obama was accused of being profligate; in truth, if anything, he hadn't done enough, and was taking the rap for someone else's failure. Others, like Brown in the UK, sought credit for 'stimulus' that was really only a mark of their own past failings. Sometimes politics can be so cruel.

The Challenges and Limitations of Monetary Policy in a Crash

Because such a high proportion of financial activity in the US was mark-to-market and registered its losses quickly, the US Federal Reserve got a strong incentive to cut policy interest rates, and did so quite vigorously from late 2007 into early 2008. What had taken Japan six years in the 1990s, the US did in two. It would be September 2008 before rates would be cut quite so enthusiastically anywhere else. The problem was that in mid-2008 many central banks were worrying that output growth was slowing but inflation was above target. Neither did it help that their macroeconomic models poorly captured the balance-sheet consequences of collapsing housing markets. Curiously, having worried so much about deflation in the early 2000s, many central bankers were now seriously downplaying the deflationary dangers. The ECB even tweaked its rate higher as late as the summer of 2008. Japan sat on the fence; with its rates already at only 0.5%, it had little room to move one way or the other without inflicting even more pain upon itself. In the US, in October 2007 Bernanke had argued: '[I]t is not the responsibility of the Federal Reserve—nor would it be appropriate—to protect lenders and investors from the consequences of their financial decisions.'[18] His caveat was that because developments in financial markets sometimes had large spillover effects on the economy, the Fed 'must take those effects into account when determining policy'. By September 2008, the caveat was all.

It quickly became clear that policymakers had lost their main paddle and were helplessly adrift. First, interest rate cuts could not generate much new borrowing and spending in a recession involving large balance sheet readjustments; the indebted were still trying to reduce their debts, and many were rebalancing towards savings. Interest rate policy became largely about taking wealth away from those with savings and giving it to those with debt. The UK's Office for National Statistics calculated than in 2009, on account of the 0.5% base rate, in the UK alone those with debt gained about £26 billion while savers lost about £18 billion. If rates were kept super-low for a few years, the transfer to borrowers at the expense of savers could easily exceed £100 billion. Protracted very low rates harmed those about to become pensioners relying on current annuity rates, as well as future pensioners who needed to save many more years of contributions in order to get the same pension out, and companies whose pension liabilities had increased. Over a decade, the UK government had introduced a menu of incentives for savers and had increasingly put the onus on individuals to provide for themselves in retirement, only now to turn round and penalize those who had. Many had not anyway saved enough for retirement, and for them this was a double hit. The biggest losers were to be found in a largely voiceless group of older savers and the thrifty; the biggest gainers were those with the biggest debts. It is readily apparent that using interest rates as a bailout mechanism suffers from all the usual moral-hazard problems.

Second, as interest rates were cut, a range of countries approached the so-called 'zero bound' beyond which conventional policies would necessitate negative nominal interest rates. Depositors and investors would avoid this by hoarding cash. Indeed, one normally tries to keep interest rates at least a little over zero; banks need to maintain a margin between what they pay depositors and what they charge borrowers, and money market mutual funds also need rates to be at least a little bit positive if they are not to become unprofitable.

Third, the rise in uncertainty caused credit spreads, liquidity premiums, and risk premiums to rise to an extent that was impossible to offset by a fall in already-low interest rates. Thus the credit crunch amongst banks was replicated in the real economy.

Fourth, slashing interest rates to nearly zero created a perverse and inequitable effect. Banks found themselves with access to nearly free money and being encouraged, because of rising deficits, to buy government bonds that returned maybe 3% or 4%. With the rate of outflow less than the rate of inflow, like basking sharks in a bath of gently warming water, banks could profit from doing next to nothing while, over time, repairing their balance sheets on the basis of a risk-free, or close to risk-free, cash flow. If problem loans sat on banks' books waiting for this process to work its wonders, it could take many years. Yet again, rescue was via wealth transfer, from average citizens, especially savers, to banks, and did not appear on the government's books.

Fifth, it was hard to target interest rate cuts. Directly subsidizing write-downs of mortgage principal for only those in trouble might help (if we ignore the difficulties in targeting the subsidy and the dangers of moral hazard). However, it was much harder, politically, to sell than an interest rate cut, the effect of which was dispersed and weaker on those suffering mortgage problems and wasted on those who were not but which at least did not show up as a government budget line.

Sixth, there were the adverse-selection—the 'lemons'—problems that were described in Chapter 4. Interest rates lose their ability to 'clear' markets when asymmetric-information problems are biting especially hard.

Finally, just as in the early 2000s, very low interest rates subsidized capital over labour, increasing the risk of a jobless recovery.

In the UK, the lucky number was 300. As Mervyn King put it in March 2009: 'In its entire 300 year history, the Bank of England has never acted so swiftly or extensively in response to an economic downturn.'[19] In November 2008, the Bank of England reduced its policy rate by 150 basis points (compared to a normal reduction of 25 basis points). By March 2009, the rate had been reduced to just 0.50%—the lowest in the Bank of England's long and illustrious history. Officials patted themselves on the back for finally, if rather belatedly, making the grade. The Fed pushed its main policy rate to 0.25% and the ECB got as low as 1%.

Deflation and Quantitative Easing

In the US, the eurozone, and Japan—half the global economy—prices were barely rising, and wages stagnating or falling. This might be good for the bottom line of an individual firm competing in international markets. However, when synchronized across entire economies, deflation pushes up the real burden of debts, makes it more attractive to delay consumption and investment to the future when prices will be lower, and sends economies plummeting. Aggressive measures were needed to keep economies away from these whirlpools of disaster and, if some were being sucked in, to pluck them out before it was too late. By early 2009, the Fed's main policy rate needed to be minus 5–6%, way beyond the reach of conventional policy measures. The only way to relax monetary policy further would involve the unconventional approach of central banks buying longer-dated government debt and private assets, so called 'quantitative easing' (QE). One by one, a number of central banks threw the QE lifeline into the dark abyss beyond the 'zero bound', crossed their fingers and hoped.

In November 2010, Sarah Palin got the monetary logic of QE nearly right in a speech billed as all about 'economics' (I kid the reader not): 'And where, you may ask, are we getting the money to pay for all this? We're printing it out of thin air!'[20] Actually, even the printing press is superfluous. A central bank first credits its own 'electronic' account with money created ex *nihilo*, 'out of nothing'. It then uses this to purchase financial assets from banks and other financial institutions by Open Market Operations (OMO). QE is *unconventional* because standard OMO involves changing the composition of a central bank's balance sheet by reducing the holdings of some assets in order to purchase other assets while holding the size of the balance sheet fixed. Instead, as a consequence of QE, the balance sheets of some central banks expanded dramatically. In market-centred financial systems, such as in the US, the logic of QE suggested buying private assets, including MBSs. In more bank-centred economies, such as the UK and Japan, government securities were the investments of choice. Standard OMO confines itself to 'risk-free' government bonds, so QE involved qualitative easing too.

The theorized benefits of QE flow out in various directions (we'll deal with the problems of QE in Chapter 11). Investors who sell government and corporate bonds and securities to central banks end up 'long' in cash paying a very low rate of return. To rebalance their portfolios, they use the cash to buy other assets, such as equities and corporate bonds, which pushes the prices of these higher. Crucially, even when the policy interest rate is near zero, the interest rates, or their equivalents, on these assets are still positive (to compensate for the risk of lending to such firms rather than depositing cash in a central bank). By pushing the prices of these assets higher, QE pushes these interest rates lower further 'along the yield curve'. Of course, the interest rates that really matter are the ones faced by corporate borrowers, adjusted for all the risks. So long as *these* rates fall and borrowers have profitable uses for borrowing, companies invest because it is now cheaper for them to do so. If consumers feel richer because asset prices are higher, they spend more too. In late 2010, because US mortgage bonds were trading at record high prices, 30-year mortgages in the US could be locked in at 4%, a record low. By helping those in debt, QE also slows the process of deleveraging, making it less painful.

By bidding up the price of government bonds, QE reduces the interest rate payable on government debt. This makes fiscal consolidation easier and, if necessary, more gradual. As a welcome side-effect for those doing QE, portfolio rebalancing involves investors diversifying into foreign assets, and so the real value of the currency of countries doing QE falls relative to other currencies. This makes the QE country's exports more competitive. Better still, if all goes well, politicians take the credit, but if all goes wrong, central bankers take the blame.

QE can also be used to break a time-inconsistency problem. A central bank would like to convince households and firms to consume and invest by promising to hold real long-term interest rates low while households and firms pay back the loans they take out to consume and invest. However, households and firms know that, as soon as growth recovers and inflation picks up (because they boosted the economy by their borrowing, investing, and spending), central banks will raise interest rates to try to hit inflation targets. Knowing that real interest rates will not stay low as promised, households and firms will not borrow, consume, and invest in the first place, and the economy will not recover. So QE is a way to commit to low real interest rates for longer; as soon as inflation appears, it takes time for all the extra financial liquidity pumped in through QE to be drained from the system, so interest rates stay low even when inflation is higher. Of course, this requires willingness to let inflation go above inflation targets in the future.

In the first round of US QE—announced in November 2008, begun in January 2009, and extended in March 2009—the Federal Reserve bought $1.725 trillion of a range of assets, including $1.25 trillion of US MBSs, as well as government bonds. In its second round, QE2—launched in November 2010—the Fed bought $600 billion of US government bonds by June 2011 (equivalent to 4% of US GDP). The Fed's balance sheet thus rose from under $1 trillion of assets to nearly $3 trillion by mid-2011, equivalent to about 20% of US GDP. Japan's programme of QE took its central bank's balance sheet from about 21% of Japan's GDP in 2007 to about 24.5% at the end of 2010. At £75 billion, the Bank of England's first round of QE was well above expectations. It was expanded in May 2009 to £125 billion, and again in August 2009 to £200 billion; then again in late 2011 to £275 billion, in February 2012 to £325 billion, and in July 2012 to £375 billion. Under the disapproving gaze of Chancellor Merkel and the Bundesbank, the ECB set up a QE programme in May 2009, half the size of what it had originally contemplated, to buy €60 billion of covered bonds.[21] Locked inside the eurozone, countries experiencing deflation, such as Ireland and Spain, were denied their own QE. Neither was QE a policy that emerging economies could try: because of the dangers of capital flight and exchange rate risk, they needed to maintain positive real interest rates, and their central banks could not take the risk of undermining any independence they had by expanding their balance sheets.

Central banks did not know how effective QE would be. It was not the sort of experiment they ever got much of a chance to try. The UK government's 2009 budget forecast presumed that £75 billion of QE would restore a 5% shortfall in nominal GDP, perhaps 1% per year over five years. One might well ask, if £75 billion could do that, what could £200 billion, then £275 billion, £325 billion, and

£375 billion do? Of course, £75 billion did not do that, which is why it became £200 billion, then £275 billion, then £325 billion, and then £375 billion.

In November 2010, when QE2 was announced, the Fed had two years of data on QE1, and argued that this showed that QE1 had lowered the yields on ten-year Treasuries by 0.3% to 1%, most probably towards the lower end of this range. In early 2011, Janet Yellen, the Fed's vice-chair, argued that, compared to a world without QE, US inflation was 1% higher, unemployment would be about 1.5% lower in 2012, and there would be 3 million more US jobs. Nevertheless, the Fed's models presumed that QE had large effects on financial conditions, and therefore model simulations tended to show a large impact. After QE2 started, the pace of US recovery flagged, which made QE look less effective. At least the pace of inflation had climbed out of the danger zone of deflation. In July 2011, in testimony to Congress, Bernanke observed that, although recovery was slow, inflation and inflation expectations in 2010 had risen by nearly 2%, helping to avoid deflation and keeping the US away from a double-dip recession. At the end of 2011, the BIS argued that the impact of QE on US ten-year Treasuries was much lower: only about 0.21%.[22]

In the UK, in September 2011, the Bank of England published its QE impact figures: yields on five-year and ten-year Treasuries 100 basis points lower, and growth boosted by between 1.5% and 2%. The Bank of England's own analysis showed, however, that the effect on the 'risky' rate of the few companies that could borrow in bond markets was small—of the order of 0.7%—and for SMEs there was no impact. The BIS begged to differ again, arguing that the impact on the risk-free rate was much smaller, more like 0.27%, and that, contrary to those promoting more QE, the effect had declined as QE expanded.[23] Announcing the expansion of the UK's QE to £275 billion, King observed in November 2011: 'I can't guarantee that it means that bank lending will rise, but what I do believe is that it won't fall as far as it might otherwise have done.'[24]

The impact of QE was weaker than hoped, in part because it was a very imperfect way to influence households and the non-financial sector, where many problem debts lay. The impact depended on those financial institutions targeted by QE *wanting* to lend more to smaller firms and households, and on large corporations wanting to hire and invest. In general, neither of them wanted to.

In the UK, base money rose fourfold relative to GDP, reaching a peak last seen some two hundred years before (how the records were tumbling!).[25] However, M4 (a much broader notion of the money supply) grew by just 2% between the third quarter of 2009 and the third quarter of 2010. It seems the velocity of circulation of money (i.e. the average number of times a unit of money is used in a given time period) simply fell to offset the rise in reserves. In the US the 'money multiplier' (i.e. the ratio between the monetary base and the money supply) fell from about 1.6 just before the crash to less than 1.0: Base money was making its way into banks, but they hoarded a lot of it. Survey after survey showed that firms were holding back on investment because of weak demand and of consumer deleveraging, and that small businesses could not borrow even if they wanted to. Instead of investing, many large firms took the opportunity to retire more expensive debt and to build their cash reserves so as to protect themselves against losses on previously-made loans and against the risks of illiquidity. The response was similar to what happened when Japan tried QE in the 1990s to save itself from the consequences of its balance sheet crash. Economies trying QE were living in what Keynes called a 'liquidity trap', where daily routine consisted in 'pushing on a string' in the hope that one day the trap would release and escape would be at hand.

If the impact caused per unit of QE was low but at least in the right direction, this may suggest that QE should have been bigger. However, central banks had fanfared the total QE numbers, as if somehow the choice of a number was much more scientific than it really was. If the Fed and others had instead proposed a target impact (much as is the case with standard OMOs)—such as a rate of inflation or a price level or a rate of nominal output growth or a level of nominal output—there would have been more room for political manoeuvre on the total QE number. Finally, in November 2011, Bernanke took the string between his teeth and hinted of a third round of QE for the US in 2012.

In 'A Treatise on Money'[26] Keynes described such activities as OMO 'à outrance'—'to excess'. Keynes, being a roundly educated man and playing a key role in the UK Treasury during and after the First World War, was no doubt familiar with the term 'attaque à outrance'—from its common usage to describe the military strategy, before and during the earlier parts of the First World War, of overwhelming the enemy. In 2008–2011, central bankers were fighting an all-out financial war. From the trenches they were lobbing anything they could get their hands on to keep the enemy at bay.

If the fight got desperate, actions lay beyond QE that might only become palatable in a truly intractable deflation. Policymakers could try to push up expectations of inflation, and not just push down long-term yields. For example, the Fed could promise that it would hold interest rates low for a long time whatever happened to inflation; this would be very risky if it triggered asset price bubbles, and so it would be hard to commit to it credibly. Or the Fed could adopt a 'price-level target', such that below-target inflation today was compensated for sure by above-target inflation in the future. Then, instead of targeting an amount of assets to be bought, the Fed could target a rate of interest on, for example, two-year bonds of, say, 2% by offering to buy as many bonds as were needed to do this; this of course meant that the Fed had to be willing to lose control of the size of its balance sheet.

Compared to the 1930s—a shameful comparison for sure—monetary policy actions were impressive and were probably the biggest factor of a discretionary nature in avoiding a repeat of the disaster of the 1930s. In the 1930s the weighted average central bank nominal interest rate of the leading seven economies stayed at 3% or more, and no other monetary measures were employed. This time the rate was pushed close to zero, and then unconventional measures were used to go beyond. It was the failure of the Fed to expand the money supply aggressively between 1930 and 1933 that made that financial crisis much worse than it otherwise would have been.[27] Indeed, it did the opposite. In an attempt to stick to the gold standard, the Fed took measures that shrunk the money supply by about a third and that generated record levels of bankruptcy. The consequence was deflation: between 1929 and 1933, goods prices in the US fell 25%, which made the real burden of debt much higher.[28] The Fed learnt the lesson, and did the opposite this time—which, of course, did not stop it from being roundly condemned by pretty much the same sort of voices that had pushed it in the wrong direction in the 1930s. Sarah Palin might have scoffed at central bankers and scattered rich linguistic pickings for budding future Palintologists to dig up, dust off, and scrutinize, but without the Feds (highly imperfect) QE, a deflationary spiral would have been extremely likely. Some say that Bernanke was cautious in pushing recovery, but Bernanke, an economic scholar of the Great Depression,[29] the right man in the right place at the wrong time, in the aftermath of the crash did more than any other single individual to prevent a re-run of the 1930s.

Impact, and Double Dip

All this stimulus was bound to leave some sort of mark, however smudged and hard to interpret. A proper evaluation needs a counterfactual of what would have happened without it. For example, even if economies ground to a halt, it could be that the stimulus worked, but that matters were so dire that the stimulus got absorbed preventing an even worse disaster, or it could be that the stimulus failed because it simply 'crowded out' other private-sector activity.

In spite of the financial crash coming in at the top of the Reinhart and Reinhart 'crisis index' range, the peak-to-trough falls were not as extreme as in average past cases. In the US, the fall in real GDP per capita[30] was about 5.4% (revised up in late 2011 to about 6.7%[31]) compared to a past average of 9.3%, and unemployment rose by 5.7% compared to 7%.[32] These figures were below those seen at the time of the Great Depression. The only other country that experienced a smaller fall in GDP per capita than the US was France, at a little over 4%. Japan experienced the highest fall, at about 8.5%, followed by Italy at about 7.5%, closely followed by the UK at about 7%, then Germany at a little over 6%.[33] The better performance of the US compared to so many past cases was because the US government maintained access to extremely cheap borrowing, whereas in past cases this access was quickly lost. This, as we shall see in Chapter 9, did not stop some in the US from trying to destroy even this key advantage.

Belying all the doomsters (that is, practically everyone), from mid-2009 the figures for industrial production turned and pointed upwards. By March 2010, global industrial production had recovered to about 6% below its previous peak.[34] Countries that had suffered big hits in their exports comprised the bulk of the recovery. This was very different from the Great Depression, when global industrial production kept falling for three years.

Seeing the spots and splashes of positive data, in countries like the US and the UK there was even talk of 'green shoots' of economic recovery. For a while, starving politicians chewed on these (sometimes to the point of hallucination). By the summer of 2010 both had withered. The US had a 5% annualized rate of increase of GDP at the end of 2009. This fell to 3.7% when measured in January–March 2010, and thence to about 1.7% in July–September 2010. It rose to about 3% in early 2011 and then collapsed. In the UK, Gordon Brown (non-UK readers will find this amazing) had managed to cling on as prime minister for nearly three years without ever being voted in. The voters had swallowed many things, but this proved one too many. It was time to cut the Gordon knot, and so in the general election of May 2010, Brown was removed. In Japan, by the end of 2010, with the expiry of stimulus measures, a healthy revival had turned into an economic contraction at an annualized 1.1%. Germany, a big exporter, saw its annualized rate of growth of GDP hit 9% before cooling to a still respectable 3.6% for the whole of 2010.

On closer inspection, the optimistic 2009 figures were not all they seemed. First came the curious workings of the 'inventory-investment accelerator' at the end of 2008 and into 2010. In a range of developed economies, in the non-financial sector, sources of external capital were scarce and costly, and the risks of being hit by a volatile market were high. In the financial sector, broad money was growing fast, whereas in the non-financial sector broad money was falling. This triggered the equivalent of a 'run' to safety in the non-financial sector. Firms cut staff, especially those on short-term contracts, under-produced for a while, and sold what inventory they could to boost their cash cushions. This registered as a collapse in economic activity in late 2008 and early 2009, suggesting that economies were collapsing much more than they really were. When the forces went into reverse, it suggested economies were recovering much faster than they really were. Then there were all the temporary stimulus measures that shifted activity from the future into 2009. For example, both the UK and the US ran car-scrappage schemes; the UK ran a temporary VAT reduction; the UK also had a stamp-duty holiday for a year on homes costing less than £175,000; and the US had a tax credit for first-time homebuyers. As policy measures went, these were, respectively: fairly dumb; costly but with some impact if not wound up prematurely;[35] about as dumb as policy gets; and ditto.[36]

After the 1929 crash, world stock markets kept falling for three to four years. Within a year of their 50% trough in the spring of 2009, world stock markets had rebounded to 75% of their pre-crash levels. It was the most pronounced bounce since 1955. Within another year or two, stock markets were within sight of their prior peaks. It was probably the most striking difference between the two crashes. Perhaps stock markets, being forward-looking creatures that had just escaped financial Armageddon, were turning early because they could see light at the end of the economic tunnel? Or maybe they were just pricing in the super-low interest rates, QE, moral hazard, and the other enriching delicacies of a thoroughly modern financial rescue? After all, on the eve of the crash, stock markets were reflecting the bubble wealth of housing and financial engineering, such that to get back to such levels so quickly was perhaps a little suspect. At the very least, it suggests that stock markets were being propped up by public-sector interventions.

Stock markets had failed to flag the crash in advance, and failed to hint at the problems soon to engulf the eurozone. The more moral hazard that was chucked by governments into the banking system, the more stock markets revelled in it. Eichengreen and O'Rourke observed: '[I]f the crisis has taught us anything, it has taught us that too much should not be made of the forecasting ability of financial markets.'[37] The past is not such a foreign country in this respect too. Between 1929 and 1932, the Dow Jones Industrial Average rose more than 20% on four occasions before eventually falling to below previous lows.

By the spring of 2010, the very worst of the predictions of doom and gloom made in late 2008 and early 2009 had not come to pass, but what did happen was far from comforting. The quick return of global trade to vigour was a surprise—and a major success. Early evidence suggests that the aggressive policies pushed by the newly established G20 played an important role in easing the credit conditions critical to flows of international trade.[38] Over 2010, the volume of world trade rose 12.4% and, by the spring of 2011, the IMF was predicting that global trade would grow by 7.4% in 2011 and 6.9% in 2012.[39]

Net private-capital flows into emerging economies recovered too; at $900 billion in 2010 they were less than their peak in 2007 but higher than in any other year. This helped emerging economies, and thereby also helped pull on the slackening recovery strings of the US and Europe. Indeed, initial panic about the impact of the crash on emerging economies turned into concern about excessive capital inflows into some of them. Meanwhile, US businesses reported record earnings in 2010—about $1.7 trillion in a year, up from about $1.3 trillion in 2009—on the back of record profit margins (as a share of GDP, the highest since 1950) caused by cost-cutting, especially via redundancies, and low interest rates that cut their borrowing costs. However, they hoarded much of the cash, which stunted growth by taking the impetus out of job creation and denying governments the taxes they needed to reduce their deficits.

By March 2010 the US was at last adding jobs, but by the summer it was losing them again. Greenspan put his finger on it in August 2010: 'Our problem, basically, is that we have a very distorted economy, in the sense that there has been a significant recovery in a limited area of the economy amongst high-income individuals...Large banks, who are doing much better and large corporations...are in excellent shape. The rest of the economy, small business, small banks, and a very significant amount of the labor force, which is in tragic unemployment, long-term unemployment—that is pulling the economy apart. The average of those two is what we are looking at, but they are fundamentally two separate types of economy.'[40] As living, breathing economic entities, the US, UK, and chunks of Europe had taken a knife and slit themselves in two. Those who lived off capital, even those who had previously misbehaved, were doing well on the back of government support. The unemployed and those living off savings were taking the pain. It was, according to Summers at Davos in 2010, 'a statistical recovery and a human recession', and in early 2011 the Institute of Directors in the UK talked of the UK's 'jobless and joyless recovery'. Actually, it wasn't even much of a recovery.

The Jobless and Joyless Recovery

The statistical journey to the bottom of the unemployment dip was bleak. In the US, by mid-2011 about 14.6 million were unemployed. Official unemployment was still over 9%. Even this was exaggerating downwards, as record numbers of discouraged workers stopped even trying to be part of the workforce and record numbers retired early (locking in Social Security at the earliest possible age of 62, even if this meant less income), claimed disability benefits, and exited from the official figures. In the US recession of the early 1980s, it took about 10 weeks on average for an unemployed person to find a new job. Now it was taking over 20 weeks. The long-term unemployed (i.e. those unemployed more than six months) numbered over 6 million, about 45% of the officially unemployed. About 9 million who wanted full-time work were in part-time work. This meant that the total unable to get the full-time work they really wanted was about 29 million. The situation had not been as bad as this since the Great Depression.

The US needed to be creating at least 100,000 new jobs a month just to soak up those entering the labour force. To achieve full employment by 2020, 22 million new jobs needed to be created to cover the 7 million who had lost their jobs in 2008–2009 and the 15 million who would enter the labour force over a decade. Bernanke told Congress that it would take five years for the US labour market to get back to normal. Even that was putting an optimistic face on things. For Obama the news was worrying. If official unemployment was to be down to 8 million by election night 2012, 200,000 new jobs needed to be created every month. In a good month, the US was lucky to achieve half of that.

In parts of Europe the situation was even worse. In Spain, with industrial output down by about a quarter, unemployment was nearly 23% by late 2011. In Ireland it was about 15%, approximately half of which represented long-term unemployment. In a range of OECD countries, rates of youth unemployment (of 16–24 year olds) were reaching new heights—in late 2011, 50% in Spain, 45% in Greece, 30% in Portugal and Ireland, 29% in Italy, and 24% in France—creating a lost generation facing poor life prospects and entrenched poverty. Indeed, the youth were absorbing a disproportionate part of the pain: in Spain, youth unemployment had been 18% as recently as 2008. With UK growth stalling, in May 2011 the OECD forecast that UK unemployment would be stuck at over 8% for at least two more years. In November 2011, UK growth forecasts were radically cut again and unemployment was heading towards three million. Youth unemployment was already over a million. In contrast, in Germany they had the lowest unemployment rate in a generation (with youth unemployment of 9%).

If growth in actual output failed to keep pace with growth in potential output (i.e. the maximum level of output that an economy can sustain without causing inflationary pressures), the long-term unemployment costs would be even higher. If potential output was hit too, the long-term unemployment costs would be higher still (and the costs of tackling deficits would also be higher).

If the recession was protracted, potential output would be harmed from at least four directions. First, from an increase in structural unemployment: a protracted recession would force a proportion of workers out of the workforce, pushing the 'natural rate of unemployment' higher. Already by May 2009 this was happening in the US; 'permanent' layoffs (of workers not expected to ever regain the same job) were at a record 53% of the unemployed. Second, from a reduction in funding for research and development that would hold back total factor productivity, as had happened in Japan in the 1990s.[40] This problem was being further exacerbated by short-sighted cuts in the relevant government budgets. Third, from the breakdown of global economic integration, especially of cross-border lending and investment: for those factors of production that are not perfectly mobile, a loss of export markets can lead to the effective loss of a chunk of capital and labour, leading to a decline in potential output. Fourth, from the harm done to the credit process.

The Congressional Budget Office estimated that the US output gap—the difference between an economy's potential output and its actual output, expressed as a percentage of its potential output—was about 6.3% in the second quarter of 2010. The OECD calculated that the UK's output gap was 4% in 2011, but in November 2011 the UK's new Office for Budget Responsibility (OBR) revised this down to 2.5%, indicating that the UK economy had been much more badly damaged by the crash than had been realized a couple or so years before. With very little room for growth before hitting the capacity buffers, there would be higher unemployment for longer *and* a bigger structural government budget deficit even when the economy recovered.

In empirical studies, evidence was mounting that past financial crises had a seriously negative impact on the growth rate of potential output, and thereby on long-term unemployment. In one study, in the five years after the onset of major banking crises the growth rates of potential output in Norway (1987), Finland (1991), Japan (1992), and Sweden (1991) were reduced by 0.9%, 0.5%, 0.4%, and 0.3% respectively.[42] In a panel study covering 190 countries, over the ten years following a banking crisis output fell by 7.5% relative to its long-term trend.[43] Applying the methodology to the data on 30 OECD economies between 1960 and 2007, another study found that, within five years, a financial crisis had lowered output by between 1.5% and about 2%.[44] If such evidence had entered into policymakers' ruminations, they would have avoided any measure that might drag out the recession longer than necessary, because of the permanent, or highly persistent, negative impact the recession would have on the level, if not the rate of growth, of output and because of the greater structural and long-term unemployment (and higher costs of tackling deficits).

Unemployment in the US and Europe was rapidly becoming not just a cyclical phenomenon but a structural one, a consequence of the structural distortions that were allowed to build in the years of debt-fuelled excess and of the harm done to economies since the crash. This was not the sort of unemployment easily remedied by standard fiscal and monetary policies. A response needed to include: pro-growth tax reform; support for research and education and job retraining; infrastructure investment; housing-finance reform to drag the emphasis in economic activity away from speculative housing investment to other forms of risk-taking and wealth creation; expanded social safety nets (especially in emerging economies and for the more vulnerable social groups in developed economies); and reform that would get the medium- to long-term fiscal house in order.

On 8 September 2011—to the repeated chorus of 'You should pass this jobs plan right away' and with a call to 'stop the political circus'—Obama thumped home his $447 billion 'American Jobs Act of 2011', his second fiscal stimulus, to a joint session of Congress. It largely consisted of extending, for one more year, already-enacted stimulus measures when they expired. At the core of the plan were cuts in payroll taxes for workers and employers, and fresh spending on infrastructure projects and on recruiting teachers. The last was especially interesting, because boosting education at all levels was the only way to turn the tide of the US's drift towards low productivity service jobs and stagnant middle-class incomes. About half of the cost of the plan came from the extension of the payroll-tax cut due to expire in December 2011. The Act also included a proposal to refinance underwater mortgages at 4%. Obama repeatedly asserted that the plan 'will not add a dime to the deficit'.[45] To cover the plan's costs, $400 billion would come from limiting the tax deductions and exemptions for individuals earning over $200,000 and families earning over $250,000. The rest would come from closing tax loopholes for oil and gas companies, from changes in the way corporate jets got taxed, and from taxes on the interest earned by fund managers.

Obama submitted the plan to the new congressional 'super-committee' tasked with finding ways to cut the deficit. He then embarked on a grand tour, making sure to surround himself, on each fresh stump, with the sort of workers and small-business owners set to benefit from the Act. The plan set a clever political trap for his opponents. Either they backed him, or they spent a year being caricatured as a Washington-based elite, out of touch with the needs of ordinary workers and small businesses. The White House splashed a clock across the top of its blog page, 'If Congress Doesn't Act, middle class taxes increase in (24 days, 09 hours, 13 minutes and 26 seconds when I last looked)'. The Senate quickly split on the part of the plan that required higher taxes on the rich. But the clock worked: days before the deadline, Congressional Republicans allowed a two-month extension (later, extended again) on condition of talks on a longer-term tax deal. The package was probably just about big enough to cut unemployment by a per cent or so and to raise GDP by a per cent or two by the time of the presidential election in 2012 if nothing more went wrong. For several months in a row in early 2012, the US saw over 200,000 new jobs created (and the official unemployment rate was down to 8.3% by February 2012). For Obama's political ambitions, this might just be enough. But then things did go wrong. Europe's economy imploded, China's problems intensified, and US job creation shrunk to 80,000 per month by mid-2012. At such rates it would be well into the 2020s before the US would be back in a similar position to that which it had enjoyed in 2007.

A Different Kind of Recession

Policymakers argued in late 2008 that it would be impossible to have recovery in the economy without recovery in banking. That's why they spent so much on rescuing banks. So, how come the banking sector pulled through in far better health than anyone dared to speculate in late 2008, and yet economic recovery in the US and in large parts of Europe was slow to non-existent, with unemployment high for years on end? If the main problem had been in the banks, economic recovery should have followed. Banks got criticized for failing to lend and for making profits exploiting easy opportunities, but their strategies were a natural response to the very poor underlying condition of the economy and to political and economic paralysis. Besides, policymakers had emphasized rescuing banks, and were much less interested in specific securities-based and market-based activities that might have been more helpful for small businesses and the unemployed. And many of the rescue measures favoured capital over labour.

In the bubble interpretation of what happened, the losses to the unemployed and to savers were a large proportion of the negative sum that exceeded the positive sum extracted by bankers and politicians in the bubble years. Those who lost the most from the wealth redistributions being used to rescue the banks were large in number, but their collective voice was small compared to the voice of more concentrated interest groups. If you were a young person staring unemployment in the face, a worker recently laid off, or an elderly person whose income from savings was decimated, you were a drop in a very large bucket or a speck of dust on a scale; if you were a major bank you had volume and weight.

If the bigger problem was the underlying poor condition of the economy, this may even suggest that there was too much bias in measures towards banks. It is difficult to judge. Politicians did not know just how high the probability was of a disastrous financial tail event, nor of how damaging the consequences would be.

Since they did not face the moral-hazard consequences of their actions, politicians had a natural tendency to be overly generous and insufficiently tough towards banks. Had the banking system been rescued differently, with less emphasis on protecting bank owners and more emphasis on creating fresh lending, especially to small businesses, perhaps sourced from newly-created 'good banks', would it have made a difference to the economic recovery? It is another issue that the economic historians will chew on. My best guess is that it would have.

Part of the explanation for the lacklustre economic performance was to be found in the nature of the recession. A popular view is that the deeper a recession, the faster the recovery, and that if policymakers prod with a bit of fiscal stimulus here and tug with a bit of monetary activism there, the internal dynamism of capitalism will propel economies back to their prior growth paths. This time the rules of economic engagement were very different. In over 90 years this was only the second episode of massive financial deleveraging to hit the US, the UK, and a large number of other developed economies.[46] When the credit bubble burst in 2007–2008, a range of problems followed.

First, lenders could not find many willing and creditworthy borrowers. The value of the collateral of many potential borrowers had collapsed and, because of asymmetric information problems, even remaining creditworthy borrowers had problems getting access to credit (those who might lend to them could not distinguish them from the much more numerous less-creditworthy borrowers). Investment and consumption were pulled down by a lack of credit. Tight credit conditions also made it harder for economies to rebalance; shifting capital from less efficient to more efficient activities often needs access to finance.

Second, with an overhang of debt on their balance sheets, with falling incomes and wealth, and with mounting job losses, many households found themselves wanting to deleverage. This created a destructive feedback loop, with collapsing asset values feeding back to make matters worse.

Third, desired savings rose. In the US, the financial balance of the private sector—the gap between the private sector's income and expenditure—went from minus 2.1% of GDP in the fourth quarter of 2007 to plus 6.7% of GDP in the third quarter of 2009, a massive 8.8% swing towards saving before stabilizing at about plus 4% in early 2012. In the UK (where the financial balance of the private sector started positive), the swing was about 6% (rising to over 9% in 2010, easing off to about 8% in 2011) of this swing, about three quarters was caused by households, and the rest was caused by the corporate sector. By historical standards, such economy-wide swings towards saving were huge, and even more remarkable given negative real interest rates. In mid-2010, the OECD calculated that in six OECD countries (the

Netherlands, Switzerland, Sweden, Japan, the UK, and Ireland) the surplus of the private sector's income over expenditure would exceed 10% of GDP in 2010, and that in a further thirteen countries, including the US, the rate would be between 5% and 10%.[47]

Most people readily understand that saving and paying off debt has benefit for an individual. But what if everyone—and worse, across many economies at once—tries to increase savings and cut consumption at the same time? Thrift that is good for one turns into recession that is bad for all. Economists call it the 'paradox of thrift'. Economy-wide swings towards private-sector surplus generate negative aggregate-demand shocks to whole economies. As Summers put it: 'In the past few years, we've seen too much greed and too little fear; too much spending and not enough saving; too much borrowing and not enough worrying. Today, however, our problem is exactly the opposite.'[48]

Fourth, a 'balance sheet' recession took hold. History teaches us that balance sheet recessions are long and painful because of years of deleveraging. Historically, deleveraging begins about two years after the start of a financial crisis, takes six or seven years and reduces the ratio of debt to GDP by about 25%.[49] Deleveraging in the worst-affected countries this time was going to take much longer because the levels of indebtedness were so much higher than in practically all previous episodes of deleveraging. The highest ratio of debt (of all kinds) to income in any previous deleveraging episode was in the UK after the Second World War, when it reached 300%. As we saw in Chapter 1, this was surpassed comfortably this time. And deleveraging is much more problematic if many countries are doing it at once.

To complicate matters, private-sector excesses were not equal everywhere. Some sectors—such as households in the US, the UK, Ireland, and Spain—would be doing a lot of deleveraging. Elsewhere—such as in Germany, Japan, and Italy—there would be little or no deleveraging. A happy ending for all would require cooperation even from those who felt they had been virtuous. In past US recessions, as the economy recovered, unemployment fell dramatically because lower interest rates encouraged dis-saving and consumption and construction. There was not a chance of this happening this time. The US, the UK, and other deleveraging countries were going to be stuck with high unemployment for a long time if policymakers were not creative in their policy responses.

In 2005, I argued that, because the collapse of a debt-based bubble is more difficult to manage than the collapse of an equity-based bubble, the heavy expansion of debt after the dot.com bust of the early 2000s came at the expense of the unwinding of more painful types of bubbles later,'[50] and that in the early

2000s the US and other economies had experienced 'a much milder recession than has historically been the case after such collapses. But the cost has been the potential for instability at a much longer horizon and the greater risk of a larger recession later.'

It is not surprising that during the crash, countries such as the US, the UK, Ireland, and Spain saw some of the biggest rises in government budget deficits (a flow per year) and government debt (a stock). All major systemic banking crises since the Second World War sent government debt rising—on average by about 86% of its pre-crisis level.[51] Once again, it pays to look at balance sheets, this time of whole economies; one can then see how the deleveraging process of the private sector leads to a rise in government budget deficits and debt. The combined financial balances of the corporate, household, government, and foreign sectors always sum to zero. Surplus flows in some sectors are matched by deficit flows in other sectors. So, when the deleveraging process began and the private sector in a range of countries swung into surplus, their governments naturally swung into deficit. Trying to stop this would have condemned whole economies to a 1930s-style Great Depression. Thank goodness for government budget deficits (they get such a bad press). Of course, persistent flows of government budget deficits lead to bigger stocks of government debt which, if they are to be repaid, at some point require governments to run larger primary fiscal surpluses; i.e. the fiscal surplus excluding interest payments must be positive.

One thing we need to be clear about. Rising government deficits and debts were the consequence, and not the cause, of the crash. They were the result of the economic policy mistakes of the past. A whole generation of politicians had lived off the backs of future generations, falsely promoting it as a mark of their economic wisdom. By 2010, Bush, Greenspan, Blair, Brown—those responsible for the legacies of public- and private-sector debt in the US and UK—were gone, even if sometimes their ghosts lingered on. Instead of swallowing the economic logic of the inevitable, those who attacked Obama and others for the high government deficits and the rising stock of government debt, dirtied the policy waters pretending that somehow Obama and others had more control over government deficits and debts than they truly did. Often the accusers were the self-same voices who had encouraged the economic imbalances that had led to the higher deficits and debt in the first place. They had been self-righteous on the way up and were not about to eat humble pie on the way back down.

Perhaps to avoid the challenges of deleveraging, policymakers could have tried to re-ignite growth in private-sector debt. However, even if consumers would have swallowed the reasoning—and, to some, the aroma was mighty tempting—reviving private-sector debt and consumer spending and pumping house prices would have simply run the danger of rebuilding private-sector debt-based bubble imbalances that would have risked another crash later. Perhaps, instead, private-sector deleveraging could have been allowed to run its course, with little government response to ease the pain. Sadly, that would have been a disaster too. Private-sector spending would have collapsed, government tax revenues would have fallen, government deficits would have risen and, sooner or later, there would have been a sovereign debt crisis anyway—brought on by those who justified their behaviour by the need to avoid such an outcome.

There were two main escape routes. The first was via net exports. The surplus income thus generated would allow the private sector in such countries to gradually satisfy its savings surge, pull off the private-sector deleveraging trick, and pay the taxes that would ultimately pull government deficits and government debt back down. This escape route required such countries to shift towards investment in the sort of activities that would create more of the products and services that emerging and other economies would demand. Meanwhile, those countries that previously over-saved—such as China, many Middle Eastern countries, and oil- and raw-material-rich countries—would have to consume and invest with a greater focus on the needs of their domestic populations and of the migrant workers who, in some cases, laboured away to create their wealth. And they needed to retreat from excessive export-led growth.

The second escape route—and like all good escape routes, it could run parallel to the first—was via public-sector investment in high-income high-debt countries, particularly in infrastructure projects, research and development, and skills and education—for lack of a better word, 'intelligent' public investments—onto which private-sector investments would piggyback as economies recovered. This would generate higher future productivity and incomes that would help to ease the burden of long-term adjustment. With all those private-sector surpluses knocking about, what was a government to do? In countries where a 5% nominal rate of growth per year was possible but nothing like that was being achieved, where governments could borrow at a rate of next to nothing, and where much economic activity was otherwise lost forever, it was logical for governments to become the borrowers of last resort and to take up the spending slack within their own economies caused by those trying to pay off their debts. Future generations were going to be bequeathed more government debt. They might as well be left assets generating a long-term rate of return that would help repay government debt. As Martin Wolf put it in the *Financial Times* in November 2010, with interest rates so low, 'Never can there have been a better time to build up public assets.'[52] With perfect timing, in November 2010 the McKinsey Global Institute released a report arguing that one of the top priorities for the UK over the coming two decades was to invest £520 billion in transport and energy infrastructure.[53] With only 15% of UK GDP going into gross investment, lower than the already very low levels of the past three decades, there was some room for manoeuvre.

In 2011, for countries like the UK, the first escape route of net exports was heavily constrained, in part by the problems in Europe (40–50% of the UK's exports were to Europe). The argument for the second escape route was getting stronger by the day. In the US, in 2010, Obama proposed a national 'infrastructure bank' to invest in key US infrastructure projects, but he quickly backed away. In early 2011 he re-grasped the nettle in his State of the Union Address, pushing for major infrastructure investments, but he backed away again. Then in his 'American Jobs Act of 2011' he slipped in some infrastructure spending. Obama quickly realized that 'intelligent' was not a word often applied in the US to public investments. Those who opposed him took the view that all federal spending was intrinsically evil, the distinction between public investment and public consumption being totally lost on them.

With firms collectively sitting on trillions of dollars in cash, it was also time to get them to spend it in ways that boosted long-term growth. In late 2011, the UK government proposed a scheme to encourage pension funds to invest in infrastructure projects. It offered a government-backed guarantee of regular long-term returns, in the hope of unlocking £20 billion of investment. It was a move in the right direction. Again, it was still not big enough, it eschewed super-cheap borrowing, and the details were still to be worked out.

If the poor underlying condition of the economy was driving bank behaviour as much as vice versa, government strategy could not just focus on banks. The US, the UK, and others in deep trouble needed to focus on a strategy to promote innovation in emerging industries and technologies such as new kinds of energy-efficient construction, biomedical tools, electric transport, and food production, and infrastructure—with an education policy to match. Tax subsides needed to switch from areas such as housing to, for example, areas such as biotechnology. The US, the UK, and much of the eurozone too needed, in a couple of words, an intelligent 'industrial policy'. So far they were getting none of this.

The Phony Economic War

Heading into 2012, in the worst-affected countries (at least outside the euro-zone), many in the population were still experiencing a phony economic war. Rock-bottom interest rates harmed those who lived off savings, but boosted the household incomes of many others, especially mortgage holders. Unemployment was high, falling very slowly in the US, and rising in many other affected countries. Nevertheless, for those who were not unemployed, it did not so far feel much like a recession. By mid-2012, those countries not yet in recession were either heading into recession or rapidly losing economic momentum. Many were starting to get a taste of the battles ahead.

The crash and the slow and difficult recovery had a message for those with an ear to listen and a mind to act. A certain kind of organization of global industrial growth had reached its limits. In the US and the UK in the years running up to the crash, as other productive activities had departed, the financial sector had expanded to fill the void. However, the financial sector's profit had come from a series of bubbles that had only temporarily boosted aggregate demand. This had all evaporated. The big issues now were what the new economic order would look like and what the transition to it would be. Over ten or so years, two synchronized rebalancing acts needed to take place. One was external, involving a complete reconfiguration of global economic activity between exporting and importing countries.[54] The other was internal. High-income high-debt economies would need to replace government spending with private-sector spending as the private sector recovered. China and a range of other countries would need to grow a properly functioning public sector and end financial repression. As countries delicately threaded their way, there would be pain, social unrest, and the chances of instability. The 1930s taught us something else: that if the window of opportunity is missed, voters eventually drift towards parties committed to national, rather than global, solutions. King observed that 'the real consequences of this crisis are only now beginning to be felt', and expressed surprise that the 'degree of public anger has not been greater that it has been'.[55] Over the next few years all would discover just how close to the surface the anger really lay.

Housing Market Meltdown: Rescue and Reform

Meltdown

In the US, for six and more years[1] problems in the housing market festered and prices fell. In spite of all the bandages and soothing ointments, the patient got worse, not better. In the first two years of falling house prices, seven million US homeowners went into foreclosure.[2] By September 2010, US average real house prices were 28% below their peak[3]—back to their 2004 level. For a while the patient seemed to stabilize, but then, as the economy stalled, prices started to fall again. By mid-2011, US average real house prices were 33% below their peak—back to their 2002 levels. The price fall was greater than in the Great Depression. Nearly a decade of supposedly guaranteed wealth gains—so reassuringly touted in the bubble-years by mortgage brokers, investment gurus, TV property show 'experts', advertisers, politicians, and other assorted real-estate seducers—had been stripped away. Three million more US home owners lined up for foreclosure in 2011. No longer paved with gold as the adverts had promised, the US was criss-crossed with streets of pain and lost delight. The dream was not meant to end this way.

The leveraged nature of house purchases (part cash-down but mostly with debt) amplified the losses to those who lost. What leverage gave, leverage took away. By early 2008, over 10% of all US home owners were already in negative equity (i.e. their home was worth less than the mortgage on it). By late 2008, US households had already lost about a third of their peak home equity, down from about $12.5 trillion in 2005 to about

$8.5 trillion. By 2011 nearly one in four US home owners was in negative equity. In the states of Arizona and Nevada it was more than one in two. The dream there was not meant to end this way.

Previous US post-war economic recoveries had housing-market recoveries at their heart. Not this time. In early 2011, the sale of newly-built homes in the US hit the lowest level since records began in 1963; at about 250,000 per month, it just about matched the numbers foreclosing. Amazingly, although it was the legacy of a decade and more of economic madness, it was Obama who took the rap for being unable to clean up yet another of someone else's messes. No, his dream was not meant to end that way.

What was the biggest factor driving property-market problems in the US? The financing tools that went wrong? The low creditworthiness of some borrowers? The lax underwriting? The regulatory failures? The list was long and all had their place on it. However, the factor associated with the most variance in mortgage-delinquency rates (for all types of mortgages) across US regions was the fall in house prices.[4] Indeed, for the 2006 and 2007 vintage subprime loans suffering unusually high rates of delinquency and foreclosure,[5] the only thing that mattered was a low rate of house-price appreciation after the loan was originated.

In the UK, between their July 2007 peak and January 2009, average real house prices fell by 20%—back to their mid-2003 level. It was a quicker, sharper fall than in the US or any time before in the UK. Most of the fall happened before October 2008, and can't be blamed on the banking collapse. Brown was fond of setting records. This was one of his more impressive ones. But, thankfully for him, with the crash in full swing, hardly anyone noticed.

By mid-2011, Irish real house prices had fallen 40% from their peak. In Dublin house prices had halved. On conservative estimates, one in eight Irish properties was empty. In Spain a million homes (many recently built) had nobody living in them. In early 2009, steep one-year real price drops were being recorded in Riga, the capital of Latvia (−60%), and in Dubai (−50%). In Ireland, Spain, and a range of other economies, house building had been one of the biggest employers. No longer. In the US, the collapse in house building contributed about 0.5%–1.25% to the already high unemployment rate.[6] Across Europe, the collapse in house building was an even bigger contributor to unemployment.

Policymakers quickly discovered that collapsing house-price bubbles are painful because they lead to loss of wealth for some, and that housing-inventory overhangs are painful because they drag prices and con-struction activity lower and unemployment higher, which leads to more defaults, which spins the vicious cycle some more. Indeed, the build-up of an inventory overhang alongside a price bubble—which well-describes the situation in the US—was especially risky because the overhang for a while absorbed, and hid, what the bubble was doing.

To the surprise of pretty much everyone, in late 2009 average UK real house prices started to rise, and were up over 10% by April 2010.[7] In the eye of a global financial storm, the Bank of England slashed its base rate to a record low 0.5%. UK house-buyers responded in the only way they knew: bidding house prices higher.[8] Ironically—and by now we have got quite used to a little bit of irony here and there—the crash furnished the super-low interest rates that, combined with slower unemployment growth than in the early 1990s, kept the number of forced sellers and of defaults in the UK low. This kept prices from falling even further. Repossessions were 46,000 in 2009 compared to their last peak of 76,000 in 1991. In the early 1990s, the non-conforming sector (i.e. those with an adverse credit history, the self-certified, and BTL) was very small. By the mid-2000s, supported by low unemployment, relatively low mortgage interest rates, and rapid house-price appreciation, it had grown to about 20%–25% of gross lending, with BTL comprising about 10%–15%. Now the non-conforming sector was being protected from a big correction by the crash-induced drop in interest rates. In contrast to the US, UK banks failed not because of defaulting mortgages but because of failures in wholesale funding and losses outside of their main area of mortgages. UK-owned banks lost on foreign mortgages 15 times what they lost on UK mortgages.[9]

In mid-2008, S&P[10] calculated that a 10% price fall from the market's peak would drive 320,000 UK households into negative equity. At 20% the number would jump to 1.2 million, and at 25% to 1.7 million, about one in seven. Small price falls would be manageable, large price falls would be much more problematic. Thus, historically low policy interest rates in late 2008 and 2009 prevented even bigger, and earlier price falls in the UK housing market, and allowed a much more drawn-out adjustment than would otherwise have been the case. Brown and the UK Treasury to the bitter end vehemently denied that dangers lurked in the UK housing market. Only the crash saved them.

In the summer of 2010, UK house prices started to fall again. Analysts and rating agencies fed their models of the UK economy with the latest information on austerity measures, collapsing mortgage availability,[11] rising unemployment, shrinking real incomes, the drastic deleveraging of households, rising taxes, and (one day) rising interest rates. And they plotted the gradual sapping away of the will of buyers to enter the UK housing market. In the housing-market slump of the early 1990s, about 1.6 million UK households were in negative equity. In early 2011 it was just over half that number. Half of these had taken their loans out in 2007, when the UK housing market peaked, and about 40% were first-time buyers.[12] In May 2011, the National Institute of Economic and Social Research, NIESR, forecast that UK real house prices would keep falling for another five years, perhaps by about 2% per year.

Before the crash I argued that investing in the UK housing market was getting increasingly risky, that a prediction of a 30% peak-to-trough real house price fall was looking perfectly reasonable, and that most of the fall would happen more quickly than in the past because, in a low inflation environment, real price falls would mostly show up as nominal price falls and feed negative momentum behaviour.[13] This seems to be what happened. UK house prices fell in the early 1990s in real terms by nearly 40% over about six years because nominal prices stagnated in the face of inflation. By 2012 a similar real price fall was looking increasingly likely, and this time it would consist of mostly nominal price falls with some real price fall on top. Eventually, unemployment would push repossessions higher, trigger forced sales, and depress prices.

In contrast to all of the above, property prices in a range of emerging economies scaled new heights *after* the crash.[14] Hong Kong notched up a 20% price rise in 2010. In China as a whole it was 15%. In Singapore it was 14%. Latvia bounced back by 27%. On the eastern seaboards of China and areas around Mumbai in India, so eager were investors to catch up on the finer points of property-market boom and bust that prices doubled in about 18 months. In August 2010, China's largest energy company confirmed that about 65 million Chinese homes had not consumed a watt of electricity in the previous six months, a strong hint that they were empty and purely speculative purchases. In contrast, Germany showed what a rational market should do, with house prices growing by a thoroughly sensible 3% in 2010, roughly matching what the economy had done.

It was starting to look as if China was next in line for a property market crash. In 2011, China was investing 47% of its GDP, about half in property building. As a result, China was even more dependent on property building than the US, Ireland, or Spain had been on the eve of their collapses. This too was a side effect of China's financial repression, because speculating in housing became one way to get around low rates on deposits. Now, property prices had turned, and sales volumes were sliding in the face of a wave of excess supply. At its peak, US average house prices were just over 5 times average income. In China the ratio in 2011 was 8–10 times—and in Beijing and Shanghai nearly 30 times. China's real-estate overhang (relative to demand) was at least as large as in some of those countries that collapsed the most in the crash. China's inventory overhang would take years to work off. A property-market crash in China would pull large sections of the Chinese economy down, especially household expenditure and external trade, and would harm China's industries for cement, power generation, and steel production (construction was using 40% of all of China's steel output). Serious fiscal repercussions would follow for Chinese local governments. Many of these relied on their monopoly control of land (the Chinese state owns all land) to boost their income by up to 40% by selling it (or rather, by selling land-use rights for up to 70 years). This was a sort of government-sanctioned Ponzi scheme since, ultimately, local governments would not be able to maintain the income flow without forcing price collapses.

A Chinese property-market collapse would hit countries such as Australia, Brazil, and Chile that had ridden China's commodity-intensive boom, and this would be happening at the same time as a second wave of recessions rolled in. With the vast majority of collateral in the Chinese banking system comprising land or property, China would be suffering its own banking crisis. Chinese authorities were caught in another trap of their own making: they could save the property market by pumping even more easy money into it and face an even bigger crash later, or hold back and the economy would grind to a halt early. In December 2011, China's Communist Party announced its intention to deflate the housing bubble in Beijing.

Housing Markets as a Source of Economic Instability

The crash reminded policymakers that housing often played a large role in macroeconomic instability. That this should come as a surprise was a surprise in itself, given the literature regarding the linkages.[15] Reinhart and Rogoff pulled another dazed curiosity from their deep hat of data, this time on 18 bank-centred financial crises in industrialized countries since the Second World War. Three results stood out. First that, on average, the greater the surge in house prices just before a crisis, the greater the subsequent fall in real house prices.[16] With real house prices indexed to 100 four years before a crisis, on average the index was approaching 115 at the time of these previous crises, and fell a bit over the next three years. In the case of the 'big five' banking crises (Spain 1977, Norway 1987, Finland 1991, Sweden 1991, and Japan 1992), the index was on average over 120 when crises hit and fell to below 100 by three years later; this time, the index for the US peaked at 130–135. Second, that for countries experiencing large capital inflows, and therefore constituting suitable comparators to the US before the crash, the build-up in equity and housing prices was the best leading indicator of subsequent financial crises.[17] Third, that when banking crises and housing bubbles go hand in hand, they tend to be a great deal more destructive than a pure stock-market-based bubble.[18]

In another study of about 120 recessions across 21 OECD countries since 1960, about 25% were associated with house-price busts, and the contractions that followed busts were 'deeper and last longer than other recessions do'.[19] Leamer argued that eight of the ten US recessions between the Second World War and the crash in 2008 were preceded by problems in housing and consumer durables;[20] the two exceptions were the economic collapse following the Korean War and the dot.com bust at the end of the 1990s.

The collapse of the Japanese stock market takes much of the popular blame for Japan's twenty-year economic malaise. Yet Japan had two bubbles. The Nikkei stock market index rose from about 10,000 to about 40,000 over just a few years in the mid-1980s, but median Japanese house prices also nearly trebled between 1986 and 1991. Indeed, the Nikkei was high in part because of the excesses of the Japanese property market. When the stock market bubble was pricked by higher interest rates, the Nikkei halved in a matter of months. Property prices took longer to turn and spent much longer falling. Median (nominal) Japanese house prices fell 40% between 1992 and 1997. In big cities prices fell by 65% and in some of the pricier parts of Tokyo by 80% and even more. The bubble-value of Japanese property wealth was vulnerable to a fall, but the debt backing it was fixed. Coupled with a strong aversion in Japan to mass default, this led to a legacy of bad debt being inflicted on Japan's financial system. Fifteen years after their 1980s peaks, both Japanese property prices and share prices were still only at about a quarter of their peak values. Japan's experience demonstrated that a fundamentally overpriced property market cannot be saved by interest rate cuts, and that the fallout can be long and painful.

In the 2000s, politicians in countries that would shortly crash had the benefit of historical evidence, plenty of case studies—of which Japan was just the most prominent—and all the necessary economic insight. And yet, confidently and in large numbers, they carried on regardless. To mark such an auspicious occasion, Reinhart and Rogoff gathered data covering eight hundred years and a vast, undulating terrain of financial boom and bust, and distilled it into an excellent book with the equally splendid title *This Time Is Different*[21] in reference to the way politicians and voters alike, the world over, had reassured themselves in the face of evidence of the blinkingly obvious variety.

Now it was time for chest-beating and *mea culpa*. Donald Kohn, Vice Chairman of the Federal Reserve, lamented: 'I and other observers underestimated the potential for house prices to decline substantially, the degree to which such a decline would create difficulties for homeowners, and, most important, the vulnerability of the broader financial system to these events'.[22] In marked contrast to the UK, super-low interest rates made little appreciable dent on the US foreclosure crisis. By the spring of 2009, even though US thirty-year mortgage rates were at record lows, access to credit was a totally separate issue from the rates at which credit could be got if one was of good enough credit quality. Deposit requirements were much higher, and many borrowers were ineligible because their homes were worth less than their mortgages, because they had lost jobs, or because their credit quality was impaired in other ways. In non-prime sectors, loan rates were still elevated and securitization markets closed. At the end of 2010, mortgage rates were even lower—thirty-year fixed rate mortgages could be got for a little over 4%—and yet the numbers of borrowers refinancing to take advantage of such low rates were plummeting. $1,300 billion was refinanced in 2009—down from the peak of $2,500 billion in 2003, when rates were at their last historic low (still, 1% higher than at the end of 2010). If US property was mispriced, it was logical for lenders to keep well away until the process of price correction had finished; because of the non-recourse nature of mortgage loans, too much of the losses on any new loans would find their way onto the shoulders of lenders.

As house prices fell, the borrowing constraints of current owners tightened as their collateral evaporated and their cost of credit, as picked up in credit spreads, rose. As we saw in Chapter 2, this 'collateral effect' had shifted with credit-market liberalization, and so it was an important effect in the UK and US, but less important in the eurozone. In Australia, Canada, the UK, and US, the collapse in equity extraction from housing negatively impacted on aggregate demand. For example, in the UK, housing equity withdrawal (HEW) swung from being about 6% of post-tax income in 2006 and 2007 to about minus 3% from the spring of 2008 onwards.[23] It was not that households in aggregate were paying down their debts more quickly than in the past; rather, it was the drop-off in housing transactions that took away opportunities to secure loans against property.[24] The pattern was a repeat of the early 1990s, only much more pronounced.[25]

Meanwhile, lower house prices reduced the need for prospective house buyers to save a deposit, and so their 'down-payment' constraints loosened. However, this benefit was offset by the collapse of the mortgage market; those who 'won' from lower long-term housing costs could not convert their 'wins' into borrowing and consumption to offset the fall in borrowing and consumption of those who had lost or who were now more constrained. In the UK, first-time buyers had been able to put down, on average, a 10% deposit and get easily 100% LTV mortgages in 2007. In 2011, they had to put down 20% on much lower LTV mortgages, even as they faced lower prices. No wonder that, in 2011, UK first-time buyers were at their lowest numbers since records began in 1974.

The US economy was hit especially hard because, as we saw in Chapter 2, the marginal propensity to consume out of housing wealth in the US was twice as high as in the UK, Australia, and Canada, and the US was dependent on a house-building bonanza. So, even if US house prices were to stabilize, this would not avoid a huge economic hit to the US economy.

The US Foreclosure Crisis and Challenges of a Response

In the US, in the boom years it had become ever easier to buy a home. To keep it was proving an altogether different proposition. Preventing foreclosures had become a high political priority. Sadly, none of the wands that Congress and the White House waved about seemed to have much of any magical effect. A Bush administration programme to get 40,000 homeowners into government-backed fixed mortgages had managed to get just 4,000 signed up by the start of 2009, and a private-sector scheme to modify loans saw 73,000 modified but 43% of these delinquent within eight months.[26]

In February 2009, the new Obama administration came up with another carrot in the shape of billions of dollars of 'incentive' payments to lenders and loan servicers—the Home Affordable Modification Program (HAMP).[27] The aim of the $75 billion programme was to reduce the mortgage payments, but not the principal (i.e. the original amount borrowed, not including the interest payments), of three to four million homeowners at risk of default. Mortgage companies, in order to participate in the scheme, were expected to drop payments to 38% of a borrower's pre-tax monthly income. The US Treasury committed to match dollar for dollar to get this down to 31% for up to five years. The repayment of the principal could be stretched, in some cases, for as many as 40 years. Servicers would receive an up-front fee of $1,000 for each eligible modification, and a fee of $1,000 per year for still-performing loans. Borrowers who stayed on time with their payments would get $1,000 knocked off the principal of the loan every year for up to five years.

And so, many of the self-same companies that got rich getting borrowers into a mess in the first place were now, according to the scheme, to receive generous 'incentive' payments to get borrowers out of it. Indeed, 21 of the top potential recipients of HAMP payments had been heavily implicated in subprime.[28] Now, like bank robbers who had returned to the scene of their crime, they were being encouraged to put some of the money back—for a fee. In policy circles the justification for this was that much-maligned principle of constrained economic optimization: pragmatism. Countrywide, the biggest subprime lender of all, might get up to $5.2 billion. Countrywide was now owned by Bank of America, along with several other failed subprime providers, such that Bank of America would obtain up to about $7 billion. Then there was JPMorgan, getting perhaps $3.4 billion, and Wells Fargo, getting maybe $3 billion. To the beneficiaries at least, it must have seemed like magic of a sort.

By mid-2011, 1.5 million mortgages had had temporary modifications under the HAMP, but 800,000 had subsequently been cancelled. Those permanently renegotiated corresponded to about three months' worth of foreclosures. Over 90% of these were at LTVs of under 105%, which meant that the HAMP was not targeting the most underwater cases. In March 2011, the then inspector general of TARP, Neil Brodsky, testified to Congress that HAMP was 'clearly a failure', that there was 'universal and bipartisan agreement' on this, and that only the US Treasury and, it seemed, Geithner and Obama were still defending the programme. In total exasperation, the courts halted foreclosures across the whole US because of abuses of HAMP. By July 2011, the government was withholding payments from Wells Fargo, Bank of America, and JPMorgan. Some old habits really do die hard.

Perhaps the Bush and Obama programmes might have worked had they been better designed. Or it could be that the task was near-impossible in the first place.[29] After all, why did banks not just voluntarily write down property prices to a little above foreclosure prices? This would have stopped defaults, kept owners in their homes, maintained the values of properties that otherwise would have quickly fallen in value if left empty, and reduced the negative impact on local neighbourhoods that otherwise would have dragged the price of other properties lower. Why did banks choose to foreclose and sell off foreclosed properties in auctions at an even bigger loss to themselves? Several problems complicated both private and public efforts to modify mortgages.

First, the incentives of loan servicers—the companies that calculated and collected payments and handled foreclosures—were not aligned with those who owned and invested in mortgage banks.[30] Servicers' fees were based on the loan principal, and so servicers benefited too little from the losses prevented by avoiding foreclosure. Servicers too worried that they would be sued by investors for being 'too generous' with borrowers (if they did nothing and so made matters worse, they could not be sued for that). And writing down one loan would impact on other lenders, since borrowers in such circumstances often had two, three, or even more loans as claims on the same asset.

Second, there were problems of asymmetric information and moral hazard. For every borrower getting a loan modification who would for sure have defaulted without the modification, lenders, who could not tell the difference, would have ended up making modifications for several others who would not have defaulted but who would miss payments so as to become eligible for modification. Unable to separate out the types, what seemed to be negative-value individual foreclosures turned out to be profit-maximizing in the aggregate.

Third, it is also possible that, in late 2008 and 2009, lenders had an exaggerated notion of their ability to recover more of the value of loans. After all, many measures were being taken to support the housing market, including: rates even lower than the historically low interest rates that had helped to create the mess in the first place; the Federal Reserve's purchase of mortgage-related securities via QE, which had pushed up their prices and reduced the interest rates on GSE-conforming mortgages; a tax credit for first-time homebuyers; and various other policies enacted by the Federal Housing Administration, Fannie Mae, and Freddie Mac.

Fourth, banks wanted to avoid modifications that would require them to mark loans down in their books. This might trigger yet more modifications that would lead to even more losses, which would eat into their capital.

Various solutions to get around each conundrum were placed on the table for policymakers to prod or (usually) simply ignore. One way around the problem with servicer incentives was to give the task of modifying a loan to a government-appointed trustee who would decide 'blind' to the exact status of the loan. To help mitigate the problems of asymmetric information and moral hazard, proposed approaches included contingent write-downs, with loans written down in increments over several years only if the borrower stayed current on payments. Or perhaps, there could be shared-appreciation schemes, such that a reduction in principal would be matched by an equity stake for lenders, with subsequent equity gains shared between homeowners and lenders. Another, voluntary, approach was to give lenders greater ability to lease out foreclosed properties to current residents at a market rate. The lender would get all of the equity. A sale would be delayed until markets had recovered. Until then, lenders would benefit from rental income. Management could be outsourced. About 20% of foreclosures were in renter-occupied investment properties anyway. However, regulators often deemed long-term leasing a non-core function of banks, and so were not especially cooperative with such solutions. To stop those who had the ability to pay but who simply wanted to walk away from a failed investment, all modifications would need strong recourse provisions attached; otherwise limited financial firepower would be wasted helping those suffering negative equity who could not refinance because of their negative equity but who were not facing foreclosure.

It was frequently argued that securitization made mortgage modifications difficult. Yet, modification rates for loans held in portfolios differed little from those held in securitized pools,[31] which suggests that servicing and pooling agreements were less of a barrier to modification than often suggested. The Congressional Oversight Panel for the TARP found that none of the securitized pools it examined that had a 5% cap on modifications had breached it. If a 5% cap was not binding, this suggests that the problem was the sheer difficulty in getting positive-value modifications regardless of the pooling or servicing arrangement.

The main difficulty with the Bush and Obama schemes was that they did nothing about the loan principal. This made such schemes, in a way, forerunners of the loan-based schemes that were to prove so ineffective in the eurozone crisis. If foreclosures were being caused only by inability to repay (perhaps because of the loss of a job or some other income shock), then a scheme to ease repayments might work. If instead, individuals were foreclosing to take advantage of the non-recourse nature of their mortgages and escape negative equity, then the policy would not work unless the principal was reduced. In one study after another, it was the low or non-existent level of equity at origination of the mortgage that was the dominant factor in the decision to foreclose.[32] In 2005, about 66% of mortgage loans delinquent for 60 days or longer were eventually retrieved by homeowners. By 2009 this percentage had fallen to only about 5%. Some couldn't retrieve. Some wouldn't retrieve.

The reluctance of Bush and Obama to write down principal was in part driven by political considerations. If government sought to write down a large part of the principal of a proportion of the population while expecting all others to keep to their repayments in full, the latter would feel punished. The politics was even worse if a portion of those being helped were seen as speculators. Marking down the principal of mortgages to the value of underlying properties would register huge losses on the books of banks or—because of the losses to Fannie Mae and Freddie Mac—for taxpayers. Many of the largest banks would not absorb the losses themselves but pass them on to the ultimate investors in pension funds. Why, some voters might wonder, should property speculators be bailed out by a government programme with the losses passed on to taxpayers and ordinary citizens in the form of lower pensions?

Perhaps, instead, as part and parcel of the normal bankruptcy procedure, the principal outstanding on a mortgage could be reduced if the value of the home against which it was secured had fallen. Doing this would reduce the monthly payments to the mortgager as well as the size of the outstanding loan. However, such proposals would not help unemployed defaulters, who made up a sizable number of those foreclosing, who could not put forward a repayment plan under a Chapter 13 bankruptcy. Investment-property speculators, who made up another sizable number of foreclosures, could already take the bankruptcy route, but chose not to; after all, when property prices are falling, it makes little sense to accept, as part of a bankruptcy deal, a reduced mortgage value that, in just a few months' time, will anyway still be more than what a property is worth. Besides, a Chapter 13 bankruptcy plan would allow three to five years to pay off a loan, compared to thirty years if the loan was modified (even forty years under some HAMP plans).

Just as one might not want to bail out the owners of a bank that had taken excessive risks, so one might not want to bail out those who had taken excessive risks to speculate in property, and none of the schemes was supposed to help speculators. The problem was that speculators coexisted alongside the innocent. If speculators could not be separated from the non-speculators, a lot of speculators might be helped for very few non-speculators being helped. Some speculators easily identified themselves by buying second or third homes and property for investment. Others simply speculated as part and parcel of the ordinary buying decision, taking on a much bigger loan than they could afford on the basis of expectations of price rises that did not materialize. If their property rose in value, they kept all the upside. The lender had made a good rate of return for granting the initial loan, but did not get to share the upside (or rather, lenders extracted the market upside by granting more and bigger loans in the aggregate, even if they did not take the upside from a particular loan). If the property fell in value, the borrower hoped to offload it back onto the lender in foreclosure.

Furthermore, as we saw in Chapter 2, even many supposedly 'non-speculative' subprime mortgages were cash-out refinancings to fund consumption. Again, why, or so many voters might wonder, should taxpayers *ex post* subsidize previous overconsumption? However, while it might seem in the interests of society to make property speculators, and those who overconsumed, face the consequences of their behaviour, not all speculators and cash-out refinancers were especially rich. The relative wealth positions of households seeking support needed to be factored in. To traverse the political minefield, a scheme had to be able to separate out the negative-equity problem from the earnings-related problem, and any attempts to write principal down had to be able to separate the deserving from the undeserving. The informational requirements for both of these tasks were extremely difficult in practice.

If all of the above did not contain political peril enough, the US administration faced a difficult timing issue. If real estate was overpriced relative to fundamentals, and deeper price cuts were on the way, a lot of public money might go on modifications, many mortgages would still foreclose, and the scheme being used would go down as a waste of taxpayers' money. Write-downs needed to be done after the price correction. However, if policymakers waited until then, they would be blamed for doing nothing to stop prices falling. Policymakers were damned if they did and dammed if they didn't. Worse, most sensible solutions needed legislation—in Washington, of all places. Perhaps because of the fights over the bank bailout and over the fiscal stimulus, and because of the looming battle over government debt, Obama and his officials were not willing to take the risk, and went instead for politically less risky options that ultimately meant that far fewer borrowers were meaningfully helped, outcomes were more arbitrary, and impact was minimal.

The US did not have a monopoly on bad ideas. In the UK, a mortgage-rescue scheme launched in January 2009 to help 6000 borrowers at a cost of £34,000 each, ended up helping just 2,600 at a cost of £93,000 each. Borrowers were given a choice between an equity loan that would reduce their monthly payments, or selling their properties to a housing association and becoming tenants. Nearly all chose the latter, much more expensive, option because they had no equity left in their properties. It is amazing how much taxpayers' money one can waste if one really puts one's mind to it.

Price Falls and Default—Not All That They Seem

Let us look a bit more closely at house-price falls, since simple intuition—that house price falls are always bad—can easily lead us astray. We consider two cases. The first case is when there is no bubble in house prices, and prices rise and fall to reflect the present discounted value (PDV) of future actual or imputed[33] rents. A fundamentals-based fall in house prices does not make the *average* household any better or worse off, but takes wealth away from those for whom the value of their house is greater than the PVD of the housing services they plan to consume, and gives it to those for whom the value of their house (if they have one) is lower than the PDV of the housing services they plan to consume (i.e. redistribution is from those long on housing to those short on housing). There is an extra complication. Property is used as collateral to support loans. Even if gainers and losers roughly even out, the average ability to borrow *is* lower because lenders charge less favourable terms to those close to, or already in, negative equity, and so the price collapse will have a real effect on the economy.

The second case is when house prices are based on a bubble. In this case the loss of bubble value to owners is not matched by a gain to anyone else, and there *is* a genuine loss of net wealth. To the extent that banks in the 2000s wrongly believed house-price rises to be fundamentals-based and not a bubble (or that banks knowingly ratcheted up borrowers' debts to exploit the bubble while it lasted), lending could be much reduced after house-price falls.

In order to understand the overall impact of house-price falls on an economy, we need to go beyond the price falls and look at the losses and gains from mortgage defaults. Here, simple intuition—that mortgage defaults are always bad—is also misleading. Mortgages embody the obligation to pay streams of interest and the principal back, which makes them both liabilities of home-owners and assets of those who do the lending (and assets of those who own the lenders, such as bank shareholders).[34] In a housing-market collapse, lenders lose only from mortgages that default, and from non-mortgage loans that default because of the collapse in the value of housing collateral.[35] In a major crash, when large numbers of homeowners default, the impact on lenders may be hundreds of billions of dollars, euros, pounds, renmimbi, ruble, rupee, and so forth—big enough to cause serious problems, but not the trillions of overall 'lost' housing equity.[36] For lenders, a degree of protection is provided by those households that do not default and so absorb the loss themselves. In the UK, this protection for lenders is strong. In the US, because of the non-recourse nature of mortgages, the protection for lenders (and foreign investors into US lenders) is much weaker.

When a borrower defaults, it is a loss to the lender but a gain to the borrower, who does not have to service the debt for its full life.[37] However, the losses imposed by defaults are concentrated in the banking and mortgage industry, while the gains from defaults are widely dispersed amongst households. Unsurprisingly, lenders are more vocal about their losses than households are about their gains. By leaving housing equity losses on the shoulders of households, much of the benefit of the Bush and Obama measures would ultimately go to lenders and not to households. Not surprisingly, households voted with their (non-recourse) feet.

Policymakers faced a trade-off. On the one hand, if households that defaulted *en masse* were relatively poor and had a high marginal propensity to spend out of current income and wealth, then removing their unserviceable mortgage debt would be good for the economy. Homeowners on average, anyway, have higher MPCs than owners of banks, and are likely to be much more credit-constrained than average shareholders in banks; a certain amount of mass default might therefore increase aggregate demand in an economy.[38] Of course, if mass defaulters are relatively well-off speculators, the logic is not the same. There is another twist in this reasoning, when applied to financial systems that securitize a lot of loans. If default risk has risen but default has not yet happened, the lenders who own the mortgages as assets mark them down, affecting their ability to lend. Meanwhile, until they default, borrowers, who treat mortgages as liabilities, keep paying, and this is a drain on aggregate demand. The two effects work to hold the economy back.

On the other hand, not forcing households to honour their debts would increase the losses to lenders, who would find their capital bases squeezed. They would have to reduce dividends, issue more equity, and reduce their lending. This would harm the economy. Letting borrowers off the hook would also encourage moral hazard amongst future borrowers (although this would be offset by lower moral hazard amongst lenders made to take more of the losses they had caused).

Policymakers had to decide whose welfare losses and moral-hazard proclivities they cared most about. Was it better for lenders' or borrowers' incentives to be targeted by being punished? On balance, it probably was best to target lenders' incentives. When banks were in trouble, avoiding harm to banks had taken precedent over preventing future moral hazard amongst banks. Yet, it was banks that had encouraged a rise in house prices and used it to ratchet up lucrative (to banks) household debt. Once locked in, it was this debt that had become problematic. Would it have been so unreasonable to expect banks, and the owners of banks, to take more of the losses? The problem was that the prior gains of lenders had already been extracted from the banking system in the shape of bonuses to bankers, so that disciplining lenders really meant disciplining the owners of lenders. The owners of lenders were ordinary people via their pensions and investments. Bankers had simply been the middle-party feeding financial resources from ordinary people to other ordinary people, creaming off a portion of the bubble they created, and now it was too late to punish them.

House prices clearly could not fall for ever. By mid-2011: US real house prices were close to their long-term trend; the ratio of house prices to rents was at pre-crisis levels; rents were rising at about 4% per year, making ownership more attractive; foreclosure levels were high but falling; and mortgage borrowing was, at last, rising. In the first quarter of 2011, for the first time since 2007, more mortgage holders caught up with their payments than fell behind. The market was getting through its correction, and policymakers were having very limited impact on this. In 2005, I argued that efforts to fight this natural correction would be futile and that it would be best to get it over and done with.[39]

Reforming Mortgage Markets and Kicking Bad Housing Habits

In many cases a few simple reforms would go a long way towards better aligning mortage-market incentives.[40] Many of these reforms were not previously pushed because they did not suit the financial sector's interests and because there did not seem to be the urgency.

In future, those earning a fee should be paid over the course of a loan and not all at the start, and there should be some claw-back in the event of non-performance of the loan. Failing this, the payment of fees over a minimal two-year horizon would catch many of the worst offenders. Rating agencies, for their part, could be required to hold on to a share of the products they rate and, for at least the first two years, there could be restrictions on selling; if the products performed well, such part-payment would come at no extra cost to rating agencies.[41]

As in other areas of life, just the fear that one might get bitten would help to concentrate the mind. This suggests the establishment of standards bodies with teeth strong enough to bite occasionally a chunk out of those who misbehave and to hold on long enough for the pain to achieve its desired effect. In the case of stock markets, brokers are responsible for making sure that they do not recommend investments that are unsuitable for their clients, and the job of arbitration panels is to grant damages to customers who suffer loss after stockbrokers sell 'unsuitable' products. Particularly aggressive brokers risk a plaintiff bar. There is no reason why mortgage brokers could not face similar 'suitability standards' and be bonded like stockbrokers, legally required to take into account borrowers' ability to repay on pain of financial punishment themselves.

High LTV loans should have compulsory insurance attached. Canadians who take out property loans at a 80% LTV ratio must take out insurance from Canada Mortgage and Housing Corporation (CMHC), a federal agency. Canadian banks have an incentive to apply strict standards to those mortgages they guarantee. Insurance brings regulatory risk weighting on such mortgages to zero, so banks have no capital advantage to fund them in speculative ways. Of course, regulators could simply make it impossible to borrow at 100% LTV or higher.

There could be a greater role for futures markets and for some forms of house-price insurance, as suggested by Robert Shiller.[42] For example, it might be possible to build into mortgages the ability for mortgage payments to go down if local house-price indices go down or unemployment goes up. Revised bankruptcy laws might include 'circuit breakers'—delays in bankruptcy settlements—when markets are turbulent, so that prices are not so quickly forced to fire-sale levels. Higher levels of prudential, including macroprudential, regulation would also reduce the destabilizing effects of mortgage markets on the rest of the economy. We will take a look at this in Chapter 12.

A redesign of the mortgage contract would help to mitigate some of the foreclosure problems and stabilize housing and mortgage markets at times of stress. For example, instead of relying on *ex post* loan modifications, which are vulnerable to time-inconsistency and problems caused by asymmetric information, pre-defined loan modifications might be built into mortgage contracts from the start. Various designs were proposed with different pros and cons. For example, a 'buy your own mortgage' (BYOM), popular in countries such as Denmark, has a 'put option' built into the initial contract. A buyer can offer, in pre-payment, the proceeds of a market sale that will pay off the mortgage even if the proceeds fall short of the mortgage's 'par value' (the degree of borrower leverage feeds into the pricing of the option). The option would be 'in the money' even for owners who found themselves underwater. This would provide a way for homeowners to buy themselves out of lopsided financial arrangements. Because the option exists *ex ante* and is transparent to the markets, it might help financial stability by reducing uncertainties about where losses lie within the financial system. The two key challenges would be pricing the option correctly (including when mortgages are pooled and securitized) and working out what to do when big price falls risk a run on BYOM options.

Another possibility, the variable maturity mortgage (VMM), maintains a constant monthly payment but has a variable amortization period that is adjusted regularly to take account of interest rate fluctuations. Structuring a contract in this way reduces the risk of payment shocks caused by resets in variable mortgage rates. In this case, the two key challenges would be calculating the maximum amortization period that would be allowed, and working out how to price and securitize variable maturity contracts. It might also be best to reserve such contract structures for lower-income homebuyers, for whom payment shock had proved so devastating. Like BYOMs, VMMs may have market-stabilization benefits. In both cases, a significant problem is that borrowers may game the system when it comes to expenditures on improving the quality of a property and the timing of a sale—but then, no solution is perfect.

Last, but not least, and maybe even the most important, preferentially advantaging housing in the tax system was supposed to encourage saving, the accumulation of housing wealth, and more stable neighbourhoods because of higher ownership rates. Instead, all too often, such subsidies simply encouraged dis-saving and consumption based on speculative price bubbles, and lowered the incentive to spend on more productive investments, such as education, infrastructure, and technology. Some, such as the UK, had done away with mortgage interest tax relief. Others, such as the US, Ireland, and Spain still retained it. US households could tax-deduct the interest on mortgage loans of up to $1 million—a regressive tax break if ever there was one—and many tanked up on mortgage debt to maximize the value of such a generous tax break. The US government had to make up for the lost tax revenues by taxing other activities more heavily, or by letting the federal budget deficit rise. For any given level of lost tax revenue, it would have been much more efficient to have redistributed tax credits towards boosting affordable low-income rental properties. In most countries there was also little capital gains tax on housing, whereas the gains from other forms of investment and risk-taking were taxed. Thus, an over-emphasis on property-based debt harmed the ability of the US and other economies to produce goods and services rather than financial products and houses. The large housing inventory overhang and the low level of housing equity (and indeed of other kinds; of investments) held by households were ample evidence of the distorted investment incentives.

Cutting tax subsidies on housing was easier said than done. First, there was a huge lobby working against it—banks, construction firms, and real-estate agencies. Second, it was difficult to change a system after many investors had sunk large long-term investments on the basis of it; changes needed to be announced in advance and to be followed by a transition period of twenty or more years. Third, such reforms were generally avoided by politicians because all of the benefits would go to future politicians, and current voters would see only their individual loss and not the collective gain. Fourth, politicians, espe-cially in the US, relied heavily on the financial largesse of those firms who would lose the most from reform.

A genuine wealth-creating economy would focus less on house prices and more on ways to stimulate entrepreneurial investments—an observation I made, to little effect, in 2005.[43] To help the cause along, in early 2010, Karen Pence, chief of the Household and Real Estate Finance section of the Federal Reserve, listed five reasons why 'housing is a lousy investment'.[44] First, housing is an indivisible asset; it cannot be sold off a piece at a time like stocks and shares. Second, unlike a portfolio of stocks and bond investments, it can't be diversified; it's a specific house in a specific neighbourhood. Third, transactions costs in the buying and selling process are very high. Fourth, it is difficult to exit the market when prices are falling. Fifth, the value of housing is highly correlated with the employment market; instead of offsetting employment risk, the ability to raise cash by borrowing or selling a home tracks employment prospects. Pence quickly got short shrift for her efforts to instil a little bit of sanity into the debate.

In the US, the GSEs were heavily criticized for their failings. Yet, govern-ment-sponsored securitization was one of the few, relative, success stories during the crash. When the markets for private-label MBSs dried up, Fannie Mae, Freddie Mac, and Ginnie Mae continued to securitize and sell mortgages to secondary-market investors. It was not because the GSEs were especially well managed. We know they were not. It was a confidence issue: investors believed that the government stood behind the GSEs and so continued to buy what the GSEs issued, which kept the mortgage market from drying up. Bernanke argued that this illustrated the need for a government guarantee of mortgages.[45] However, he also made clear that such a backstop would need reform of the GSEs. The key to this was dealing with the conflicts of interest between the private shareholders of the GSEs and the rest of society. The GSEs were also less willing, than they might otherwise have been, to raise capital and to expand operations during the crash because the extra capital would have diluted the value of the capital of current shareholders.

In 2008, Bernanke proposed a menu of options.[46] First, to fully privatize the GSEs and to establish a public insurer partially underwriting their portfolios. Second, to replace the GSEs with a system of 'covered bonds', a popular option in Europe, secured against high-quality pools of mortgages and other assets. Issuers would have to hold reserves bearing full exposure (beyond certain limits) to repayment. This would encourage them to issue and hold lower-risk mortgages in their portfolios. The GSEs could then manage the asset pool in the covered bond to adjust for under- and over-performing collateral. Third, to keep the GSEs but to get rid of their private ownership and to organize them explicitly as a public utility. This could involve the expansion of the role of the GSEs to cover housing functions currently performed by the Federal Housing Administration and Ginnie Mae (in addition to Fannie Mae and Freddie Mac). The first and second options would require a return for investors sufficient to generate an adequate pool of capital. The third option would require reliable underwriting and pricing systems—and measures to prevent capture by industry.

In February 2011, in the US a White Paper proposed the wind-down of the GSEs and three other options for government support of the mortgage market. First, to limit the engagement of the Federal Housing Administration to providing access to mortgage credit for poorer borrowers only. Second, to combine the first option with a guarantee over mortgages, at prices that would only make the guarantee competitive if a private market was not functioning. Third, to make government the last-ditch insurer of the mortgage market, paying out to the holders of mortgage securities only when private insurers got wiped out. There would be a transition period during which the GSEs would pull back on the size of loans they guaranteed and would raise the price they charged. This was a turn-up for the books. In the competition to decide who had failed the least, the GSEs had lost, and the role of the largest US banks in the mortgage market would henceforth be further enhanced.

House-Price Bubbles and the Reform of Monetary Policy

The other key area for reform that impinged on house prices was monetary policy, which had ridden triumphant before the crash. The twin-headed beast of the business cycle and inflation had been slain. The hero was monetary policy with its sling and just one stone. Especially virtuous was monetary policy's modern incarnation, inflation targeting, an 'information-inclusive strategy for the conduct of monetary policy'.[47] It was argued that changes in exchange rates, bond prices, and house prices would be reflected in current inflation, and that targeting a particular rate of inflation would make the economy more stable. On this, there was considerable consensus in monetary policy circles. Blanchflower penned the obituary: 'The whole idea that we just need to control inflation looks to be dead and buried.'[48]

In retrospect, it was a mistake to believe that, on its own, low, stable goods and services inflation was necessary and sufficient for achieving wider financial-system stability and full employment. As a result of such wishful thinking, money and credit came to be seen only in terms of their impact on standard measures of inflation, and not in terms of their impact on asset prices— especially house prices. Yet rising house prices are a kind of inflation, because they are the rising future cost of consuming a unit of housing services. There had been warnings that because assets, especially housing, are used as collateral in loans, this risked asset price bubbles and consumer debt booms[49] and, combined with the narrow focus on institutions, this risked systemic dangers.[50]

Under the intoxicating influence of inflation targeting (with some 'efficient-market' thinking mixed in to make the concoction that bit more potent), no attempt was made to deal with rapidly rising asset prices, especially in housing, even though it was known that losing control of asset prices would risk future inflation and deflation: when nominal asset prices go out of line with nominal income and with nominal prices of goods and services, balance is eventually re-established either by the prices of goods and services rising to meet the new asset prices (i.e. there is inflation) or by the collapse of asset prices (i.e. there is deflation). Asset price bubbles thrive in environments of low and stable inflation: the removal of interest rate surprises encourages the risky behaviour that feeds bubbles. In 2005, the BIS warned of the dangers of inflation-targeting: 'If positive supply shocks push down inflation, such that policymakers have no reason to tighten credit conditions, then the greater capacity of financial systems to supply credit and debt will be matched by greater demand. Such circumstances could create a boom and bust cycle in the financial system which would, in turn, generate headwinds that could feed back and weaken the real economy in various ways. And if the starting point for this process were already low inflation, the outcome might be an unwelcome disinflationary process that would be more malign than one generated by positive supply shocks alone'.[51] Such thinking was so hopelessly out of touch with the mood of the time, it could only ever expect to be ignored.

Inflation/deflation had not gone away. It had changed its disguise and gone into hiding. Rising house prices were the perfect cover; nobody was looking there. Instability had not gone away; price and output volatility were suppressed in one period, but they reappeared in a later period via asset prices and especially house prices. Regular low-level volatility morphed into long periods of near-flat volatility followed by very great volatility.

Neither was inflation targeting always what it seemed. For much of the 2000s, the inflation target in a range of countries was, in large part, achieved because of global economic imbalances. For example, in the UK in the years before the crash, services-based inflation was running at about 4%. However, goods–price inflation was zero or negative because of the impact of imports and 'globalization', so that the overall index was on target. In 2011, with goods-price inflation running at about 4% and service inflation at 3%, the target was decidedly more difficult to hit, and policymakers allowed themselves not to have to hit it.

Apparent 'success' in dealing with the aftermath of the dot.com bust only further encouraged policymakers to adopt a confident hands-off approach. They did not spot that volatility had only been tamed in the early 2000s at the cost of even greater volatility at a much later date, via a different asset class: housing. As Blanchard observed: 'We now realize that economists and policymakers alike were lulled into a false sense of security by the apparent success of economic policy ahead of the crisis.'[52]

Until the crash, the conventional economic wisdom (or perhaps the wisdom of those who made economic convention) was that central banks should not lean against asset price bubbles, but come out after the crashes to clean up the mess. Greenspan argued that policymakers should react only if asset price bubbles threatened price stability—and by 'price stability' he meant the prices of current-period goods and services. He argued that those trying to spot and prick a bubble could not possibly identify a bubble for certain, and know that they were deflating one. If they got their bubble prognostications wrong, they might dampen a healthy economic expansion that would never have led to a crash. If they acted alone, they would risk holding back their own country's economic growth. Even if they could work out that there was a bubble, lengthy and unpredictable time lags, between a policy action and its impact on the economy, would risk instability; if a policy action started to work only after a bubble had burst 'naturally', the fallout might be worse. Greenspan was far from alone. As Mishkin observed: 'It is hugely presumptuous to think that government officials, even if they are central bankers, know better than private markets what the asset prices should be.'[53] Such thinking has a long pedigree. Princeton economist Joseph Lawrence 'achieved minor notoriety'[54] by declaring, shortly before the crash of 1929, that: '[T]he consensus of judgment of the millions whose valuations function on that admirable market, the Stock Exchange, is that stocks are not at present over-valued . . . Where is that group of men with all-embracing wisdom which will entitle them to veto the judgment of the intelligent multitude?'[55] Those who called a bubble a bubble and argued that bubbles should be dealt with, were mavericks, eccentrics, who had broken a golden rule of economic etiquette—like swearing in church.

To make matters worse, policymakers treated all types of bubbles—whether in share prices or house prices—the same. In truth, while it was certainly right to be sceptical of measures targeted at 'stabilizing' share prices, it was careless to apply the same logic to housing markets. First, volatile house prices are often more damaging for an economy than volatile share prices. Second, it is easier to work out that house prices are misaligned than it is to work out that share prices are misaligned. Third, it is easier to dampen (through prudential tools) house-price volatility than share-price volatility. In particular, most ordinary people do not buy shares on margin, whereas they do in the case of housing; they spread their purchase of stocks and shares (for example, through their pension schemes) over a lifetime, and so benefit from some smoothing of volatility, but they sink their house purchase at one point in time and take the risk of volatility.[56]

However, politicians are not enthusiastic bubble prickers at the best of times. When economies are strong, or even just apparently strong, politicians find easy ways to justify higher asset prices in order to avoid the act of pricking. Indeed, they treat high asset prices, especially house prices, as confirmation of the wisdom of their economic ways. When economies are weak, politicians are even less willing to prick a bubble, fearing that it will make matters worse. House-price bubbles are surprisingly popular too. Across huge swathes of the planet, taking deliberate actions that would cause pain to a few now, in order to avoid a lot of pain for many later, who would never appreciate the pain they were spared, was one act of political insanity too far. The more natural political tendency was to favour after-the-event rescue over prevention. This bias in policymakers' actions created the famous 'Greenspan put' in housing: with no policy action when housing markets are overshooting upwards, but plenty of action to protect households and financial firms when housing markets are collapsing, price bubbles are encouraged to be even bigger.

Perhaps, macroeconomic stability needs a higher inflation-rate target. In the UK, the previous 2% target was based on the notion that unstable inflation, and not inflation *per se*, is the danger, and that a lower inflation rate is more likely to be a stable inflation rate. A 2% target, it was reasoned, was more likely to create stability than a rate even just a few per cent higher (if one allows for improvements in quality and changes in consumer choices, a 2% target is pretty close to an effective target of 0%). At higher targeted rates, overshooting errors—perhaps caused by economic lags—would create inflation volatility that would unhinge inflation expectations and risk inflationary behaviour.

The crash demonstrated that excessively low inflation-rate targets carried dangers too. Low-frequency high-impact instability is more difficult to dampen when the ability to set interest rates much below inflation has been lost. Adjustment then has to come through non-conventional monetary measures or through unemployment. If a 2% inflation rate target was associated, on average, with a 5% policy interest rate, then a 4% target would be associated on average with a 7% policy interest rate. This would give an extra 2% wiggle room. Because financial markets condition their behaviour on what they know to be the wiggle room, a higher inflation-rate target, or so the logic goes, would reassure the markets that central banks can respond when house prices crash.

However, matters are not quite so straightforward. If inflation was, say, 4% on average, then prices would double every 15 years. This is a much quicker doubling than at 2%. More problematically, if the inflation-rate target in the past had been 4%, inflation would have been coming in below target for most of the 2000s, and policy interest rates would need to have been lower, perhaps as low as 2% or 3%, to try to stimulate inflation. Real interest rates would have been even more negative, and asset price bubbles even bigger! Given the underlying global imbalances and deflationary pressures, a higher inflation target would not have helped if the only tool at policymakers' disposal was an interest rate. We should also note, incidentally, that moving to a higher inflation-rate target in the aftermath of a crash would not be advisable; it would send out the signal of intention to let debts be inflated away, which would risk panicking bond markets. In a crisis, an inflation-rate target would also be problematic because it is not possible to adjust for missing the target. At such times, targeting a price-level *path* would be better because it would allow for any early underachievement to be offset by a later overachievement and vice versa.

Central banks chose not to lean against asset price bubbles, especially in housing, in part because they had conditioned themselves into having just the one policy tool (the short-term, usually overnight, money market rate) and the one target (current-period price stability).[57] Of course, the interest rates that really mattered were those on 12-month corporate loans or, in the US, on thirty-year mortgages. However, the links were felt to be strong enough to be able to influence the overall financial situation through the one interest rate. There were those who argued that asset price bubbles could be dealt with through suitably modified inflation-targeting regimes, because the effects of asset price bubbles showed up in output gaps and inflation.[58] There were others who argued that expecting matters to resolve naturally, and therefore adopting a policy of 'benign neglect',[59] was just too dangerous, and that central banks needed to respond when deviations from asset price fundamentals seemed significant. But this would need new tools. Before the crash, the creation of such tools was totally off the political cards.

With just the one policy tool, the twin goals of price stability and asset-price stability were in competition with each other. If a policy interest rate is used on its own to tackle the inflation embedded in asset prices, then only a small proportion of the policy rate is set on the basis of current one-period goods-and-services inflation (since goods-and-services inflation would constitute a small part of the inflation index that is being targeted) and the majority of the policy rate would be set on the basis of the future inflation that is embedded in asset prices (which would constitute most of the index being targeted).[60] In 2003–2005, if the UK had set its short-term policy interest rate consistently higher in order to tame its property-market excesses, a big rise in short-term interest rates would have been needed. The growth of domestic demand would have fallen short of that needed for inflation to be on target, unemployment would have risen, inflation would have fallen, and at some point deflation might even have taken hold. This would not have affected long-term interest rates on world capital markets or stopped 'irrational exuberance' in the US. The exchange rate would also have appreciated and economic harm would have been inflicted by a collapse in exports. The UK, acting alone, would have suffered higher unemployment and real economic damage for very little gain.

In the 1990s and 2000s there was plenty of debate about more tools but, at a time when price stability seemed to have been achieved, the minimalist approach suited the mood of the time. The disagreement was polite. Those who wanted more tools would be listened to, but only after the current way of doing things had first shown its limitations by crashing. The key issue after the crash was to supplement the interest rate tool with new macroprudential tools that would limit bank lending over the cycle. These might, in particular, include requirements on bank capital from a macroprudential perspective, targets for credit aggregates, and limits on LTV. Standard goods–and-services price stability would be the target of the interest rate. Financial stability would be the target of the new macroprudential measures and capital requirements. We will return to this in Chapter 12.[61] Those who argue that new tools would impose costs would do well to reflect that when the crash came, the single interest-rate tool *was* supplemented by 'unconventional operations' that had large and unpredictable costs.

Another option was to extend inflation targeting so as to include a target for asset price inflation, especially of house prices. Of course, this would compel policymakers to make judgements about the sustainability of house-price levels. Before hastily dismissing this, sceptics should ask themselves what would have happened if they had heeded the warnings of those who argued in the mid-2000s that house prices were overvalued.

After the crash, macroeconomists ventured out of their bunkers in a refreshingly self-critical mood. Willem Buiter, to make sure that his readers could not possibly entertain the slightest doubt, titled one of his blogs 'The unfortunate uselessness of most "state of the art" academic monetary economics'. Robert Solow, a Nobel laureate, wrote: 'I am left with the feeling that there is nothing in the empirical performance of these models that could come close to overcoming a modest scepticism. And more certainly, there is nothing to justify reliance on them for serious policy analysis.'[62] Marcus Miller, and Joseph Stiglitz, another Nobel laureate, described one of the key macroeconomic workhorses as: 'ill-suited to understanding the origins of the crisis or designing measures to solve it'.[63] But theirs was not a counsel of despair. Many of the ideas that needed to be incorporated into macroeconomic models had been around for a while. A 'Great Moderation' mindset had given little incentive to include some of this thinking, and the crash had injected renewed vigour into those pushing to incorporate it into, and thereby improve, the modelling. Three things became clear. First, in the future, central banks were going to have to pay a lot more attention to asset prices, especially house prices. Second, new tools would be needed to supplement the interest rate tool. Third, monetary policy was going to have to become a lot less target-driven and much more nuanced—that is, it would have to involve a return to the sort of world from which policymakers thought they had escaped in the early 1990s. No longer would monetary policy be the easy path to economic paradise.

9
Austerity and the Battles Over Sovereign Debt

Debt in a Balance Sheet Recession

The years of abundance were over. Years of famine were about to ravage the land. In a range of advanced economies, the deleveraging of the private sector and the rebalancing of the economy were going to take a long time. The government sector was going to be the shock-absorber in the short run as the stock of sovereign debt first rose, and then fell when the private sector recovered. More sovereign debt was inevitable, but exactly how much? If attempts were made to rein it in too quickly, economies would collapse, private-sector deleveraging would take even longer, the decline in tax revenues would make the pile of sovereign debt higher. Financial markets would panic, propelling interest rates higher, and prospects for future growth would be harmed. Yet, if sovereign debt was reined back too slowly, panic about its sustainability would kick in before private-sector deleveraging was over. The interest burden would grow, the pile of sovereign debt would end up bigger, and an even greater future tax burden would harm investment and growth. Finding the sweet spot between these two painful economic realities became the Golden Fleece of macroeconomic success or failure. Of course, not everyone was looking.

Policymakers struggled with a deep irony. Debt had been at the heart of the crash. How could debt have a role in the recovery? Crucially, the two types of debt were not the same. Much of the first was private-sector debt, secured against housing as collateral. The second was sovereign debt, secured against the tax-raising powers of governments. If private-sector debt had become riskier than sovereign debt, the overall economic cost could be made lower by easing adjustment in the former by temporarily accepting more of the latter. Both types of debt carried risks. On the one hand, private-sector debt difficulties would show up in millions of acts of default, rapidly declining asset prices, and feedback spirals that would send economies even further towards deflation. On the other hand, sovereign debt difficulties would involve whole governments defaulting or, short of that, the burden on taxpayers rising. The challenge was to steer a path between these two risky possibilities. It was clear before the crash that the US, the UK, and others needed to be creating a fiscal cushion to withstand the crash.[1] Failure to do this was about to impose a very heavy cost.

There are two components to the cost of sovereign debt—capital repayment and interest payments. Stable 'rich-world' governments don't worry about capital repayment because when a tranche of sovereign debt comes up for repayment, a new tranche can be issued. The burden of interest payments is a function of the interest rate charged on a country's sovereign debt and the ratio of that country's stock of sovereign debt to its GDP. For long-term solvency, any current fiscal deficit needs a larger primary fiscal surplus later. This can be achieved by some combination of: a fall in non-interest public spending; an increase in the tax burden (at any given level of GDP); or higher growth which pulls the fiscal costs of unemployment down and generates higher tax revenues (without pushing up the tax burden at any given level of GDP). There is no free lunch, but sovereign debt is less burdensome if it is repaid from the proceeds of growth.

Many standard arguments against running temporarily higher government budget deficits are much less applicable in a balance sheet recession. It is usual fare in economics that budget deficits 'crowd out' private-sector investment: governments compete against the private sector for real resources; this pushes up the interest rates that the private sector must pay; this reduces the amount of investment that the private sector can do; and this reduces economic growth. However, in a balance sheet recession, economies are awash with private-sector savings, exceeding what the private sector wants to borrow (and interest rates cannot work to align the two). In the US, the UK, and in a range of other OECD countries, this excess flooded into government bond markets. This pushed bond prices higher and bond yields lower, even as the supply of new government bonds was rising.

If not now, then perhaps eventually, like Peter at the gates of fiscal Heaven, bond markets would divide those in the queue into the 'fiscally responsible' to be rewarded with lower long-term interest rates, and the 'fiscally profligate' to be dammed to higher long-term interest rates forever (or until default, a form of purgatory). Sovereign debt is a confidence trick. It is not backed by any physical collateral. One set of creditors must believe that the debt can be rolled over in the future to another set of creditors. If growth is low and the interest rate on the debt is high, then higher taxes and government spending cuts will eventually be proposed as the way to get the level of debt back down. As the political cost of such measures rises, the likelihood that they be carried out decreases. The bond market prices this in, and the judgment can be harsh. As one of President Clinton's advisors, James Carville, once observed: 'I used to think that if there was reincarnation, I wanted to come back as the president or the Pope or a 0.400 baseball hitter. But now I want to come back as the bond market. You can intimidate everybody.'[2] Yet, in the years immediately after the crash, the bond market did not seem that intimidating. Even in the spring of 2011, ten-year government bonds were trading at about 3.4% in the US and only a little higher, at 3.6%, in the UK. Outside of the eurozone, most developed-country governments could borrow long term at half the real yield of a decade earlier. By late 2011, interest rates on ten-year government bonds were under 2% in both the US and the UK, and real rates were negative. Such low rates reflected the bond market's view that the US and the UK were struggling with the deflationary consequences of burst credit bubbles, and not that their default was imminent.

Maybe danger could be read from the rising costs of insuring sovereign debt. Yet, by the spring of 2011, the cost of insuring $10 million of US sovereign debt for five years, at about $45,000 per year, had halved since the spring of 2009. The cost was about $1 million for an equivalent amount of Greek government debt. Indeed, according to the market, the US was the fifth safest of 156 countries, and the safest of all G20 countries. Germany, France, and Australia were all deemed far more likely to default than the US. Furthermore, for countries with a low ratio of sovereign debt to GDP, the spreads on CDSs on their sovereign debt had, on occasion, risen because of high short-term funding needs. On the other hand, in countries with high ratios of sovereign debt to GDP, CDS spreads had hardly moved. This suggested that, at least within a range, the issue was less about the size of the outstanding stock of a country's sovereign debt and more about that country's short-term funding (i.e. debt roll-over) needs. Regarding bank debt guaranteed by governments, the spreads were higher than on sovereign debt because of the extra risks, but much lower in the case of countries such as the US, the UK, and France than, for example, Greece and Ireland. In 2011, financial markets were not worrying that the US, the UK, France, and others might be unable to make good on their sovereign debt commitments.

Like the argument that the universe is turtles all the way down,[3] the retort would be that, although the bond market looked relaxed now, just wait and see, it will deliver its punishment eventually. In this case, worries about sovereign debt boil down to worries about sudden crises based on self-fulfilling beliefs.[4] These are triggered the very first moment that it becomes clear that the welfare of holders of sovereign debt will, at some future date, be ranked lower than the welfare of everyone else. Backwards induction[5] from that date brings default forward to the present. Above a particular level of sovereign debt (the 'trigger' point), bond markets panic, interest rates charged on sovereign debt shoot up, and the burden of sovereign debt rises. This necessitates higher taxes and spending cuts. This, in turn, raises the domestic political pressure to default. Bond markets panic even more—and the self-fulfilling loop starts all over again. Shouldn't levels of sovereign debt be cut early so as to establish credibility with financial markets and to take away the risk of even being near to such a trigger point?

But crisis models are our friends as well as our foes. What if the cost caused by premature austerity is great, and the current situation is nowhere near the trigger point? What if premature austerity reduces both public- and private-sector expenditure and income (in a deleveraging economy facing grave uncertainties, the risks are already tipped in the direction of the private sector cutting its investment)? This would pull tax revenues down and unemployment costs up, push sovereign debt higher, and take economies closer to such trigger points. The very thing that politicians strive to avoid, they bring about by striving!

It matters too who owns a country's sovereign debt. In countries such as the US and the UK, a large amount of the savings that were needed to finance budget deficits were being generated domestically by private sector deleveraging. Payments being made by one group, via taxation, to cover the interest costs of sovereign debt, were being picked up by another group, who owned the debt, in the same society (and the two groups partly overlapped). The more of a government's debt that is held domestically, the less likely is default since: the high yields on the debt are recirculated domestically, the benefit of reneging is lower, and the domestic political fallout of reneging is higher. In the spring of 2011, about 62% of outstanding real US federal debt was owned by US individuals and government institutions (including social security, the US civil service, and military trust funds). This figure included 7% held by the Federal Reserve.[6] The rest was held by foreign nations, including China (China's 9.5% holding was lower than much media coverage suggested). If the residents of a country were cutting their consumption and their borrowing and perfectly willingly putting their savings into government bonds of that country, they were offseting their own aggregate-demand-diminishing behaviour with an increase in aggregate demand by another route. If they were happy to do so at very low interest rates, why should the government not take advantage? One could see in the figures the increasing reliance of the US on sovereign wealth funds and foreign central banks.[7] This was something that needed to be watched. However, in a world beset by all kinds of risks, it was not a major cause for alarm. In the UK, most of the debt was also long-term such that the risks of debt roll-over were low.

Nevertheless, although governments such as those of the US and the UK had found it relatively easy to sell their debt by tapping, at very low cost, domestic savings and sovereign wealth funds, this would not go on forever. One day the shift of demand back to higher-yielding corporate debt would push Treasury yields higher. Furthermore, because of QE some governments had been the biggest buyers of their own debt; one day this prop would be removed too. And, some governments had benefited from inflows of capital caused by a 'flight to quality' and a 'flight to liquidity', which had offset the forces that were tending to increase their government borrowing costs. As these flows reversed, their borrowing costs would rise. The US in particular benefited from its status as the global reserve currency, making it the safest financial port in the storm into which, at times, many crowded; eventually they would want to leave.

In the early 1990s, Japan's banking crisis cost the Japanese government $1 trillion, and Japan's sovereign debt crept higher. There were worries that yields on Japanese government bonds would shoot up. However, like many countries in economic trouble after the crash, Japan was facing a balance sheet recession. The Japanese government was not competing against the private sector for funds, and a large proportion of Japan's sovereign debt was held in domestic hands. Twenty years on, the Japanese government, in spite of having sovereign debt at over 200% of its GDP and having lost its triple-A status, was still able to fund itself with ten-year bond yields of under 1.5%. Japan's experience tells us that there are costs and dangers from too little sovereign debt, as well as from too much sovereign debt, during a balance sheet recession.

Finally, it matters whether budget deficits are 'active' (used for pushing recovery and paying for investments that are key to growth, rebalancing, and putting the unemployed to work) or 'passive' (caused by high unemployment and slow growth leading to tax revenues that are insufficient to cover public spending). Unfortunately, the ballooning budget deficits in many countries were increasingly becoming passive.

In mid-2009, Christina Romer, Chair of the President's Council of Economic Advisers and a scholar of the Great Depression, warned of the dangers of repeating the mistakes that prolonged the Great Depression.[8] She observed that we have come to think of the recovery from the Great Depression as slow because full employment was not achieved until the outbreak of the Second World War, but how a closer inspection of the data reveals that recovery was fast after the policy disasters of the early 1930s. Initially, politicians of all persuasions, from communist to free-market capitalist, mistakenly clung to the simple intuition of balanced budgets and money backed by gold. Then, in the four years after Roosevelt took office in 1933, US GDP growth averaged 9% per year. Twelve million jobs were created in about five years, and unemployment fell from 25% to 14%. It was the most rapid sustained growth the US has seen in peacetime. Then, in 1937, the fiscal stimulus was removed, and social-security taxes were imposed for the first time. The budget deficit was reduced to about 2.5% of GDP.[9] The Fed, fearing that, once recovery was under way, there would be another speculative credit binge and that excess reserves would make it difficult to fight inflation, doubled reserve requirements on banks. The Fed had misread the situation. Banks were still very risk-averse after the financial panics of the early 1930s, and were holding large reserves, way beyond the legislated requirement, as an extra cushion. The result was a double-dip recession. Romer argued that a similar premature urge to withdraw measures might backfire. Just about the worst thing policymakers could do was to emphasize only deficits, have no strategy for dealing with the surpluses generated by the deleveraging process of the private sector, and forget the importance of growth and of economic rebalancing for getting levels of future sovereign debt lower.

Sadly, by 2010, the economic sea was getting treacherous. Navigation was becoming more erratic, and Romer's fears were starting to come true as, all across the world, leading politicians took to treating economies like households—along strict Dickensian lines: 'Annual income twenty pounds, annual expenditure nineteen nineteen six, result happiness. Annual income twenty pounds, annual expenditure twenty pounds ought and six, result misery.'[10] The was followed by the usual fallacy of composition—that because the result of an act is good for a single household, a whole economy of households performing that act will lead to a good collective outcome.

The US Long-Term Sovereign Debt and Short-Term Stimulus Problems

In late 2003, I wrote that the US risked a fiscal crisis in the future if it did not get a grip on its long-term fiscal weaknesses.[11] The risks were threefold. First, underfunded entitlement programmes: Social Security, which covers pensions; Medicare, which is government-run insurance to pay for healthcare provided by the private sector for seniors and the permanently physically disabled; and Medicaid, which is health insurance for the poor. Second, the implicit promise to bail out Fannie Mae and Freddie Mac. Third, high levels of military spending.

Two trends, long known about, were set to drive US sovereign debt much higher if nothing was done. The first was the impending retirement of 'baby boomers'—about a quarter of the population. This was set to push the ratio of beneficiaries per 100 workers from 30 to about 47 by the 2030s.[12] The second was the growing cost of medical care, which over four decades had consistently risen by about 6% per year, way beyond the rate of inflation. The appetite of US healthcare for gobbling up-public- and private-sector GDP—currently 20%, and twice the OECD average—was alarming, and all efforts to control its eating habits had failed. Thus, Social Security, Medicare, and Medicaid expenditures were set to grow from 44% of non-interest government spending to 65% by 2030. According to the US Treasury, the long-term shortfall on Social Security alone was about $43 trillion.[13] Mary Meeker (who was not all that her name might suggest) estimated that total US government unfunded liabilities were about $75 trillion.[14]

The US had had plenty of time to start the adjustment. President George W. Bush, a baby boomer himself, encouraged by Vice President Dick Cheney ('Reagan showed that deficits don't matter'[15]), did the opposite. Despite having the opportunity to get US national debt to zero by the end of the decade, Bush instigated unfunded permanent tax cuts that totalled several trillions, turned a $2 trillion government budget surplus into a huge budget deficit, doubled the $5.7 trillion national debt, left little or no productive investment to show for this, and lived off the largesse of the Chinese and off the biggest US property bubble in history. Bush replicated what Brown and Blair were doing: running budget deficits at the top of the economic cycle and grabbing as much as possible from the next generation of politicians and taxpayers. Bush justified the tax cuts for the very richest with the notion that this would stimulate US job creation and growth. For once, we can taste the results: a decade of no net job creation, the stagnation of middle-class incomes, growing inequalities that contributed to the severity of the crash, and no fiscal cushion for when the crash came. Bush's actions were not out of step with the mood of his times; twice, electoral love had proved blind to such blatant economic folly.

Unfortunately for Obama, polls in mid-2010 showed that voters were even more worried about jobs and inflation than about the budget deficit. The record swing away from Obama in late 2010 was not a vote for austerity, but a protest vote against unemployment at more than 9% and against the bank bailout. No president since Franklin Delano Roosevelt had been re-elected with unemployment over 7.2% and rising. Reagan managed it because the rate was falling.

Early in 2011, the impact of federal discretionary stimulus was coming to an end. US states were embarking on severe spending cuts and tax rises to balance their budgets. Local governments in areas blighted by the foreclosure crisis were finding their property taxes vanishing just as they were facing some of their greatest ever demands. The extremely weak response to super-low interest rates and QE suggested that the US economy was even more structurally vulnerable than it had been in the 1930s. With its economy slowing again, the US needed more short-term federal stimulus matched with a credible long-term deficit-reduction plan. Markets would have accepted more fiscal stimulus in the short-term if the long-term risks were being tackled. Alas, the US political elite, with rare exceptions, conspired instead to conjure up an entertainment that was something between a pantomime and a game of chicken.

Obama went first, submitting to Congress in February 2011, a budget that did not stabilize the ratio of US government debt to GDP in the long term. He handed the task of working out how to achieve this to a commission. The National Commission on Fiscal Responsibility and Reform (the 'Bowles–Simpson Commission') proposed a target of $3.9 trillion deficit reduction over a decade, with the goal of stabilizing, and then reducing the ratio of US sovereign debt to GDP. The bulk, 80% of the deficit reduction was to come from the reform of entitlements. The remaining 20% was to come from higher tax revenues due to slightly higher tax rates for the wealthiest, to capital gains and dividends being taxed at the same rate as ordinary income, and to the gradual elimination of tax exemptions and subsidies such as for home-mortgage interest, employer-provided healthcare and other fringe benefits, ethanol, private jets, and various expenditures exempted at some time or another by some politician or another for some political advantage or another. More revenues, lower tax rates at the margin, fewer economic distortions—a useful contribution to long-term fiscal stability, one might have thought.

The US tax code was ripe for reform. Over the years, it had been nibbled here and pecked at there until it had become one gigantic sieve, notorious for its inability to collect much revenue. The White House calculated that in 2011, US households on average, paid just 14.4% of their income in federal tax, the lowest in 60 years. Some of the richest individuals benefited from some of the lowest effective tax rates of all. A report from the US Internal Revenue Service in April 2011 found that in 2007 the super-rich, the top 400 highest income earners, by structuring their tax affairs to take advantage of lower tax rates on capital gains and on dividends than on income, paid an effective tax rate of just 17% (down from 26% in 1992). Multibillionaire Warren Buffet, calling for the super-rich to pay a bigger share of the tax burden, pointed out that his overall tax rate was lower than that of his secretary. In early 2012, Republican presidential hopeful Mitt Romney (estimated net worth $190–$250 million) revealed that he had paid only 13.9% in federal income tax in 2010. This was less than the average American wage-earner. Such a low rate was perfectly within the rules, so long as every opportunity in the tax code to avoid paying tax was sufficiently rigorously applied. According to the OECD, adding up all sources of tax, the US tax burden was about 25% of GDP in 2010. In contrast, the rates were about 35% in the UK, 36% in Germany, and 48% in Denmark.[16] Amongst OECD countries, only Chile and Mexico had a lower tax burden than the US. What was so unreasonable about filling some of the US budget deficit gap with a little bit more tax revenue?

A few simple measures could make a dramatic improvement. If federal tax receipts were to go up to 18% of GDP, which was their average over the previous forty years, a third of the US annual budget deficit would disappear. If the Bush-era tax cuts were allowed to expire, the average American family would pay about $1,500 per year more, which would supply a $3 trillion deficit reduction over ten years. The IMF, in a 2010 study of 30 industrial countries that had closed their budget-deficit gaps since the 1980s, found that they achieved it through spending cuts and tax increases in roughly equal measure.[17] Unfortunately, the US electorate and their politicians were inimical to such practical reasonableness. Polls regularly reported that voters were consummate masters of doublethink, wanting government debt to be cut but unwilling to countenance for themselves fewer entitlements or higher taxation to do it. Obama ignored, or felt obliged to ignore, his own commission's proposals.

Republicans understood the contradiction and based their dramatic 2010 mid-term success upon it. They promised to cut $100 billion dollars off the current year's budget deficit, and they fed too off the declining political fortunes of Obama. By now, Obama was clinching deals that offered increasingly little to those who had voted for him in 2008, and many of his natural supporters kept away from voting.

However, there was a new voice on the political block. The Tea Party, the tail that now wagged the Republican dog with an energy that bordered on the manic, was outraged—or at least made a good semblance of being outraged, which was really the point—and threatened a government shutdown if it did not get its way. With just an hour to go, the proposed cuts finally gravitated to

$78.5 billion. Processing this number alongside fourteen trillion dollars (the level of US federal debt in mid-2011) and a division symbol through a calculator revealed just how surreal the political debate had by now become.

The Tea Party was a creature of its times. It reflected the view of those in the US population who felt that the US government spent too much of their tax dollars protecting the rich and powerful (the bank bailout had not helped), and who were angry at the way Washington had treated them over the years. The Tea Party had worked out how to channel all that anger in a machine for manufacturing protest against 'big government' and against all those who represented it. With few real policies on anything, the Tea Party was anti-establishment in ways that were remarkably establishment. In the 'financial engine of the Tea Party'[18] (in Romney's words) sat two billionaire petrochemical brothers, Charles and David Koch, at whose behest the party exploited the heavily gerrymandered primaries system to gang up on, and oust, moderate Republicans in the 2010 mid-term elections. The phalanx of talk-radio and TV news channels that promoted the Tea Party's agenda knew that any suggestion of intelligent compromise would have killed the story and caused audience ratings, and advertising revenues, to plummet. Instead of conservative politics being promoted as the art of the possible, it *had* to be portrayed as an endless struggle. The unorthodox 'no compromise' message, now something of an orthodoxy amongst those who believed in it, pulled in money from disgruntled rich donors. The Tea Party took Obama at his word and turned it on its head, in a political philosophy based entirely on the audacity of nope.

The Tea Party, not the sort to miss an opportunity to make life even more difficult whenever at all possible, ruled out cuts in popular programmes like Medicare and Social Security and in military spending. The cuts had to be applied to a sliver, just 12% of the federal budget. Playing fantasy war on the head of such a precarious fiscal pin meant cutting some of the investment that were most needed for long-term growth, such as in infrastructure and education. Some of those now threatening to destabilize an already fragile economy were the very same people who had encouraged the policies that had drained the government of resources in the first place. Having generated fiscal problems, they were now cynically using the crash to slash programmes they never really liked, while still stubbornly refusing to deal with the long-term fiscal challenges. The rise in crash-related budget deficits was a skirmish at the edge of a much bigger war, but it suited some to treat this as the war.

In his 2008 campaign, Obama had promised not to raise taxes on the middle classes. Average voters liked the idea of soaking the rich—in polls, 70% were in favour—so long as they did not have to pay any more tax themselves. Now

Obama was trapped. Imposing higher taxes only on those making more than $250,000 per year was not, its own, going to solve the long-term fiscal problems. And every time Obama talked of investing in infrastructure, education, technology, and competitiveness, he simultaneously undermined himself by sticking to low ratios of federal tax to GDP. Obama had been heavily attacked in late 2010 by those in the Republican Party who saw the sane rebalancing of the fiscal books by tax revenues as akin to drinking poison. Those who suggested that Medicare needed reform, had been chided with claims that they promoted 'death panels'. Every time Obama had tried to scatter the Tea Party hordes, up had sprouted even more of them. The president who says 'Yes we can', but knows that he can't, wasn't about to offer them an arm or a leg again.

Some way had to be found to separate serious deficit hawks from those who merely squawked and pretended to have feathers so that they could pick off the weak and score ideological points. At the start of April 2011, up sprang Paul Ryan, the Republican Chair of the House Budget Committee, with a plan: 'The Path to Prosperity'. The plan was based on spending cuts only, and proposed getting the primary government deficit in balance by 2015, and federal government spending down to 20% of GDP by 2018. The 20% was, somewhat improbably, below the historic average even though the population was aging. Ryan claimed that, over ten years, his plan would cut $5.8 trillion of spending and $4.4 trillion of deficits compared to the Obama budget announced in February.

All the emphasis in the Ryan Plan was on medical costs. Starting in 2022, no longer would the government pay the majority of the cost of treatment covered by Medicare, (for those born since 1957); this programme would be replaced by health-insurance 'vouchers' (although Ryan avoided the word 'voucher') the value of which would be capped to rise no faster than inflation. Ryan argued that competition between insurers would drive health-care costs lower. Medicaid would be given to states in block grants, on the supposition that they would manage the funds with more of an eye to costs than the current programme, which passed most of the cost on to the federal level. Obama's health-reform plans would be scrapped. The need to eliminate tax loopholes and deductions was mentioned, but none were identified. Social Security, the biggest entitlement of all, was not discussed. The notion of raising revenue through more tax, even if marginal tax rates were lower, was ruled out, although cutting the top rate from 35% to 25% for both individuals and businesses was ruled in. 'We don't believe a lack of revenue is part of the problem, so we will not be discussing raising taxes,' declared Senate Republican leader, Mitch McConnell, leaving a meeting between Obama and Republicans in the White House in mid-April. Perhaps McConnell's thinking was being clouded somewhat by his belief that, whatever it took: 'The single most important thing we want to achieve is for President Obama to be a one-term president.'[19]

To some, lower taxes had become an article of faith that no amount of evidence could budge. It was conveniently forgotten that after Reagan—a hero to the Republican Party—had pushed through his 1981 tax cuts, the budget deficit went from 2.5% to nearly 6% of GDP, and the nominal stock of US sovereign debt rose from about $900 billion to about $.2.8 trillion. Ryan seemed to presume that tax cuts could only have the opposite effect. George H. W. Bush was voted out after only one term, in part because of his efforts to clean up after the Reagan budget deficits. His son was not going to be so foolish. Neither did some wish to remember that after Clinton raised taxes, almost exclusively on the wealthy, as part of his 1993 deficit-reduction plan, there followed the longest economic expansion in US history, and with it, the first government fiscal surplus in 30 years. Indeed, the knowledge that the government's finances were on a stable footing boosted confidence and investment, which did the rich no end of good.

There was only one thing wrong with the Ryan plan. It was not going to work. The plan's optimistic figures were based on a surge in growth and a big fall in unemployment, caused by lower taxes; this had never happened before. For all its claims to the contrary, the plan also failed to tackle, head-on, rising healthcare costs. The non-partisan Congressional Budget Office showed that private health-insurance coverage tended to cost more than public coverage, and so healthcare costs would still keep rising. The problem would simply be shifted to retirees, who would face rising treatment costs and a falling proportion of those costs being covered. The scheme would become a chronically under-funded voucher scheme, and there would be political pressure to increase the effective value of the vouchers or to simply abandon the scheme altogether.

The Ryan plan was a curious political proposition. In polls, two thirds of respondents opposed any change to Medicare or Social Security. Indeed Medicare was popular amongst Republicans. To give him credit: Ryan might have found himself deeply unpopular when being deeply unpopular was a necessary prerequisite for doing anything remotely economically sensible. Yet, by proposing far greater cuts to discretionary spending than those of the Democrats (two thirds of the cuts were to fall on programmes that especially helped the poor), the plan was not going to get through the Democrat-controlled Senate, and even if, against all the odds it did, it was anyway going to be vetoed by Obama. Unfortunately for Ryan, the plan could all too easily be caricatured as dismantling Medicare and Medicaid and using the proceeds to cut taxes for the rich.

Obama repeatedly shied away from putting a long-term fiscal plan on the table. Sometimes he hinted he knew what to do. One day in May 2011, passing through London, off-guard but still careful enough to leave out the word 'tax', he observed: '[W]e have to make sure we take a balanced approach that is a mixture of cuts but also thinking how we generate revenues.'[20] Accused of allowing himself to become a hostage to Republican agenda-setting, it was time for Obama to act.

A week after Ryan's announcement, Obama released his own plan for cutting $4 trillion of deficits over twelve years.[21] Approximately 70%–80% was to come through spending cuts. The rest was to come through higher tax on wealthier Americans, the 2% or so earning $250,000 or more per year. Cost control for Medicare would be via a new independent commission, as proposed in Obama's previous healthcare bill, with a target set for Medicare to grow no faster than GDP plus 0.5% per year. Military spending would be cut. The proposal was astonishing in many ways. It floated ideas that were anathema to many Democrats, including cutting Medicare, Social Security, and other key social programmes, in return for a miniscule concession on taxation from Republicans and the Tea Party. Obama was risking his party's wrath, and even its fragmentation, to edge towards the middle ground.

The plan was immediately rejected by the Republicans, almost entirely because of the intransigence of their Tea Party elements. Obama's own Democratic colleagues were also furious that the package was so tilted towards cuts, and, they felt, gave the upper hand to Republicans. Of the 193 Democrats who had survived the 2010 cull, about 70 were in the progressive, liberal wing of the party, and their revolt against the state of negotiations was growing. As a telling example of the games being played at the expense of economic recovery, the Republicans had rejected a compromise deal that harmed Obama within his own party and that would have ushered in the largest ever cut in the size of the US government—in preference for a smaller deficit reduction plan, of $2 trillion, conditioned on no tax rises, not even those related to the removal of inefficient tax loopholes.

The Debt-Ceiling Fight

Even more absurd, the US government imposed on itself a debt ceiling of $14.3 trillion—which was approaching fast. The Obama fiscal stimulus and the bank bailout contributed less than 5% of the stock of outstanding US sovereign debt; most was the result of the economic follies of the past and of the recent recession. By 2 August 2011, the US Treasury was going to lose its authority to borrow. In the past, raising the debt ceiling had usually not been a problem. Indeed amongst Republican presidents, Reagen had done it eighteen times, and George W. Bush seven times. This time, high on its Tea, the Republicans were determined to use the vote on raising the debt ceiling to leverage yet more short-term cuts. Those leading the charge clearly had no conception of how financial crises work. The last thing a government should ever do is cast doubt on its willingness to make good on its financial obligations. At best, this would raise the costs in non-default states, which would harm the economy. At worst, it would trigger default. The financial markets were treating the US as far from broke. Days before the possible default, the ten-year US Treasury yield was under 3% and government bond auctions were well-covered. Perhaps the markets were sending out a false signal, waiting to panic only if the US ran off the cliff and tested the effects of fiscal gravity. More likely, the markets were signalling that the biggest risk of all was political failure and lack of recovery. If so, why deliberately endanger the US economy by threatening to make its government broke? If difficulties in rolling over sovereign debt trigger higher borrowing costs and crises, this was madness.

The Tea Party saw things differently. In their view, other US voters, less enlightened than themselves, were just one cleansing default away from seeing the light and converting to the true economic faith. Like hardened end-time believers, those in the Tea Party would not just tolerate default; they were actively willing it on, only too eager to hold the full creditworthiness of the US government hostage to get their pound of political flesh. A disaster they brought on by their own antics would provide the very evidence they needed to justify their beliefs. If the next financial crisis had a trigger point, the Tea Party sure seemed in a hurry to find it.

On 31 May 2011, the Republican-controlled House of Representatives vetoed the first bill to raise the debt ceiling by $2.4 trillion. Utah Republican, Jason Chaffetz, member of the House budget committee, told Fox News: 'It's what they asked for . . . they're going to see it go down in flames.' Just to flex its muscles, in late July 2011 the House passed a bill to cut $5.8 trillion of spending over ten years, but including no tax rises. The Democrat-controlled Senate scheduled a vote to shoot the bill down (in flames, presumably). Obama, in a surprise late move, backed the fiscal-reform plan of the so-called 'Gang of Six', three Republicans and three Democrats who had gallantly been negotiating to implement some of the Bowles–Simpson plan in the face of the derision heaped on them by many in their own parties. This was meant to reduce the deficit by $3.7 trillion over the forthcoming decade. The move seemed to get the support of Republican leaders in the House, but the plan was too late and doomed by its tax-raising component (it would raise $1.2 trillion in new revenues over ten years).

In April 2011, the IMF had expressed severe doubts about the ability of the US to tackle its long-term fiscal trajectory. In April and June, S&P and Fitch had warned that not raising the debt ceiling would threaten financial stability in the US and the world. In mid-July, S&P declared: '[O]wing to the dynamics of the political debate on the debt ceiling, there is at least a one-in-two likelihood that we could lower the long-term rating on the US within the next 90 days.' They added that political debate in the US had 'become more entangled' with 'an increasing risk of a substantial policy stalemate enduring beyond any near-term agreement to raise the debt ceiling'.[22] None of the rating agencies was passing a strictly economic judgment on the US. After all, US taxes were at their lowest levels in decades, so if the US had a political will, there would be a way. The judgment was regarding the political inability in the US to achieve a viable economic solution.

A temporary loss of triple-A status could probably be managed. Those countries, such as China, that held large quantities of US Treasuries, would not dump their stockpile overnight, because that would hurt them too. However, US taxpayers would pay a price. In February 2011, the Congressional Budget Office calculated that even just a 1% increase in the interest rate faced by the government would add $1 trillion to its borrowing costs over a decade. This would swamp the discretionary cuts now being fought over. A default would lead to financial and economic collapse. Long-term interest rates would rise, unemployment would rise even further, and the budget deficit would be even bigger. Federal payments to US states would shrink, forcing them to make emergency arrangements that would cause local economies to spiral downwards.

Modern finance presumes there is a risk-free rate of return at the heart of the financial system to act as the reference point for pricing assets and derivatives. For decades, this risk-free rate was backed by the 'full faith and credit' of the US government. With that gone, those who used US Treasuries as collateral would have been forced to cut their trades, sparking a wave of deleveraging. If this had led to a credit crunch, it would have been a repeat of 2008, but without the US being available to bail the financial system out. Matters were so serious that Obama's first duty of care was to restate the absolutely obvious: a default would be a disaster.

The US political system was based on a paradox inside an enigma, wrapped tightly up inside a media bubble. It allowed numerous checks and balances, and it relied on compromise between Democrats and Republicans, yet both were sharpening their distinctions rather than blurring them. Obama knew that hitting anyone other than the rich with higher taxes would get him branded the 'tax-and-spend' president, who had gone back on his word. In an environment of negative election campaigns—where the point was not about winning but about making sure that that the other side lost—votes in favour of spending cuts or of tax rises generated ammunition for campaigns against incumbent politicians. In the 2010 mid-term elections, the Republican Party had filled its ranks with dozens of freshmen on a mandate to shrink the government at any cost. Now, marvellously uninterested in producing actual results, with their sense of purity triumphing over the merely practical, they too were trapped—humiliation being the penalty for compromise. With neither side giving, neither side could give. The Democrat and Republican parties were like two huge clashing rocks. All those who tried to sail between, risked being crushed.

In mid-July, having given up on trying to strain the Republican Party of its Tea Party elements, the House speaker, Republican John Boehner, and Obama were working on a 'deal' that would raise $800 billion in revenue in exchange for huge spending cuts. It got quashed by those Boehner sought to lead (as one veteran political commentator put it: 'Sixty to 100 of the Republicans he leads are damn near nuts'[23]). It also fell apart because Boehner (it was later revealed) insisted that Obama's 2010 healthcare overhaul be gutted.

The true fanatics at the heart of the Tea Party declared that if any of those newly elected in the 2010 mid-term elections under a Tea Party ticket voted for a bill that did not include the cuts they demanded or did include the tax increases they opposed, it would be viewed as betrayal. By now they had lost all sense of self-restraint, and didn't seem to care that, in this democracy at least, the White House and Senate were controlled by Democrats. Instead, they elevated financial-market provocation into something of a new art form, using the threat of a US sovereign debt default as the ultimate weapon to extract concessions that could not be gained by the democratic process. For those of a nutty disposition, the point wasn't to pass laws, but to create clear contrasts to be used as political ammunition in the next election campaign, not to take responsibility and act, but to abrogate responsibilty, force the other side to act, and then complain.

In late July 2011, with default just days away, behind-the-scenes talks were edging towards a compromise. The notion, it seems suggested by McConnell, was to allow Obama to raise the debt ceiling on his own initiative, in return for more modest spending cuts, and to allow a vote on it up to three times before an election, the results of which the president could veto. The Republican Party would get its chance to register disapproval, and so not lose face. Budget reform would wait. McConnell knew that if the US defaulted and this was blamed squarely on the Republicans, it would contain the seeds of Republican political destruction. Obama too faced dangers. He had repeatedly said that he would veto a partial deal, but his room for manoeuvre was narrowing by the day.

At the last moment, on 2 August, an agreement was cobbled together: the Budget Control Act. Enough Republicans in the end realized that to vote the deal down would get them blamed for driving the US into the arms of default. As last-minute compromises usually go, the deal was the worst of all worlds. When Obama and Boehner had nearly reached their $4 trillion 'grand bargain' in July—admitedly skewed towards spending cuts—they were close to sending a signal of political seriousness about tackling the long-term fiscal issues. The final deal conveyed no such signal. The debt ceiling was raised by $2.4 trillion, enough to avoid another squabble before the next presidential election. However, the issues that would shape the long-term path of national debt—tax revenues, spending on health, and an aging population—had been left to be fought over another day. There would be $2.2–2.5 trillion of spending cuts over the coming ten years, about $1 trillion agreed upfront and about $1.2–1.5 trillion to be determined by a bipartisan congressional supercommittee by late November 2011. If that committee failed to agree, a range of automatic cuts would come into effect, starting in 2013. Supposedly, this was to enforce bipartisan cooperation (but who was kidding who on that one?). A cut of $600 billion in 2013, about 4% of US GDP, would plunge the US in a double-dip recession. The very expectation of this would harm investment and consumer spending.

The political pain of allocating the cuts was avoided. Nor did the sums make any sense. Federal discretionary spending was supposed to fall to 5.4% of GDP in 2021. Yet, discretionary spending had averaged about 8.7% over the previous 40 years. The lowest it had ever been was 6.2% in 1999, but even that was after a decade-long boom and not a decade of decline. And there was no way the US fiscal problems could be put in order by cuts only in non-defence discretionary spending (loosely, those regular functions of government that are not defence, social security, or healthcare). These components currently stood at about 4.4%. The Congressional Budget Office, on a plausible set of assumptions, calculated that the budget deficit would still be in the region of 7.5% in 2021, so the sums could never add up even if *all* of the 4.4% was slashed. But slashing the 4.4% would require slashing the education, infrastructure, and public investments needed for recovery and long-term growth.

The US had made honouring its debts a political issue. No wonder then that although the debt ceiling had been raised, S&P did as it had promised, and downgraded the US (and, in late November 2011, Fitch put the US on negative watch for downgrade). Even with the downgrade, in September the rate on US ten-year gilts briefly hit a record low of 1.67%. At the end of 2011, the rate was still hovering under 2% and, by July 2012, was back down to 1.62%, a rate not seen since just after the Second World War. In late July 2011 there was a small upwards blip in the annual probability of US default (from about 0.8% to 1%, as derived from five-year CDSs). Otherwise, the market's view of the chances of the US defaulting was the same in mid-2012 as it had been in mid-2011. This was not what one would expect of an economy heading towards default, but more like what one would expect of an economy heading to become like of Japan which had struggled for 20 years with its balance sheet problems.

Perhaps predictably, at the end of November 2011, the bipartisan congressional supercommittee split itself down party lines, failed to reach aggrement on how to apportion the cuts, and bounced the problem back to Congress. The stage was set for a year-long political fight over automatic cuts (or their veto) in the run up to the 2012 presidential election. As their respective bargaining chips, the Democrats had the scheduled automatic expiration of the Bush tax cuts, and the Republicans the automatic $500 billion cuts in Pentagon spending over ten years. Congress and the Senate avoided all this by approving, in mid-September 2012, a $1.05 trillion spending bill to keep the federal government going till 27th March 2013.

The policy vacuum at the heart of US government was creating huge uncertainty for investors and consumers regarding the path of future fiscal policy at both federal and state levels. This was denting confidence and holding back recovery. In the spring of 2011 there had been signs, at last, of some private-sector revival and of the labour market reaching a turning point. By the summer of 2011, US politicians were doing their level best to extinguish this flicker of hope. If, from the start, the Democrats had been more proactive on the long-term fiscal issues, they would have starved of support those pushing for deep early cuts, and this would have sucked most of the poison out of the debates on the need for short-term stimulus. Obama, by failing to articulate and push early for what needed to be done, had ended up achieving less. Afraid to anger his own party, Obama had angered them anyway.

Both sides were procrastinating over long-term fiscal issues, to avoid having to make potentially unpopular decisions. They had already slipped into an 18-month election campaign—as fatefully as a patient might into a deep coma. Perhaps, they hoped, the key issues could be left until after the 2012 election. However, those issues were going to be just the same in 2013, and the difficulties even greater. The only window of opportunity for progress was going to be when the patient awoke in the first few months of a new presidency. Obama, if still president, would need to do something brave right at the start of his second term (the calm response of financial markets in 2011 even suggested that this was understood).

To Obama, the political dilemma must have been clear. He could have pushed for a long-term budget solution within his fist term, that involved painful reforms in entitlements and tax, but this would have risked voter wrath (including amongst his own supporters) and diminished his chances of a second term. That outcome, in his eyes, would have led to economic and social disaster because newly-empowered Republicans would have pushed the US even further towards the policy mistakes that had deepened and lengthened the recession of the 1930s. To break free, why did Obama not employ a smidgen of his famed oratorical skills to transform the economic narrative? His own bipartisan fiscal commission and the so-called 'Gang of Six' had cleared the path before him. The IMF, rating agencies, and others had all issued warnings that could have been turned into a call for action on the long-term debt issues. Obama wasn't helped much by an electorate that couldn't see just how much their current woes were the payback for the previous excesses for which that they had voted in their droves.

Perhaps Obama was judging that the single-minded simplicity of some of his opponents would become a liability. Indeed, within five months of the 2010 mid-term elections, those in the US population taking a negative position on the Tea Party had risen from 25% to 50%. Maybe Obama's chosen political route was to let the Republicans, under the heady influence of the Tea Party, wield the axe or take the US to the brink of default, and then respond once the potential damage was understood by the electorate. Perhaps, like a long-distance runner with a canny strategy to outfox the field and win, Obama was letting the pack run ahead and exhaust itself in the hope that, unable to believe its luck, the Tea Party would push self-indulgence to the point of Republican Party annihilation. For such a reportedly cautious president, it was a risky strategy and, perhaps, an audacious hope.

The UK's Austerity Experiment

In the UK, the smooth rhetoric of election time quickly gave way to the harsh reality of cuts. In his emergency budget of June 2010, the new Chancellor of the Exchequer, George Osborne, claimed that the UK had already lost the financial market's confidence. Seemingly oblivious to the peculiarities of a balance sheet recession, he introduced the most severe spending cuts in the UK since the 1970s, equal to a fiscal tightening of 7% of GDP over four years starting in the spring of 2011, and loaded into the later years (2% in 2014, and 2.8% in 2015).

This, he claimed, would eliminate, by 2015, the structural budget deficit (the bit left when economic growth is normal), and would be the sure route back to growth. Another 300,000 public-sector workers would go. Most families earning over £18,000 a year would have their tax credits cut and face higher National Insurance premiums (a tax on income). Child benefit would be frozen for three years, and the pay of public employees for two years. Mind you, Osborne was buoyed by the predictions of the new Office for Budget Responsibility—a recovery in GDP of 2.1% in 2011 and of 2.6% in 2012, inflation comfortably back under 2%, exports booming, and a positive trade balance contributing a third of growth even as government spending and investment were being cut back.[24]

An efficient programme of cuts would emphasize the relative inefficiency of what was being cut. Government announcements indicated little danger of such logic being applied. A range of alternatives—investment in science, new transport, and infrastructure; measures to boost youth employment; a major house-building programme—could wait. According to the Micawber school of economics, it was wiser to do such investments later when the interest charges would be higher, and the impact on growth and unemployment lower.

Falling dutifully into line, the new deputy prime minister, Clegg, contrary to all his earlier objections (such is the inebriating effect of power once supped), pushed the same message at his party's annual conference in late 2010. The £81 billion of cuts was somewhat bigger than the figure of £6 billion that just a few months before he, Cameron, and Brown had flicked back and forth for the entertainment of TV viewers in the pre-election debates. Now, the pill was sugar-coated with talk of the 'Big Society', a phrase cleverly coined by the new prime minister, Cameron. Unlike concrete spending programmes, the 'Big Society' could not be measured, and so nobody would ever know two or three years' later if society had got bigger, and who to hold to account if it had not.

To plump out the distortion some more, in his 2011 New Year address, Cameron claimed: '[W]e are clear that the alternative—indecision and delay— would mean taking unacceptable risks with our economy, our country, and our people.' Given the enormity of the dangers if he was wrong, one might expect some clear articulation of just what the 'unacceptable risks' were. Cameron, like Brown before him, seemed incapable of seeing that he could be taking unacceptable risks with the economy, the country, and its people even while he was posing as doing the opposite.

At the end of January 2011, Osborne asserted that the mere expectation of deep spending cuts had prevented a sovereign debt crisis in the UK.[25] It was an extravagant claim, based on such a flimsy pile of evidence. In his budget speech in March 2011 Osborne even claimed that the UK's long-term interest rates were close to those of Germany because of the expectation of cuts. However, the UK had a combined public- and private-sector debt much greater than Greece, never mind Germany, and was running a government deficit (10.3% in 2010) about three times the size of Germany's. Even more bizarrely, the difference between interest rates in the UK and interest rates in Germany had not budged since before the fiscal plans had been announced and, indeed, before Cameron, Osborne, and Clegg had come to power. The UK was not in the eurozone precisely so as not to have to match the policies being imposed on the eurozone periphery. This was a point lost on Osborne. Perhaps he was not such a break from Brown after all. It seems that, in the UK at least, with only the occasional short-lived exception, part of the job description of a Chancellor of the Exchequer is to have a streak of self-delusion.

Policymakers were embarking on the biggest experiment ever to test 'Ricardian equivalence'.[26] This is the notion that households assume that higher government spending today means higher taxes tomorrow, and therefore they cut consumption today to save to pay the higher taxes tomorrow—which renders governments powerless to alter the path of the economy. However, Ricardian equivalence presumes that household income is held fixed and that capital markets are perfect, so that households can borrow as much as they want at the same rate as the government. After a severe crash, when households are rapidly deleveraging and extremely credit-constrained, such logic needs to be treated with a generous pinch of caution. If large spending cuts mean that taxes will later be lower, and that the private sector will be stimulated to fill the gap, then cuts will stimulate recovery. But if cuts depress the prospects of the private sector, reinforce recession, and even trigger deflation, then Ricardian equivalence will *not* hold, and the burden of budget deficits and long-term debt will be even higher. Worse, if growth collapses, markets might come to believe that the only way out will be to inflate the debts away. This will, in glorious self-fulfilling fashion, bring on the very panic that those driving austerity say they are most keen to avoid.

In spite of the monetary stimulus of two years of near-zero interest rates, massive QE, and the much-vaunted boost to the economy caused by the mere expectation of large spending cuts, UK GDP shrank by about 0.6% in the last quarter of 2010. Construction and business investment shrank by about 2.5% apiece. In spite of the benefits of a falling pound to help revive exports, the trade deficit rose. In the first quarter of 2011 there was a shock collapse in business investment of over 7%. Only a tiny rise in GDP kept the UK from declaring an official recession. Indeed, if exceptional items were stripped out, the UK was already heading back towards recession. In the second quarter of 2011, a measly 0.2% rise in GDP indicated that the UK economy was treading water. A low-to-negative rate of economic growth was going to make no discernible dent in the unemployment figures and was going to eat into tax revenues and knock the debt-reduction plan off course. The seriousness of the situation was dismissed with another fallacy of composition: '[It] doesn't change the need to deal with the nation's credit card', proclaimed Osborne.

Osborne deliberately had no plan B. That, it seems, would be 'indecisive'—apparently an 'unacceptable risk'. As economic growth ground to a halt, Osborne declared: 'To back down now and abandon our plans would be the road to economic ruin. We will stick to the course. We will secure our country's stability. We will not take Britain back to the brink of bankruptcy.'[27] Just how near the UK was to bankruptcy was not explained (for all its faults, the UK was nowhere near). Jonathan Portes, director of the NIESR, accused Osborne of 'scaremongering' and described his logic as 'fundamentally flawed'. Richard Lambert, the departing head of the Conservative-leaning Confederation of British Industry, lobbed a shot over Osborne's bow by arguing that it was wrong to presume that the policy of cuts would deliver growth.

At the end of May 2011, Cameron declared: '[I]f you look [at] what has happened in Greece, Portugal or other EU countries you have often seen those bond rates increase. That is the risk we would have run if we had not set out on the path of deficit reduction.'[28] Perhaps Cameron knew that contrasting the UK's economy with that of Greece or Portugal was utterly preposterous, but he did it because he wanted to win a debating point or two (and, by now, the search for arguments was getting desperate, and any straw /άχυρο/palha would do). Or perhaps he did believe that the contrast was appropiate. It is not clear which is worse.

The main reason the UK had much lower interest rates than Greece or Portugal (or Ireland and Spain, who had long been running government budget surpluses) was because the UK had its own currency and could always create enough money to repay its debts. Eurozone countries had lost this ability, and this exposed then to a genuine risk of default, which pushed up their borrowing costs. The UK was also not obligated to bail out the euro, and the value of the pound in other currencies could fall to help the UK's economic recovery. In the UK it was inflation, and not default, that would ease the debts away if ever they became totally unmanageable. Yet UK interest rates were low because the bond market believed that UK medium-term growth and inflation prospects were very suppressed, and this was going to keep UK monetary policy very loose for a long time. In Cameron's defence, we hould add that if the world economy collapsed because of all the shenanigans in the US and Europe, then borrowing for the UK might get more risky. Perhaps tougher austerity was being forced on the UK by the foolishness of others. However, this was not the justification Cameron used and, in the eurozone, he was supporting the self-fulfilling errors that were bringing the disaster on.

All surveys in mid-2011 indicated that UK business confidence was rapidly shrinking, taking with it any desire to invest or hire. The UK's construction industry was hit especially hard. The numbers of small businesses defaulting on their loans shot up. A string of retail chains suffered sudden falls in sales and profits. It seemed that individuals and firms *were* reacting in advance of austerity measures, in negative and destructive ways, and that pessimism was begetting more pessimism. Indeed, when interest rates are close to zero, and huge amounts of unconventional monetary stimulus are needed in order to have any discernible impact, it is entirely predictable that prematurely aggressive austerity will do more harm than good (high-school and undergraduate economics students will recognize a world with a flat LM curve). Even the IMF started to worry about the 'contractionary effects on private domestic demand and GDP' of austerity.[29] It published analysis of 173 cases of fiscal consolidation and found that, consistantly, it resulted in economic contraction. The conclusion was: 'Fiscal consolidations that are unduly hasty risk prolonging the jobless recovery in many advanced economies. So countries with the scope to do so should opt for a slower pace of consolidation combined with policies to support growth.'[30]

The Experiment Failed

At the end of November 2011 the results were in. In a budget statement to Parliament, Osborne was forced to add £158 billion to the five-year forecast for government borrowing that he had made just a year before. This was much more than the size of the cuts supposedly to reduce the budget deficit. Government debt, instead of peaking at 70.3% of GDP, would now peak at 78% (even this figure was based on optimistic growth projections). The private sector would have to generate even more future tax revenues to fill the government's even bigger financial hole. Surely, this was opposite of what Osborne's policy was meant to bring about. Osborne should have learnt from Keynes who, facing fairly similar economic conditions, observed: 'The engine which drives Enterprise is not Thrift, but Profit.'[31]

The public finances were being hammered by low growth and rising unemployment, which were pushing tax (especially income tax) revenues down and benefit payments up. According to the OBR's 'optimistic' forecast (for they had 'pessimistic' ones too), the UK economy would be 13% smaller by 2016 than forecast by the UK Treasury in 2008. In the spring of 2011, the annual probability of a UK sovereign debt default (as derived from five-year CDSs) was about 0.8%, which was a little bit higher than that of the US. By early 2012, the probability of a US default had fallen, but the probability of a UK default had doubled—a blunt contradiction of the claim made by Cameron that the UK's austerity policy was going to reduce the risk of default.

Even if sovereign debt one day reached 80% of GDP, if that was all the debt to worry about, a sovereign debt crisis was avoidable. The problem was that, as Fitch put it, the UK had 'become the most indebted of any AAA-rated sovereign with the exception of the US'.[32] If the UK lost its triple-A status, it would be because of its combination of public- and private-sector debts. Yet the government never talked about the impact of austerity on the burden of private-sector debt.

Evidence was also mounting that the potential growth of the UK economy had been much lower than it had seemed in 2007, and that it had since been harmed. When the economy eventually recovered, there would be weaker growth in output and in spending, larger budget deficits, and yet more pressure for austerity. Then, as output tried to recover to its pre-crisis levels, there would be more pressure for interest rates to rise because of the lack of spare capacity pushing up inflation. The OBR predicted that it would take the UK at least another six years to eliminate the structural deficit, two more than Osborne originally contended. If the eurozone collapsed, this would stretch out even longer. The UK's sovereign debt was heading towards £1.5 trillion by 2017 (higher, if the eurozone collapsed). Cameron asserted that getting UK sovereign debt lower was 'proving harder than anyone envisaged'[33]—which wasn't strictly true. It was becoming ever clearer that monetary policy could not on its own salvage the economy, yet Cameron, Osborne, and Clegg were betting everything on a monetary policy rescue.

Over 2011, UK real household disposable income fell by about 1.2% and, in the first three months of 2012, by a further 0.9%. The UK's Institute for Fiscal Studies, IFS, reported that median incomes would not go above those of 2002 until 2015. This was much worse than in the Great Depression. As well as public spending cuts, inflation had eaten into UK consumption, which by late 2011 was 1.7% weaker than the Chancellor had expected in March 2011. Tax rises had also eaten into disposable income (VAT, a form of consumption tax, had gone back up from 15% to 17.5%, and then to 20%). In his March 2011 budget, Osborne had predicted that in 2012 the economy would grow by 2.5%. Now the OBR was predicting 0.7% if the eurozone did not deteriorate. Many other forecasters felt that Osborne would be lucky to see zero. The UK was still not moving towards rebalancing. Net trade was still negative, which meant that any improvement in the economy hinged on business investment. In March 2011 the OBR had predicted that over 2011 there would be a rise of 7% in business investment; now it was forecasting a fall of 0.8%.

In response to the dramatic deterioration in the UK's economic fortunes, Osborne pushed through cuts totalling another £36 billion by 2017. He scrapped an increase in child tax credits, and instigated a second two-year ceiling on public-sector pay rises of 1% per year, for 2013–2015, generating a total public-sector real pay cut of 16% over five years. And he accelerated the increase in the retirement age. The OBR revised its prediction of the number of public-sector job losses as a result of government policy, from 400,000 in the five years 2011–2016 to 710,000 in the six years 2011–2017.

Cameron and Osborne switched from claiming that the UK benefited from not being like Greece and the eurozone, to blaming Greece and the eurozone for the UK's problems. Certainly, the eurozone's woes were harming UK exports and growth; however, the UK's slowdown and the fresh rises in unemployment had started roughly when Cameron, Osborne, and Clegg had announced their economic strategy. At that time the economy was growing; so they could not attribute the dramatic deterioration of the UK's public finances to the eurozone's problems in 2011.

The coalition government had based its political hopes on a short, sharp economic shock followed by recovery, as the private sector rushed in to fill the gap left by the shrinking of the state. An election in 2015 immediately preceded by tax cuts and optimism would sweep Cameron and Osborne back into power. By 2011, the outcome was utterly unlike what they had presumed just a few months before, and it spoke volumes about the naïve economic thinking at the heart of their strategy. By mid-2012, the UK economy had experienced its worst four years, outside of war, in at least 100 years, and its slowest recovery since the 1930s—and this, even though the bulk of the austerity was yet to come. Markets that had priced in a rise in interest rates assuming there would be a recovery, switched to presuming low interest rates for much longer. Plan A had not gone according to, well, Plan A. Yet, Cameron, Osborne, and Clegg had insisted that there was no Plan B, reasoning that if they relaxed their strategy, the markets might punish the UK. By now, perhaps they were right. But, if so, that was their own fault for setting flexibility up to be seen as failure. Fitch was heading towards downgrading the UK's AAA credit rating. If that happened, Cameron, Osborne, and Clegg would struggle to pin that on the previous government and would only have themselves to blame. They were stuck. To back down would be an admission of failure that would gift a win to their opponents.

At the end of December 2011, UK ten-year government bond yields went below 2%. The last time that had happened had been in 1897, the year Queen Victoria celebrated her diamond jubilee. Portes observed: 'Our current historically very low level of interest rates is—just as in Japan—a sign of economic failure, not success.' Many parts of the business community that had initially cheered were starting to have their doubts. In January 2012, the UK's national debt hit £1 trillion for the first time. It wasn't going to hover there for very long.

Two years into a seven-year austerity drive, the UK needed a new strategy based on investment and growth. Because potential output had been damaged by the crash, it was also necessary to craft ways to increase the long-term capacity of the economy. The construction sector was one of the worst-hit and had some of the greatest spare capacity. Better infrastructure would raise the lagging productivity of the UK economy, which would raise future tax revenues, which would help to pay for the initial investment. Instead, the Comprehensive Spending Review of 2010 announced a 30% cut in public investment, from £59 billion in 2010–2011 to £45.4 billion in 2013–2014. Because of the recession, government spending was rising, and not falling: trying to stick to a deficit reduction target by slashing public investment was perverse.

In November 2011, after a very long and eventful journey, the penny had finally dropped. Even then, the 'National Infrastructure Plan' involved only a $5 billion direct boost to government infastructure spending over 2011–2015, which was way too small and did not even offset the already announced cuts in public investment. Even more bizarrely, this was to be funded by austerity cuts. Osborne also announced a plan to encourage about £20 billion from pension funds to fund infrastructure projects, by backing such projects with government guarantees. Such financing was more expensive than government borrowing. The problem for Osborne was that the costs of infrastructure projects were up-front, but their payoffs were off in the future. Taking advantage of super-cheap borrowing would have registered as a short-term rise in the budget deficit. Thus, Osborne found himself paying homage to Brown, exploiting off-balance-sheet accounting practices to hide the fiscal truth, even while he was committing the country to higher long-term costs. Perhaps, it might be argued, by not raising the official deficit figure, the government would be less likely to cause panic in the financial markets. However, this presumed that financial markets would not work out the higher costs and the higher implicit deficit for any explicit deficit figure. If others had been able to put their government's balance sheet on the line and it had not registered as government spending, Osborne could do this too. 'These are guarantees. We are not borrowing this money,' he declared as he got out his spoon and started to dig.

Financial initiatives needed to target small businesses in ways that the bank rescue had failed to. So Osborne announced a £5 billion National Loan Guarantee Scheme for SMEs—equivalent to a subsidy of about £50 million per year—with up to £15 billion more held in reserve for later. It was modest progress, if a little late in the day. Recognising the upcoming storm, in June 2012 Osborne announced £140 billion in subsidised funding for banks (equivalent to nearly 10% of GDP).

Why did Cameron, Osborne, and Clegg find themselves repeating the fiscal policy mistakes of the 1930s and of Japan in the 1990s (Japan repeatedly tightened fiscal policy before private–sector demand was strong enough to sustain recovery)? With super-low interest rates, sound credit, and a floating currency, they had every reason to boost demand, yet they chose not to. And why were the resources of the state used to cushion the deleveraging process of banks but not the deleveraging of other sectors of the economy? (and many bank owners, especially unsecured bank bondholders, were pardoned their share of the burden) Repeatedly, the answer was to stop the financial markets from panicking and propelling the burden of UK debt higher. Again and again, the logic turned out to be flawed and efforts to adhere to it caused the burden of debt, and the risks of default, to rise anyway. Did Cameron, Osborne, and Clegg really believe the logic? If so, they were doing a lot of economic damage in the name of false logic. Or did they not believe it but they had different motives, such as their desire to rapidly shrink the public sector, using the fallout of the crash as cover. Krugman and Wells observed: 'Supposedly responsible policy makers are sounding more and more like the priesthood of some barbaric cult, demanding sacrifices in the name of some invisible gods.'[34]

Global economic growth shrunk from an annualized 6% in early 2011 to 4% in late 2011, and then to a predicted 3.3% in 2012,[35] mostly because of the economic and political problems in the US and Western Europe. Economic historians will be interested to know whether this was part of the natural economic dynamics of adjustment after the crash or the result of policy errors. Sadly, history will record that error played a significant part. Compared to the 1930s, much more emphasis this time will be on the failures of fiscal policy than monetary policy.

The Challenge for Western Leaders

Despite the fight over the debt ceiling, in 2012 the US was growing more than the UK or the eurozone. For all the talk of austerity, US economic policy had been nowhere near as austere as some had hoped. In the UK, much of the austerity was yet to come and growth was flat or even dipping. In Japan, the fiscal stimulus had withered and the economy was stagnating again. China was in trouble too, as we shall see in Chapter 11. In the eurozone, austerity was biting hard, and many European economies were contracting fast. We shall turn to this in the next chapter.

In the short-run, a fiscal boost was needed to sustain demand. Instead, cranking up of austerity risked bringing on the very thing politicians said they most feared—collapsing private investment, another recession, worse budget deficits, and a second big crash. In the long-run, the key challenge was going to be how to persuade the current generation, the old as well as the young, and not only the rich, to sacrifice—including by investing for the long-term, not consuming so much, and paying more tax—for the sake of future generations. Worse, it was not a winning political hand to promote sacrifice, having bailed out the wealthiest section of society, the financial elite, who had gone straight back to making huge bonuses as usual.

For years, the largesse of the Chinese and growing fiscal imbalances at home had allowed Americans to pay low taxes, dis-save, and live beyond their means. Now they would have to balance the books by taxing themselves instead. But try telling that to the average voter. On the political stump in 2008, Obama had argued: 'Change will not come if we wait for some other person or some other time. We are the ones we've been waiting for. We are the change that we seek.' But changing the habits of a lifetime is difficult. Trained for 30 years and more in a never-never sweet shop where increasing numbers of goodies could be swallowed whole without ever the need to face the bill, it was time for a truth test. No longer could voters express a preference for more and more and then punish those who had the temerity to suggest that they should pay for it.

The Eurozone Crash

The Flood

In 2010, financial panic spread across the eurozone—the block of countries, seventeen at the time of writing, that share the euro as their common currency. Some called it the debt crisis at the periphery.[1] One did not realize until then how big a periphery Europe had. From the azure waters of Greece to the emerald meadows of Ireland—with Portugal, Cyprus, Spain, and Italy in between—one by one, countries tripped headlong into debt traps. So accustomed to crises and crashes by now, hardly anyone questioned why anything appeared out of the blue. In mid-2007, the market regarded the likelihood of any eurozone country defaulting as close to zero; the interest rate spread (i.e. the difference) between ten-year Greek government bonds and ten-year German government bonds (the borrowing premium that a riskier country like Greece had to pay compared to what less-risky Germany had to pay) was only 0.26%. It was a sign that investors were remarkably confident in the Greek economy, or astonishly complacent, or convinced that, come what may, Greece would be rescued. Even at the end of 2008, the ten-year spread was still only 2.25% and, at the end of 2009, it was only a little bit more, at 2.4%. Right up to early 2010 there was little mention, in political discussion or the media, of the conflagration to come.

At the launch of the euro, the priority had been to establish the new currency's credibility. For this to be achieved, it was felt that each country entering the euro should tie its hands behind its back and rule out entirely a range of appealing policy options—flat-out exit from the euro in times of trouble being the most extreme. Gone forever would be the self-fulfilling speculative attacks that pick off weak currencies in an exchange-rate mechanism that investors know can be broken. Countries would understand that if they indulged in public- or private-sector profligacy, they could not devalue their currencies to escape the consequences. Nor could they dig themselves into economic holes assuming that they would be saved by others in the eurozone. Alas, it was an experiment most noble in purpose but perhaps a little naïve. Politicians, in both the periphery and the core, had been digging.

Greece and the Launch of the First Rescue Programmes

If digging had been an Olympic sport, Greece would have taken the gold. More industrious than most, the Greek government had contrived ingenious ways to hide the hole. In 2004 it was discovered that the Greek government had repeatedly under-reported its budget deficit, which in 1999 had not been 1.8% but 3.4%, and in 2003 not 1.7% but 4.6%. Greece compounded its fiscal vulnerabilities with a system of government that rewarded the well-connected and punished the enterprising and honest. Greece's political system was ripe for reform with or without a crisis.

In mid-2009, the IMF prepared a draft report highlighting the risk of Greece defaulting. Greek officials complained, and the final report, while critical, played down the risks. Five months later, Greece's new prime minister, George A. Papandreou, eager to shake his predecessor's skeletons out of the closet, revealed that the budget deficit was not 6%, but more like 12%. Eurostat gave the figures the once-over and settled on 13.6%, which was more than four times the EU limit—and one of the highest in the world. Even this was later revised up to 15.8%. The stock of Greek sovereign debt was approaching 120% of Greece's GDP, and heading towards 145%–150% by 2013.

The rapid fiscal deterioration in Greece was because the crash and the global recession had compounded a domestic fiscal error. Greece's economy grew in real terms by over 4% between 2001 and 2006 (about 7% per year in nominal terms), which was faster than the European average. However, Greece had entered the euro with a ratio of government debt to GDP of just over 100%. Instead of using the proceeds of growth to run a primary budget surplus and to reduce the ratio, the Greek government had done the opposite. Investors reasoned that Greece could sustain higher levels of government debt because: its economy was set to grow much faster than in the past; they were protected from loss because Greece could not devalue and undermine the value of their investments; and Greece could take advantage of record low interest rates. Greece had spent most of the 1990s with the drachma discount rate hovering in the 14.5% to 21.5% range. From 2002, the rate was a totally improbable 3.25%. The strategy left Greece without a fiscal cushion.

When they joined the eurozone, countries such as Greece had ceded their monetary sovereignty to the ECB. They had lost any ability to cut interest rates or to use their own programmes of QE. They could not generate higher inflation to boost nominal output and drag their ratios of sovereign debt to GDP lower. They could not devalue to boost their exports and to replace lost domestic demand with fresh external demand. They had three options. They could try to 'devalue' internally by cutting wages, pensions, and other costs. This would be difficult for one country to do in good times; if many tried it together, it would lead to deflation, which would make matters worse for all. Or they could write-down some of the debt as lost for good. Or they could seek temporary transfers, or even permanent ones (i.e. bailouts), from others in the eurozone. Citizens in Germany and France had joined the euro on the under-standing (article 125, the 'no bailout condition', of the Lisbon Treaty) that they would never be asked to make transfers to other member states in trouble. In their eyes, transfers looked like Greece, Ireland, Portugal, and others avoiding the austerity measures that they had brought upon themselves. The Germans and French said 'nein' and 'non'—and other less printable things.

By early April 2010, the markets—fearful that Greece might not be able to roll over its sovereign debt—were demanding 4% more on ten-year Greek government bonds than on ten-year German government bonds, and 5%–6% more on two-year Greek government bonds than on two-year German govern-ment bonds. In late April, Greek sovereign debt was downgraded, and higher borrowing rates were plumping Greece's pile of sovereign debt ever volumin-ously. Greece could not grow fast enough to generate the larger primary budget surplus that was needed to pay the interest costs and thereby stop the pile from growing faster than its GDP. Such sad fiscal logic spun the debt trap wide. As the projected ratio of Greek sovereign debt to GDP grew, more Greek tax revenues were needed just to service the debt. This led to more austerity which depressed private-sector investment and spending, which reduced tax revenues, which pushed the budget deficit higher. This sent borrowing costs even higher, to compensate for the increased risk of default, which pushed the projected ratio of sovereign debt to GDP higher still. And the cycle started all over again.

On 3 May Greece was thrown a €110 billion rescue package—€80 billion from eurozone members, €30 billion from the IMF. For all the talk of 'bailout', the money was not given, but lent at 5.2%. A loan was deemed compatible with the Lisbon Treaty in a way that a direct transfer was not (in fact, both were legally questionable). The notion was to take Greece temporarily out of the sovereign bond market, relieve it of high interest rates caused by the risk of default, and break the cycle. The loans would be released in tranches as austerity targets were met. In Germany—and, it's worth reflecting, in Greece too—talk of debt restructuring and direct fiscal transfers was still utterly taboo. Germany was facing a key regional vote in May, and Chancellor Merkel would not have helped herself by encouraging such talk.

Two fears tormented policymakers. First, that default by a small country on its sovereign debt would act like a thread which, if pulled, would unravel the whole European garment. Second, that if the conditions placed on private-sector creditors were too harsh, bond markets would panic, and default would happen anyway. Greece, Ireland, and Portugal would be small explosions on the periphery; as a percentage of the eurozone's GDP in 2010 they were respectively 2.6%, 1.7%, and 1.9%. Spain, at 11.4%, was an altogether different proposition. European banks were holding nearly a trillion euros of Spanish debt, half of it on the books of German and French banks, and it weighed heavily on the minds of politicians in Berlin and Paris as they struggled to sleep at night.

And so, on 9 May 2010, the eurozone member states agreed to a temporary €750 billion safety net for the eurozone (additional to what had been agreed so far for Greece). This had three components. First, the European Financial Stability Facility (EFSF), which has authorised to borrow up to €440 billion by issuing bonds backed by the guarantees of eurozone members to lend to those members in difficulty, subject to conditions negotiated with the European Commission. Second, the European Financial Stabilisation Mechanism (EFSM), which was able to borrow up to €60 billion using the budget of the European Union as collateral. Third, up to €250 billion from the IMF. With Germany as its largest backer, the EFSF carried a triple-A credit rating; even in the summer of 2011 it was able to borrow at just 3.3%. Greek sovereign debt yields fell. The dragon had been placated by a potion of sorts. It would not stay dozy for long.

Ireland and the Launch of the European Stability Mechanism (ESM)

In our Olympics of the financially absurd, Ireland took the silver—but only just. Ireland had not so much been digging as building and piling high—housing and private-sector debt. Ireland's banks had more than happily obliged, a property bubble being their financial bezzle of choice. Biggest and grandest of all was the Anglo Irish Bank, whose smooth-talking CEO, Seán FitzPatrick, king of the Dublin business and political scene (the two were sewn up at the seam), had a sham-Midas touch that left his victims with ersatz gold. Astonishingly, nearly all of Anglo's €72 billion loan book was to property developers and builders. As property prices crashed, so did Anglo. To its shareholders' delight, the profits of Anglo Irish had swelled from €42 million in 1987 to €1.2 billion in 2007. Now they had collapsed, to record the largest corporate loss in Irish history (€12.7 billion over the 15 months to March 2010). Anglo Irish's shares had peaked at €17. By December 2008, they were worth about the same as the paper they were printed on: 22 cents. Property developers and politicians had scooped off copious supplies of financial oil to grease their fast-spinning wheels, and now they had crashed. The Irish people had borrowed to the hilt because that was what everybody did, and bought brand-new two-up-two-downs, that were later worth half what they had paid, because that is what everybody did. The Irish had perfected the bubble-art of making money out of nothing, getting rich selling houses to themselves.

Courtesy of Anglo Irish, FitzPatrick even amassed, over eight years, secret personal debts that peaked at €87 million. By December 2008, his skills at hiding the truth had reached their limits and, by July 2010, the financial emperor with no more than a *Trifolium dubium* to hide his meagre financial modesty was bankrupt. The bailout of Anglo Irish alone cost Irish taxpayers at least €34 billion. FitzPatrick—a strange gift of God who rode the Celtic Tiger until the poor creature was dead—was not quite an Irish Madoff, but he came close enough.

Irish politicians did not allow their bankers to take all of the discredit. Brian Cowen, the Irish Taoiseach, in words reserved by *The Times* of London for only the most special of occasions, was a 'dismal failure'.[2] In September 2008, in his haste to throw a blanket guarantee over the senior creditors of Ireland's banks, Cowen had not bothered to process the numbers inside his head, and so had not worked out that, by turning such huge private-sector liabilities into huge public-sector liabilities, Ireland's public finances were going to be—in the financial jargon—stuffed. Mind you, Cowen had been pressured by European leaders to protect senior bank creditors on the presumption that it would prevent contagion to banks in Germany, France, the UK, and Spain. As the support for banks flooded through to the Irish government's books, its budget deficit hit 31%, before falling back to about 10%. Total outstanding Irish sovereign debt had been a completely safe 25% of Irish GDP in 2007. In 2010 it was approaching 100% and heading towards 125% by 2013.

The Irish people were not all innocent victims. For 14 years, the fictions and fantasies of Fianna Fáil had suited many of them just fine. Election after election, they had voted in those who touted bubbletrope and fairytale, and would soon enough have booted out anyone who tried to yank the punch bowl from beneath their noses. They happily rode interest rates pitched low to suit post-unification Germany, and France; indeed, real interest rates were negative for long stretches in the mid-2000s. In 2007, Ireland's saving rate was minus 5%. For such a small country, Ireland had been remarkably successful at convincing banks, especially in Germany, France, the UK, and Spain, to lend to it. Some of the lending was used to boost its industries—Ireland's export performance over 1999–2008 was about 20% better than the eurozone average, and a great improvement on the years before the euro—but much was wasted pumping real estate.

In December 2009, the Irish government had pushed through an austerity budget that included €15 billion of spending cuts over three years, a 15% reduction in public-sector pay, and the goal of getting the budget deficit down to 3% by 2014. The Irish people took their fiscal amputation with an unexpected degree of equanimity. Perhaps they were numbed by the anaesthetizing effect of collective national economic guilt? The Irish economy went from years of real GDP growth of 6% to a fall of about 12% between 2008 and 2010.

Nothing in life lasts forever, and the EFSF had a life expectation that took it only to 30 June 2013.[3] Fortunately, mortality does wonders to concentrate even the most distracted of political minds, and at the EU summit in October 2010 a permanent replacement for the EFSF and the EFSM was agreed, the European Stability Mechanism (ESM). Less fortunately, feeling the need for a futile gesture—something that would raise the whole tone of the crisis—Germany's Angela Merkel, with France's Nicolas Sarkozy at her heels, pushed for a private-sector sovereign-debt bail-in, via collective-action clauses in all eurozone bonds issued from 2013. As Merkel put it: 'We must keep in mind the feelings of our people, who have a justified desire to see that private investors are also on the hook, and not just taxpayers.'[4] In polls, only 20% of Germans thought that bailing out Greece was right, and across the German political spectrum the dominant position was that sovereign bondholders should share the burden. Merkel was desperately trying to hold a coalition together, and deviation from this position would have been dangerous for her. The IMF was also taking the view that a negotiated voluntary restructuring of Greek sovereign debt was 'Unnecessary, Undesirable and Unlikely'.[5]

Merkel was raising an important issue. A permanent long-term crisis-reso-lution mechanism risked creating moral hazard by lowering the costs of default for countries that followed unsustainable policies. Yet, trying to pin such clauses in place while in the jaws of a crisis was, to say the least, precarious. One might think that bonds issued before 2013—and not covered by such clauses—would be safe. However, this ignores the lamentable rigours of backwards induction. If by 2013 countries were still experiencing difficulties in sovereign debt sustainability, any sovereign bonds issued then would have to promise very high rates of return because of the risk that such bonds would one day default. But these rates would make the debt-sustainability problem worse. Hence, those who invested before 2013 in sovereign debt knew that in 2013 its rollover was going to be difficult, and that other eurozone members would either have to bail *them* out or renege on the promise not to default. By backwards induction, high yields, to reflect such risks, would have to be priced in *now*. Killing off the euro with a proposal to save it was probably not what Merkel intended.

For all her tough words, Merkel was travelling the well-worn path that policymakers had followed during the global bank rescue. The clauses targeted only investors in sovereign debt, not the senior creditors of banks. To suggest that those who might buy sovereign debt should be punished for the misbehaviour of banks that happened before they appeared on the scene was ridiculous. That they should be punished because of financial contagion caused by current policymakers was even more bizarre. The idea that, in the process, moral hazard at poorly disciplined German and French and British and other banks would be encouraged by a supposedly strict Germany, beggared belief. Perhaps the previous bank rescue constrained Merkel. Senior creditors in big US banks had been protected from taking their richly-deserved losses. Coordinating the wiping out of all senior creditors across all failed banks globally had proved impossible. Perhaps, as a consequence, it was just too difficult to force losses on senior creditors in some eurozone banks without causing panic at other eurozone banks. Or perhaps the fact that many of the senior bank creditors were German was playing tricks in Merkel's mind.

The first rescue package for Greece kicked the can a little further down the road, but policymakers were soon again upon it. On 28 November 2010, they tried to repeat the trick, with a €85 billion package for Ireland, carved out of the EFSF. As Irish luck would have it, this coincided with work on the replacement ESM. Some even claimed that Ireland was bounced into needing a rescue because the commotion over collective-action clauses panicked Irish sovereign bondholders. Rescue was again in the shape of loans, at 5.8%, and tweaked with some sleight-of-hand: €67.5 billion was committed by the EU and the IMF, Denmark, Sweden, and the UK (after all, UK banks accounted for a quarter of the lending in Ireland at its peak and would face heavy losses if Irish banks defaulted), but the Irish government also agreed to use €17.5 billion taken from its own national pension reserve fund and other cash reserves. Since the IMF was charging just 3% on its portion, the average 5.8% indicated a decent enough return for European contributors (the UK was getting a good rate of return from lending to prevent its own banks from facing the consequences of their previous reckless lending).

Happy Response—Not

If policymakers had hoped for a happy ending, they were not to get it. The day after the EFSF was announced in May 2010, two-year Greek bond yields fell to less than half of what they had recently been (although they were still high) and two-year Irish bond yields fell by about two thirds. After the Irish rescue, the fall in both of these yields was minuscule. Indeed, *even with* the rescue package in place, ten-year bond yields for Greece, Ireland, Portugal, and Spain were over 11%, 9%, 7% and 5% respectively. The potion was losing what little strength it ever had. The problems were at least ninefold (bear with me; European policy-makers like to stack their problems high, and I may even have missed some).

First, the rates payable on the loans to Greece and Ireland were higher than any realistic rate of growth of their economies, and so the ratio of their sovereign debt to their GDP was going to rise further, and the debt was still not going to be fully repayable.[6] Second, the size of the ESM was not big enough to rescue a big country or to deter speculative attacks. If it had been several times bigger from the start, it would have ended up cheaper because it would have had the power to frighten financial markets and to kill off self-fulfilling speculative pressures and so keep the rates on sovereign debt lower.[7] The lack of a sufficiently large once-and-for-all solution was uncomfortably reminiscent of policy-making in 2007–2008. Third, by officially recognizing that sovereign debt creditors would be 'on the hook', higher yields would follow on the eurozone bonds of *any* countries at risk. Fourth, if countries ever had to make good on their commitment to the collective guarantee, this would involve a real transfer of resources, which would be a violation of the Lisbon Treaty. The financial markets knew the political problem this would cause, and priced it in now. Fifth, rescue was concentrating on the symptom of the problem (sovereign debt) and not the cause (bank debt). Sixth, the rescue facility was not flexible enough to buy bonds on secondary markets, and so it could not undermine speculators. Seventh, as in 2007–2008, policymakers got it into their heads that if only they concentrated on liquidity issues, the solvency problems would somehow disappear. Eighth, the ESM was not divorced from political processes. Any measure needed approval of all member states, and could still be amended later. The extra uncertainty raised the costs. Ninth, both the EFSM and ESM were loan- and not grant-based mechanisms.

Grants reduce the indebtedness of recipient countries, which benefits their creditors whose claims are henceforth more likely to be repaid. Instead, ESM loans were set to be senior to the claims of other creditors, and if current loans under the EFSF got converted into ESM loans they too would become senior. Investors therefore knew that the burden of any future restructuring was going to fall disproportionately on any remaining (and by then junior) long-term creditors. Their claims were devalued immediately. Ironically (and European policymakers were big on irony) a larger official *loan* programme implied that less would be available for private creditors *if* the programme did not work. As the programme got bigger, but not big enough, investors would sell off the long-term sovereign debt of countries that were at risk but not yet in the programme. The risk premiums on remaining sovereign debt would rise. This would push up the financing costs of countries at risk, and increase the pressure on them to enter the mechanism. Even countries whose problems were manageable might be forced to be 'saved'.

Yields on Greek bonds fell on 10 May—but were much higher than they had been when the proposed rescue package had been much smaller. Then yields rose over subsequent months, in spite of the size of the rescue package. The May 2010 Greek rescue package guaranteed all two-year Greek sovereign bonds, and their spread over similar German bonds should have fallen to zero. Instead, the spread eased to about 7%, and was soon on its way back up as the markets priced in the high probability that the programme would default before its replacement in 2013. According to the economics literature, official lending in a crisis only lowers sovereign bond yields if it acts as a catalyst to pull new private-sector lending in and encourages reforms that generate higher future primary budget surpluses.[8] Instead, the financing part of the Greek and Irish rescue was triggering a crisis because the financial lifeguards were pulling the victims out with a rope looped around their necks.

Write-downs would force Germany, France, the UK, and others to recognise the losses of their reckless banks. However, recapitalizing their banks would have involved an up-front cost. Loans were politically easier even if a bad economic solution. Germany, France, the UK, and others would eventually have to recapitalize their banks at an even greater cost, but that was for another day and, maybe, for another set of politicians.

Of course, the situation could have been much worse. And so it was. Only €80 billion of the ESM's capital was to be paid in. The rest was callable. If an ESM-creditor asked for funds or even defaulted and wiped out a chunk of ESM capital, other shareholders in the ESM—including those who might need to be rescued—would have to pay in new capital. Germany and France, because of their triple-A status, could guarantee their portions of any shortfall; however countries that had lower credit ratings because they might default would have to put actual cash in. The biggest backers of the ESM after Germany and France were Italy and Spain. If Italy or Spain got into trouble, would the other one really honour a commitment that would push up their own borrowing costs and risk of default? If both Italy and Spain needed to take rather than contribute, the burden would shift onto Germany and France. Germany could probably bear the strain. France, whose guarantee came to about 10% of its GDP, was already running a budget deficit of about 7% of GDP, and would risk its own triple-A status. Only the finely honed art of European political compromise could have contrived such an ingenious way to spread a crisis.

Next came Portugal. Financial markets had reacted well to Portugal's strategy to delay austerity and concentrate on structural reform and on getting its finances in order through growth. The markets swung against Portugal only when uncertainty regarding the EFSF and the ESM escalated, bond yields around the periphery rose precipitously, and Portugal pushed hard on the austerity brakes. In early April 2011, with the Portuguese economy shrinking at about 1.3% per year, its official unemployment rate rising to over 11%, and yields on five-year Portuguese bonds touching 10%, Portugal joined Greece and Ireland in the eurozone intensive-care ward. On the principle that if the patient isn't hurting, the treatment isn't working, eurozone finance ministers attached austerity measures to Portugal's €78 billion loan package that were even harsher than those that had triggered the recent collapse of the Portuguese government. In July 2011, Moody's downgraded Portugal to junk status. Portugal needed structural reform, but surely it was now a victim as much as a culprit.

The Not-So-Innocent Eurozone Core

Those in the eurozone 'core', such as Germany, thought of themselves as the innocent victims in all of this. Over the 2000s, they had been cool and industrious, building export industries, and reforming their labour markets and welfare systems as they went. As far as they were concerned, like squirrels who refused to store for winter, others had scoffed all they could and lazed in the midday sun. If others were now hungry and burnt to a crisp, Pech gehabt!

The truth was a little more complex (and Germany took the bronze). Those now struggling had effectively tied themselves, like countries in the 1920s, into a new gold standard. Nominal exchange rates were fixed after the launch of the euro, but real exchange rates had diverged dramatically. Helped by very low inflation, unit labour costs in Germany had barely risen. In Greece they had gone up by nearly 50%. In Ireland, Spain, Italy, and Portugal it was about 40%. The result was a persistent German balance of payments surplus, which grew from about €50 billion at the launch of the euro to nearly €200 billion in 2007, and a balance of payments deficit across the rest of the eurozone of almost exactly the same proportions. Had it not been for the 'artificial' fix of the euro, the German Deutschmark would have appreciated and stopped this from happening. Germany flooded the rest of Europe with cheap money (just as China, because of its undervalued currency and chronic trade surpluses, had flooded others, especially the US, with cheap money). This fed a mix of genuine investments, real-estate bubbles, and private and public consumption, as banks in the core lent huge amounts to the periphery, in a sort of European version of subprime, but without all the fanfare. Outside of Greece, the explosion of debt was almost exclusively private-sector debt. German politicians did not challenge the chronic imbalances, the undervalued German currency, and the reckless lending that pumped periphery imports, which were, of course, German exports. Thus, over the 2000s, Germany built up a growing stock of claims against the rest of the eurozone via its banking system. Like China, Germany would lose on a portion of the claims eventually.

This was eerily reminiscent of an earlier European era. In the 1930s, surplus countries faced no penalty for accumulating gold, just as countries such as Germany in the 2000s faced no penalty for accumulating reserves. In the grip of the Great Depression, surplus countries such as the US and France refused to pursue expansionary policies or to lend directly to countries such as Germany, while deficit countries—including Germany, the UK, and Italy—were supposed to adjust by devaluing their economies 'internally' because the gold standard meant they could not devalue 'externally'. Then surplus countries refused to supply emergency support for banks that failed because of the contraction. In September 1931, the UK came off the gold standard, pursued expansionary policies and grew—on average by over 3% per annum between 1931 and 1938. Those that stayed on the gold standard, including Germany, shrank. Greece, Ireland, and Portugal in 2010 found themselves in a similar predicament to Germany in the 1930s. Back then, Germany was weighed down by impossible-to-pay reparations demands after the First World War and its banks were undercapitalized after the hyperinflation of the 1920s. Brutal austerity, in an effort to devalue 'internally', made Germany's debt burden worse and contributed to internal political disaster. If Germany had learnt the lessons of its own economic history it would not be repeating the same mistakes now that the tables were turned.

If government profligacy had been the main *cause* of the eurozone crisis, there would have been a surge in government budget deficits after the euro was launched. Yet, with the exception of Greece, fiscal balances were on average *better*. Portugal, after entering the euro, maintained about the same government budget deficit, of about 3.7%, as it had in the late 1990s, which was an improvement on the early 1990s. Spain went from a government budget deficit of about 4% of its GDP to an average budget surplus (over 2000–2007) of about 2%. Ireland was in budget surplus before and after entering the euro. After its entry, Italy averaged about the same budget deficit as France: 2.7%. The Germans, on 2.2%, were more 'profligate' than Spain or Ireland (no wonder Cameron only mentioned Greece, and never Spain or Ireland, in his dire prognostications). Greece had its faults, but, contrary to all the stereotyping, even Greece was paying about a third of its GDP in taxation and government employment of the workforce was only about the European average of 20%. It had more small entrepreneurs per capita than anywhere else in Europe, and its workers on average worked longer hours than German workers.[9] How could Greece and, at a pinch, Portugal, together comprising only about 4.5% of eurozone GDP, possibly explain a crisis threatening the global economy? How could government profligacy totalling about 0.2% of eurozone GDP (20 cents in every €100 of eurozone activity) have such global repercussions? If Spain and Ireland were included in the 'zone of profligacy', a crisis caused by a group of countries that started in collective government budget surplus was being exacerbated by profligate Germany.

Those in trouble had experienced the biggest current account imbalances and floods of capital in the eurozone, as surpluses in the core were intermediated to the periphery by banks. On average, as a percentage of yearly GDP over 2000–2007, the capital account inflows were about 9.4% for Portugal, 8.4% for Greece, 5.8% for Spain, 1.8% for Ireland, and 1.3% for Italy.[10] Even for Greece and Portugal the capital flows had been much bigger than government deficits. The problem was that the capital flows were prone to a sudden reversal of investor sentiment.[11] This had now happened and, just as in the US and the UK, it had been compounded by a swing towards saving as the private sector deleveraged. In Ireland, the (gross) household savings ratio swung from minus 5% of GDP to about plus 18% in mid-2010. Corporate deficits evaporated, and government deficits rose, just as had happened perfectly naturally in the US and UK.

However, quite unlike in the US and the UK, this triggered risk of sovereign debt defaults because the straightjacket of the euro sent sovereign debt interest rates soaring. It was not profligacy, but the institutional design of the euro that was causing the difficulties.

The euro had encouraged the huge capital flows, but had simultaneously taken away the ability of countries to respond to sudden stops in capital flows. This needed the firepower of the core. Germany was happy to take the upside from the capital flows and the boost to trade caused by its entry into the (inefficiently operating) euro, but preferred that the systemic risk conse-quences of the euro (the *quid pro quo* for the benefits to exist) stay on the shoulders of the periphery. Unlike China, countries in trouble did not have large foreign-exchange reserve buffers to protect themselves. They found themselves vulnerable in ways that were very similar to those experienced by countries in South-East Asia in the late 1990s when capital flows suddenly stopped and went into reverse.

At the outbreak of the eurozone crisis, financial institutions in Germany had an exposure to the banks and private sector of Greece, Ireland, and Portugal that totalled about €230 billion (more than €400 billion when Spain was added in). Those in the UK had an exposure of about €200 billion, and it was €150 billion apiece for France and the US (the US exposure was mostly to non-bank and corporate lending), €90 billion for Spain, €25 billion for Italy, and €80 billion for the rest of the eurozone combined. A write-down on some of these exposures would have caused large losses for German, British, and French banks and insurance companies, and the need for some of them to be recapitalized. It was not just that a few struggling countries had huge financial obligations, but that a few large countries were heavily exposed to them.

It suited those in the core to insist that sovereign-debt holders, and not bank-debt holders, take losses. Because of a strong 'home bias', it was banks in Greece, Ireland, and Portugal that owned most of the sovereign debt of their own countries. A 50% haircut on their sovereign debt would wipe out about 70% of the equity of Greek banks, 50% of the equity of Portuguese and Spanish banks, and 10% of the equity of German and French banks.[12] Yet, a collapse of banks in Greece, Ireland, Portugal, and then maybe Spain, Italy, and Cyprus would necessitate cross-border bank recapitalizations from Germany, France, the UK, and others. Why were the Germans so reluctant to help small eurozone countries in trouble if the alternative was a loss for their own financial insti-tutions of maybe €60 billion to €100 billion, and losses for German taxpayers that would be much higher if panic spread?

The eurozone's problems had their roots deep in dysfunctional banking systems, nourished by a generous watering of macroeconomic mismanagement and political hubris. Now, fully ripened, debt and property bubbles had burst. Bank solvency problems transmogrified into sovereign-debt solvency problems—the eurozone manifestation of the global banking crisis. Eurozone leaders were fighting a German and French and British (and other) banking crisis disguised as a sovereign debt crisis. They were trying to bail out their own banks through a loan-based rescue of governments at the periphery.

Nor was the ECB entirely blameless. For years it had accepted the bonds of different eurozone governments on the same terms as those of Germany. For their part, banking regulators everywhere treated eurozone sovereign debt as riskless. Banks that were required to hold 'riskless' assets to meet their regulatory requirements had loaded up their balance sheets with the sovereign debt of 'periphery' eurozone countries, happy to earn the tiny extra returns (thus, Greek banks were satisfying their prudential requirements when they loaded up on Greek sovereign debt). When it all went wrong, what had been supposedly low-risk turned out to be surprisingly high-risk. Banks found themselves holding too much sovereign debt that had turned 'toxic', in much the same way as many banks in 2007–2008 had found themselves holding assets they thought were risk-free but that carried (credit) risk after all. There was a collapse in the market for sovereign debt (similar to the collapse of the interbank market in 2007–2008 after subprime lending turned toxic) and the premiums on sovereign debt shot up.

As part of its liquidity measures, the ECB bought up enormous quantities of debt (bank and sovereign) of eurozone countries in trouble, especially of Greece, Ireland, and Portugal. By late 2011, it was holding about €35–40 billion of Greek government bonds. If the ECB made a loss on these, it would pass it on to member countries in proportion to their shares in the ECB's capital. As a consequence, the ECB was unwilling to support sovereign debt defaults on which it would lose and that would require it to be recapitalized by member governments.

The ECB was an independent central bank but, unlike other central banks, it did not have a state to back it. It was bound by rules that forbade it to lend to governments. It had unlimited capacity to print money but meagre resources to take losses. It was the euozone's fire station, except that it was not connected to any water supply. Consequently, those in trouble were left to face much higher borrowing costs than they ever would have faced had they kept their own central banks (nobody made a big fuss about this when they joined the euro). By late 2011, the ECB had spent less than 5% of eurozone GDP on buying up European bonds. This was much less than what the central banks of the US, the UK, and Japan had done buying up their own government bonds. So, despite being exposed to losses (although earning a nice profit if the bonds made it to maturity), the ECB had not done enough to prevent eurozone borrowing costs from soaring.

Concerned about inflation in the eurozone core, in April 2011 the ECB even started to raise its policy rate from its record low of 1%, to 1.25% and then to 1.5% in July. Higher interest rates would make debt sustainability in the periphery more problematic, and this would hit especially hard those countries, such as Spain and Ireland, where variable-rate mortgages made up a high proportion of the stock of all mortgages. ECB interest rate policy was signalling that debt write-down was more likely to be effected by debt restructuring than by inflation, and that the ECB, despite all its attempts to achieve the opposite, would take a big loss itself. Yet the ECB was indicating that it did not want to face such a loss either. Perhaps this is what Rogoff meant by policy that was 'inconsistent, incoherent, or both'.

Politicians in the 'core' had strong incentives to procrastinate. Under the terms of the ESFS, official loans to eurozone members in trouble ranked equal to the claims of other creditors. A default during the EFSF phase would mean that Germany, France, and others would have to make good on their guarantees. This would register for them as government spending. Merkel would be dragged through the German constitutional court. The politics in France would be messy. Under the terms of the ESM, official loans would be senior to the claims of other investors, and so private creditors would take the first losses. This gave current politicians a strong incentive to delay resolution at least until 2013 when the ESM came into effect. Sadly, like oil and water, politicians and financial economics don't mix. Forward-looking financial markets would understand that private-sector creditor protection after 2013 would be weaker, and so the risk of default before then would be high. Meanwhile, the markets would impose heavy borrowing costs on countries in trouble which would make everyone's costs high. Then the markets would force resolution earlier than politicians were planning. In places like Germany and Finland, voters did not want a bailout (not even one based on loans), but they did not want a messy default and forced recapitalization either. Procrastination was the path of least domestic political resistance at each individual step, even if it ended up costing more.

Ireland, Iceland, Greece, Spain, and Italy

If any country was fundamentally strong, it was Ireland. It had a highly educated workforce and good infrastructure, and it was the destination of the bulk of US direct investment into Europe. Yet by the spring of 2011, Ireland had been in recession for three years. Its domestic demand and investment were down 27% and 60% respectively from their pre-crisis levels. Ireland was unable to control its own money supply, which had therefore been collapsing since March 2010, and deflation had been pushing up the real burden of its debt. In April 2011, stress tests revealed the need for another €24 billion of capital to buttress Irish banks. The Irish government dipped into the EU-IMF fund; this pushed the total cost of its bank bailout to over €70 billion. Moody's cut Irish government debt to one notch above junk. It was just another case of twisted financial irony. Big global banks that had misbehaved received, courtesy of government guarantees, multiple notches of credit-rating upgrades worth tens, and maybe hundreds, of billions of dollars. Countries such as Ireland, on the other hand, got multiple notches of credit-rating downgrades because they were small and had taken on the burdens created by misbehaving banks.

As if to rub salt in the wound, Iceland ran a referendum to decide whether to repay the debts—running at eleven times its national income—of its private failed banks. Unsurprisingly, rather than lock themselves into debt servitude to foreign treasuries forever, Iceland's voters said no. Bank bondholders had to take a large haircut, and banks had to be restructured. Iceland also responded with capital controls, and the IMF allowed it an extra year to borrow and spend before austerity kicked in. For all the alleged risks engendered by such behaviour, by late 2010 Iceland was emerging from recession, on track to pay off its remaining debt, and with access to international capital markets. At 7%, its unemployment rate was high by its own standards, but low in comparison to Greece and Ireland. In February 2012, Fitch upgraded Iceland to 'investment grade' (from BB+ to BBB−). In 2011, the Icelandic economy expanded by 2.6% and Iceland exited its IMF aid programme. Of course, Iceland also had the benefit of its own independent currency, the króna, falling by about a quarter to boost its exports.[13] The lesson seems to be that if debt restructuring is inevitable, it is better not pretend otherwise, and to get rid of unsustainable debt as soon as restructuring becomes inevitable. And, perhaps, that the governments of small countries like Ireland did not have to shoulder banks' losses.

The big difficulties lay in Greece, which was in its fourth year of recession. In 2010, the Greek economy shrank by 4.5% and it missed all its austerity targets.

The Greek government released a statement saying that this was 'mainly the result of the deeper-than-anticipated recession of the Greek economy that affected tax revenue and social security contributions'. Salvation via internal devaluation was not happening. The more Greece tightened, the more domestic demand was crushed and investor confidence shrivelled. Tax revenues collapsed, even further reducing Greece's ability to service its debts. The bond market showed its disdain: borrowing costs soared, which made the budget deficit worse. It was clear that Greece needed to write-down some of its sovereign debt, but the ink of each new agreement was barely dry before the next one was being squeezed through the political rollers, and a year of skating around the facts had worn a huge hole in policymakers' credibility. By now, Greek unemployment was officially expected to hit 17%–18% by the end of 2011, but the true rate was at least 5% higher. With youth unemployment over 45%, no wonder that one of Greece's biggest exports was its young and educated; an economy cannot empty itself of its talent for long without undermining its long-term growth potential and making its sovereign debt even less sustainable.

The original timetable had Greece raising half its financing needs in 2012 with a full return to capital markets in mid-2013. This was utterly unattainable. The Greek government had a financing gap of at least €90 billion out to 2014. Greece needed to borrow more or to restructure its sovereign debt with a large write-down. In April 2011, Wolfgang Schäuble, the German finance minister, was severely criticized for openly suggesting the latter. The markets were pricing a default in, but politicians, especially of the German variety, could not yet talk openly about default. Jean-Claude Trichet, president of the ECB, ruled out any notion of debt restructuring, arguing it would cause a eurozone bank meltdown similar to that of late 2008.

Under normal circumstances, Spain should have been safe. Spain's core problem was not its sovereign debt, which was only about 60% of its GDP in 2010 and was projected to rise to only a little over 70%—lower than the ratios of 'safe' Germany and France, and the UK. Unlike Germany, Spain was running a budget surplus. Unlike Greece, Spain had played by the fiscal rules. However, Spain's ratio of private-sector debt to GDP was 170%, and most household debt was at floating rates, such that higher interest rates quickly fed through to higher household-debt servicing costs. Spain's banks had borrowed about $110 billion from British banks, $160 billion from French banks, and $180 billion from German banks. Much had been wasted on politically-driven projects and on a house-building frenzy. If panic had set in, even a safe-looking Spain would have needed financial help. And, so too would have the banks in the countries of those that had lent to Spain.

As a pre-emptive move, the Spanish government had, early on, pushed through expenditure cuts, labour-market and savings-bank reforms, public-sector pay cuts, pension freezes, an extension of retirement age, a rise in VAT, and cuts in regional programmes. With official unemployment over 20%, did Spain need to become another victim? In March 2011, Spain's bond yields had been falling, and the answer seemed to be no. By July 2011, the painful contortions to finalize the terms of the next Greek bailout sent Spain's ten-year borrowing costs over 6%, a euro-era record, and the answer seemed to be yes.

In the decade to 2010, Italy was the third slowest growing economy in the world (4% in real terms over ten years, but ahead of Zimbabwe and Haiti). As a result, Italy had the rich world's third-biggest sovereign debt to GDP ratio, of about 120%. By mid-2011, with its ten-year bond yields over 6%, Italy was being dragged ever-closer to the inferno. If it went in, the eurozone would not have been able to muster sufficient resources to pull it out. Italy approved an austerity package of €45 billion for 2011–2013, and then got on with approving another that took the total thus far to €60 billion (and then another at the end of 2011 and yet another in 2012). The Italian finance minister Giulio Tremonti observed, in exasperation: 'Salvation does not come through finance but from politics. But politics cannot make any more mistakes . . . Just as on the Titanic, not even first-class passengers can save themselves.'[14] In May 2011 Mario Draghi, Italy's departing central-bank governor (off for a spell as president of the ECB), denounced Italy's 'vested interests oppressing the country in so many ways', and poured scorn on the social and economic record of Italy's free-spending prime minister Silvio Berlusconi. Berlusconi had done very well financially while the Italian economy and its people had done abysmally. It was perhaps a shame that Draghi waited till he was leaving. What Draghi dare not say about Berlusconi, the *Economist* magazine splashed across its front cover on 9 June: 'The man who screwed an entire country.'

Italy held (as of December 2011) €1.9 trillion of outstanding sovereign debt. At least, the maturity profile was such that Italy could sustain expensive bond auctions for a more prolonged period than Greece or Ireland; however, in 2012, it still needed to roll over about €350 billion (equivalent to nearly 30% its GDP). Italy's personal-savings rate was high, and its private-sector debt low; unlike Ireland and Spain, it had no speculative housing bubble. More of Italy's sovereign debt was owed to its own people than was the case in many other countries in trouble. Italy's problem at the close of 2011 was essentially one of illiquidity and not of solvency. If European politicians were merely competent, they would stop the former becoming the latter.

In 2010, the average ratio of sovereign debt and budget deficit to GDP of the eurozone was 85% and 6% respectively.[15] This compared favourably with the US where these figures were about 84% and 11%. The figures for Germany were 83% and 3.3%, and for France they were 82% and 7%. Indeed, the government budget deficit of the UK was higher than Spain (9.2%), Portugal (9.1%), and Italy (4.6%). Had the eurozone been a country such as the US, it would not have suffered any speculative attacks against its weaker parts (which in the US are protected by federal transfers) and interest rates in the periphery would have stayed low. If European policymakers had stopped triggering spirals of panic, damage would have been limited to at most Greece and, if the worse came to the worse, Portugal. Indeed, if handled well, Greece could have been used to draw a line in the sand.

By mid-2011, Ireland's situation was improving. It was achieving a current account surplus of 3%–4% of GDP, at least in part because of an upward trend in exports (and not just because of recession). It did not need to borrow from international markets until 2014. Its debt to GDP ratio was going to peak at about 110%, which was entirely manageable given its underlying economic strengths. Its banks, now recapitalized and with their problem assets dealt with, were out of danger. Domestic demand was shrinking but, at last, the Irish economy was growing. Why threaten Ireland by making a complete mess of Greece? As Vines and Watson put it in the *Financial Times*: '[A]n Irish success story of the kind we think is underway will come to be seen as a precious and crucial trump card for the eurozone debt strategy. It gives the lie to fears about a generalised transfer union. And it illustrates that adjustment in the eurozone is feasible'.[16] Instead, the higher borrowing costs facing Greece, Ireland, Portugal, Spain, Italy, and Cyprus, and others were because of self-fulfilling contagion at work in a system that lacked a collective mechanism to smooth over bumps in the fiscal road, locked inside an exchange-rate straightjacket, and run by politicians whose rudimentary competence in financial economics had long ago reached its limits. Being small, fiscally struggling, fish in a tank of hungry financial sharks, prodded and stirred by the sharp stick of austerity, with next to no room for manoeuvre made Greece, Ireland, and Portugal especially vulnerable.

Euro Break-Up or Default?

Discussion increasingly focussed on the possibility that the eurozone was about to break up? Could Germany, maybe along with the Netherlands, Austria, Finland, and France, leave the euro to a Mediterranean bloc? As a result,

Germany would avoid the long-term risks of inflation and keep its monetary independence. Those that remained inside the eurozone could stick to their contracts in euros, regain some policy flexibility, reduce their interest costs, and avoid years of deflation, high unemployment, and domestic political strife. Or could it be the other way around—weaker economies leaving the euro one by one?

It sounded easy, but nothing could have been further from the truth. The switch to the euro had been planned over many years and was smooth. Just talking of a break-up risked causing bank runs inside weaker countries as bank accounts got drained to avoid being converted into less valuable currencies; signs of this could be seen already in Greece and, increasingly, in Cyprus, Spain, and Italy. All kinds of capital controls and restrictions would have been needed, even though they would have been in contravention of the rules of the single market (unless countries like Greece and Ireland exited from the single market too). To stop cash from crossing borders by the boot-load, treaties on border-free travel would have had to be suspended. There would have been years of legal challenge from those who found their money trapped on the wrong side of any divides that opened up. Existing contracts written in euros—on anything from property leases to payments for industrial imports, backed by collateral anywhere in the eurozone—would have ended up needing to be settled in another currency backed by collateral in that country. Foreign banks and pension funds would have sued for losses on government bonds that collapsed in value. If Greece had gone first, other countries in trouble would have had their access to capital markets frozen, as investors tried to work out who would be next. Trade would have collapsed. For a country to get out of the Lisbon Treaty but stay within the EU would have needed the unanimous agreement of all other EU members. The much more drastic measure of exiting the EU would only have needed only a majority vote (but it would have needed also EU subsidies and payments to be completely untangled). Surely, exiting the EU so as to get out of the Lisbon Treaty more easily would have been an overkill for those who wanted to leave the eurozone?

Neither would a strategy of *Alleingang*—going solo—have been in the obvious long-term interests of Germany. The German currency (a new Deutschmark perhaps?) would have heavily appreciated. Germany's huge current account surplus would have disappeared. With one in six jobs dependent on exports, German unemployment would have risen. German banks would have made heavy losses on loans and investments repaid in heavily depreciated euros, and would have needed to be rescued by German taxpayers. According to the Bundesbank, in mid-2012 German banks had just over €800 billion exposure to banks, companies and the public sector of other eurozone countries; a bailout of its own banks would have sent Germany's debt-to-GDP ratio rising at the same time as Germany would have been suffering a huge income loss. If the eurozone had broken up, it is not obvious that the single market would have survived. If beggar-thy-neighbour trade wars had followed, all, including Germany, would have been hurt.

If break-up was economically and politically too costly—which does not mean it was not going to happen—it was less costly to work out as early as possible what proportion of sovereign debt could realistically be repaid by Greece, Ireland, and Portugal, recapitalize those European banks that suffered losses, and work reform and growth strategies around that. The role of the EFSF (and then the ESM) would have been to stabilize sovereign debt, that of the ECB to stabilize banking systems. A month or two is a long time in European politics, and by June 2011 Germany was openly discussing a restructure of Greek sovereign debt. The 'type' of debt restructure, and whether a particular measure would be deemed a default for credit-rating purposes, became the focus of a grimly fascinating, if not entirely conclusive, policy debate.

A 'market-friendly' default seemed challenging. In this game of chicken, if bondholders had refused, would European officials really have gone through with their threats? If larger haircuts were to be achieved, actual default, and not just threatened default, would probably have been needed. Several factors, however, suggested that sovereign bondholders might have agreed 'voluntarily'. First, offer prices could have been close to current market prices. Second, many bondholders were institutions, amenable to a little bit of creative political pressure. Third, in contrast to many past emerging-economy crisis, many sovereign bonds (over 90% in the case of Greece) were written under local law. Besides, in past cases in emerging economies, usually only a small fraction of creditors had taken the risk of free-riding when a reasonable offer was on the table. Ten years after Argentina's default, those who had held out had not received a cent. In the cases of Pakistan, Ukraine, Uruguay, and the Dominican Republic, exchange offers implemented before a formal default were used as a way out.[17] Argentina, Russia, and Ecuador used exchange offers but waited until after they had defaulted.

To allow Greece to benefit from its efforts at growth, another option was GDP warrants. Instead of imposing an interest charge regardless of the state of the Greek economy, repayment could have been linked to Greece's capacity to service its debt.[18] The Greek government would have allocated, say, 4% to 5% of any growth in its nominal GDP towards payments to its creditors in proportion to their initial holdings. This would have stopped rising interest rates from triggering a collapse in the Greek economy.

Solution after Solution

Germany, against the wishes of the ECB and the French (whose banks were heavily exposed to Greek sovereign debt), wanted the next Greek loan to be conditional on private-sector sovereign bondholders taking some losses. EU officials were working on a 'selective default', aiming to get Greek sovereign debt—then at about €340 billion, or 160% of Greek GDP—down to about €255 billion, or 120% of Greek GDP. The ECB said that it would stop supplying liquidity to Greek banks against the collateral of Greek government bonds if European policymakers pushed a solution that involved Greek default, which would have harmed the ECB. To avoid any deal being deemed a selective default, France, for a while, pushed the idea of a bank levy to cover the losses on the banks' part of any deal. The banking sector was against a levy. The German government did not believe that a levy would raise the necessary funds. It would have needed agreement across the EU and national parliaments, which hardly seemed likely. And it would have been difficult to target payments at those holding Greek bonds. Other cracks were opening up. Sarkozy (and Cameron and the US) wanted the ECB at the centre of any expansion of the EFSF; Merkel did not. The ECB itself repeatedly resisted a bigger role because of its lack of resources and the limits to its powers enshrined in EU treaties.

On 21 July 2011, an agreement was at last reached, in the shape of a 'voluntary' rollover, or 'exchange' plan. Greece would get a €109 billion loan at a rate of about 3.5%, on terms ranging from 15 to 30 years. At least the combination of longer maturities and lower interest rates made the debt more sustainable. The private sector had finally been put 'on the hook', with a 21% cut in the net present value of Greece's sovereign debt (about €50 billion by mid-2014, assuming a 90% take-up). Fitch said that this would be deemed a selective default. Trichet, at the ECB, performed a U-turn and allowed the deal on condition that in the case of a selective default, eurozone governments agreed to post €35 billion in collateral with the ECB. Ireland and Portugal got a 2% cut on the rate charged on their EFSF loans and the freedom to extend them from 7 to 15 years. This would save Ireland about €1 billion a year in interest costs.

No European ointment is ever applied without a strategically placed fly— several, if at all possible. First, the size of the EFSF was not increased. By late July 2011, the EFSF had already committed €145 billion to Portugal and Ireland and €73 billion to the second Greek package, leaving only about €220 billion of the initial €440 billion in the pot. And so, in spite of a range of new powers, the

EFSF was still not big enough to guarantee that cash would always be there to pay out sovereign debt holders and protect Spain or Italy. In glorious back-wards-induction fashion, the markets would price this in.

A novelty was introduced, in the shape of a flexible credit line for the EFSF. This allowed it to buy distressed government bonds on the open market of any eurozone country and not just those already part of an EFSF programme. This was intended to help prevent speculative attacks. Members of Merkel's own Christian Democrat Party and its junior coalition party, the Free Democrats, objected. They hardly needed to bother. With the EFSF no bigger, the new powers were pointless.

To be safe, Greek sovereign debt needed to be cut by much more than 21%. A reduction to the eurozone average (85% of GDP) would have needed €140 billion, or about 2% of eurozone GDP. It seems that the private sector's participation had to be sufficiently big to please the political classes, but the selective default had to be sufficiently small so as not to rip a painful hole in the losers' balance sheets. Such compromise necessitated an even bigger bailout further down the road. Forward-looking bondholders knew this. Greek two-year government bond yields fell from 40%, but only to about 28%, a reflection of the still high risks. Greece had to agree to an even harsher set of austerity measures. Maybe Greece could have used the deal as a springboard to bring its sovereign debt to 120% of GDP by the end of the decade, putting it on a par with Italy. That would have required Greece's damaged economy to run a 'primary' budget surplus of about 5% per year by mid-decade; the shadows of flapping pigs' wings could be seen dancing across the stones of the Bundestag and the Acropolis.

If eurozone politicians had believed that Greece was capable of servicing its sovereign debt, they would have backed the scheme more fully and taken the payoff in the shape of lower interest rates for Spain and Italy. Payoff would have been immense at little extra cost. Perhaps, at heart, they knew that Greece would default. Moody's certainly thought so, cutting its credit rating for Greece by three notches to one above default, assessing the chance of Greece defaulting as 'virtually 100%'. The finance minister of Greece shortly observed: 'We should not be the scapegoat or the easy excuse that will be used by European and international institutions in order to hide their own lack of competence to manage the crisis.'[19]

The proposed changes in the structure of the EFSF would have needed agreement in national parliaments. Astonishingly, the details about the neces-sary legal change to the fund's structure was not going to be hammered out until after European politicians had first had their 2011 summer break. They needed it. But speculators don't take summer breaks, and just days into August the markets were in spirals of panic again. To ease market pressures, the ECB, opposed by Germany's Bundesbank and various members of its own governing council, intervened to buy government bonds of Ireland and Portugal, but not of Spain or Italy. Spain and Italy were much too big for the ECB to have had any worthwhile impact.

Much of the funding of eurozone financial institutions had become very short-term.[20] This was similar to what happened in mid-2008. The 90 banks that went through the European stress tests needed to refinance €5.4 trillion of debt over the following two years, equivalent to about 45% of EU GDP. In the past, because default was effectively ruled out, it was easy to roll over even such huge sums. In less than a week in early August 2011, overnight deposits at the ECB doubled, as nervous banks preferred to dump excess funds there than in the interbank market. It was reminiscent of the hoarding amplification mechanism we saw in Chapter 4. As short-term bank funding costs shot up, so did the chances of a new credit crunch, not unlike that of 2008, except worse because of the lack of firepower to stop it.

In Brussels, at the end of October 2011, Europe's leaders peered over the edge of the precipice, and were frightened enough to agree to a new three-part package, the details of which would be worked out by the end of November. First, banks holding Greek sovereign debt would take a voluntary 50% haircut (the ECB again insisted it would not write-down what it had lent to Greece). Second, the bailout fund would be boosted to about €1 trillion by somehow leveraging, four or five times, its remaining funds. Two possibilities were on the table. One involved offering insurance to purchasers of eurozone bonds, which, if it inspired confidence, would lower borrowing costs. The other involved a 'special investment vehicle' into which large private and public investors, such as China, could invest. The half-life of each new piece of rescue thinking was getting shorter, and the notion of the leveraged EFSF lasted about a week. Third, banks would be recapitalized to guard against future government defaults. The European Banking Authority (EBA) calculated that about €106.5 billion of fresh capital was needed by June 2012 (in early December 2011, the EBA revised the figure up to about €115 billion to reflect the collapsing value of government bonds held by banks). German banks got off lightly, required to raise €5 billion in new capital (revised up to €13 billion). The bigger the write-down for Greece, the bigger the recapitalization needs would be. Many banks embarked on fire sales of assets (to the tune of about €950 billion over two years) to try to raise the additional capital, which made recovery in the eurozone even less likely. In order to allow the deal through, Germany insisted on new government budgetary discipline built into a new treaty.

By November 2011, eurozone countries were being treated as if they were wheat and chaff, the later being blown away by ever more punitive interest rates. With European politicians regularly jousting over how to split the pain between sovereign bondholders and taxpayers, no wonder that yields on ten-year Italian government bonds hit 7.6%. If at some point the Italian government had lost access to bond markets, Italian banks would have been wiped out by their losses on Italian sovereign debt. Many non-Italian banks (especially French banks) were exposed too. On 30 November, with the interbank funding market frozen, the ECB announced an agreement with the Fed to slash the rate at which the Fed lent short-term dollars to the ECB (dollar swap lines) to on-lend to eurozone banks (the Bank of England also announced a new lending facility for banks). In the first week of December the ECB lent $50 billion in 84-day loans. This was on top of the ECB's euro lending, secured by the assets of banks. The ECB insisted that the risk of such lending (against collateral, even if of increasingly weak quality) stayed on national banks' balance sheets. The German finance minister, Schäuble, reversed his previous position, and voiced support for increasing German resources to the IMF. The eurozone was rich enough not to need the IMF, but the involvement of the IMF allowed countries like Germany and the UK to avoid the political discomfort of explicitly lending to the eurozone periphery.

Central banks, not eurozone leaders, had taken away the chance of a huge bank run—for the time being—by injecting enough liquidity to keep the critically-ill patient stable, while eurozone leaders thrashed around working out what to do next. However, that meant the ECB was propping up banks that were propping up governments that had previously propped up their banks. What would happen when the banks ran out of eligible collateral and could no longer borrow from the ECB? To stop the inevitable bank runs, banks might have ended up in temporary state ownership. But if Spain or Italy had rescued a big bank, this would have pulled down the creditworthiness of its government, which would have reduced its ability to protect other banks, which would have set off a contagious panic to all banks—a death spiral between a sovereign debt crisis and a banking crisis. Quite preposterously, problems in Greece, a country the size of Nevada, had been allowed to threaten even the US. And so, ahead of the next European summit, Geithner did his own grand tour of European capitals, with the quaking voice of Obama ringing in his ears: 'Europe is scaring the world.'[21]

At the December 2011 European summit, Merkel pushed with all her hands and feet to get agreement on a 'fiscal stability union'. For a moment she must have thought she was within millimetres of rolling her prodigious stone to the top of the hill. Government budgets were going to be 'balanced or in surplus', which in practical terms would mean a structural budget deficit of never more than 0.5% of a country's nominal GDP. Apparently, the rule was going to be fixed within the legal systems of all countries and, if Merkel had got her way, the European Court of Justice would have been empowered to police public spending and budget policies of the 17 eurozone countries, and there would have been quasi-automatic fines for fiscal sinners.

This was no fiscal union, and instability would have been its only legacy. Instead of an inter-regional insurance mechanism with countercyclical flows, it would have institutionalized in perpetuity a procyclical adjustment mechanism that would have made recessions worse. The private sector in the periphery was heavily deleveraging. Therefore, to get the sum of private and current account deficits close to zero could only have happened if the periphery had increased its exports and import substitution, or if it had an even worse recession. With the periphery collapsing, what was the likelihood that exports to Germany from places like Greece would rise (which would require the relative deterioration of the competitiveness of Germany), or of the whole eurozone becoming much more competitive and hence exporting more to the rest of the world? To use another of those technical economic words: zilch.

Even more bizarrely, Germany was able to borrow at unprecedentedly cheap rates and could have been offsetting the collapse of aggregate demand in the rest of Europe, yet it was embarking on its very own aggregate-demand squeezing policy to cut its own deficit. There was still no backstop for Italy and Spain, no eurobond, and no bigger role for the ECB. All this might have had the feel-good factor in Germany, but the whole enterprise was doomed to fail and this was going to harm Germany too. And it was clearly preposterous to assume that eurozone politicians would ever stick to self-imposed budgetary discipline. They never had under the previous Stability and Growth Pact: when Germany and France breached the pact in 2002 and 2003, they suspended legal provisions against themselves. The US had repeatedly failed to stick to fiscal discipline. And the UK, under Brown, never had: he redefined the economic cycle and shifted financial activities off balance sheet. Under Merkel's leadership, Europe was about to do what the US had done in the 1930s: force an even worse recession and deflation on itself, and export it to the rest of the world. Merkel, demonstrating consummate political skill but appalling lack of economic insight, had managed to lift the blame away from Germany, an undervalued Deutschmark, banks, capital flows, investor panic, and the institutional faults of the euro, and to unload it all onto sovereign debt and the faults of individual eurozone countries in trouble. In the process, the demonizing of Greece by Merkel, Sarkozy,

Cameron, and others turned a marginal solvable problem into an existential crisis for the whole eurozone, and raised the spectre of political turmoil in Europe.

In mid-2012 it was the turn of Spain. Spain was experiencing a much bigger balance sheet recession than even the US and UK. Its private sector had cut its debts by over 17% relative to GDP since the third quarter of 2007. This had been offset by a swing of about 12% in public-sector debt and a fall in the current account deficit. The Spanish economy was collapsing and needed to let its automatic stabilizers work. Germany said no. Too much austerity would send the burden of Spain's private-sector debt rocketing. A treaty that forced Spain to collapse in an effort to hit quickly a 3% budget deficit target would have threatened the whole eurozone.

Merkel did a complete about-turn on her demand that private-sector creditors take losses on any future sovereign debt restructuring; the involvement of private-sector creditors in Greece would be 'an exception', she declared. Perhaps someone had finally explained to Merkel that countries in trouble needed to roll over their sovereign debt as cheaply as possible, and that the bonds of struggling eurozone countries could not be made less attractive than bonds in any other debt market. Merkel's learning on the job was turning out to be expensive for Germany. Sarkozy also did an about-turn, accepting that sanctions would be much more automatic. By now, Sarkozy had worked out that in this particular *pas de deux*, France's role was to hide how strong Germany was, Germany's role was to disguise how weak France was, and that Germany was going to get is way in the end.

Merkel hoped that the new 'fiscal stability union' would require only a quick and narrow change to the EU treaty, backed by all 27 EU members and applied to the 17 in the eurozone. Instead, the weight of the pitiless stone proved too much for Merkel and it came crashing back down again on to the European plain (actually, Prime Minister Cameron had run up to the top of the hill and pushed, by vetoing a Europe-wide treaty). Instead, there would be an accord with penalties for those breaking budget deficit rules, backed by a treaty between governments. Within days, several countries that had signed up were making clear how little fiscal sovereignty (notably in relation to independent tax policy) they were prepared to relinquish.

It would be nice to report that Cameron's veto was because he had concluded that the 'fiscal stability union' was based on a misdiagnosis of the causes of the eurozone crisis and that the pursuit of the wrong set of policy tools would bring on disaster. However, the deeply flawed deal was apparently, in his opinion, not good enough for the City.[22] An EU effort to supply the IMF with an additional

€200 billion also fell short. The UK refused to loan up to €30 billion unless others in the eurozone put in more. The US, needing congressional approval, declined. This left the EFSF vulnerable to downgrade (also because a key contributor, France, was by now vulnerable to a downgrade). British taxpayers would have been on the recapitalization hook if the EFSF was not big enough to stop problems from escalating and if UK banks made losses in Ireland and Spain. Half of UK exports were to Europe, and this was lining up to be the next big external shock that would knock the UK's economy off course.

Within days, the ECB launched is Long Term Refinancing Operations (LTRO) scheme, which lent money to banks at about 0.75% for three years in the hope that they would buy up the high-yield sovereign debt of countries in trouble. On arriving at the ECB, Draghi had reversed the interest rate hikes of his predecessor and reinterpreted the mandate given to the ECB as allowing it a bigger role in preventing an imminent credit crunch. In its single biggest liquidity measure, the ECB leant €489 billion to just over 500 banks. They dumped their new liquidity right back in the ECB to earn a paltry 0.25%. This was QE by any other name. At the end of December, Italy could sell three-year debt at about 5.6%, much below the record high of 7.9%. The rate on its ten-year debt fell to about 7%, below the previous record of 7.6%, but Italy could not sell all the ten-year debt it offered. The LTRO had taken away the fear of imminent financial collapse. However, just like the liquidity measures discussed in Chapter 5, cheap loans prevented runs on solvent banks but did not get rid of the problem of insolvent banks.

A week on from the December 2011 summit, Fitch put Belgium, Spain, Slovenia, Italy, Ireland, and Cyprus on negative watch (i.e. a 30% chance of downgrade within 18 months), on the basis that 'a "comprehensive solution" to the eurozone crisis is technically and politically beyond reach', that '[o]f particular concern is the absence of a credible financial backstop', and that 'this requires more active and explicit commitment from the ECB to mitigate the risk of self-fulfilling liquidity crises for potentially illiquid but solvent Euro Area Member States'. In January 2012, S&P downgraded France's triple-A rating, and cut the credit ratings of Italy, Spain, Cyprus, and Portugal. S&P declared that: 'Austerity risks becoming self-defeating.'[23] In mid-February Moody's cut the credit ratings of Italy, Spain, Portugal, Slovakia, Slovenia, and Malta, and put France, the UK, and Austria on negative watch. The new head of the IMF, Christine Lagarde, warned of the dangers of repeating the mistakes of the 1930s and urged eurozone leaders to scale up the size of its rescue funds. The World Bank president, Robert Zoellick, talked of 'a tinderbox out there in both political and economic terms'.[24]

In late February 2012, to the very last moment, the second Greek bailout looked in jeopardy. In 2011, Greece's GDP had contracted by 7% and industrial output by 11.3%. Unemployment was at an all-time high of 21%. The Greek primary fiscal deficit had fallen to less than 1% of Greek GDP, which meant that most of the rise in Greece's debt-to-GDP was because of higher borrowing costs and the collapse in GDP. Creative ways had to be found to keep within the €130 billion limit agreed at the October summit, yet still, supposedly, meet the target debt-to-GDP of 120% by 2020. The ECB agreed to forgo profits on its holdings of Greek bonds, giving about €15 billion of extra wiggle room. Other central banks agreed to a similar course of action with their few remaining Greek sovereign bond holdings. Private-sector creditors agreed to a bond swap generating an effective 54% write-down, about €107 billion, on €200 billion of debt. Greece agreed a further round of €3.3 billion of spending cuts in 2012, or about 1.2% of GDP, and to a new law prioritizing repayments to creditors over spending on social services. The deal would be policed on the ground by EC inspectors. The minimum monthly wage of €751 would be cut by 21%, and that for the under-25s by 32%. By now, austerity had cut pay and pensions in Greece by 40%. A secret report (by IMF and European economists), and therefore quickly leaked, showed that if Greece did not grow, its debt could easily settle at 160% of GDP by 2020 even with the deal. Greece was not about to attract capital flows to grow and prosper, and investors were being annihilated by uncertainty and industrial decline. Greece was going to be back for more debt reduction in a political vacuum where the willingness to provide any more resources was shrivelling by the day. At the end of February 2012, the ECB pumped a further €530 billion liquidity into about 800 European banks.

Many ordinary people in Greece were sympathetic to the need for political reform, but they no longer trusted eurozone leaders bearing gifts. Instead of developing a strategy to harness the democratic process towards reform, eurozone leaders alienated potential political allies inside Greece by infantilizing the lot of them and prioritizing external pressure. Greece was heading towards parliamentary elections in May 2012 and already those that agreed to the deal were scraping record lows in the opinion polls. Even if eurozone leaders drove another disastrous outcome, ordinary Greek people, and not those who had benefited from exploiting the largesse of the Greek state in the first place, would get the blame. Surely, there would come a day when having the economy destroyed by the incompetence of outsiders would no longer be politically tolerable. Economic reform takes time and, in its early days, often makes matters worse by closing down unproductive capital and making labour redundant. Ordinarily, the negative side-effects can be cushioned by lower interest rates, depreciated currencies, and the expansion of other sectors to absorb displaced workers. None of this was possible. Reform was only going to work if there was growth to support it. Greece needed to clear the slate and put in place a rescue fund to revive its economy. Reform needed to be driven by rewards rather than threats and more punishment.

On 7 June 2012, Fitch—blaming 'policy mis-steps at the European level' that had 'aggravated the economic and financial challenges facing Spain'[25]—downgraded Spain's credit rating by three notches, from A to BBB. On 11 June, eurozone leaders announced a €100 billion Spanish bank rescue. On German insistence, the link between bank insolvency and sovereign insolvency, instead of being broken was reinforced: the credit line was to Spain's government and not to its banks and, if fully drawn, would have added about 9.5% to Spain's debt-to-GDP ratio, pushing it over 90%. Spanish sovereign bond yields rose. The bond market was also spooked by the possibility that the rescue funds would rank higher than private bondholders if Spain defaulted. Irked by the market's reaction, European political leaders, in their emergency summit in late June, agreed that, once operational, ESM funds would, after all, be available to directly recapitalize banks (including, retroactively, Spanish banks). Merkel made a U-turn, but not for long: by late 2012, Germany and its Dutch and Finish allies were insisting that recapitalisation by the ESM would still require a full sovereign guarantee, and so the bank-sovereign insolvency feedback loop continued to spin.

To square some of the conflicting aims, a 'banking union' quickly found its way to the top of the political agenda. This entailed spreading across the eurozone the burden of underwriting banks, in exchange for which the ECB would become supervisor of all eurozone banks, with powers to intervene over the heads of eurozone members when their banks failed. Again, Germany grabbed a spanner—insisting that the ECB's role be limited to just large, mostly border-straggling, banks. Key details remained tricky. Slow bank runs were draining euros from banks in Greece, Spain, and Italy, and depositing them in banks in Germany (by August 2012, Spain's central bank had borrowed nearly €450 billion, equivalent to about 40% of Spain's GDP, just to replace the fleeing euros). A credible eurozone-wide deposit guarantee scheme, promising to honour the full euro value of bank deposits even if a country left the eurozone, would have stopped bank runs. However, it would have been very expensive if countries left the eurozone, and so it was not clear that it could have been made credible. Officials in Brussels proposed setting up a common fund paid from levies on banks to fund a eurozone-wide bank resolution regime. Yet, no fund was ever going to be big enough, and a government back-stop was still going to be needed. Surplus countries, Germany prominent amongst them, knew that they would find themselves shouldering the lion's share of an implicit public guarantee of banks. The problem was the timing. Other countries wanted to see a German financial commitment quickly, but Germany was unwilling to mutualise bank liabilities without first obtaining from other countries a commitment to tougher fiscal discipline.

Germany was in a curious position. The struggle over Spain made it clear that protecting all unsecured private bank creditors – a key German condition of all previous rescue loans – was no longer possible. When Iceland's banks were not rescued, the creditors of those banks paid the price. If eurozone banks were not rescued, the net creditors were going to be the banks, insurance funds and pension funds of surplus countries, notably Germany. Savers in Germany, and other surplus countries, had to choose between having what they were owed by debtor countries defaulted upon, or being bailed out by the ESM. For all the rhetoric to the contrary, Germany was going to be the biggest beneficiary of mutualising bank liabilities.

Politics in the End

Financial markets wanted collective European responsibility for financial and budgetary policies. Public opinion in many eurozone countries did not. Financial markets wielded the power of economic life and death. Public opinion shaped what was politically doable. We can but guess at some of the motives driving policymakers. In March 2011 all three German coalition parties voted against allowing bond purchases by the ESM, and Merkel's own supporters were objecting to anything that smacked of a 'transfer union'. Merkel must have been worrying about her 21-seat majority. If that evaporated, never mind the eurozone, she would be gone by 2013. In France, President Sarkozy, facing elections in 2012, was trailing in the polls to Marine Le Pen of the far-right Front National on an anti-Europe scorecard. In Finland, to counterbalance the rising popularity of the 'True Finns'—an anti-immigration party that rejected the idea of rescuing 'squanderers'—mainstream parties took harder lines too. The True Finns polled just 3.7% of the popular vote in 2007, but 19% in the 2011 election, turning 5 seats into 39 seats in parliament with commensurate losses for more centrist parties.

In 2012, if Merkel had softened her stance on Greece, it would have caused ructions in her party. Merkel, repeating the experience of some politicians who failed to act before the global financial crash, found that the more she let the problems escalate, the more she could look heroic tackling them: in the summer of 2012, Merkel's domestic approval rating soared to nearly 70%. Merkel was also taking a hard line in part because of the dangers of a rightward political swing. In many countries, austere economic thinking was being matched by the rise of nationalism and an increased hostility towards immigration and minorities. If the rise of the far right in Germany was matched in France, Netherlands, Finland, Hungary, Austria, Greece, and elsewhere, Europe would be back in 1930s territory.

Everywhere, centrist governments were holding back on sensible solutions for fear of tempting domestic political fate and because they could not, or would not, convey how the national interest would be enhanced by early resolution of the problems in Greece, Ireland, and Portugal. Merkel repeatedly failed to make the case to the German people for taking actions that had an up-front cost that would avoid an even bigger cost for Germany in the long term. Even then, she stuck with the wrong diagnosis of the problem. Perversely, Germany grew 3% over 2011, on the back of the euro's problems. Half the growth in German exports between mid-2009 and mid-2011 came courtesy of the collapse in the time euro. Floods of capital from the panicking periphery into Germany pushed ten-year German bond rates down to about 2%, and two-year bond rates, for the first time ever, to zero, easing Germany's own budget deficit problems; the same capital movements that were crushing Italy, Spain, and Greece were temporarily boosting Germany and making its citizens even less willing to save the euro from collapse. At the periphery, voters were hardening in their opposition to the policies of those living in the false paradise at the core. In elections in Portugal there was a swing to the far left. In Greece and in Spain the people rioted, and the future seemed to be only more blood, toil, sweat, and teargas. Spain's embattled socialist prime minister, José Rodrígues Zapatero, was forced to call an early election, which he lost to Mariano Rajoy. In November 2011, Italy's Berlusconi was booted out. In May 2012, France's Sarkozy was removed. In late 2012, Greece was heading towards default or exit from the euro in 2013 or 2014.

European leaders were ignoring the dreadful lessons of European history, with potentially dire consequences. Just as the reparations after the First World War crippled Europe and propelled it towards war (Keynes had warned of the dangers in *The Economic Consequences of the Peace*), so too now it was impossible to imagine Greece, Ireland, Portugal—and, heaven knows, Spain and Italy—being squeezed through the austerity mangle for long enough to pay off their foreign creditors, without this entrenching a deep depression and causing a great deal of political unrest, and even war. As Keynes had pointed out, a country's ability to 'pay' reparations is a function of its economy's ability to produce goods

THE EUROZONE CRASH **285**

and services to satisfy reparation demands. High reparation demands might sweeten the mood of the victors, but they make no economic sense if those economies trying to make reparations are destroyed in the process. The victors become victims too. All across Europe, political leaders were creating a waste-land and calling it peace.[26]

Three inconsistencies sat at the heart of the European dream. First, persistent imbalances and the lack of ability to adjust exchange rates to take the imbalances away. Second, the possibility of sovereign debt defaults at the country level. Third, the lack of a fiscal union to enable cross-border burden sharing via transfers; the need for this had been recognized from the start.[27] Embracing the lot was failure to establish workable economic governance.

Prior to the euro, careless monetary and fiscal policies caused exchange rates to fall, which led to higher interest rates for the culprits. That is, currency markets acted as the brakes on public- and private-sector profligacy. In a currency union the brakes supposedly came from credit markets—that is from financial institutions, and especially banks. Countries that wanted to be profligate inside a currency union could not simply print more money but would have to borrow it and would find their loan costs rising. Policymakers reasoned that with banks disciplining private-sector excesses, their job was to concentrate on rules to rein in public-sector excesses and guard against inflation. Little did they think that one day the problem might be the excesses of banks and deflation—and they left many countries to self-police and to break the fiscal rules anyway.

Instead, over the 2000s, credit markets drove interest rate differentials close to zero to nothing, and showed no signs of inflicting punishment until way too late. The reasons were as described in Chapter 3. First, many of those working in finance had short-term horizons. They pocketed a regular short-term interest differential as profit and bonus, and left the tail default risk for others. Second, like the errant countries, they pushed their luck, presuming the EU would protect them from default because of the systemic dangers. They were right. But it was not systemic reasoning: Germany, France, the UK, and others did not wan their banks to take the losses they were due. The euro did not take the risk of financial contagion away. It transformed it from exchange-rate risk into credit risk—which first sat lightly on the shoulders of banks and then more heavily on the shoulders of governments and finally on the shoulders of the eurozone itself. Instead of a currency crisis, there would be a sovereign debt crisis.

One day, sooner than many had been expecting, the eurozone was going to be forced to choose between fragmentation or a minimal fiscal union. The latter would involve a central mechanism for discretionary fiscal policy, perhaps with a budget of 1% of eurozone GDP, and a eurozone treasury with the power to override national policies. This would require a treaty change. The size and duration of the ESM would need to be bigger, and there would need to be credible conditionality clauses attached to loans to counteract moral-hazard tendencies, and a sovereign debt restructuring mechanism. Independent councils of auditors and fiscal experts to supervise and regulate would be needed to supplement ineffectual markets and voters in their disciplining efforts. For three years, Europe's leaders—just like their counterparts in Japan after its economics collapse in the 1990s—had failed to clean up the balance sheets of their banks. It was time for banks, and their owners, to absorb their losses.

The only way to stop destructive cycles of ever-higher sovereign borrowing costs at times of stress would be via pooling part of the debt of all eurozone countries. This would require a common eurozone bond, a eurobond, under the aegis of the ECB acting as lender of last resort. The ECB would replicate for countries what a lender of last resort does in banking, and, just as in banking, the confidence that there is a lender of last resort would be enough that the ECB would hardly ever need to act. Allowing individual-country bond markets inside a monetary union was always risky. Governments that have their own currencies can issue bonds and so guarantee that liquidity will always be there to pay out the bond at maturity, because they can get their central bank to create the money to do it. Inside the eurozone, nations found themselves issuing debt in an essentially 'foreign' currency. They were effectively downgraded to the status of emerging economies.[28] This created a system open to contagion, with bank-run properties at its core; nations suffering liquidity, and maybe solvency, problems triggered runs against other nations that otherwise would have been safe. Non-pooled systems as epitomized by the EFSF and ESM, which relied on countries guaranteeing each other's debt, had proved an unmitigated disaster. Every time one got into trouble, it set off contagious risks of default that caused rates on the sovereign debt of others to rise—from small countries like Greece, right the way up to Spain and Italy.

Merkel repeatedly ruled out eurobonds, at least as a quick fix to the crisis; on 2 December 2011, she told the Bundestag that 'discussion about eurobonds is pointless'. Merkel had also convinced Sarkozy, who added: 'Germany and France are in complete agreement that eurobonds are in no case a solution to the crisis'.[29] Yet the European Council president and many eurozone countries remained in favour. Germany worried that prematurely pooling debt would create moral hazard and reduce the pressure on the weaker members to reform their fiscal ways and would result in Germany paying higher interest rates. This worry was not dissimilar to the fear of creating moral hazard in a banking system with a lender of last resort. As in the case of banks, moral hazard risks could be mitigated by incorporating discipline mechanisms. One proposal[30] was to condition eurobonds rates on key macroeconomic performance metrics such as debt-to-GDP ratios. Rates would be lower than panic rates in the market but still give good incentives because the rates would fall as performance conditions were met. Besides, in a system that had not pooled debt, Germany had ignored indiscipline anyway. Could it be that pooled debt might have given Germany more incentive to discipline those such as Greece before it got too late?

Economic history teaches us that a crisis is never over until it's over (which is rather annoying when one is trying to finish writing a book about it). As the eurozone journeyed through 2012 and into 2013, it was in for a steep recession. A wave of sovereign defaults, similar to the ending of the Latin American debt crisis of the 1980s, was going to sweep in. If in the process the eurozone broke apart, it would be because politicians failed. Maybe instead, the crisis would give the impetus to put in place the institutional mechanisms to support the euro. A euro that, for the short-term gains of Germany, lifted the countries on its periphery on a euphoric wave of debt and, when the flows receded, spat them out every ten years as insolvent was not a euro that was ever going to last. Merkel and Sarkozy and others had worked out that to sustain the euro, closer economic coordination and political oversight were needed. Whether such an arrangement could be made to work, with its implied losses of national sovereignty, in a Europe scarred and polarized by economic battles, was far from clear, and perhaps it was too late. Only time would tell. But time was running out.

Global Rebalancing and Instability

What Next for China?

As the US and Europe struggled and tore themselves in strips, elsewhere new configurations of economic power and new potentials for instability were emerging. Growth was low, and sometimes negative, in countries suffering from balance sheet recessions, but high in China, India, Brazil, and in a range of emerging economies. There was increasing talk of a dual-speed global economy, of currency wars and trade disputes, of the decline in the role of the US dollar and the rise to prominence of the Chinese renminbi, of inflationary and deflationary pressures, and of the dangers when unwinding super-loose monetary policy.

China was going to be important for what would happen next. On 17 August 2011, US Vice President Joe Biden, in a joint meeting in Beijing with his Chinese counterpart Xi Jinping, declared: 'I am absolutely confident that the economic stability of the world rests in no small part on co-operation between the United States and China . . . It is the key, in my view, to global stability.' It is an all too familiar story. A rising superpower drew finance in from abroad and invested it in manufacturing capacity. Millions of workers were pulled from the countryside to work in the new factories. With production far greater than the country could consume internally, it exported its massive industrial overcapacity to others. Its trade surplus ballooned. Its holdings of foreign-exchange reserves set new records. These funded the trade deficits of those buying its goods. The strategy seemed to work—until the crash of 1929 brought the US to its knees.

In the 1930s, the US faced two options. It could, to borrow Andrew Mellon's phrase, have 'liquidated' its manufacturing and labour capacity. Or it could have replaced the lost external demand for its goods and services with new internal demand. It tried to do neither and, instead, passed the Smoot–Hawley Tariff Act of 1930. Foreign goods were to be kept out, the US was to go back to exporting, the surpluses were to return, and the burden of overcapacity was to be bounced back onto 'foreigners'. Rebalancing was to be done some other time on some other day. Of course, this is not what happened. The 'foreigners' raised their own barriers, and batted the overcapacity problem back. International trade collapsed. Unable to see the value of expanding its own domestic demand, the US liquidated. And the mess was splashed all over the history books.

If policymakers had learned the lessons of those books, both the US and China would, by 2009, have been dancing to a different tune. The US could choose to invest in its future (including in infrastructure, new technologies, and human and social capital) or it could return to its addiction to overconsumption based on imports and persistent balance of payments deficits. China could use its excess capacity to supply its own domestic consumption and allow its currency to appreciate, or it could go back to favouring its export sector with state-subsidized finance and currency manipulation—its very own, beggar-thy-neighbour, Smoot–Hawley.

After the crash, for a while, global economic imbalances seemed to improve. However, this was largely because US imports fell and China's current account surplus plummeted, from about $430 billion in 2008 to about $260 billion in 2009, because of the collapse in global trade. When global trade bounced back, so did China, with a current account surplus in 2010 of about $300 billion (about 5% of its GDP). As rates of global growth fell over the course of 2011, China's current account surplus shrunk again. By June 2011, China had boosted its foreign-reserve holdings to $3.2 trillion (about two-thirds dollar-denominated), well ahead of the next highest holder, Japan, holding about $1 trillion. Global reserves holdings rose by $2.2 trillion over 2009 and 2010, taking total global holdings to about $9 trillion.

Surely, by now China must have realized that its reserve holdings were a more than adequate cushion, and that they were imposing a heavy cost on itself: a yearly loss of about 1.5% of GDP, and the risk of a huge loss at some future date when the value of the cushion collapsed. China's build-up of reserves continued to drain demand away from Western goods and services. In the spring of 2011, China's State Council, at last, openly talked about how to reduce the accumulation and diversify the holdings. Zhou Xiaochuan, China's central-bank governor, even declared that China's reserve holdings were well beyond anything China would ever need, and that it was time for them to be reduced.

Size was not the only issue. If China were to invest in US productive assets, instead of holding its claims against the US in the shape of reserve holdings and US government bonds, this would help the US to reconfigure its economy. China's strategy was also forcing the US towards using more QE in part to force onto China internal inflationary pressures so as to try to get China to push up global inflationary pressures (and the emphasis on QE in the US was also because of the loss of appetite for greater fiscal stimulus).

In a curious, but helpful, twist, China's sovereign wealth fund, the China Investment Corporation, announced in late 2011 an interest in using some of its $400 billion to invest in infrastructure projects in those countries that had crashed, so long as stable returns were guaranteed. Some in the US and Europe baulked at the notion of China 'buying up' chunks of infrastructure projects, but it made perfect economic sense as part of global economic rebalancing. To revive demand in the US, Europe, and elsewhere, it would help if Western demand for China's goods was compensated by Chinese demand for Western investments including physical assets and equities. China would reduce its reliance on export-led growth, and allow its population to get more of the fruits of such investments. This would help the West to grow, to reduce its unemployment, and to pay off its debts.

Meanwhile, in the US, news items started to appear praising US consumers every time they were back in the shops, even though re-igniting a US consumer boom based on Chinese and other imports was hardly the way to go. Worse, those in the US traipsing through their local malls seeking consumerist relief tended to be in the top 25% of the income distribution. If escape from economic malaise included innovation and investment, even that was being killed off by sagging economic confidence and by the political games in Washington.

If countries with huge balance of payments surpluses and with spare savings did not accommodate the needs of those who were trying to deleverage, the deleveraging process would take longer and drag out the economic damage.[1]

The problem was once again the politics. In China, internal structural reform was needed to increase consumption and reduce savings, and to create proper safety nets, pension systems, and social infrastructure. This would take time. The unbalanced model of economic development of many oil-rich Arab countries seemed even less amenable to a quick fix. For years the rich elites of such countries had benefited from the uncritical support of the West, and any reform that might have challenged them had been stimied. At last, in the spring of 2011, grass-roots pressure for reform burst forth unexpectedly. The leaders of those countries did not want to hear it—because it involved them losing some of their personal wealth and power—but a good package of reform measures could only improve the chances of long-term economic stability both for themselves and for the rest of the world.

The Chinese government was sticking to its well-worn path of compromise in order to suit China's corporate and political elites. The power of narrow interest groups was amply demonstrated by the way China's 4-trillion renminbi stimulus package inefficiently targeted state-directed lending, although only about 30% of the value added in China was by state enterprises. Most of this pumped China's construction and property bubble, encouraged overinvestment in sectors that already had overcapacity, and further pumped the current account surplus. None of it was targeted at strengthening China's social safety nets. In 2011, 90% of China's growth came from fixed-asset investment, much of it trophy infrastructure projects. One day, the surge in credit was going to lead to a surge in bad debts. But that was going to be a problem for a new batch of leaders. An emphasis on capital-intensive projects was even undermining employment goals and efforts at social stability.

China faced complex domestic political pressures. Yielding to foreign powers would have been was seen as weakness, and Chinese leaders found themselves under domestic pressure to look 'strong'. China was also able to use its huge reserve holdings for geopolitical purposes, which included lending tens of billions to favoured governments and enterprises without ever needing to go through the sort of political processes that would be faced in the US or Europe. Thus, China became a bigger lender to developing countries than the World Bank, and was becoming the dominant foreign power in Africa, especially in the exploitation of raw materials.

In one international meeting after another, calls for China to reform its economic ways were muted. Other countries running big balance of payments surpluses, such as Germany, had little desire to draw attention to an issue that might get them accused of doing essentially the same. For oil-exporting countries, business as usual was far too congenial to risk rocking the boat. Countries such as Japan and South Korea knew that: their currencies would probably rise if China was forced to let its currency rise. They were not going to encourage that.

A few years before the crash, I explored why it would probably take a long time for China to allow its currency to revalue (or to float and appreciate).[2] In brief, the argument was based on a currency-crisis model that pitched the welfare of the Chinese government and of its social and political elites against the welfare of the rest of Chinese society. The longer China held out, the greater the build-up in its reserve holdings. This stored up an even greater loss for

China when revaluation finally materialized (China would lose on the conversion back into its own currency). At some moment in time, speculators were going to realize that, however much the Chinese government committed to holding its currency down, the costs of its actions would, at some future moment in time, come to outweigh the benefits to the Chinese government. Backwards induction from that future moment would bring the 'crisis' forward to the first moment when this was understood. Even more capital would flood in, taking the one-way bet that the currency would rise. This would push up inflation and other costs, and revaluation would be forced. Adjustment was likely to be delayed in China, way beyond the timescales that would be socially optimal for China and the rest of the world, because the 'protest cost' imposed by China's non-elite population on Chinese elites was very weak, and because, as the pile of its foreign-exchange reserves and US sovereign debt holdings grew, the political costs of allowing a loss on those holdings also grew. China took care not to undermine the US financial position because it would undermine its own holdings of US dollar reserves and US government debt; this was often conveiently ignored in debates about China's motives. An earlier revaluation would encourage investment in China's non-tradable sector, help reduce its reliance on exports, and avoid some of the long-term dangers that might otherwise make China's path of economic emergence go awry like that of Japan. Instead, China delayed, and found itself trapped.[3]

Perhaps the hand of the Chinese government was at last being forced. Real exchange-rate appreciation can come about either because a country's nominal exchange rate appreciates or because of a difference between the rates of inflation of itself and of those countries it trades with. In China, in 2011, consumer-price inflation was running at about 5.5%, well above the rate of inflation in the US. Therefore, for China, real exchange-rate appreciation was happening much faster than nominal exchange-rate appreciation. Looked at in another way, each dollar that was converted to be spent in China was buying less and less both because the nominal amount of renminbi it bought was falling and because each renminbi was buying less and less in China as Chinese domestic prices were rising. By holding its currency low artificially, China had imposed lax monetary policy onto its own economy, leading to over-investment, bubbles, and inflation. This would eventually force an adjustment.

Indeed, the internal politics in China was dictating that the Chinese government avoid high inflation. By 2011, Chinese officials were becoming increasingly sympathetic to the notion that an appreciation of the renminbi against the dollar and other currencies would help to neutralize imported inflation and inflation created by domestic credit booms, and that maybe this would help avoid a later bust in China. As a result, China started to pull back gingerly from holding US federal debt. Between July 2009 and the end of 2010, China's holdings went from being 13% to being under 10% of all holdings of US federal debt held in public hands (of course this often got interpreted the other way: as a sign of problems in the US). China was starting to adjust, albeit slowly, largely under the *force majeure* of rising domestic inflation.

In 2011, as US politicians played an astonishing game of fiscal brinkmanship, the lesson for China, as the largest foreign holder of US Treasuries, was that it was time to stop investing so heavily in the paper assets of the US, and wiser to invest in its own people and allow its currency to float freely. It would be costly for China's leaders to admit to their past economic mistakes and to crystallize a loss, yet the benefit to the Chinese economy would ultimately outweigh that cost—and help the world economy as well. This was difficult to achieve while those who had made the mistakes were still in power. A change of Chinese leadership in late 2012 was an opportunity to change economic course.

Another key to making the growth of countries such as China more balanced, and hence of achieving a more balanced global economy, would be the growth of a more 'sophisticated' Chinese financial system, capable of more efficiently channelling domestic savings *within* China and so encouraging Chinese domestic demand. And—just when we thought we had achieved irony-overload—China and others would benefit too from the lessons learned after the crash about how to design 'better' financial systems.

If patterns of global economic activity did not change so that demand in the US could be sustained without the prop of a lending boom, then the US would eventually find itself in a similar position to Japan, a country that battled deflation for the best part of two decades. It was in the long-term interests of both the US and China to avoid this, and to cooperate like they never had before. According to the principle of comparative advantage,[4] the only thing the US, the UK, and others needed to worry about was productivity. Politicians, goaded by a popular economic misconception about 'competitiveness' (namely, that somehow the US is 'in competition' with China), regularly get this wrong.[5] Growth in productivity, not 'competitiveness', ultimately drives living standards. If productivity in China, or India, or elsewhere was higher, it would benefit the US, the UK, and other countries. If China increased research and innovation and made itself more energy-efficient and environmentally friendly this would be to the benefit of all. Instead, the interacting weaknesses of all the major global economic players were magnifying, not correcting, global economic inbalances.

Currency and Trade Wars

Dealing with global economic imbalances would have generated a win-win situation, but those expected to take an economic loss in the short-term needed certainty that others would coordinate. Yet coordination was getting ever more difficult because the needs of different economies diverged, and policymakers usually had the mandate to stabilize only domestic variables, which barred them from taking into account spillovers onto other countries. In South Korea, in October 2010, G20 finance ministers issued a forlorn statement: '[U]ncoordinated responses will lead to worse outcomes for everyone. Our cooperation is essential. We are all committed to play our part in achieving strong, sustainable and balanced growth in a collaborative and coordinated way.'

Some of the biggest risks surrounded currencies. In the 1920s, in a time of little money, trade protection was all about exporting deflation. In 2011, in a time of much money, trade protection was about preventing nominal exchange rates from rising by limiting capital inflows, and therefore about exporting inflation[6] and stopping overheating. The modern equivalent to Smoot–Hawley was the use of currency policy as a form of industrial policy, or, for those who like their words a little blunter, exchange-rate manipulation as hidden export subsidy.

More than forty countries had pegged themselves to the dollar, or close to it in a so-called 'dirty float', with the intention to import stability. Instead, they were feeling the effects of the monetary policy that had been pitched for the rescue needs of the US and therefore way too loose for their own domestic circumstances. Capital was flowing into these countries, taking a punt on the usual one-way bet (if their currencies were forced to break the dollar peg and rise, speculators would gain). Capital inflows into emerging economies are often thought of as good news, because this enables them to invest and grow. However, these flows were pushing up asset prices and generating inflation in their recipients. Share prices in China, Brazil, and Indonesia more than doubled. In Hong Kong, house prices shot up 50% in about a year, in spite of curbs on mortgages. If some of these asset price rises were 'bubbles', they would cause challenges when they collapsed.

There were problems also for those countries whose exchange rates were floating. Brazil's annual current account surplus with the US (of about $15 billion) turned into a deficit (of about $6 billion) as a consequence of the dollar weakening against the Brazilian real. The finance minister of Brazil, Guido Mantega, coined the term 'currency war' and pinned the blame on the US and, to a degree, China. Other countries—South Africa, Turkey, and India—headed towards widened current account deficits. The fall of the dollar sent the euro rising to over $1.50 at the end of 2009. Investors scurried to mark down their growth forecasts for the eurozone. Over 2009 the renminbi also fell by about 14% against the euro because of the fall of the dollar. The role of US policy in aggravating problems in the eurozone often went unremarked.

Every time the dollar fell, the prices of metal, oil, and grain rose for those countries tied to the dollar. This effect was being reinforced by surges in demand from fast-growing emerging economies, by adverse supply conditions, especially for food, and by energy price spikes due to political instability in major oil-exporting regions. Key victims were the poorest food-importing countries in Africa and South Asia. Food inflation in India in 2009 and 2010 was running at about 14% per year. With food taking up a much higher proportion of household budgets in India and Africa than in the US and Europe, the pain was especially intense for the poor. Rapidly rising commodity prices were stoking inflation in emerging economies and stagflation (i.e. low growth and high inflation) in advanced economies, especially those with large debt overhangs.

As in all the best policy battles, each side took to blaming the other. China blamed the US for driving down the dollar via QE and for exporting its troubles. The bubble had gone from US housing and banking onto the shoulders of the US government, and now, via QE, onto China and other emerging economies. Because of China's desire to hold its currency down, the excess supply of dollars due to QE that was now finding its way to China had to be absorbed by the PBOC creating more renminbi, buying up the excess dollars, and increasing even further China's foreign-exchange reserves. The extra renminbi in circulation pushed up Chinese inflation and asset prices. If China had pushed up its interest rates to defend itself against asset-price bubbles and inflation, it would have simply pulled more financial capital in. China had two main options. It could have tried to limit lending by imposing higher reserve requirements. China did this numerous times; by July 2011, large Chinese banks needed to hold 21.5% of their deposits in reserve with the central bank (Peru also adopted higher bank-reserve requirements to try to limit lending).[7] Alternatively, China could have allowed its currency to rise and taken a loss on its huge foreign-exchange and US sovereign debt holdings. China faced an appalling dilemma. Let inflation and asset price bubbles rise and risk a crash later, or try to avoid bubbles but risk a loss now.

The US blamed China. To the US (although it was rarely spelled out) the more complete picture was that the problems had gone from China to the US housing market to the US government and then back to China via QE. Normally we would think that a fast-growing economy with the world's largest current account surplus should see its currency rise, and we would regard it as rather odd if, instead, it pegged its currency to that of a lower-growth economy. Yet, for many years up to about mid-2005, the renminbi had been pegged at just over 8.25 to the US dollar. Between 2005 and 2008, the Chinese government allowed the renminbi to appreciate by about 20% against the dollar. Then, concerned at the impact of the global downturn on its export sector, China held the rate fixed through 2008 and 2009, before letting it appreciate again. According to purchasing power parity (PPP), which says that a currency's price should reflect the amount of goods and services it can buy, the renminbi was still undervalued by about 40% in 2009. Many accused China of manipulating its currency in ways that harmed countries such as the US. Obama threatened: 'If the Chinese don't take actions, we have other means of protecting US interests.'[8] However, he did not spell these out. At the IMF's governing body meeting in April 2011, Geithner accused the IMF of not using its existing tools to tackle China on its exchange-rate 'manipulation'. He also argued: 'We will never seek to weaken our currency as a tool to gain competitive advantage or to grow the economy.' He wasn't entirely convincing: a falling dollar was a natural side effect of near-zero interest rates and QE, whether intentional or not.

Indeed, it was a little too convenient for China to blame its domestic inflation and real-estate bubbles on outsiders. By November 2010, the US had only managed to raise its broad money (as measured by seasonally adjusted M2) to about $8.8 trillion. Meanwhile, the central bank in China had pushed Chinese broad money to about $10.5 trillion. Yet, the Chinese economy was a third of the size of the US economy. On a measuring stick that stretched to the trillions, this made US QE look rather modest. In truth, China was confronting the consequences of its own loose monetary policy and rapid credit expansion, onto which the US had, for sure, introduced a few uncomfortable waves of QE. China's booming economy was less about improved economic prospects than about a massive monetary shock of China's own making. China had built for itself a huge shadow banking system. Much of the expansion of finance in China had been unregulated, and when loans went wrong, China's high rate of growth made the problems seem manageable. Like the US before it, China risked having its very own subprime disaster and ending up at the centre of the next banking crash. If that happened, the two-speed global economy would become the no-speed global economy.

Other countries were also engaging in excessive credit expansion and were overheating. Brazil, Columbia, India, Indonesia, and Turkey were especially vulnerable because credit per head had more than doubled in real terms in about five years, and much of the credit had gone into real estate. Argentina, Brazil,

India, and Indonesia were suffering from inflation problems. In Russia, the oil-fuelled trade surpluses were dwindling, and with them the easy money that had boosted social spending and incomes, especially under Putin.

According to the Fed, the US could only get its government budget deficit and sovereign debt levels back down if other sectors of its economy, chiefly exports, expanded as a per cent of US GDP. Attaining this, the Fed reasoned, via a fall in the nominal exchange rate of the US was surely preferable to achieving it via inflation. Using QE to help achieve domestic stability was rational even if it imposed a negative externality on other countries. In the Fed's eyes, it was anyway time for a coordinated appreciation of emerging economy currencies so as to help the rebalancing process along, and China and others needed to cooperate.

Yet China saw the same matters through a different, domestically-orientated, lens. Wen Jiabao, the Chinese Premier, warned in October 2011: 'Do not work to pressure us on the renminbi rate . . . many of our exporting companies would have to close down, migrant workers have to return to their villages. If China saw social and economic turbulence, then it would be a disaster for the world.'[9] In China's eyes, the US needed to be less belligerent, given that it was the US political elite that was at fault because it had, over several decades, created and fed so much of the mess in the first place. After the crash, the US thought that it was able to get away with super-low interest rates, to benefit in a very one-sided way from the 'exorbitant privilege' of the reserve-currency status of the dollar, to take advantage of super-loose policies such as QE that emerging and less-developed countries could not risk copying, to hugely favour its big failed banks, and to export a large part of the costs of its past failures to other countries. And it expected those who suffered the consequences to not complain.

As various rounds of QE further weakened the dollar, some countries sought ways to retaliate. In 2010, Japan, South Korea, and Thailand intervened in their (spot) currency markets. Brazil, Chile, and Peru kicked off the new year of 2011 in similar vein. Brazil imposed a 2% tax on inflows into its bond markets and equities, and warned that a currency war risked turning into a full-blown trade war. Of course, as each tried to make its currency the only one that did not rise, the effort was self-defeating. Worse, it risked more aggressive measures, including genuine trade protectionism and subsidies that discriminated against foreign firms. A bout of protectionism would damage global supply chains, and it would take years to recover from the wounds. Sadly, the shifting of currency battles to centre-stage was a consequence of politicians, especially in deleveraging countries, refusing (often because of domestic politics) to take the necessary steps towards rebalancing that we discussed in earlier chapters. It was also a

side-effect of de-emphasizing fiscal policy and putting all the weight on monetary policy.

Many emerging countries started to argue their right to use short-term capital
controls and trade controls (such as tariff barriers) to protect themselves. After
all, the ability to use QE was lopsided, and the use of super-low interest rates in
the US was to the detriment of other countries. Many wondered what was so
wrong with a few of their own 'lopsided' measures. Support for capital controls,
although only as a last resort, came from an unexpected quarter. In February
2011, the IMF issued a report promoting global guidelines on capital flows.[10]
Rogoff was diplomatic but firm: 'These are very tough intellectual questions to
which there are no crisp answers, but there is a good case for emerging markets
to limit inflows to prevent a crisis in four or five years' time.'[11] In the past, the
IMF had taken a harsh stance against such controls; it was getting soft in its
old age.

Indeed, a growing number of economists, having waded through one of
the more treacle-like confluences of international economics and politics, were
starting to argue for 'sensible' capital controls. Capital controls could not be used
to defend a fundamentally unsustainable currency peg, but they could be used
to buy time to deal with short-term economic disturbances. Evidence showed
that controls on capital flows could make domestic monetary policy more
independent, change the composition of capital inflows, and reduce exchange-
rate pressures.[12]

The Fall of the Dollar and the Rise of the Renminbi?

The truly sick patient of the global economy, the US, survived in part because of
the global reserve-currency status of the dollar. Strange though it may seem to
some readers, but every time there were economic problems anywhere in the
world, even if heavily shaped by failures in the US, the US was the safe haven of
choice for investors. In late 2008, after the collapse of Lehman, the dollar rallied
as many investors scrambled to get away from emerging markets and commod-
ity-linked currencies. In 2010, when the eurozones' problems intensified, the
dollar rallied again for no other reason than its status as 'safe haven'. The global
role of the dollar also allowed the US huge leeway for its QE operations. Yet the
dollar was on a path of long-term decline, its safe-haven status taking new
knocks every day. Investors were diversifying away from the dollar and holding
more emerging-market currencies, gold, and other commodities.

Global reserve-currency status presents to its holder a trade-off between domestic stability and international stability. Over the years, the US had prioritized the former at the expense of the latter with a cheerful alacrity that bordered on the reckless. What was going to happen when the issuer of the world's reserve currency was in relative decline itself—its creditworthiness in question, its currency no longer seen by investors as a safe haven, its economy suffering from greater inflation expectations and financing risk than other economies, and with investors seeking yield in emerging markets and commodity currencies?

Perhaps the US needed to reflect on the experience of the UK?[13] By the outbreak of the First World War, the US economy was already twice the size of the UK economy, yet the dollar had absolutely no international role. The UK had been the first industrial superpower, a big exporter, and a big investor globally. This first-mover advantage locked in sterling as the global reserve currency. Central banks held their reserves in pounds, not in dollars. No foreign bonds were issued in dollars. US exporters and importers got their trade credits in London and did their business in sterling. The US lacked the market infrastructure to allow the dollar to play much of an international role. The US had neither a central bank nor a liquid market in the trade acceptances which were used to finance exports and imports. The UK's continued pre-eminence as holder of the global reserve currency seemed assured. Then, in 1924, the Federal Reserve System was set up. It immediately set about creating a highly liquid market in trade acceptances. The strategy was quite deliberately 'interventionist'—almost an infant-industry approach to creating a market. The confidence of investors was built. By the late-1920s, New York was the leading source of trade finance in the world. The Fed eased off on its support, private investors were allowed to take over the market and, by the end of the 1920s, central banks held more reserves in dollars than in sterling. In less than a decade, a new international currency, the dollar, had ousted the market-leading product, sterling.

Now, by becoming the world's biggest, and most inefficient, debtor, the US had weakened its claim to global reserve-currency status. Perhaps the biggest irony of the Bush years was that the president who launched two wars to assert the US's global hegemony ended up hastening its decline by other means. What saved the US from losing its reserve-currency status was the lack of any viable alternative to the dollar and the fact that the US had a veto on any mechanism, such as via the IMF, to create a dollar replacement.

Much has been written about the possibility that China might establish the renminbi as a leading international currency. During 2010 and 2011, the Chinese authorities encouraged trade conducted in renminbi, with Hong Kong as the designated offshore centre. The rate of growth in the use of renminbi was startling. We can be a little more sanguine: the high growth rates were from a very low base; China could not be home to an international reserve currency under its current economic and political regime; trading on the Chinese foreign-exchange market would first need to become much easier (China had a raft of capital controls); and China's financial markets would need to be more accessible (there was little point buying renminbi in Hong Kong if assets could not be bought in China). Given China's caution about liberalization of its financial system, this seemed like a several-decade long project. Perhaps the process might be self-fulfilling and quicker, and might result in China being eventually forced to open up and give greater access to its currency and markets. The very openness and liquidity would make it increasingly difficult to sustain Chinese corporatist ways, and this would hasten the need for reform in China. Until then, in the competition for the least-ugly safe asset, the dollar would invariably win.

Ultimately the biggest threat to the US was not from China and 'abroad' but from within, from its own political elites and their inability to deal in even remotely sensibly ways with difficult (but not irresolvable) economic problems. To heap blame on China and 'the others' seemed easier, and even felt thera-peutic, although it was damaging self-indulgence.

Whither Emerging Economies?

Before the crash it was often argued that emerging countries had decoupled their economies, and the fates of their investors, from the economies of more developed countries. This argument turned out to be entirely fallacious. Eco-nomic and financial integration had made emerging economies more, not less, vulnerable. The first route was via demand for their exports. As we saw in Chapter 7, some emerging economies took the biggest early economic hits after the crash, because of their high exposure to the collapse in global trade, but were among the first to recover. Then they were vulnerable again in late 2011 and early 2012 as the eurozone wobbled.

Moreover, the funding for banks in many emerging economies had been primarily sourced from abroad. A domestic interbank market was not a prom-inent feature in the financial landscapes of such economies; so, when the crash came, the standard liquidity-enhancing provisions found in more advanced economies were not possible. Central banks in emerging economies eased liquidity problems by providing foreign currency. Some had large foreign-exchange reserves they could tap to do this. Others relied on currency 'swap lines' with the central banks of more advanced economies and on IMF facilities. Because of the dependence on cross-border lending, the refinancing needs of emerging economies were high.

The other big problem was the knock-on effects on emerging economies from rescue measures in developed economies. First, many developed-economy governments offered support to their domestic financial institutions on condition that they increased or maintained domestic lending. This 'home bias' was a form of protectionism to the detriment of emerging economies. Second, bank guarantees provided by governments in more advanced economies out-compete anything that the governments of emerging countries could offer. It was too risky for emerging-economy governments to 'mortgage' themselves in the way the US and European governments had done in order to provide such guarantees. As a consequence, for a while, emerging countries experienced deposit outflows from their banks. Third, because of currency-risk and country-risk, there was usually a higher regulatory capital charge on the cross-border exposures of developed-economy financial institutions; getting rid of these exposures was a quick way for such institutions to improve their capital ratios. Fourth, by the spring of 2009, very risk-averse investors were shifting away from emerging economies into mature-economy bond markets, deeming them higher quality in a crisis; it was a highly variable effect. Fifth, foreign-exchange swap markets were impaired, which reduced the ability to use assets denominated in foreign currencies as collateral to access central bank facilities.

Nevertheless, once the fickleness of international investors and the side-effects on emerging economies of rescue efforts passed, the crash created also opportunities for many emerging economies. Many took an economic hit no bigger than that of the early 1990s recession. Big populous emerging economies, such as China, Indonesia, and India, proved far more resilient than many expected. In China, output stalled, did not fall, and then bounced back: indeed, China overtook Japan to become the world's second-biggest economy. India and Brazil powered ahead in terms of their GDP.

Mature economies very rarely grow on a sustained basis at more than 2% or 3% per year in real terms, which is roughly their long-term rate of productivity growth. After the crash, they were facing large public- and private-sector debts and, in many cases, such as the US, demographic effects that were increasingly working against them. In contrast, it is not extraordinary for emerging economies to grow at 8% or 9% per year in real terms, because the process of economic catch-up allows them to take advantage of existing technologies, without uncurring the costs of developing them from scratch, and to avoid the cost of maintaining old infrastructures. In many emerging economies (although not all, with China being a notable exception), favorable demographics meant that young workers generated savings and surges in investment.

Nevertheless, high rates of growth in emerging economies were going to eventually ease. As labour shifted from low-productivity agriculture into much higher-productivity manufacturing, and then into services where productivity improvements were slower, technical innovation was going to be needed eventually to sustain emerging-economy growth. When emerging economies did eventually slow, it was going to impact upon highly-indebted developed economies relying on the imports of emerging economies to pull them through. When would this happen? One set of authors found that, among countries experiencing sustained catch-up growth, there was a critical threshold—a little below $17,000 per person at purchasing power parity (PPP) in 2005 prices— beyond which growth dropped significantly, from about 5.6% to 2.1% per year, once all the catch-up advantages were exhausted.[14] Western Europe, Japan, Singapore, South Korea, and Taiwan went through something like this. However, experiences varied. Some countries, such as Japan, experienced slowdown in steps. Other countries, such as the US and the UK, were able to keep growing for longer than average before slowdown set in.

According to such studies, China would hit the threshold in about 2015.[15] China had a number of risk factors associated with a higher probability than average of slowdown, including: a low ratio of workers to dependants (because of past population policies); a low level of consumption as a percentage of GDP; rising and unstable inflation; and an undervalued currency. The reason for the last is unclear, but it may be that an undervalued currency reduces the incentive to invest in innovation, and leads to imbalances that eventually harm growth. There were, however, offsetting factors. China had openness to trade, and it might one day allow economic development to shift inland and innovation to be nurtured on the coast.

One particular group of emerging economies was already in trouble. Among the countries often referred to as 'emerging Europe' there were those in a periphery beyond the periphery—countries such as Latvia, Hungary, Bulgaria, and Romania—who had deemed it some sort of fashionable rite of economic passage to stuff themselves full of bank debt. Many of them had reasoned that since they were going to join the euro anyway, there was no reason to pay high interest on debts in local currency when cheap borrowing was available in euros and other currencies. These countries had wondered what elixir the Irish and others were imbibing that had allowed them to expand at 7%–9% per year, and whether they could have some too. Of course they could, but it was powerful stuff and easily went to one's head. In some of these countries, the growth of private-sector debt had been even greater than in the US and in the UK. Many had been running large balance of payments deficits that they offset with inflows of foreign-currency mortgage lending and property buy-outs. Banks, in particular in Germany, the UK, Switzerland, Sweden, Italy, and Austria had not been backward in coming forward with cheap loans.

All these flows had now evaporated, leaving such countries facing a dilemma similar to the one that had been faced by those countries that got into trouble in the Asian financial crisis. They needed to attract external finance to cover large current account deficits while, at the same time, rolling over maturing government debt, and they had to repay their private-sector foreign-currency debts. They could not transfer private-sector risk into sovereign risk, as the US, the UK, and the eurozone had done. They could end their currency fixes to help to fix their trade imbalances, but that would make the costs of servicing and repaying their foreign-currency denominated debt much higher in local currencies, increase defaults, and reinforce domestic deflationary pressures. Or they could keep their currencies strong to help pay their foreign-currency debts but, as a result, their exports would collapse and depression set in. Hungary and Romania drifted in the direction of the first option, allowing their currencies to lose about 20%–25% of their value in 2009. At the end of 2011, official unemployment in Hungary was nearly 10% and a million homeowners had seen monthly mortgage repayments rise by a third over 2011. By January 2012, all three main credit rating agencies had cut Hungary's credit rating to junk status. Hungary's new government lurched towards authoritarianism, rewriting the constitution so that its 52% vote in the general election in 2010 would have given it 75% of the seats in parliament, and would have made it victor in the 2002 and 2006 elections that it lost. It took the judiciary under party control and forced opposition-supporting media outlets to close. Was this a taste of the Europe to come?

Latvia demonstrated just how challenging adjustment through austerity could be. Nearly 90% of Latvia's debts were in foreign currencies, and owed mostly to Swedish and Austrian banks. Over two years, Latvia turned around its huge external current account deficit by means of public-sector pay cuts and austerity, but its GDP fell by 20%, unemployment rose to nearly 25%, its real-estate market plummeted, and its government budget deficit was still nearly 8% at the end of all the pain.

To complicate matters, German recovery was turning out to be important for countries such as Poland and the Czech Republic, that had integrated themselves into German manufacturing supply chains. The Czechs had also borrowed and lent much more in their own currency, and used foreign investment to promote exports and not so much to pump property bubbles. As a result, the Poles and the Czechs were not especially sympathetic towards others in the outer reaches of Europe.

At some point there was going to be a political fight over the repayment of the debt of these countries. When the dollar was devalued by Roosevelt in 1934 (from $20 to $55 per ounce) he annulled the 'gold clause' that indexed payment of US bank loans to the price of gold. The equivalent act in the 2010s would push the debt burden back on to the original lenders, usually European banks; this would wipe out a chunk of their capital. For many in the periphery beyond the periphery, the incentive to repay was not exactly strong. Many post-Soviet economies had been restructured to benefit foreign investors, not domestic residents. In Latvia, for example, labour had been paying about 50% tax (labour, employer, and social tax) even though property taxes were set at less than 1%. As asset price inflation had driven labour to migrate, Swedish and Austrian banks had benefited. Was it so unreasonable for the owners of such banks to face the consequences of their poor investment decisions?

However, threats not to repay in full would have been be met with credit-rating downgrades and higher borrowing costs. But, as in the eurozone, there were limits to the political feasibility of enforcing repayment when all knew that it was to benefit foreign banks. One lesson from the eurozone debacle was that, even if write-down is inevitable, it practically never happens until after a longh delay that pushes the cost even higher, and that it sometimes takes protests and the fall of governments to create the impetus to negotiate the terms of debt write-downs.

Inflation, Deflation, or Default

In 2005, I wrote that the path of recovery for economies such as those of the US, the UK, and Europe, would be a delicate balance between the risks of deflation and the risks of inflation.[16] It seemed a curious notion at the time, but it was the logical consequence of having, on the one hand, a collapsing bubble-infested balance sheet and debt overhang (which are deflationary), and on the other hand, huge government deficits and unconventional monetary policy (which tempt inflation). After the crash, investors started to mirror the complex set of risks in their behaviour. There was a rush into government bonds, which crushed yields. This indicated worry about deflation. But there was also a rush into gold—an asset that central banks could not create more of and a liability of none of them—which suggested that gold was being used as a hedge against inflation because of fears that heavily indebted countries would one day inflate their debts away. The price of gold quadrupled from its pre-crash low.

It was difficult to evaluate the balance of long-term risks between inflation and deflation. Central bankers had to act in a world where the trajectory of the thing they most cared about, inflation, was very unclear. They had no reliable way to asses the impact of all their unconventional monetary policy. They knew that it might be difficult to reverse such measures, but they did not know how difficult. If the private sector started to believe that sovereign debt burdens were getting so high that inflation might be used to eat the debt away, long-term inflation expectations would rise.[17] But if the private sector developed long-term deflationary expectations and started to postpone investment and spending, this would feed the very deflation that central banks feared. Nor was it clear what had happened to potential output. If potential output had fallen significantly, then the output gap was perhaps less negative than evidence was suggesting, and disinflationary pressures being overestimated, and inflationary pressures being underestimated. In the 1970s, the impact on potential output was underesti-mated and therefore so too were the inflationary pressures. By late 2011, the evidence was increasingly pointing to a similar collapse of potential output in many heavily-leveraged countries, and to long-term inflationary pressures. Yet this was dancing with other forces that pointed to deflation.

China had been like a giant factory—or at least the end of the production line—for the world, and especially for the US. It was rapidly becoming clear that in the future China would no longer be exporting deflation but inflation. The US and other countries would have to offset this with lower domestic inflation or contend with higher inflation too. Nevertheless, the inflationary pressure from China on developed countries was lower than often argued. First, only about 10% to 15% of the final price of export goods 'made in China' represented value added in China because of the 'end-of-the-production-line' phenomenon. Thus, Chinese labour costs could go up quite a lot with only a modest impact on the price of goods. Second, Chinese productivity levels were going up, which was allowing Chinese wages to rise without pushing up prices. Third, some production was shifting to lower-wage economies (Bangladesh, Vietnam, Indonesia, and India), and this was pulling global inflationary pressures back down.

There was a difference of opinion as to what was causing the inflation that surged in 2010 and 2011 and as to what, if anything, it suggested about the future. China and the ECB both blamed loose monetary policy, especially in the US. The ECB tightened its policy and emphasized the need to maintain its own credibility. The Fed and the Bank of England blamed high demand from fast-growing emerging economies and oil price rises that were beyond their control. In the UK, the rise in VAT had temporarily pushed up domestic inflation, and the 25% decline in the value of the pound (itself a function of monetary policy choices) was pushing up import prices. Yet, despite inflation of 5%, and real earnings falling, there was no upward wage pressure, which suggested that domestic inflationary pressure was low. With all the domestic risks on the downside, the Bank of England kept interest rates very low. The Bank of England had loosened its policy in the years before the crash, using the excuse that falling import prices were pushing inflation lower. Now it was using the excuse of rising import prices to justify the same loose policy (and to support the rebalancing towards exports), and it had missed its inflation-rate target every month since January 2010. This had the hallmarks of a 'Greenspan put' in the making, and suggested that the Bank of England was taking risks with its credibility.

Inflation is the friend of those lumbered with high debts. Like hungry moths left in a cupboard full of smart suits for long enough,[18] inflation eats away the real value of the debts of government and of the private-sector. Again, some self-fulfilling logic can be used to tell a story of future inflation. As the level of sovereign debt rises, the economic and political costs of keeping the promise to repay the debt in real terms weigh more heavily against the economic and political benefits of keeping the promise. At some point, markets come to believe that at some future moment politicians will simply conclude that it is politically less costly to monetize some or all of the debt forever and absorb the cost in terms of higher inflation. The 'crisis' is triggered (by a process of backwards induction) the first moment this is realized. The rates at which governments are able to borrow rise to reflect the heightened risk. The yearly stream of tax revenue required to cover the stream of interest repayments rises. Just one or two per cent more borrowing cost translates into tens of billions of pounds or dollars or euros of tax yield transferred from current public spending to paying off the previously acquired debt.[19] Rollover of government debt becomes more difficult. Pressures rise on governments to raise taxes and to cut spending. This encourages governments to inflate, and instils expectations of inflation. This feeds back to raise borrowing costs. And so on. This could happen even in a recession or a jobless recovery, resulting in 'stagflation'. Thus, even if inflation is currently low, a government might need to persuade markets that it will repay its debts in real terms. Even if unemployment is high, a government might need to play tough with interest rates.

The dynamics also depends on who owns sovereign debt. If the debt is mostly held by domestic residents, most of the interest payments and eventual capital repayment go from one set of domestic residents to another. Sticking to real repayment means placing the welfare of those holding more sovereign debt over those holding less. Typically, those holding more tend to include the relatively well-off, savers, the elderly who have built up life savings and are shifting out of equity investments into fixed investments, and pension investors of all ages whose pension funds have invested in government bonds. To the extent that sovereign debt is held externally to a country, inflation helps to pass the costs on to 'outsiders', and so is more acceptable to an electorate.[20]

When emerging economies face debt that has reached unsustainable levels, inflating the debt away or defaulting and negotiating new terms has frequently been the escape route. The economic impact of a write-down is similar to inflation; a loss of value is imposed on the lender, with the inflation specific to that lender. A default is a way to pass the burden on to foreigners. Emerging economies capable of 8% or 10% or 12% rates of economic growth per year can more easily get over default than countries with much lower potential growth rates. Within a few years, the healthy prospects for new investors (precisely because the unsustainable debts have been taken away) prove enough to get over the impact of the prior default on previous investors.

Would the default option ever be available to the US? The answer ought to be 'no'. The risks of a financial market meltdown and the loss of the dollar's global reserve-currency status would be just too high a price for the US to pay. The very fact that the damage would be so large is indeed what stops it from happening in the first place (although, as we saw in Chapter 9, the high price of default also means that it can be used as a political weapon). If default is ruled out, the US (and the UK and others) would have to absorb the cost of their debt internally. The only way to avoid this would be to inflate the value of the debt out of existence. The extremely low interest rates in 2012 suggested that this was still a highly unlikely scenario.

The Downsides of QE

Nowhere did the debate over inflation and deflation get more animated than in arguments over QE. A full evaluation of the impact of QE needed to incorporate the longer-horizon effects, which were fiendishly hard to measure. According to George Osborne, before he became the UK's finance minister, QE was 'a desperate government's last resort' (which, actually, was a pretty accurate description of it). It was not the purpose of QE to finance budget deficits. Yet, one hand of government was issuing debt to fund its budget deficit, while the other, via QE (QE2 in the case of the US), was buying it. By mid-2012, two-thirds of the recent increase in the stock of UK government debt had been monetized in this way and the Bank of England's balance sheet had ballooned to about £350 billion.

This blurring of the boundary between monetary policy and fiscal policy had its risks. If unwinding QE makes deficit financing more difficult, political pressures not to unwind might undermine central-bank independence. If central-bank independence is key to the credibility of anti-inflation policy, control of inflation would become more difficult, and QE would one day lead to higher interest rates that would knock on to the borrowing costs of both the government and the private sector. Worse, if long-term interest rates started to rise simply because of the fear that this might happen, monetary authorities would end up chasing their tails, pumping ever harder on QE to restrain the rise, but this would just make fears worse. No wonder that Germany's Chancellor Merkel got her claws out ('Merkel Mauls Central Bank'): 'What other central banks have been doing must be reversed.'[21] The ECB had 'bowed to international pressure with its purchase of covered bonds', she growled. 'We must return to independent and sensible monetary policies, otherwise we will be back to where we are now in ten years' time' she announced.

The risk was probably lowest in the case of the ECB and greatest in the case of the US. The ECB, even after the expansion of its holdings in late 2011 and early 2012, had lower holdings than the US to offload back onto the market. In the US, later rounds of QE involved purchasing long-maturity debt. If such actions were reversed by simply allowing gilts to mature (perhaps to avoid registering losses) the process could take a long time. The notion seemed to be that the Fed could speed the process up either by selling back assets it had bought, or by raising interest rates and giving incentive for banks to deposit funds back into the Fed. If worse came to the worse, the Fed could raise reserve requirements. The problem, as always, was the politics. The Fed was a creature of the US Congress and increasingly becoming an off-balance-sheet dependency of the US Treasury. If, some years later, it proved impossible to get agreement on tax rises or spending cuts to repay government debt, Congress—and the electorate—might simply find inflation the easier political route. And if at that point, emerging economies were exporting inflation (instead of exporting deflation as in the past), it would seem, all the more, the sensible thing to do.

QE was just another form of borrowing and its costs would show up eventually. If the balance sheets of central banks were to be shrunk back later, markets would need to absorb both the normal supply of government bonds and the running down of the central bank's assets. QE pushed down bond yields in the short run, but the cost was in terms of pushing up bond yields at a later date. If the Fed and the Bank of England at that later date were to make big losses in the process of shrinking their balance sheets, they would find themselves dependent on their Treasuries for bailouts. The Fed made big gains on its 2008 and 2009 asset purchases because such purchases were done at low prices that then rose. Losses on its later purchases, which were mostly government bonds, would probably be more salient in the minds of voters (in late 2010, at the time of QE2, ten-year rates were only around 2.6%, and so the Fed was buying government bonds at high prices). If losses contributed to sustained fiscal deficits, the chance of ratings downgrades might follow. QE was also the latest twist of the 'Greenspan put'. If central banks always jump in to protect markets from the deflation downside, but are less willing to act on the inflation upside, markets price this in, which exacerbates moral hazard and future bubbles.

One way to reduce some of these negative impacts would be to have— designed and built in from the start—an explicit exit strategy from QE, includ- ing policies for raising bank reserve requirements and selling debt to the public. But how could such a commitment be made credible? And would politics not interfere with any notion of surgically precise exit strategies? Unclear exit strategies lead to unclear strategies for businesses, because investors are unable to know whether it will be interest rates or taxes that will go up, or public spending that will be cut.

QE helped banks to satisfy tougher liquidity requirements. Some said QE was also a back-door recapitalization. However, there was little, or no credit expansion to show for such benefits to banks. Cheap money inflated asset prices artificially and sent reported profits soaring. The US stock market shot up 22% in 2009. Bank share prices rose, and the banking system registered itself as safer. But if bubbles in asset prices were being used to repair bank and corporate balance sheets, and generating problems in emerging economies and for developed economy bond markets, what would happen when such bubbles collapsed? If banks that otherwise would have been insolvent were avoiding being closed down, would they just dump their losses at a much later date, and hope to be rescued then?

As a source of virtually free money, QE gave investors the ability to speculate in foreign currencies and equities, oil, gold, industrial metals, bonds of emerging markets and commodity-producing countries, grains, and food. Price spikes in many markets acted as indirect taxes that harmed growth. Bill Gross, king of the bond market, advised: 'Shake hands with the government... their checkbook represents the largest and most potent source of buying power in 2009 and beyond. Anticipate, then buy what they buy, only do it first'.[22] Bankers and investment managers paid themselves generous bonuses on reported profits that were entirely artificial and had nothing to do with their superior investment skills.

In the face of a balance sheet recession and the collapse of aggregate demand, and up against the 'zero bound', fiscal policy was the only option that had any real traction. Yet, one by one, policymakers were gluing the fiscal levers off. QE was no silver bullet for battered economies on the ropes, and yet desperate governments were increasingly having to rely upon it.

In the US, a tax credit for investment in physical-capital or for job creation could have provided the same inducement to investment as a fall in long-term interest rates caused by QE, but without some of the longer-term risks and negative side-effects of QE. Even better, firms would have had to invest to get the tax credit, and so the credit would have been a more reliable device to reduce the cost of investment. QE, for all the heated debates over it, was, nonetheless, politically far easier than a tax credit that would have to go through Congress and register in the government's budget.

Similarly, it would have been more efficient to inject resources directly into infrastructure investments and pay back when the economy recovered—than to give all kinds of indirect speculative gains to those with the ability to exploit QE but whose behaviour only occasionally led to a positive increase in infrastructure. Why not create government-backed infrastructure banks with the same long-term burden as QE? By mid-2012, it was surely time to think beyond QE, and of ways to get central-bank money into the hands of those who were credit-starved. The most effective way to takle the liquidity trap was to inject cash directly into the pockets of citizens rather than indirectly via banks. Being 'new' money, it would not add to the deficit. So far, policymakers were avoiding taking this more direct route.

Some of those who pushed for fiscal tightening did not seem to understand that the monetary levers would have to stay loose for longer to overcompensate. Yet, with Congress and the Senate locked in fiscal deadlock, and the UK government stuck, for political reasons, with a plan that was not working, the Fed and the Bank of England were the only organizations able to move on anything. If there was inflation later because of QE, current politicians would not be on the hook. It was a bit too easy politically to push austerity and walk away from the problems that, as a consequence, central bankers would have to deal with later. Strange, too, that policymakers favoured a monetary approach that boosted the bonuses of many of those who broke the financial system in the first place, rather than favouring a fiscal approach that would do more to help the victims. All options created risks, but the risk to the unemployed and the poor was not high on the list of concerns.

Through 2009 and 2010, the finer points of slow or fast removal of QE were batted back and forth. However, by mid-2011, with the US economy stalling and practically every fiscal-stimulus instrument stuck in the political sidings, a new round of QE, called QE3, was about the only approach they had left that might move. Inflation was not much of a concern. Despite the rise in import prices, inflation expectations stayed low and wages showed no signs of rising and setting off an inflationary spiral. Increasingly, there was little choice but to offset the deflationary forces of tighter fiscal policy by using more QE, for all its long-term costs. Reversing an even bigger QE3 one day would be harder than reversing QE2, for sure, but not doing it at all risked an even deeper economic contraction. Eventually, in mid-September 2012, the Fed launched QE3, and pitched it as an open-ended purchase each month of $40 billion in agency MBSs.

Something Bigger Out There?

Was an even bigger disaster possible? Certainly it was possible to conjur up gratuitous disaster scenarios, involving new bubbles bursting, debt and deficits rising, and economies so utterly dislocated that it would be extremely difficult for them to get out of their mess. We saw in 2007–2008 that stability can hide instability, that when measures of risk on a range of assets are driven very low, risk can still be very high. What if policymakers were creating conditions conductive for the next crisis? If a bond bubble was expanding, when it collapsed there would be nothing left in the policy armoury. Interest rates could not go any lower, and once private investors were trying to sell government bonds as fast as central banks were trying to buy them, QE would lose its power too. If the dollar collapsed and financial markets were hit, banks would be in a new crisis. It would be a rerun of 2008–2009 but worse, because deflation would be a reality, fiscal policy would be lost, monetary policy not working, and international cooperation blown to bits. Policymakers needed watch their step, needed to be more cooperative with each other, and needed to expand their policy tools to include fiscal stimulus and growth. Otherwise, there really might be even worse nightmares out there.

Banking Reform

The Race to the Bottom

The first rule of sound financial regulation is that the one doing the regulating should outsmart the one being regulated—and not the other way around. It is not an easy rule to follow. The one being regulated invariably has more to lose than the one doing the regulating. In the years before the crash, it did not help that, instead of being on a relentless mission to think up ever smarter ways to outwit their opponents, financial regulators were in a race to the bottom.

First, in the US, came the Garn-St Germain Depository Institutions Act of 1982. The full title sounds familiar: 'An Act to revitalize the housing industry by strengthening the financial stability of home mortgage lending institutions and ensuring the availability of home mortgage loans.' As President Ronald Reagan signed it into law he quipped, 'All in all, I think we hit the jackpot!' He was right. Many thrifts tanked up on risky loans and gambled on the basis of the federal insurance of their deposits. The S&L crisis of the 1980s followed sure enough. Next, in the UK, came the 'Big Bang' reforms of 1986, with the aim being to help banks compete against their foreign rivals. Then, most notable of all, in the US in 1999, key provisions in the UK Banking Act (the Glass–Steagall Act) of 1933 were dismantled, as part of the Gramm–Leach–Bliley Act. Down came the firewalls between commercial banks, investment banks, and insurance companies. Up sprang new combinations of all three. Larry Summers, US Treasury Secretary, said it would 'better enable American companies to compete in the new economy'.[1] Policymakers were warned of the dangers. Investment banks would drill through to the government guarantee attached to commercial banks and use it to subsidize their own risk-taking beyond what was socially optimal,[2] and wholesale and retail banking would concentrate into fewer and bigger too-big-to-fail (TBTF) banks.[3] The promised land of economies of scale and scope, greater diversification, 'one-stop' convenience—and more profits—proved a somewhat more enticing prospect.[4]

President Bill Clinton, it is said, now regrets not regulating the over-the-counter (OTC) derivatives market. When, between 1993 and 1996, the market doubled to $28 trillion (by 2008, the market had grown another twenty-fold),[5] Clinton worried enough to appoint Brooksley Born, a highly experienced financial lawyer, to head the Commodity Futures Trading Commission. She quickly warned of the dangers from lack of transparency and oversight. Greenspan, guardian angel[6] of financial markets, keen to demonstrate the age-old principle that convictions are far more dangerous than lies, at one Congressional hearing after another warned that prying too closely would result in the loss of business to foreign competitors.[7] Summers added that even the request for more information would 'cast the shadow of regulatory uncertainty over an otherwise thriving market, raising risks for the stability and competitiveness of American derivative trading'.[8] Summers did not do irony, and so did not spot that if merely enquiring about the facts was a risk to stability, this might suggest that the OTC market hung by a thread. But if so, why be deliberately ignorant of just how thin that thread might be? Robert Rubin, Summers' predecessor, and Arthur Levitt, then Chair of the SEC, joined Greenspan and Summers in their anti-Born chorus. In 2000, Congress, having taken stock of the wisdom of its oracles, and keen to ensure collective responsibility for the ensuing disaster, enacted the Commodity Futures Modernization Act. Like a fishmonger's knife, the Act was used to gut Born's agency of its ability to regulate the OTC market. As Born put it after the crash, 'Recognizing the dangers...was not rocket science, but it was contrary to the conventional wisdom and certainly contrary to the economic interests of Wall Street.'[9]

The British *do* do irony and so, in 2002, Greenspan was knighted by Queen Elizabeth II for 'services to financial stability'. Rubin went on to head the executive committee of Citigroup, where he contributed with rare distinction to its demise. 'You were either pulling the levers, or asleep at the switch,' observed the chair of the FCIC when Rubin appeared before it (Rubin did not help his case by saying that he knew nothing of the dodgy investments that brought Citigroup to its knees, despite having been paid some $126 million for services that might, not unreasonably, have included knowing).[10]

After the crash, Rubin greatly regretted that he 'did not recognize the serious possibility of the extreme circumstances that the financial system faces today'.[11]

Summers—thoroughly re-educated[12]—reflected: '[T]here's no question that with hindsight, stronger regulation would have been appropriate.'[13] Meanwhile, Levitt lamented that 'All tragedies in life are preceded by warnings. We had a warning. It was from Brooksley Born. We didn't listen.'[14] Perhaps reasoning that those who create a mess should help to clean it up, Obama appointed Rubin as a key economic adviser and Summers as head of the National Economic Council. In 2009, Born was awarded the John F. Kennedy 'Profiles in Courage Award', which allowed Caroline Kennedy to opine that 'Brooksley Born recognized that the financial security of all Americans was being put at risk by the greed, negligence and opposition of powerful and well-connected interests'[15] and allowed the rest of us to marvel at the whirring inner mechanisms of the US Democratic political establishment.

To Gordon Brown, Greenspan was a hero and, in a rare moment of modesty, quite simply 'the man acknowledged to be the world's greatest economic leader of our generation'.[16] Greenspan's philosophy of unfettered markets fell into eager hands that shaped it into a new regulatory model for the UK, the 'Better Regulation Action Plan'. In 2005, Brown instructed Parliament that: 'Best practice risk-based regulation now means more inspection only where there is more risk and a light and limited touch where there is less risk ... [I]t is also right to lessen the burden of regulation'.[17] In its full excruciating glory one paragraph sticks out: 'In a risk-based approach there is no inspection without justification, no form filling without justification, and no information requirements without justification. Not just a light touch but a limited touch. Instead of routine regulation attempting to cover all, we adopt a risk-based approach which targets only the necessary few. A risk-based approach helps move us a million miles away from the old assumption—the assumption since the first legislation of Victorian times—that business, unregulated, will invariably act irresponsibly. The better view is that businesses want to act responsibly. Reputation with customers and investors is more important to behaviour than regulation, and transparency—backed up by the light touch—can be more effective than the heavy hand.'[18] The 'Better Regulation Action Plan' was all about inaction.

To an economist, 'risk-based' suggests a model of risk, into which data are fed, out of which warning signs come, with a set of tools primed to extinguish problems before they get out of hand. Instead, 'better regulation' meant only the few already suspected would be collared for inspection. Brown praised the UK's FSA, which had 'already done valuable work on adopting a risk-based approach', and he welcomed 'the thinking it is doing about how it can further reduce the burden of financial regulation'. After the crash, the chief executive of the FSA, Hector Sants, spoke of the political pressure exerted on the FSA to adopt light regulation: 'I think the prevailing climate at the time and indeed, right until the crisis commenced was that the market does know best.'[19] Since best practices should be shared generously with one's European neighbours, Brown continued, 'And we will challenge the [European] Commission to ensure that existing regulations are reformed so that they can be implemented in a risk-based way'. Brown had made a career out of dragging innocent little words kicking and screaming into sentences where they would otherwise be too embarrassed to be seen ('vigilant', 'prudent', 'boom', 'bust', and 'stability'). Now it was the turn of 'risk'.

In June 2007, weeks before the interbank market seized up and the shadow banking system collapsed, Brown made sure to clarify that 'risk-based' meant less regulation by talking about 'enhancing a risk-based regulatory approach, as we did in resisting pressure for a British Sarbannes–Oxley after Enron and Worldcom'.[20] The US Sarbanes–Oxley Act of 2002 had sought to strengthen corporate accounting practices and investor protection after two glaring examples of businesses that, unregulated, had forgotten the bit about reputation, and invariably acted irresponsibly. Mervyn King observed: 'Indeed, just before the financial turmoil broke out in the summer of 2007, there was a debate in New York about the need to follow London's example of unfettered markets if they were not to lose ground.'[21] Two high-profile reports argued that the competitiveness of US investment banks was being harmed by not matching Brown's 'light-touch' financial regulation.[22]

Believers everywhere were to discover that the clay out of which their object of devotion was made was of but the weakest consistency. Greenspan reflected: 'Those of us who have looked to the self-interest of lending institutions to protect shareholder's equity—myself especially—are in a state of shocked disbelief.'[23] Brown, one of the more recalcitrant of sinners, and with a keen instinct for self-preservation, licked off his spots, slapped on some stripes, and blamed a 'new and largely unregulated global financial system [that had] developed in the 20 years before the crisis' (a shame perhaps that this overlapped with his 11 years as UK finance minister and prime minister). For good measure, he lamented that: 'Submerged beneath the surface was an unseen, unregulated shadow banking network that ... operated far outside normal rules and procedures.'[24] He was 'furious to discover that other major banks too were recklessly using their customers' own money to speculate',[25] outraged by the 'shocking recklessness and irresponsibility of the banks that he believes contributed to the depth and breadth of the crisis' and the 'failure intrinsic to unregulated global markets', and bemoaned that 'regulators and governments have failed to keep pace'.[26] To sit at the helm of UK financial regulation for over a decade, to fail to see what everyone else could see, and to push for softer regulation of risky financial activities anyway might itself smack of a certain degree of recklessness.

The Push to Reform

Everything changed in September 2008. Washing the seeds back into the bottle was not going to be easy. With politicians pondering the different tiers in the capital structures of banks, the only tears the public were really interested in were those in the eyes of bankers. Confused and angry at the way the financial gods had turned, they demanded an occasional blood-letting on the high altar of political sacrifice. Obama was a pretty good High Priest: 'We want our money back, and we're going to get it,' he declared. 'If these folks want a fight, it's a fight I'm ready to have,' he railed. 'Every single dime' of the bail-out money would be recovered, and 'Never again will the American taxpayer be held hostage by a bank that is "Too Big To Fail".'

Bankers could live with the public's anger. Money, after all, is a powerful analgesic. Politicians could not. They were torn between, on the one hand, the need to look as if they were responding to the outrage, so as better to preserve their own endangered political skins and, on the other hand, the need for global coordination. The result was hasty, country-by-country reform proposals, each with its own set of dedicated followers (who sometimes changed their minds). In the US, in mid-2009 Geithner unveiled a plan to regulate OTC derivatives. In the UK, in late 2009 a levy on bank bonuses was announced, quickly followed by similar announcements in Germany, France, Belgium, Denmark, Cyprus, Austria, Portugal, Hungary, and Sweden. Like throwing a pebble into a deep pool of raging discontent, the notion quickly spread that the political elite was on the public's side. Then, since it was bad form to bail out rich bankers and not look to be wanting the money back, in January 2010 Obama proposed a levy to recover $90 billion from banks over ten years. In the UK there were to be stress tests run by the FSA, living wills, and a new leverage ratio. The European Commission put great store on the idea of clamping down on hedge funds and private equity, and was keen on bonus taxes too.

Perhaps the biggest tree-shaking of all came in January 2010 when President Obama announced 'a simple and common-sense reform'. He declared: 'Banks will no longer be allowed to own, invest, or sponsor hedge funds, private equity funds, or proprietary trading operations for their own profit, unrelated to serving their customers.'[27] This new 'Volcker rule' was received well by some in London (Lawson, Cable, and King), and so the UK Treasury took to referring to them as 'hot-heads'. Warming to the badge of disapproval, the still-in-opposition Conservatives (even Osborne) leapt enthusiastically to the idea of splitting up banks, before backtracking and emphasizing instead the need for 'global cooperation'. Obama's announcement followed suspiciously quickly on the heels of Goldman Sachs declaring 'business as usual', which political poison meant a $16.2 billion bonus pot, a 37% increase on the year before, a cool half million dollars on average per Goldman Sachs banker, and much more for the select few. For a bank that would have been dead but for a series of government subsidies, it was brazen stuff. Obama hadn't got to where he got without spotting an own goal. Democrat voters disliked Wall Street. Mid-West Republicans disliked a liberal elite seen as selling out to Wall Street. What better than to trap the Republicans in Congress into opposing something that would make them look to be on the side of Wall Street?

As the US, Europe, Japan and others charged off in different directions, occasional respite appeared in the shape of a trickle of reports and papers that, over time, turned into a torrent of regulatory reform proposals.[28] The urgency of the flow reflected another dilemma. Time and thought were needed to get reform right, yet reform needed to be locked in while politically feasible. Avinash Persaud warned: 'In each of the last seven international financial crises, plans for a radical shake up of international regulatory or monetary arrangements made surprising progress, only to be tidied away and stuffed in the bottom drawer once the economy recovered.'[29] Already by September 2009, reform plans in the US were being stripped back under heavy pressure from the banking industry. After all, this was an industry used to spending $250 million per year on lobbying, most recently to stop legislation tightening up on sub-prime, and it had to find somewhere new to spend its money.[30] As Obama put it in September 2009—recognizing a political hoop when he saw one—'Time is the enemy of reform.'

And so—perhaps taking the 'too-big-to-fail' logic a little too literally—the US 'Dodd–Frank Wall Street Reform and Consumer Protection Act' came in at over 2,300 pages and was signed into law in July 2010. The Act also bought into being a new 'consumer protection bureau'. Since breaking up is so hard to do, the 'Volcker rule' was watered down, such that by late 2010 easy ways were already being found to get around it.[31] Europe (but not the US) brought in new bonus regulations. The European Union drafted a new directive ('Emir') to create clearing houses for derivatives, and issued new insurance rules ('Solvency II'). The Financial Stability Board—the regulatory arm of the G20—proposed extra capital requirements, and 'living wills' for the most systemic global financial institutions. In September 2010, the Basel committee announced new minimum capital adequacy and liquidity ratios ('Basel III'). Some argued that large financial institutions had pushed the new rules off and that, having escaped the pot, many were soaking in a warm bath of moral hazard, from the soothing comfort of which they sought to shape regulatory possibilities at a more leisurely pace. In September 2011, the UK's Independent Commission on Banking (ICB), the 'Vickers Commission',[32] pulled the plug out (or so they hoped) with a proposal for ring fencing, higher minimum capital requirements than the new Basel rules, and 'bail-in' bonds for when banks got into trouble.

We need to step back from the fray for a moment. Many reforms are possible, but not all are high priority and, as anyone who writes legislation knows, it is easy to craft impressive-looking volume out of very little weight. The standard justifications for banking regulation are threefold.[33] First, problems of asymmetric information. Because of their own limited resources and experience, depositors are not good at monitoring the banks that take their money,[34] investors often only get to know the quality of what they invest in after they have invested, and borrowers may be misled. Second, externalities that are not captured by the private interests of those in banking. Financial firms overdo actions that are privately beneficial but harmful to others, and underdo actions that enhance system-wide stability. Like 'pollution' and 'pollution abatement', regulation is an attempt to create incentives to avoid the former and encourage the latter. In particular, unlike in most other industries where the failure of one firm advances others, the failure of one bank often increases the chances of other banks failing. Third, the usual issues of antitrust and the restraint of monopoly power.

Our benchmark for judging regulated outcomes should not be an idealized one. In the real world many contracts are incomplete (e.g. in simple banking models, the amount of consumption committed in a deposit contract at a particular date to those withdrawing at that date is not contingent on the state of nature at that date) and markets are incomplete (i.e. it is not possible to trade at one point in time all the commodities that will ever exist in the economy, distinguished by time and state, and contingent on all future uncertain events). As Allen and Gale put it: '[I]t is not enough merely to show that there exists a welfare-improving policy. We also need to characterize the policy and show that it can be implemented. A badly designed intervention could make things worse. If the welfare-improving policy is too complicated or depends on information that is unlikely to be available to the policymaker, such mistakes are likely.'[35] This, of course, is not the kind of helpful advice policymakers generally like to hear. In particular, what is the right amount of regulatory cost for society to bear on an on-going basis to avoid the cost of a particular 'amount' of crash on an occasional basis? If banks take on too little risk, crises may be avoided, but a per cent or two less growth per year because of inefficient capital allocation generates a significant welfare loss.

Let's return to the paradigm of insurance. Bailouts are the result of governments insuring (often for free or a very low charge) the retail deposits (deposit insurance), wholesale deposits (liquidity insurance), or equity (capital insurance) of banks. As a side-effect of giving governments such an 'insurable interest' in banks, moral hazard is created: knowing that they are protected, banks take bigger risks. Governments may threaten to be tough, but when a crash comes it is not credible to be tough—policy is not 'time-consistent'—and so banks take the risks anyway. Reform is all about reducing the government's insurable interest, charging an efficient risk-adjusted fee for the insurance services that governments provide to banks, making policy more time-consistent, and reducing moral hazard and the incentives to create tail risks, and thereby the frequency of crashes.

Capital, Leverage, and Liquidity

One way to reduce the insurable interests of governments is for banks to hold more capital. It might help to think of this extra capital as a higher excess on the insurance 'policy' between a government and a bank, such that the bank absorbs more of any loss before the government pays out on the 'policy'. The usual line of attack against this is that it raises banks' funding costs, which harms their customers. However, from society's perspective what matters is the social cost of bank capital—the cost adjusted for the incidence of, and damage done by, crashes. If banks can borrow at artificially low rates because of a government subsidy, taking the subsidy away would raise the cost charged to those taking excessive risks, but this would generate savings elsewhere—for taxpayers no longer on the hook. And financial firms would stay away from excessive risks. The BIS, taking a median estimate of 60% of cumulative output losses for an economy caused by a 'typical' crash, argued that even just 1% reduction in the annual probability of a crash would generate, on average, about 0.6% of expected output per year in benefit.[36] If output loss was the sole metric,[37] this was probably an overestimate of the potential benefit of more capital in the US and the UK where 60% cumulative loss of output was beyond what was seen in the crash (although, as growth rates collapsed in 2011, the impact could approach such a figure in some countries). The problem was that the losers from such reform were concentrated, vocal, well-resourced, and living in the here and now, but the winners were diffuse and living in the future.

There was a range of benefits from having banks hold more, and better quality (i.e. more loss-absorbing), capital. First, the biggest contributor to the 'equity premium'[38] demanded by bank equity holders is the risk of extreme tail events like crashes which wipe equity holders out.[39] If the incidences of tail events were lower, the equity premium and the overall cost of capital would be lower, and economic growth rates higher.[40] Even this exaggerates downwards; today's equity risk premium is based on the already existing, generous, and largely free, insurance of the state. Second, banks would suffer less from debt overhang problems and find it easier to raise funds at times of incipient crises. Third, it was not lending per se that policymakers wanted to encourage, but higher-quality lending. Much lending had been poor-quality because the capital structure of banks had been skewed towards debt. Fourth, it would help offset tax distortions that treat equity as non-tax-deductible and debt as tax-deductible, which encourages banks to hold too much debt in their capital structures (of course, the more direct route is to overhaul tax codes). Fifth, it might offset some of the perverse incentives created during the crash; by repeatedly protecting bank creditors, debt would henceforth reign supreme in the capital structure of big banks unless something was done to offset this. Finally, if banks and borrowers could better withstand periods of economic and financial stress, uncertainty would be lower, and investment and growth higher.

It was still not possible to say how much capital was 'optimal' or what the right distribution across equity and debt in the capital structure of banks was, nor indeed when the capital should be added. In November 2010, 20 senior financial and banking economists proposed that if at least 15% of banks' total (non-risk-weighted) assets were funded by equity, 'the social benefits would be substantial. And the social costs would be minimal, if any.'[41] In December 2010, international regulators, as part of Basel III, increased the minimum requirement for common equity from 2% to 4.5% of a financial firm's risk weighted assets (RWAs).[42] The tier-one-capital requirement would increase from 4% to 6%. There would also be a new 'capital conservation buffer' of 2.5%, which would bring the total common equity requirement to 7% (more than triple what it had been before the crash), tier-one capital to 8.5% and total minimum capital requirement to 10.5%. Banks would be able to draw on the 'capital conservation buffer' in times of stress, but, as it shrank, they would face constraints on earnings distributions. The changes would be phased in between January 2013 and 2019, and were in addition to a stronger definition of capital and higher capital requirements for trading, derivative, and securitization activities that would be introduced at the end of 2011. A non-systemic financial firm meeting its minimum common equity, capital conservation buffer, and maximum 2.5% countercyclical buffer (to be discussed below), would have 9.5% common equity and 13% total capital. Those deemed systemic would hold more equity and capital than this, but how much more had yet to be determined.

If more capital imposed a big added cost, the Swiss authorities didn't seem to mind. They increased their total capital requirement to 19%. Maybe they were reflecting on the fate of Ireland and Iceland, the only two other countries with higher ratios of bank balance sheets to GDP? Perhaps 19% simply reflected what 'market forces' dictated banks should hold to keep the confidence of investors in a country with such a high ratio and without the advantage of a large government to bail banks out? In terms of bank assets relative to the size of its economy, the UK was next, and so it was not surprising that the UK's ICB also recommended minimal capital adequacy ratios higher than the new Basel rules.

Banks would still not be holding enough capital if a crash happened. Could a time-consistent way be found for governments to refuse to inject capital at such times? There were two main options. If unsecured bank creditors faced bail-ins when banks made losses (just as creditors do in other industries), they would be forced to write off part of their claims or accept equity instead when banks made losses. Crucially, a bank would not need to be bankrupt to do this. The ICB in the UK, the EU as part of its new directive on bank resolution, and the Dodd–Frank Act all promoted the idea of bail-ins. One step in this direction involved making bank depositors senior to bank bondholders, which the ICB also promoted.

Then came various forms of private-sector insurance and 'contingent capital', such as via contingent convertible bonds. These so-called 'cocos' would pay a risk-based insurance 'premium' to the holder (equivalent to an extra bit of capital held by the bank in good times), and generate a large payout (i.e. a large chunk of capital) to the bank from the holder if a systemic crash materialized.[43] This sounded simple enough, but the practical challenges were great.

First, the conversion of bonds into equity would need to be triggered by a public signal of a 'systemic' event and not by a signal reported or controlled by a bank. Second, unless the insurance premium and payout were proportional to the systemic risk a bank imposed, it would continue to leverage its position to improve its own return at the cost of others.[44] Third, like earthquake insurance, payout would depend on a rare event for which data are sparse, and pricing such bonds would be difficult (if the bonds were traded so as to 'discover' a price, this would require the market for them to be liquid at all times). Disaster myopia would rule. Fourth, newly created moral hazard (since banks would be insured against bad states) would need to be priced in, and there still would have to be supervision to stop banks taking excessive risks. Fifth, there was a danger that bonds would convert when there was no need[45] or not convert when there was a need (for example if the public signal was an index of bank share prices or bank capital ratios). In particular, capital ratios tend to be lagging indicators, only falling when a crisis is happening or has already passed. Sixth, regulators would still need to use discretion, and they would be lobbied hard. Legal challenge would be rife.

We are not ended. Seventh, such insurance might be treated as a top-up of a state bailout anyway. Eighth, premiums might have to be higher to compensate for the possibility of an adverse selection of those seeking insurance. Ninth, banks might free-ride on other banks, and such schemes would therefore need to be compulsory. Tenth, forcing bigger banks to hold more capital insurance than smaller banks might signal that bigger banks would not be allowed to fail under any circumstances, while smaller banks would be, making the TBTF problem worse. Eleventh, such schemes might generate a sense of entitlement; what if the efficient solution *is* that some banks are not saved? Twelfth, the returns to 'crash' bonds would fall at the same time as the returns on all other investments, making them less attractive to pension and sovereign wealth funds. This seems to suggest that the IMF, or similar, would have to underwrite such schemes; if so, the trigger for pay-out would need to be outside the control of the IMF. Finally—we got there in the end—it is not entirely obvious that private capital would materialize in a crash even if contracts were in place to provide it. What if the market for contingent capital dried up (and the 'system insurers' anyway preferred a government bailout in a world where not bailing them out would not be time-consistent)?[46] All these caveats are making us quite giddy. The lesson would seem to be that we should tread carefully with all schemes, emphasize the simple and robust over the complicated, and that, perhaps, robustness might be better served by a structural solution.

The only G7 country not to have bailed out or guaranteed its banking system was Canada. Perhaps this was because it had a leverage ratio of 5% applied to all banks, and limits on mortgage lending. In early 2010, the US Treasury pushed the idea of a stricter leverage ratio, and the new Basel III capital requirements were supplemented by a leverage ratio too, initially set at a 'test' rate of 3%. This would nevertheless face challenges, in particular regarding how such ratios would be implemented when banks' assets and liabilities spanned jurisdictions. And countries would try to break global agreements on leverage to steal market share. Banks lobbied hard against the Treasury's proposal, and it failed to make it through the Senate.

The lack of harmonized liquidity ratios was a huge regulatory gaping hole. The task now was to internalize to financial institutions the systemic risk caused by liquidity problems caused by their maturity mismatches, and incentivize them to use more long-term funding. The best way to get rid of liquidity risk is to hedge across time—that is, allow more time to sell assets and reduce the need for quick sales. This was one area where simple changes in rules on funding could go a long way and be relatively easy to monitor.

The Basel Committee developed two new minimum liquidity standards.[47] First came a 30-day 'liquidity coverage ratio' (LCR). Global banks would have to hold enough 'unencumbered, high quality liquid assets' to offset the net cash outflows that might be encountered in an acute short-term 'stress scenario'. The initial stress scenario was built upon shocks experienced in the crash (though not a worst-case scenario).[48] Then there was a 'net stable funding ratio' (NSFR) with a time horizon of one year, which related to the proportion of long-term assets funded by long-term, stable funding. At the time of writing, none of these new ratios had gone into operation, but they were a definite improvement on what was there before. Had such rules been in place and Bear Stearns been forced to stick to them (by selling off some of its MBSs or never acquiring them in the first place), it might have survived.

Again, a key issue was how to reduce the insurable interest of government via time-consistent liquidity arrangements in a crash.[49] There were four overlapping possibilities. First, banks (perhaps while fulfilling some of the new rules) could increase their own 'self-insurance' by, for example, holding more government debt, which does not carry the credit counterparty risk of other sorts of assets; the excess on the liquidity insurance policy between a bank and a central bank would be higher. Nevertheless, liquidity problems could probably not be too long-lived, and there would be free-riding in a voluntary system. Furthermore, some countries in the eurozone suffered because their banks were holding too much home-country sovereign debt. This hinted at further limitations. Second, private insurers could provide access to liquidity. However, this would not help in times of particular stress when risks became correlated, and it would probably concentrate risk in a few hands. We saw above some of the challenges of insurance in the case of capital; similar issues would arise in the case of liquidity. Third, the central bank could be the market maker of last resort. This happened in the crash, when hosts of special liquidity schemes took assets off banks' books. The chief downside was the creation of moral hazard and the risk of big losses being borne by central banks. In future there would have to be more predefined rules regarding the size of support, what would be accepted as collateral, and what fees and haircuts would be demanded.[50] Fourth, the Treasury could provide insurance against credit counterparty risks.[51] This had been widely done, with governments guaranteeing the highest-grade mortgage-backed securities. Again, the terms on which this would be done in the future and the consequences for moral hazard were the key issues. Although the new Basel rules improved provision of liquidity in normal times—and so would reduce the chances of crashes—very little progress was made on determining how liquidity would be provided if a crash happened anyway.

Too Big to Manage, Too Big to Regulate

Capital and liquidity rules operate a bit like tax rates (think of how tax rates influence pollution behaviour and not the amount of revenue they raise). The two key challenges are acquiring the information to set them efficiently, and withstanding lobbying if they have discretionary elements; after all, once a 'tax-rate' line is drawn in the sand, bankers, like highly trained fleas, have an instinctive desire to jump beyond. This brings us to a fundamental question. Is it more time-consistent to regulate behaviour caused by bad incentives caused by the structure of banking or to change the structure of banking so as to change the incentives and not to have to control behaviour quite so much? Often an insurable interest is forced onto governments by banks being too big (or connected) to fail (TBTF).

In 2008, just 145 banks each controlled assets over $100 billion, totalling 85% of all of the assets of the top 1,000 banks in the world.[52] Of all government crash support, 90% went to just these banks. With perhaps half a dozen key individuals per bank, about a thousand people were at the heart of the crash. The very top of the size distribution was even more skewed. In 1998, the five biggest banks controlled 8% of the banking assets of the top 1,000 banks in the world. By 2008, it was 16%.[53] Following multiple mergers, the combined assets of the five largest banks in the US—Bank of America, Citigroup, JPMorgan Chase, Wachovia, and Wells Fargo—swelled from $2.2 trillion in 1998 to $6.8 trillion in 2007.[54] By 2009 in the US just four banks—Bank of America, JPMorgan Chase, Citigroup, and Wells Fargo & Co.—controlled 46% of the assets of all FDIC-insured banks, up from about 38% at the time of the crash. Bank of America, fresh from its near-death experience, had $2.25 trillion in assets, 30% up from the year before. The top three US banks controlled about 8% of domestic bank deposits in the mid-1990s, 20% on the eve of the crash, and

30% just after. The pattern repeated itself elsewhere. In 2011, just six banks controlled over 90% of all UK current account deposits, and in Germany seven banks controlled 68% of all German current account deposits. Governments even encouraged the mergers and takeovers that brought this about— JPMorgan Chase with Bear Stearns, Bank of America with Merrill Lynch, Wells Fargo with Wachovia, Lloyds TSB with HBOS, and Commerzbank with Dresdner Bank.

The dinosaurs had come close to extinction, but, having swallowed some of their rivals, they were quickly back roaming the land, fatter and more ravenous than ever. In previous crashes based on excess debt, a prerequisite for recovery involved the shedding of excess banking capacity. A good rescue would have stripped this out of big failed banks. Yet, on the contrary, the more reckless were given a competitive advantage, and smaller, better-managed banks denied market share they might have won from big mismanaged banks. Only the tiddlers were allowed to drown, taken over by regulators and 'resolved'. Schumpeter was on to something with his idea of 'creative destruction',[55] but it clearly did not apply to big banks, who liked to impose capitalism red in tooth and claw on others, but were a little less enthusiastic about having the principle applied to themselves.

To the big, big is invariably beautiful. However, our best evidence indicates that the economies of scale in banking are exhausted at a fraction of the current size of the biggest global banks.[56] Evidence on 100 mergers and acquisitions indicates no strong efficiency gains.[57] Cross-activity mergers haven't created economic value,[58] diversification is overrated,[59] and a study of 800 banks across 43 countries found that equity markets even valued conglomerates lower than the sum of their separate parts![60] Had many banks simply grown beyond what could be managed? Stiglitz thought so: 'It has long been recognized that those of America's banks that are too big to fail are also too big to be managed. That is one reason that the performance of several of them has been so dismal.'[61] Time and again, from Rubin, Prince, Fuld, Goodwin, and Hornby downwards, once-lionized bank executives who, with ravishing strides, had controlled huge financial empires, whimpered in their testimony that they did not fully understand what was going on inside their own banks.

Many reasoned that beyond a certain size and complexity they simply could not be allowed to fail. If one thinks of the TBTF as a clever poison pill—let us die and we will take you with us—one quickly gets the gist. If, in future, banks, and not taxpayers, were to bear the true cost of the risks they took, the curse of the TBTF would need to exorcized. The TBTF could borrow more cheaply than the non-TBTF because the promise of a government bailout made it less risky to lend to the TBTF, and so another goal needed be to create a more level playing field for smaller banks. There are three ways to reduce governments' huge TBTF insurable interests: to regulate; to resolve; or to break up and shrink.

It could be that if regulation of the TBTF was tough enough it would act like a tax on size and complexity, and create incentives to be smaller and less complex. Geithner thought so: 'In sum, our proposals will provide...an intensity of government oversight that will serve as a strong disincentive for firms to become too big, complex, leveraged, and interconnected.'[62] Yet, it was difficult to believe that government regulation alone would do this. The sort of capital rules that would tax the TBTF involved discretion that the TBTF would surely gang up against.

Perhaps, instead, new resolution mechanisms would make it easier for the TBTF to die? King was even blunter than usual: 'If banks screw it up and make bad decisions they should be allowed to fail. In my view, there is no way you can run a system on any basis other than that.'[63] In a healthy banking system, the likes of Lehman, Bear Stearns, Northern Rock, HBOS, Citibank, and AIG would die with minimal inconvenience to others. With survival only of the fittest and death of the dumbest, perhaps next time some would not be so dumb? This might involve 'living wills' or 'shelf bankruptcies', with legal clauses written into all contracts a financial institution signed with other parties, stipulating orderly arrangements after its unfortunate, but necessary, demise. The whole point of financial death is to wipe out owners and give them more interest in not dying in the first place. Worthwhile banking activity would survive, and many bank workers would be employed inside new institutions crafted out of the old.

A raft of knotty practical issues floated to the surface. Resolution would need radical simplification of corporate structures and capital market networks (for example, Goldman Sachs had 900 subsidiaries including in the Cayman Islands, Mauritius, Panama, and Liberia,[64] and Citigroup cross-guaranteed its debt across different parts of the company, with nearly $500 billion in deposits at foreign branches compared to a little over $300 billion in US deposits). The application of conventional insolvency policy to banks might entail assets being auctioned to the highest bidder, but this presumes that those who value them the most can raise the finance to buy them; this cannot be presumed to hold in a crash. With bankruptcy laws varying across countries and types of financial institutions, who would be in charge? What if large banks were simply sold to other large banks? And would resolution be enforced when several large banks were in trouble together even if it risked systemic collapse? Living wills would have to be reviewed by regulators on a regular basis, with powers to force changes to clauses not deemed credible. What would be the punishment for being economical with the truth about the nature and extent of exposures to other financial companies? In booms, would regulators use their powers or come under pressure to use a light touch? I am sure the reader has already worked this one out for themselves.

The Dodd–Frank Act talked of funeral plans and orderly liquidation procedures for the systemically important. The FDIC would get new powers to wind down failing non-bank financial groups and there were fine words about the costs of wind-down being forced onto shareholders and bank creditors. However, there was no power to manage orderly resolution at the global level. Even S&P made it clear—because they priced it in their ratings and spelt it out in writing—that the US government would almost certainly bail out the TBTF rather than use any new wind-down powers. Besides, allowing big banks to fail has generally not been the American way. Over recent decades the average attrition rate (the percentage that on average die per year) amongst US banks was less than 0.1%, and even this was mostly on account of smaller banks failing (for hedge funds, in contrast, it was about 5% and rose to about 10% in the crash).[65] For all the talk of free-market capitalism, large banks got to use the government to protect themselves from death.

The third option was structural. Break-up could be physical or legal. The latter would involve a firewall between different departments of the same bank, a boundary line on one side of which financial institutions would be eligible for government support in the event of a crash, but on the other side of which they would not be. The objective would not be to remove all, or even most, risks, but to take away the tail risks, the ones that cause the crashes.

Of special interest are large universal banks that take in retail deposits, covered by a government guarantee, in one division, and maximize the value of the guarantee by using them to cross-subsidize and boost profits on their investment banking activities, and for whom punishment is not time-consistent. The reader will find no sympathy here with the notion that financial institutions should not engage in risky investment activities. It is just that those doing such activities should use their own money and that of their investors and not rely on a government subsidy to achieve their high returns.

In the end, the US settled on containment and not structural reform. The Dodd–Frank Act proposed not to divide banks by function but to limit the ability of bank holding companies to use deposits to fund investments in proprietary trading, and they would not be allowed to bail such investments out. However, the language was highly diluted. This was in part because the distinction between banking and investment products is sometimes fuzzy. For example, it might be thought that deposit-taking should be protected by the 'insurance' of the state but wholesale-funded activity should not be; but wholesale money often comes from pensions and mutual funds—that is from individuals who deposit their savings. And some proprietary trading is to protect bank customers (in much the same way as airlines hedge fuel prices to reduce their uncertainty). US regulators came up with a complex list of rules to define a proprietary trade, to try to separate buying and selling for a bank's own account (banned) from buying and selling—'market making'—on behalf of customers (permitted). Quickly, the cup of treacle ran over.[66]

After the US backed off (and Switzerland too, since its new, higher, capital ratios applied to whole, and not ring-fenced, banks) the UK was the last to show interest in separation. In September 2011 the ICB (the 'Vickers Commission') proposed 'ring-fencing' the domestic retail services of UK banks (the payments system and the provision of credit to households and SMEs)—to be overseen by their own independent boards of directors—leaving global wholesale and invest-ment banking outside the fence. Both parts would be separately capitalized. The fence was 'flexible' (a concept apparently introduced at the last minute); depending on how banks funded themselves, they would be able to set the fence wide enough to enclose large corporate clients or narrow enough just to cover retail customers and small businesses. Inside the ring-fence a capital cushion of up to 20% would be needed, comprising equity of 10% of RWAs and up to 10% of additional capital in the shape of bonds, and there would be a 4% leverage ratio (up from 3%). It would still be possible to move funds over the fence so long as the rules on minimal capital requirements were met. In the UK, between £1.1 trillion and £2.3 trillion of banks' assets would sit inside the fence and be protected by government insurance, and about £4 trillion would sit outside. Thus the average insurable interest of the UK government would be reduced.

Another key feature of the ICB's proposals was the insistence on bail-ins. For example, Barclays and HSBC, being potentially globally systemic, would need to hold bail-in bonds equal to about 17% of their RWAs. Other large UK banks would need to hold bail-in bonds equal to between 10.5% and 17% of their RWAs. Within the fence, depositors would rank higher than senior creditors in the event of insolvency.

Banks quickly argued that depositors and borrowers inside the ring-fence would lose out when proprietary traders lost access to depositors as a source of cheap funding. This suffered from a string of logical problems. First, it was the chunks of hidden government subsidy that made some forms of risk-taking profitable. If an investment were not profitable without the subsidy, it should be allowed to wither away. If it were profitable, it would migrate into the sort of financial institutions that take risks without such subsidies, such as hedge funds, which have the appealing property of being able to die with a reliable degree of alacrity. Second, if depositors wanted exposure to such risks, they would be able to get it via some other route. Currently, facing limited liability, depositors chase extra returns even if these are only because a bank is taking bigger risks on the back of the government guarantee of its deposits. Since depositors hardly ever monitor banks, the TBTF are essentially taking advantage of a class of 'investors' who do not monitor them. If others funded such risky activity and bore any losses, they would more rigorously monitor risk-taking and demand greater return, which would be more efficient. Third, the biggest beneficiaries were those who engaged in the risky activity, who turned the TBTF subsidy into bonuses for themselves. With a ring-fence in place, if banks did not pay their investment staff so much, the extra costs would fall on shareholders, in the shape of lower dividends, and not onto depositors and borrowers. Higher costs of capital would apply to investment banking and not obviously to the rest of the real economy. Fourth, the overall level of risky activity was higher than socially efficient precisely because that was the way to extract the value of the TBTF subsidy. Fifth, the subsidy disadvantaged those who lent to genuine wealth-creating SMEs whose investments did not match the short-term, high-margin and highly collateralized lending that best extracted the subsidy. If a ring-fence really did stop government subsidies of retail banking activities advantaging international dealing and short-term lending over local long-term investment, maybe banks would show more interest in long-term investments that would help the economy recover. Sixth, many of the profits in the pre-2008 era were phony; no cost argument should be based on these. Finally, if a ring-fence led to fewer crashes, depositors and borrows would benefit.

The ICB calculated that the yearly cost to the UK economy of the implicit TBTF subsidy was about £3–4 billion (on a conservative estimate), and the yearly cost of the reform package to UK banks was about £4–7 billion. So, *even if* banks passed on to their customers £3–4 billion of the costs, it would just equal the average gain to society by not having to pay the TBTF subsidy.[67] Even if all the £4–7 billion cost was passed on to bank customers, it equated to just fractions of a per cent of a £6 trillion pile of assets. But if the yearly cost passed on to bank customers was less than £3–4 billion, and more of the cost showed up in lower bank bonuses, then bank customers and society would be better off. The banks (and the media) made a meal of the extra £7 billion 'cost' to society, but the real net cost to society was much lower, and, on balance, *if* crashes were avoided, there was almost certainly a net benefit. UK taxpayers had already paid £7 billion multiple times over consequent on their losses on their equity stakes in large UK banks and the damage to the economy.

Nevertheless, a ring-fence was no panacea. Practical challenges in making it workable involved legal complexities regarding corporate governance, dividend payments, and intra-bank relationships of various sorts. For example, how could the directors and managers of a holding company be accountable to its share-holders if the retail division had a truly independent board of its own? Previous experience of firewalls had not been encouraging either. Even with a ring-fence in place there still was no way to resolve large financial firms that operated in multiple jurisdictions. Critically, would the ring-fence be time-consistent? If in a crisis the ring-fence was likely to be ditched to stabilize the banking system, banks would continue to price in the subsidy of the state (in this light, the extra loss absorbency courtesy of bail-ins would make the ring-fence more time-consistent). In 2007–2008, much financial activity in segregated companies quickly found its way back onto the balance-sheets of regulated companies, and investment banks like Goldman Sachs and Morgan Stanley were allowed to come inside the government insurance fence. It is sobering to reflect that while the crash involved universal banks like Citi, UBS, and RBS, some of the biggest victims, such as Lehman Brothers, Bear Stearns, Washington Mutual, Northern Rock, and AIG were not universal. For them, a ring-fence was a non-issue. Even those universal banks that failed, often failed because of bad decisions— such as the ill-judged acquisition of ABN AMRO by RBS—that light-touch regulators did not challenge.[68] In the summer of 2012, numerous banking scandals illustrated the inability of the industry to police its own information flows. This suggested that it would be difficult to create impenetrable ring fences. And then the government anyway set about watering down the ring-fence proposals.

By now, much was going on globally in terms of capital and liquidity reforms. If such reforms had been in place, the owners of RBS and Lloyds TSB, and not taxpayers, would have had to take more losses and so would have changed their behaviour. This suggested that, even with ring-fences in place, a lot of the work would be done by other reforms. In the run-up to the announcement of the ring-fencing, headlines regularly reported that this, that, or the other bank (or more precisely, Barclays, HSBC, and Standard Chartered) might relocate from the UK if the ICB was too tough. Within days, such banks were saying that the higher capital requirements were manageable, and that, maybe, London was not so bad after all.

Macroprudential Regulation

The biggest priority of all was to tackle excessive risk-taking at the global level. 'Macroprudential' regulation (or 'systemic' regulation, depending on the literature) recognizes that credit booms lead to busts. Thinking about 'macroprudential' regulation was not new. The BIS was talking about it in the mid-1980s.[69] Then, almost eight years to the day before the crash, the general manager of the BIS made a speech about 'marrying the micro- and macroprudential dimensions of financial stability'.[70] A thankless crescendo of BIS voices[71] trilled away until the next speech, in 2006, by the next general manager of the BIS, 'Marrying the micro- and macroprudential dimensions of financial stability: six years on';[72] for nothing much had changed. Just days before the collapse of Lehman, the BIS even circulated a 'macroprudential' framework.[73] The IMF had been thinking about macroprudential issues for a long time,[74] and a number of economists had been gallantly hammering away; Goodhart and colleagues had long warned of a range of dangers that subsequently were core to the crash, such as the joint-introduction of Basel II and the new International Financial Reporting Standards (IFRS) mark-to-market accounting system that would generate procyclical capital adequacy ratios.[75] However, macroprudential regulation 'would have been seen as a tax on the success of the investment banking community and the City'.[76] Challenging the status quo 'would have presented nearly insurmountable political and intellectual difficulties'.[77] Big banks reasoned that since there was to be regulation anyway, it might as well be the sort that favours the big, interconnected, and systemic, and can act as a barrier to entry. Regulation that 'targets only the necessary few' was much more agreeable.

There are two sets of drivers of positive-feedback mechanisms in financial systems that generate macroeconomic procyclicality. The first are limitations in risk measurement. Since it is difficult to distinguish underlying trends from the transitory—especially if the financial and real economy are highly interconnected—short-term measures of volatility and default rates get fed into financial decision-making processes. The second are a range of incentive issues, two of which stand out. The first one is the 'principal-agent' problem between providers and users of funds: providers are less informed than users and so use collateral and margin requirements to discipline users. However, this 'solution' creates a new set of problems in the form of a direct link between asset values and funding. The second one is the conflict between actions that are rational for the individual but collectively bad. For example, microprudential logic may say that a bank should sell assets in a bust to improve its balance sheet, but if all do, fire-sale prices harm the balance sheets of all.

Macroprudential regulation is about making banks presume that they are the source of more risk than they think they are, and to hold bigger 'buffers' when microprudential logic says risk is low and smaller buffers are fine. This, it is argued, reduces the amplitude of the credit cycle and the chances of crashes. At times when credit expansion is deemed 'excessive', policymakers would tighten some combination of capital adequacy requirements, leverage ratios, the growth rates of various balance-sheet items such as total assets, total private-sector deposits, bank lending to the private sector, loan provisioning, minimum liquidity requirements, loan-to-value ratios, and so forth. A 'hard-wired' rule would help policymakers tighten even as economies are booming; they blame the rule. In a slump this would work in reverse; in 2012 with banks extremely risk-averse and holding back on lending, macroprudential logic dictated lower capital requirements even as all the talk was of tougher standards. Like the recent fiscal battles, tougher long-term requirements were needed precisely so as to be less tough in the recession. It sounds straightforward enough, but operationalizing such apparently simple macroprudential logic is challenging.

First, systemic risk is not just about size but also about the interconnected nature of banks. Using the pollution analogy, and sticking just to capital, a capital charge would have an 'own' component related to a bank's own risk and a variable 'system' component reflecting the bank's contribution to systemic risk, directly or by acts correlated with the financial difficulties of other banks. Adrian and Brunnermeier[78] proposed a measure of this 'externality' affect, CoVaR, the value-at-risk (VaR) of the financial sector conditional on a particular bank being in distress. Standard VaR relates to the risk that a bank inflicts upon itself. The percentage difference between the VaR and the CoVaR of a particular bank is a measure of the degree to which it contributes to (or is correlated with) overall systemic risk. However, as the IMF observed: 'In many cases the information needed to detect systemic risks is either not collected or not analyzed with systemic risk in mind, especially those data needed to examine systemic linkages, as this requires information about institutions' exposures to one another.'[79]

Second, there is a potential conflict between macroprudential rules, to control the level of lending, and inflation-targeting rules, that work by controlling the price of lending.[80] If the 'technological frontier' of an economy was shifting outwards, mechanistically applying macroprudential tightening would harm the opportunity to improve society's welfare while inefficiently pushing inflation lower. Central banks would find themselves trying to push the rate of inflation up by reducing interest rates. As Blanchflower explained, 'Central bankers might have one foot on the accelerator, whilst simultaneously applying the hand brake.'[81] So, macroprudential rules need discretion. Yet, it is often difficult to evaluate the true nature of technological advances until much later. In the late 1990s, many argued that the technological frontier of the global economy was moving forward because of advances across technology, economic policy, risk-management, and emerging economies. Facing a difficult signal-extraction problem, politicians deemed rapidly rising share prices a measure of the collective knowledge of these advances and of their policy prowess. In the run up to the crash, regulators had enough discretionary powers to stop the build-up of excessive leverage and risky mortgage-related activities, but they chose not to. If discretionary macroprudential tools had been in place, in both the late 1990s and mid 2000s there would have been heavy lobbying for a particular interpretation of the facts, and it is not obvious that macroprudential tightening would have happened. What would the institutional arrangements be to shield macroprudential decision makers from political pressure?

Third, there will continue to be regulatory arbitrage and 'disintermediation' to get around the rule. As macroprudential capital ratios rise, profits from cheating while everyone else cooperates rise, and there is the usual shift towards activities that are relatively less targeted in any rule. Since systemic riskiness rises with size, variable capital ratios would act like a tax on size. Big financial firms, like turkeys canvassed for their views on Christmas dinner, have an incentive to lobby against such things. Perhaps, if the countercyclical capital charge was used sparingly, some of these effects could be lessened.

Fourth, in a crash some mechanism would still have to be in place to provide capital. Spain had 'dynamic provisioning' requiring more capital to be held when credit grew 'excessively', but Spain did not avoid an almightily housing bubble. Spain avoided a credit crunch in late 2008, but 'dynamic provisioning' could not cope with the eurozone crisis.

Spurred on by the US Treasury,[82] the Dodd–Frank Act was the first time US regulators had openly talked of regulating 'systemically' risky financial institutions. The Act proposed a Systemic Risk Council, and that financial institutions with assets over $50 billion would be deemed 'systemically' important. Large hedge funds, asset managers, private equity firms, and other 'non-bank' lenders with assets under $50 billion might be nominated onto the systemic list if their leverage and risk exposures made them systemic. Eighteen months after the Dodd–Frank Act was signed, in part because of heavy lobbying, neither the list nor the rules were written. The US Treasury and the Fed wanted a handful on the list. The FDIC would have the job of winding-down and so wanted many on the list. Furthermore, the Dodd–Frank Act did not entertain the notion of raising or lowering capital requirements as financial conditions changed and so was not especially countercyclical, and would do nothing to counter speculative bubbles. The Act also continued the practice of treating financial firms relative to the losses they created for themselves and not the costs they imposed on others. Thus the Act talked systemic but did not fully walk the systemic path. The UK set up a new macroprudential Financial Policy Committee (FPC). What bite the new institutions would have, and how shielded they would be from lobbying, was yet to be seen. At least, greater systemic surveillance was useful.

The Basel committee instigated a new element of macroprudential capital: a countercyclical buffer, in a range of 0%–2.5% of common equity or other fully loss-absorbing capital, above and beyond the new minimums. This would kick in when a country was deemed to be experiencing excess credit growth, and would be 'adjusted according to national circumstances'.[83] Local discretion had logic: asset price and credit cycles tend to be national, and capital ratios need to differ according to where assets and liabilities are. However, the opportunities for bank lobbying are obvious. The maximum extra capital cushion was not especially big.

Of Bonuses, Governance, and Incentives

For years the rewards at the very top of banking ballooned, but no president or prime minister ever dared complain. Just before the crash, US bank CEOs were earning 500 times the median US household income. Turner talked of 'an economic crisis . . . cooked up in trading rooms where not just a few but many people earned annual bonuses equal to a lifetime's earnings of some of those now suffering the consequences.'[84] He was wildly exaggerating. Why, the trading chief of Citigroup, Thomas Maheras, made nearly $100 million over just three years tanking his bank up on all its disastrous 'toxic' assets—a bonus every *week* equal to what some of those now suffering the consequences earned in a lifetime. Having burned his company down, the CEO of Citigroup, Charles Prince, managed to escape the flames (on 4 November 2007) with $38 million in bonuses, shares, and options (and a pension of $1.74 million a year). The Chairman of Merrill Lynch, Stan O'Neal, posted $8 billion in losses over August and September 2007, and, no doubt reckoning that a mighty impressive feat, grabbed $161.5 million as he slammed the gate behind him. Andrew Mozilo, under the terms of his $67.5 million SEC fine (that Countrywide paid a chunk of courtesy of an indemnity clause in his employment contract) never even had to acknowledge wrongdoing. With net worth of $600 million and the criminal investigation dropped, he got off essentially scot-free. Even as the Lehman wreck dissolved beneath his feet, Dick Fuld did not pay back any of the half billion dollars he pocketed between 1993 and 2007. When Rubin turned up for his first day in the Obama administration he was not asked to pay any of his $126 million back. During the US S&L crisis, it was not golden handshakes all round; it was handcuffs—a thousand pairs to be precise. This time, one failed banker after another, the golden parachutes fluttered open, they eased themselves to the ground and off they ran. If this was the punishment for failure, what on earth was the reward for success?

Much debate has concentrated on the sheer size of payments (and we often forget that the riches piled up for the few and not the many), but size is not everything. Greed and folly played their part, but so did bad incentives. Faults included pay excessively linked to short-term results at the expense of long-term value, a lack of provision for clawing back payment when things went wrong, and limited liability as far as the eye could see. Reward in the shape of shares or options on shares, because of the heavy use of debt, became a leveraged bet on the value of banks' capital. And bonuses were easily extracted from mark-to-market profits generated by holding net long positions in mark-to-market assets (mark-to-market pulls profit forward into the horizons of those getting paid now). Worse was the incentive to target activities where a bubble was easy to generate but hard to prove until too late. Many engaged in no more than writing glorified catastrophe insurance on the back of a housing bubble, spreading widely the social costs while narrowly concentrating the benefits on themselves; for every dollar extracted, multiple dollars of lost GDP, welfare, and unemployment followed for others. All too often it was ridiculously easy to make huge bonuses from the tiniest speck of skill, and sometimes from no skill at all, in a banking system that gave birth to a spattering of dancing stars and an equally fine sprinkling of dullards, who all demanded, and usually got, their stellar rewards.

Various reforms seem obvious, and some have already been enacted. For example, Europe limited the cash component of senior bankers' bonuses to 20%, with the rest share-based and spread over several years. US regulators (for a while anyway) proposed that senior executives defer half their bonuses for three years and put in place special measures (such as bonus-malus accounts) for those taking on higher levels of risk. Another route was to link bonuses to banks' bonds (of course, so long as this meant a loss in a crash, which was not at all obvious). Nevertheless, bankers are always hungry, and by late 2011 attempts to control pay in one component, such as bonuses, quickly saw pressure to raise it in another, such as base salaries. And even if there were multi-year bonus horizons, they would never be for more than a few years.

It was politically convenient to forget that the most efficient way to pay bankers involved a large proportion of performance-based reward (i.e. a bonus) and not a flat payment. The key was to relate the size of the 'bonus' to risks taken and to asset performance (especially loan performance), and not to equity returns. Indeed, 'bonus bashing' often deflected attention from more radical reforms which could not so easily be reversed once the therapy of 'bonus bashing' was ended, by which time equal enforcement of global rules on compensation would be difficult. Banks that pay a fraction below the 'going rate' lose key staff. The biggest constraint on that 'going rate' will not be the initiatives targeting bonuses, but all the other reforms.

If creating tail risk became more difficult because of higher capital and liquidity requirements, bonuses would fall. Breaking up and slimming down banks would reduce the ability of bankers to take advantage of nothing more than a bank's size or TBTF status to boost a bonus; some of the worst excesses and most inappropriate bonuses happened in simple areas of retail and com- mercial banking and not in the supposedly complicated 'hot' areas, because pay was related to size and rate of expansion. With macroprudential regulation in place, banks that would pay out big bonuses in a boom would have to put aside more capital.

There was a rich morphology of others orbiting beyond bankers who failed to discipline bad behaviour. Many bank boards were wholly inadequate. Non- executive directors, drawn from a very shallow pool, hardly ever held bank executives to account or vetted key appointments. Bank risk officers had poor day-to-day contact with senior decision makers because they themselves did not have senior positions. At Allied Irish Bank, three successive chief internal auditors presented evidence of corrupt practices to the board, and each time they were ignored. The reporting structures at HBOS and Citigroup were so bad that their boards had not a clue what some of the high-risk team were up to. Many shareholders—in all the textbooks, the next bastion against foolishness— behaved more like speculators than owners. Surely, 20%–30% return was not possible without extreme risks being taken? Yet, many shareholders did not think that decisions that we now know were dumb were dumb. Indeed, bank boards and risk officers knew that investors would punish *them* if they tried to stop activities that were highly profitable. Managers drew their bonuses off the same frothing cauldron as those they sought to manage. No wonder that the banks the market 'favoured' in 2006 made the worst returns during the crash, those with more shareholder-friendly boards performed badly, and those banks in countries with more independent supervisors fared better.[85]

This suggests a whole raft of possible governance reforms, including the following: separate risk and audit committees; non-executives with more rights and responsibilities to challenge audit-committee auditors; auditors that are regularly changed; improved international accounting standards; chief risk officers with stronger roles in company governance;[86] more attention to 'key-person' risk (that is, when only a few employees really understand what is going on in a particular line of business); limits on the number of directorships held by board members; division of the role of chairman and chief executive; greater availability of reliable public information to help boards and investors alike perform due diligence; a lifetime ban and the stripping of honours of failed bankers; and prison for many more of the corrupt.

For all their vaunted sophistication, methods of risk evaluation—both internal to firms and external via CRAs—were seriously flawed. Up to 60% of the securities that the CRAs rated as triple-A were subsequently reduced to junk. In particular, since measures of risk were inferred from asset price volatility, there was an illusion of safety on the eve of the crash because volatility was very low. This had strong ideological roots. If prices are always efficient, markets are always liquid (so that asset prices always follow 'random walks'), and interactions on asset markets are irrelevant, then using market prices to evaluate value and risk[87] is 'efficient'. In reality, risk is more a 'behavioural' phenomenon, lumpy and non-linear, with tipping points and discontinuities. As a result, tail risks were massively underpriced by financial firms in their self-insurance (e.g. their own holdings of liquidity), in their public insurance (i.e. the insurance 'premium' they paid for deposit, liquidity, and capital rescue programmes), and in their private insurance (e.g. catastrophe bonds).

Yet, if efforts are made to model tail risks properly, a number of problems arise. First, even though tail events are more frequent than predicted by normal probability distributions, they are still infrequent. With no prior history, new financial instruments are especially vulnerable;[88] nobody really had any experience of default on securitized pools of subprime mortgages. Second, if there are strong competitive pressures, bankers will anyway gravitate away from fully insuring against tail risk. Year after year, the insurance 'premiums' eat into profits yet create no payoff. Then when the tail outcome materializes, central banks and Treasuries step in anyway. Third, as we saw in Chapter 3, bankers engage in activities—increased leverage, larger trading books, more tail-heavy instruments, greater business diversification, the writing of deep out-of-the-money options—that *create* tail risks. Tail risk is big in banking, because those in banking like it that way.

One possible solution might be to incorporate stress tests into the credit-ratings models of the CRAs, allowing for more extreme events than suggested by recent data. Of course, there would be arguments over what scenarios to use. Could CRAs withstand lobbying and give a highly risky activity a poor rating even if it is highly profitable? Several ways have been proposed to deal with CRAs' conflicts of interest. One is to switch payment for ratings from borrowers to investors; however, it is still the case that once a rating is known, everybody knows it and the incentive to pay for it is weak. Another is to enhance the role of reputational issues and the loss of franchise value of CRAs. Another is public disclosure of ratings methodologies and the criteria for downgrading so that deviations from models can be spotted.[89] A simple incentive might come from standardized ratings definitions combined with a portion of results-based 'reward'; ratings firms would put a portion of revenues in a common fund that would be distributed according to how accurate their ratings turned out to be. More complicated perhaps would be to encourage other agencies to compete and break the oligopoly of rating agencies. The signs were not good. In the US, the SEC put on hold the creation of the new Office of Credit Ratings, a key reform in the Dodd–Frank Act. CRAs continued to give credit ratings to financial institutions while openly admitting to not having a clue about swathes of still-opaque activities.

The CRAs were not the only ones facing conflicts of interest. Surely it is absurd that the financial industry gives millions every year to those supposed to be tough on it? Three of the five biggest donors to US political parties in 2008 were Goldman Sachs, Citigroup, and JPMorgan.[90] In the UK half of Conservative party funds came from those working in banks, hedge funds, and private equity firms. Investment banks also faced potential conflicts of interest on many different levels. Operating between different groups of their customers—that they served variously as advisers, market-makers, underwriters, or as fiduciary—they could exploit knowledge of their customers' order books to make a profit on their own proprietary trading, keep the best investments for themselves, and sell the worst to their clients. Motivated by generous fees, they issued securities for mergers and acquisitions that generated no benefit for their clients in the long run, and miss-sold credit risk protection. In July 2010 Goldman Sachs was fined $550 million, the largest fine in the SEC's history, for selling bundled-up mortgages the selection of which involved a powerful client taking a trading position that would benefit from their collapse. The shame is that many of the specialist firms and hedge funds that could challenge investment banks, and are small enough to fail, have been lumped together and branded as shadowy.

Although certain kinds of derivatives played a prominent role in the crash, in many cases the real problems were the leverage that was used to turn some into massive wrong bets, the creation of huge opaque exposures, and the way some, such as CDSs, were exploited for their tail-risk possibilities by financial institutions that were TBTF. The solution was to create greater (post-trade[91]) transparency of derivatives trading, and to reduce counterparty risks via central clearing facilities. Better risk management, closer alignment of capital to risk, and better regulation would do the rest.

The shadow banking system, where many of these risks had their genesis, was the product of the profit-making strategies of large regulated banks, a symptom as much as a cause. If regulated banks were better regulated and had their TBTF status stripped away, the symptoms would improve. If shadow banking activities have (indirect) recourse to government insurance, such activities should be on the balance sheets of banks (i.e. banks should pay the 'insurance fees' for the government's protection of such activities by applying capital and liquidity rules to them).

A year after the Dodd–Frank Act was signed, more derivatives were to be standardized and to go through clearing houses, and many were to go onto electronic exchanges to be more transparent. However, international harmonization was a long way off; major differences had developed across countries regarding collateral requirements and the structure of the new market. And what if the central counterparty might itself become insolvent and reliant on government support in the face of large, systemic events? The Dodd–Frank Act failed also to single out for reform important parts of the shadow banking system and markets that were systemically important. In particular, the counterparty risk caused by the opaque system of repos was at the heart of the contraction of liquidity, yet there was no plan to have repos cleared and settled on a centralized, transparent market. Money market mutual funds—that provide a service that mimics commercial banks but without the capital requirements, reserve requirements, and charges for deposit insurance—needed to be brought under the umbrella of commercial banks, and to be treated more like ordinary mutual funds, with redemption value reflected on day-to-day market fluctuations and not a fixed dollar price. One problem was that the Act also sought to regulate by type of form and not by function, which invited new organizational forms to emerge outside the rules.

Global Regulation and Regulation Globally

Some say there needs to be a new 'World Financial Organization'. When thinking of the US Congress ceding oversight of American banks to a 'World' body, the words 'Hell' and 'freeze over' float freely across the page. The IMF and the World Trade Organization have no mandate for this. If a key role fell to the IMF, it would first need meaningful reform, with its seats, votes, and quotas reconfigured to better reflect reality on the ground. If perchance Hell one day did freeze, it is unrealistic not to expect strong US pressure to shape the standards of the new international body. If such a body had existed in the 2000s, surely the US would not have allowed it to police the hugely profitable subprime activities of some of its biggest financial firms. After all, as a spokesman for Bush and Paulson once observed, 'It's very difficult thing to say as a national policy goal that we're going to limit the success of an American firm.'[92]

What would be the international rules? Basel II was a sophisticated mechanism for introducing risk weighting into the capital requirements of banks, and the result of 15 years of intense deliberations. Yet it neglected macroprudential risks, failed to put any weighting on off-balance-sheet exposures with a maturity of less than a year, and was not concerned with market-liquidity risks or funding-liquidity risks at all. One might conclude that Basel II was a form of regulatory forbearance. Realizing that they were going to be regulated anyhow, banks went along with, and did their best to shape, Basel II in a way that avoided much tougher rules. In the spirit of 'light-touch', Basel II emphasized self-regulation and the internal models of banks, and banks took full advantage to get the weights as low as possible. In the face of growing risks, Basel II reassured and soothed, a blindfold to the senses and a muffle to the voices of the sensible.

Regulatory systems were also fragmented. As well as putting the Glass–Steagall Act out to grass, the Gramm–Leach–Bliley Act of 1999 shifted the focus of oversight away from the Fed (restricted henceforth to overseeing bank holding companies). Alongside the Fed and the US Treasury, the US had five federal depository institution regulators as well as state-based supervision, a federal securities regulator (the SEC), alongside a range of other state-based agencies, a federal futures regulator, and more than 50 state-based insurance regulators—and still the US crashed. Few regulators had the itch to scratch much below the surface, and plenty of bankers fell, or found ways to fall, between the cracks.

The UK was an even sadder case. In 1997 Brown replaced a bipartite system—based on the expertise and market knowledge of the Bank of England

and the access to cash and political authority of the Treasury—with a tripartite system including a new organization, the FSA, a Treasury satellite. According to Brown, its architect, it was 'a world-leading example of how to regulate financial services'.[93] Let's not beat about the bush: it was a disaster. At one fell swoop the arrangement split the macro, systemic, economic central bank from the micro, individual, prudential, legal, and accounting FSA. The Bank of England ended up notionally in charge of financial stability but without access to the detailed knowledge of the goings on inside individual banks that would enable it to perform that function. Thus, Northern Rock drifted towards disaster without the regulatory dots being joined up in one place, with no more than the sounds of clashing bureaucracies and political buck-passing to see it on its way. An internal review of March 2012 revealed an ill-prepared Treasury under Brown ('the financial sector had not been a high-priority area of the Treasury's business for a number of years') and squabbling at the highest levels between it and the Bank of England. In spite of its new responsibilities, the Treasury had only three people covering financial stability. The Old Lady of Threadneedle Street had been nobbled in the interests of 'light-touch' regulation. In Iceland (and elsewhere) similar politicization of regulation, and the overly close personal relationships amongst key actors, severely weakened regulatory vigilance.[94] The UK's Financial Services Bill scrapped the FSA from 2013 and passed its supervisory powers back to the Bank of England's subsidiary body, the Prudential Regulatory Authority (PRA). The Bill allowed the government in future to seize failing banks and wipe out shareholders. For the first time the chancellor would be able to direct specific liquidity to specific entities in trouble. The new FPC would direct the PRA to take action against potential financial instability.

The other big 'institutional' issue is the level at which regulation should be performed: by 'home' or 'host' supervisory authorities? The key problem is that international financial institutions are international in life, but national in death.[95] Crisis management is expensive and paid by national Treasuries and taxpayers, who, naturally enough, expect to have control. When the US authorities bailed out AIG they spent some $40–50 billion on non-US counterparties, but this was not likely to be the norm. This suggests strong host-country regulators with global coordination. The 'efficient frontier' of financial regulation for each country varies too; why penalize less developed countries with a more complex system than they yet have the skills to run, harming their financial development?[96]

One of the biggest gaps remains the lack of a cross-border resolution authority for dealing with the failure of large global banks.[97] Such an authority would define in advance who would be in charge of winding which bits up and what monies would be used. The harmonization of bankruptcy laws or cross-border liquidation rules is at least ten years away. Warnings were issued in the run-up to the crash, but ignored. This suggests that global early warning systems should be encouraged that move beyond models based on foreign-exchange markets to include also models for banking and debt crises and the linkages across different types of crisis and countries (contagion).[98]

The biggest challenge as always will be regulatory arbitrage, as less strict regimes seek competitive advantage over more strict regimes. Some in the G20 'remain hesitant to lean too hard on banks they consider vital to their national economies'.[99] One of the limitations that surely played on the minds of the UK's ICB was that the foreign rivals of UK banks would continue to receive the state subsidy that the ICB was seeking to take away from British banks. Europe's proclivity for universal banking, combined with EU law allowing any EU-authorized bank the right to set up a branch anywhere in the EU, means that without an EU-wide agreement, banks can avoid break-up imposed in one country by locating their head offices in another country and managing activities in the potential break-up country as the local branch. If, for example, tougher rules on US proprietary trading applied only to domestic US banks, banks would just move their 'prop' desks to the jurisdiction of another (such as Europe or Asia), since it would be impossible for the US to ban a US-incorporated bank from operating a prop desk elsewhere in the world. Next, we shall hear that because of this, such rules should not be tougher in the first place.

The Dodd–Frank Act was not the end, just the end of the beginning. Regulators now needed to write the rules—depending on who was counting, between 225 and 400 of them. Yet, after a year, only 55 had been finalized, and of 67 studies required by the Act only 32 were complete. Many of the rules needed international agreement, which was elusive. Perhaps if big banks had been forced to shop around to find a better deal on the trillions of dollars of free insurance and subsidy they got from governments, and if policymakers had swept more big failed banks to their deaths and allowed smaller, more successful, rivals to expand, then big banks might have viewed some of the issues differently.

Progress was being squashed from two directions. First, a thoroughly investigated Act would have taken too long and been derailed, but a more quickly written Act was easier to attack (to much glee, lobbyists got Bernanke to admit that the cumulative impact of all the different measures had not been studied). Second, as Barney Frank observed, 'The climate for being critical was aided by the fact that the recovery's been slow.'[100] Just like with the fiscal problems, the issue was the timing. In the long-run, tougher discipline was needed. In the short-run, with banks cautious and not lending, there was no need to hastily ramp up the capital and liquidity buffers. Yet, banks were doing little to help the recovery, and the rallying cry of choice for those who opposed tougher regulation was that 'burdensome' regulation would snuff out recovery. By late 2011 even Geithner was going around urging policymakers not to be too vigorous, and he was getting help from a Republican majority in the Congress in no mood to provide the budget to get the job done quickly. Elsewhere, for all the talk of tougher regulation, much had failed to materialize, and global coordination was elusive.

It is sometimes said that an occasional crash is the price to be paid for a more dynamic financial system and higher economic growth. If only this were so. A quick flick of the US Financial Crisis Inquiry Report—with its umpteen eye-popping accounts of self-serving, unethical, irresponsible, manipulative, flat-out greedy financial practices, should disabuse even the most generous-minded reader. In the 1930s, a bit like today, Wall Street hated the new regulatory environment. Something we now regard as obvious—nationwide deposit insurance—was vehemently opposed until after the calamitous bank runs of the early 1930s created an atmosphere conducive to its legislation.[101] Ultimately, though, Wall Street was one of the biggest beneficiaries of the reforms, because they instilled greater confidence in financial systems. Today, like then, with no bubbles to rely upon for future high returns, investor confidence will be more important than ever.

In 2011 'Occupy Wall Street' groups sprung up all over the world. Many were dismissed as anti-capitalist. This missed the point. The general public had cottoned on that financial systems were rigged (the LIBOR scandal of the summer of 2012 seemed to further confirm this). They had watched wealthy bankers abuse the public's trust and strip any and all social sacraments of everything but the mere satisfaction of their own cravings. They had seen rescue efforts that used dishonest scales, and weights that favoured bankers over everyone else. The biggest enemies of a dynamic financial system were not amongst the protesters but within the financial institutions themselves, amongst capitalists who had gone out of their way to try to destroy capitalism.

Banking is too complex and evolving for any reform measure to be the last word. But we don't seek a perfect solution. It is better to have the practically doable over the theoretically grand, to prioritize fixing the few major problems, and to keep it as simple as possible. As the famous ecologist Nelson Hairston once remarked, 'If it's not worth doing; it's not worth doing well.'[102] And as the famous physicist Albert Einstein once observed, 'Any intelligent fool can make things bigger, more complex, and more violent. It takes a touch of genius—and a lot of courage—to move in the opposite direction.'

Closing Thoughts

As we picked our way through the causes and consequences of such explosive events, a range of deeper and more troubling questions left their trails across our minds. Why did public policy have so little to say about the dangers as they were growing? The costs turned out to be astronomic. Why was so little done to ward off disaster before it was too late? Why were those who worried not heard, and those who were heard not worrying? Did a crash really have to happen *before* there was political capital to be made out of doing anything about it? Perhaps the fundamental question is not why the crash happened, but why it was allowed to happen.

In November 2008, Queen Elizabeth, passing through the London School of Economics, was treated to an explanation of what had caused the crash. She enquired, not unreasonably, 'If these things were so large how come everyone missed them?'[1] In the summer of 2009, a group of eminent economists put together a three—page letter to respond to the queen's concerns.[2] It talked of the 'psychology of denial' that gripped both the financial and political establishment, and of 'financial wizards' who thought they had worked out new ways to spread risk globally—an idea that had been no more than 'wishful thinking combined with hubris'. 'In summary,' they concluded, 'Your Majesty, the failure to foresee the timing, extent and severity of the crisis and to head it off, while it had many causes, was principally a failure of the collective imagination of many bright people, both in this country and internationally, to understand the risks to the system as a whole.' Once upon a time, the Tower of London would have beckoned.

What the letter did not mention was that the failure of collective imagination was wilful. Many researchers and thinkers *had* identified key dangers. The problem was getting political leaders to act. In Chapter 1 we saw that there had long been heated debates about global imbalances, but nothing was done. In Chapters 2 and 3 we saw the mounting evidence of reckless mortgage lending, unsustainable housing booms, and the malign use of financial instruments, and yet these were met with denial and political inaction. The dangers of excessive debt and leverage were clear, but it was not politically convenient to make a fuss. Leverage equalled risk, but also profits for financial institutions, and growth and tax revenues for governments. Deleveraging would cause asset price falls and recessions—and that was a problem for somebody else, some other time on some other day. The mechanisms of the crash, described in Chapter 4, if not their severity, were understood by a range of economists. The absence of rescue strategies, and the presence of hindrances for rescuers if a crisis came—problems we analysed in Chapters 5 and 6—were tolerated. We saw in Chapter 8 the discussions regarding the overly narrow-focus of monetary policy; many understood that an interest rate on its own could not tackle key dangers and that new tools were needed, but such concerns were ignored. The long-term fiscal sustainability issues, discussed in Chapter 9, were already known about. The mistakes in setting up the euro, described in Chapter 10, were clear in advance. The global tensions that would follow a crash, described in Chapter 11, were already lurking in the wings. In Chapter 12 we saw how individualized risk and light-touch regulation ruled the regulatory roost, and how the rituals of regulatory oversight often hid the lack of actuality of oversight; perhaps, that was their point. We saw no shortage of proposals for dealing with global systemic risk, yet monitoring systemic dangers got nowhere. There was much discussion of macroprudential regulation, and some progress in a range of Asian countries (Thailand, India, Hong Kong), Latin America, Eastern Europe, and Spain but not in the US, the UK, Iceland, and other countries at the heart of the crash. We are so used to having had a crash, we hardly remember just how unfashionable, how utterly unacceptable, socially and professionally, it was to speak loudly of the dangers, and how the prevailing mood of the people, markets, business leaders and their educators, politicians, and the media, reassured and favoured those who ignored the risks, and made those who expressed their concerns feel like spoil-sports.

Wilful ignorance bordered on the blasé, even the downright bizarre. On 8 March 2006, in The Hague, another queen, Queen Beatrix, received the diplomatic letters that installed Roland Arnall, founder and chief executive of America's largest subprime mortgage lender, Ameriquest, as the new US Ambassador to the Netherlands. It was just in the nick of time. In early 2006, Ameriquest was fined $325 million for abusive lending practices: cold-calling the poor and persuading them to take on crippling subprime loans juiced with hidden rates and fees, forging documents, and pressurizing appraisers to inflate home values so that more and bigger loans could be made. The elderly and minorities made especially profitable targets. Many of the 5 million who borrowed from Ameriquest in 2005–2007 lost their homes. Such predatory behaviour was not perhaps the sort of thing one might expect of a diplomat. Yet Arnall, a billionaire thanks to such malfeasance, the largest single fundraiser for President Bush ($12.5 million between 2003 and 2005, having previously been a major long-term donor and fund-raiser for the Democrats) and co-chair of the 2004 Republican Convention, for acts of such inspired generosity was recommended for the posting by President Bush on 1 August 2005 and was deemed worthy by the Senate on 6 February 2006.

In such a world of moral eccentricity, what chance was there for any efforts to make it safer? For example, in March 2002, well before the crash, the IMF launched a new initiative to promote 'financial stability as a global public good'. Its task was 'to identify potential systemic weaknesses that could lead to crises' and formulate a 'comprehensive strategy aimed at safeguarding the stability and integrity of the international financial system . . .'[3] In its first quarterly 'Global Financial Stability Report',[4] the first of many published before the crash, numerous risks that subsequently played key roles in the crash were identified. There was concern about 'credit risk transfer mechanisms [that] could develop to be a source of financial market risk' and worries that 'the relatively low degree of financial disclosure and market transparency about these instruments and markets—and about who owns the credit risk—would seem to pose some risk that market participants might have difficulty in accurately gauging the nature and extent of the credit deterioration'. Intense competition from large global financial institutions had 'strengthened the linkages among the major financial systems and financial centers' and 'may have increased the potential for spillovers across financial institutions and centers'. Financial institutions were 'now more exposed to market, liquidity, and counterparty credit risks' facilitated by 'the rapid growth of the global over-the-counter (OTC) derivatives markets'. Off-balance-sheet (shadow) special purpose vehicles were especially worrying, 'particularly the extent to which such vehicles genuinely remove risks from the balance sheet of the originating entity rather than merely disguise them'. In conclusion, 'The higher dependence of balance sheets on traded financial assets—in the context of greater indebtedness—is a potential source of risk.' Does this sound a little familiar?

Perhaps policymakers were also lulled into a false sense of security by their apparent successes in dealing with a string of potential disasters in the 1990s and early 2000s. The first batch included the collapse of the European Exchange

Rate Mechanism (ERM), the Asian financial crisis, the collapse of a range of financial institutions—the most notable of which being Barings and the hedge fund Long-Term Capital Management (LTCM)—and crises in Russia, Asia, and Mexico. The early 2000s witnessed the aftermath of the dot-com collapse, the September 11 attacks, Argentina's sovereign debt default (the biggest in history), record corporate defaults in the US, and the failure of Enron, a huge dealer, market-maker, and liquidity provider in the OTC energy derivatives markets. Each time the systemic consequences were somehow contained. As OTC derivative contracts rapidly unwound, the exposure of counterparty credit risks did not seed disaster. CDSs against defaults seemed to cope. Many concluded that the global financial system was naturally more robust and self-correcting than it truly was, and that there was always time to fix problems. Greenspan argued that such episodes 'suggest a marked increase over the past two or three decades in the ability of modern economies to absorb shocks' and that 'the increased resiliency now clearly evident arguably supports the view that the world economy already has become more flexible'.[5] He even gave credit to the US's massive secondary-mortgage market as a stabilizing force, keeping the US economy afloat by allowing homeowners to spend on the back of rising property prices. Politicians promoted such thinkers, because they said what they wanted to hear.

The collapse of Enron—until then the largest US Chapter 11 bankruptcy in history—is especially salient. Enron was a pioneer in the accounting shenanigans that masked excessive leverage. Enron's extensive off-balance-sheet transactions were not spotted by shareholders, analysts, and creditors until too late, and so market discipline was ineffective. Enron was not required to put aside prudential capital against trading risks, or to disclose information on its risks to counterparties or about market conditions in those markets in which it played a key role. Its OTC derivatives activities (in energy, credit, and other financial derivatives) were essentially unregulated. Its auditors faced conflicts of interests because they were also Enron's consultants. Does this sound familiar?

Enron should have been the canary in the coalmine. Instead, when it keeled over, this was treated as a sign of vitality. Significant losses were forced on to financial institutions and institutional and retail investors, yet systemic problems did not materialize. There were worries that not all the instruments used to hedge credit exposures to Enron would cope. But, in spite of a long and bumpy ride, they mostly did. To finesse its barbaric feast, Enron pulled its auditor, Arthur Andersen, to its corporate death. Enron's CEO, Jeffrey Skilling, was fined $45 million and given a 24-year sentence for fraud. Surely, many regulators reasoned, in future the Enrons of this world, and those who connive to help them, would know to look out for themselves.

The respectable alibi for letting 'self-interest' drive self-regulation in the banking sector was the so-called 'efficient-markets hypothesis' sitting at the heart of modern finance. If many are making wrong forecasts, perceive risk as being low when in fact it is high, and lose, then in will step a class of 'smart' investors who will bet on the basis of more correct forecasts and better understanding of the risks. In so doing, they mend the market's inefficiency and, even, stop it from arising in the first place. The crash taught us that such simplistic thinking does not hold. First, contrarian investors, using other peoples' money, need to attract more money to keep their positions going. When inefficiencies last a long time, contrarian investors will not survive. Second, as we saw, many of those who make silly investment decisions do not lose anyway. Third, politicians undermine the value of betting against silly investors and, yet, it is not time-consistent for politicians to refuse to intervene. The true reasons for 'efficient-market' thinking rarely swam close to the surface. Partly they were ideological, partly plain profitable, partly just political. The 'efficient-markets hypothesis' was the sanctifying cloth to hide the nakedness of 'light-touch' regulation, and all the benefits that it would bestow.

How did politicians come out of this sorry saga? On the whole, not very well. In the run up to the crash, in the US Republicans were in power, and in the UK it was 'new' Labour. If it had been the Democrats and Conservatives, it would have made no difference. All were prostrating themselves before the new financial deities. The disaster for the US was that Bush hadn't a clue about the dangers and left it all to Greenspan. The disaster for the UK was that Blair and Brown got both the financial-sector understanding wrong and the public finances wrong, and they got the first wrong because if helped to solve the riddle of the second. Bankers might have lit the fuse, but they had plenty of help to pile the gunpowder high.

At least the US held a major banking enquiry looking into the causes, especially in the US, of the financial crash. The UK did not hold a full independent enquiry into the failings of its banks and political leaders. In mid-2012, the UK government finally announced an enquiry, but it was ring-fenced to cover only LIBOR manipulation and not the wider failures. To the relief of all political parties, it was to be a political (i.e. parliamentary) enquiry, and not a judge-led enquiry. It was not too late to hold such an enquiry.

There were unique features to the crash—such as the role of asset securitization—but it broadly resembled the boom–bust of past crashes. As the crash approached, policymakers' responses also followed the pattern of past systemic crises and crashes. There was a long period of denial. Then a period of regulatory forbearance and generous liquidity support to deal with insolvent financial institutions in the hope that they would recover. Problems with bank capital were ignored for as long as possible and bank restructuring delayed. The stress on the financial system and economy eventually proved too much and action was finally forced. Then, as the crash unfolded, some of those who had floundered the most now found themselves hauled into the rescue ark and treated to overly generous hospitality by those (often their friends) who steered it. After the crash, as the rescue vessel settled and its contents were released back into the wild, one was left wondering if the new regulatory landscape had not been reshaped with the interests of banks, and not those of the general public, uppermost in mind. Efficient, risk-taking, entrepreneurial, genuinely wealth-creating activity is critical to the functioning of a modern capitalist economy. This was subverted, before, during, and after the crash. Many of the responses to the crash were so rewarding for banks that the penalty for generating crashes was taken away. We should care too that the banking system attracts a lot of human talent from other areas of the economy, and that if a huge chunk of that is wasted doing silly things, the true opportunity cost is the loss to society of what that talent might otherwise have achieved.

Surely, the size of the underlying crash this time was even greater than in 1929, and the financial system pushed much closer to the edge (take the policy environment of the 1930s and do the experiment). For all of the inability of its politicians to act, the economy of the US was structured so as to allow economic stabilizers to work and for much bigger deficits to cushion the blow. At least the basics, such as deposit protection, were in place. If the US had forced itself to stick to 3% to 4% government deficits, as in the 1930s and the eurozone from 2010, it would have created an utter disaster for itself and the world.

The crash highlighted the evolution in financial and macroeconomic risks. Up until the late 1990s, financial crises were based more frequently on inflationary shocks. Starting then, and paralleling the shift in the relative power of capital over labour, came a shift towards financial crises based on deflation and over-investment, a pattern similar to the late 1920s. Then, as now, stagnating wages and inequality meant that the increased growth of output was not absorbed, and a surge in borrowing filled the gap. In both cases, a stock market boom turned sour as investments turned out not to be as profitable as had been hoped. This time, the process was kept going for longer by masking the stock market collapse with an even bigger debt bubble.

The stability of the Great Moderation was presented as good for all, yet most of the spoils of the Great Moderation went to capital. The social conflict that would otherwise have been caused by the victory of capital over labour was dampened by the rise of debt. That shield has now gone. Many of the bitter social battles today, and to be harvested in the future, were bottled during the Great Moderation and have, perversely, been made worse by the further skewing of income, wealth, and power towards the rich and powerful after the crash. Inequalities and economic injustices were tolerated in the years before the crash on the premise that, somehow, this allowed more sustained prosperity than the alternatives. The collapse of the Great Moderation and the post-crash divergence between the fates of the super-rich and the vast majority[6] has shown this to be false.

The years before the crash were marked by the fight between capitalism and Soviet-style communism. Capitalism triumphed. The crash has served to redraw the battle lines as between liberal democratic capitalism and nationalist authoritarian capitalism. Emerging economies, including those in Eastern Europe, Asia, and Africa, are starting to find the latter attractive. In China, the elite do what they feel they need to do to preserve their interests, without the encumbrance of a democratic process. In the US and Europe, as we have seen, what is economically possible is increasingly shaped by what is politically possible, which is a function of the biases of voters and the poor quality of much debate. As the dangers get more global, all too often the people are turning inwards towards more narrow national interests. After the crash, Obama might have been the most powerful man in the world, but, as we repeatedly saw, his capacity to make and remake policy was heavily constrained. European leaders were increasingly finding the same.

Generations come and generations go. As memories fade, what has been will be again, and what has been done will be done again. The point of books such as this is to keep collective memory alive, to preserve some of the bitter after-taste of the past in the present, in the hope that it might serve as guidance or as a warning. More than ever, we need people willing to arm themselves with the lessons of the past and to 'speak truth to power'. In this, we all have our part to play. Let us not repeat the same mistakes next time.

ENDNOTES

Preface

1. Remarks to Joint Session of Congress, 24 February 2009.
2. According to Simon & Schuster's promotional material for *Beyond the Crash*.
3. Farlow, 2004*a*, 2004*b*, 2005.
4. Brown, 2010*a*.
5. *Financial Times*, 2004.
6. A copy has helpfully now been placed on the Internet.
7. *Daily Telegraph*, 2010*a*.
8. *Daily Telegraph*, 2010*b*.
9. A government's budget deficit is the difference between that country's government spending and government receipts in a year expressed as a percent of that country's gross domestic product (GDP) for that year. It can be measured including or not including the interest paid on government debt. The total deficit, often just called the 'deficit', is spending plus interest payments on the debt minus tax revenues. The primary deficit is the difference between current government spending and total current revenue from all types of taxes.
10. Farlow, 2003.
11. The fourth paper looked at 'Risk Premia in Housing Markets', and took the standard notion of financial risk premia—that investors need some 'extra' return as compensation for volatile asset prices—and argued that the near-zero risk premia in many housing markets only made sense if house-buyers and banks believed that house prices could not fall. The paper reviewed evidence of past house-price volatility to argue that this made no sense. The fifth paper (referenced many times in the third paper) looked at 'Global Banking Liquidity, Mortgage Markets and Housing'. Some of this material has found its way into Chapters 2 and 3.
12. Galbraith, 1954.
13. Freidman and Schwartz, 1963.

Chapter 1

1. Most scholars now feel that the role of trade wars in causing the Great Depression has been a little exaggerated. Trade was only about 5% of US GDP, a much smaller percentage than it is today. Of course, that means that perhaps we should worry more about the potential consequences of trade wars today.
2. Chancellor of the Exchequer's Budget Statement to Parliament, 16 March 2005.

3. Bernanke, 2004.

4. Kim and Nelson (1999) and McConnell and Perez-Quiros (2000) were among the first to note the reduction in the volatility of output. Blanchard and Simon (2001) showed that the variability (as measured by standard deviations) of quarterly growth in real output and inflation had declined by half and two thirds respectively since the mid-1980s. They observed that one interpretation of the data could be that there was a single structural break in the mid-1980s. Bernanke accepted this interpretation of the data, with 1984 as the break point.

5. When I use the term 'leverage' on its own I am referring to the ratio of liabilities, such as debts, to assets. When I intend 'leverage' to refer to the ratio of debt to income, I mention income.

6. Crafts, 1999; Collins and Bosworth, 1996.

7. So, credits are recorded for exports, and for interest, profits, and dividends on assets held abroad, and for transfers received. Debits are recorded for imports, and for interest, profits, and dividends on foreign holdings of domestic assets, and for transfers paid.

8. Figures from IMF, Currency Composition of Official Foreign Exchange Reserves (COFER).

9. We need to allow for capital depreciation too.

10. Farlow, 2005, p. 51.

11. All the savings data is from the Bank for International Settlement.

12. Brenner, 2006.

13. Ibid.

14. Seignorage is the difference between the value of money and the cost to produce it. In particular, the US can print dollar notes for next to nothing yet, in order to hold them, foreigners must provide goods and services at the face value of the notes. The US effectively gets a huge, revolving, interest-free loan from the rest of the world.

15. Eichengreen, 2011.

16. Farlow, 2005, p. 55.

17. This, of course, is what national-income accounting tells us will happen. The issue here is who has claim on the hoard and in what it is invested.

18. Sometimes 'inefficient' asset price bubbles even help to unlock credit constraints.

19. Galbraith, 1954.

20. World Economic Forum, 2011, 2012. See also Atkinson and Morelli (2011).

21. Economic Policy Institute.

22. Bernanke, 2005a.

23. Taylor, 2008.

24. Caballero, Farhi, and Gourinchas, 2008.

25. Rodrik, 2008.

26. Fisher, 1933.

27. The Federal Reserve did so by, for example: (1) acting rapidly when confronted with the zero bound, as discussed in Reifschneider and Williams (2000); (2) providing forward guidance regarding short-term interest rates, as discussed in Eggertsson and Woodford (2003); (3) expanding the Federal Reserve's balance sheet through purchases of longer-term securities, as discussed in Bernanke, Reinhart, and Sack (2004).

28. Fuhrer and Madigan, 1997; Reifschneider and Williams, 2000; Ahearne, Gagnon, Haltmaier, Kamin, et al. 2002.

29. Obviously a change in interest rates takes time to favour the 'right' sort of investment, and the impact on jobs in the short-run may be distorted by previous investment decisions.
30. Greenspan, 1996.
31. McKinsey Global Institute, 2010.
32. Case-Shiller Home Price Index.
33. Broadbent, 2012.
34. Meckling and Jensen, 1976; Stiglitz and Weiss, 1981.
35. Rajan, 2006.
36. See the series of papers on this topic by Hart and Moore (1994, 1995, 1998, 1999, and 2007).
37. Farlow, 2005, p. 25.
38. See Hart, 1995, p. 141.
39. The only possible contender was the collapse in international trade finance that followed the assassination of Archduke Ferdinand and his wife, Sophie, duchess of Hohenberg, in Sarajevo on 28 June 1914.
40. Stiglitz, 2006. For the Iraq war, as of 2006, the conservative estimate was of $1 trillion, with the 'moderate' estimate of $2 trillion.
41. *The Guardian*, 2010.
42. Obstfeld, 2005; Obstfeld and Rogoff, 2001, 2005, 2007.
43. Bean, 2008.
44. King, 2009*a*.
45. *The Economist*, 2004.
46. See Chapters 2 and 8 for important caveats and nuance.
47. *The Economist*, 2004.
48. Minsky, 1986.
49. Greenspan, 2005*b*.

Chapter 2

1. Shiller, 2009.
2. Congressional Oversight Panel, 2009*d*, p. 5.
3. *It's a Wonderful Life* was voted number 11 in the American Film Institute's '100 Greatest American Movies of All Time'.
4. Fleckenstein, 2005.
5. The headlines got ever more inventive: 28 May 2002, 'Going through the roof'; 29 May 2003, 'House of cards'; 20 April 2005, 'Will the walls come falling down?'; 16 June 2005, 'After the fall'; 16 June 2005, 'In come the waves'; 8 December 2005, 'Hear that hissing sound?'
6. *The Economist*, 2005.
7. All figures are S&P/Case-Shiller Home Price Indices.
8. The index was at 100.59 in January 2000, and at 206.15 in May 2006.
9. United States Census Bureau data.
10. Shakespeare, *The Merchant of Venice* Act 3, Scene 2: 'Thus ornament is but the guiled shore To a most dangerous sea.'
11. Barker, 2004.
12. BBC, 2010.

13. Soros, 1988.
14. Figures from The Center for Public Integrity, based on 350 million loan applications.
15. Muellbauer and Murphy (2008) report 0.07–0.09, while Carroll, Otsuka, and Slacalek (2006) and Slacalek (2006) report 0.09.
16. Muellbauer, 2007.
17. European Central Bank, 2009; Muellbauer and Blake, 2009; Miles and Pillonca, 2008; Honohan, 2008.
18. Aron, Duca, Muellbauer, Murata, and Anthony, 2011.
19. Attanasio, Weber, Blow, Hamilton, and Leicester, 2005; Benito, Thompson, Waldron, and Wood, 2006; Muellbauer, 2007.
20. Muellbauer and Murphy, 2008.
21. Aron et al., 2011.
22. Muellbauer and Murphy (2008) show this for the UK. See also Muellbauer (2007).
23. Muellbauer and Murata, 2008.
24. Greenspan and Kennedy, 2008.
25. Joint Center for Housing Studies at Harvard University, 2006, p. 36, Table A6.
26. Weale, 2007.
27. Muellbauer and Murphy, 2008, p. 14.
28. Ibid., p. 15.
29. A Ponzi investment scheme pays returns to investors from a combination of their own money and investments of the next generation of investors. Such schemes are named after Charles Ponzi who used the notion to much personal benefit in the 1920s.
30. Foote, Gerardi, Goette, and Willen, 2008; Sherlund, 2008.
31. BBC, 2009a.
32. Prepayment is a risk because when mortgage debts are paid off early the new financing may be cheaper for the borrower but the original lender gets less because the payments that would have been made would have been above the market rate. Prepayment reduces the upside of credit and interest rate variance for the lender. To compensate, a prepayment penalty is often included in the loan.
33. When securitization dries up, the accuracy of LP data falls, and when subprime specialists go out of business, the accuracy of HUD data falls.
34. Demyanyk and Van Hemert, 2008.
35. Mayer and Pence, 2008.
36. Mian and Sufi, 2009.
37. Gorton, 2008.
38. See Committee on the Global Financial System (2006) and Bank for International Settlement (2004, Chapter I).
39. Gerardi, Lehnert, Sherlund, and Willen, 2008; Ellis, 2008.
40. Demyanyk and Van Hemert, 2008.
41. Cagan, 2007.
42. See Benito, Thompson, Waldron, and Wood, 2006.
43. LoanPerformance data. The exact figures in the first quarter of 2007 were 33.7% and 7.3%.
44. Avery, Brevoort, and Canner, 2007.
45. Cagan, 2007.

46. The number of homes vacant or for sale as a percentage of homes that are owner-occupied or vacant and for sale.
47. Ellis, 2008.
48. Moody's Investor Service, 2008.
49. Demyanyk and Van Hemert, 2008. The task was performed on a database of half of all US subprime loans issued between 2001 and 2007.
50. Bucks, Kennickell, and Moore, 2006.
51. Ellis, 2008.
52. Demyanyk and Van Hemert, 2008.
53. The Center for Public Integrity, 2009.
54. Jaffee, 2009, pp. 61–82.
55. *The Banker*, 2003.
56. *Boston Globe*, 2009.
57. *Business Insider*, 2009.
58. The Center for Public Integrity, 2009.
59. See, for example, Barrett (2008), *Wall Street Journal* (2008), Congleton (2009), and Leonnig (2008).
60. *New York Times*, 2003.
61. Kiff and Mills, 2007; Blundell-Wignall and Atkinson, 2008.
62. Ashcraft and Schuermann, 2008.
63. See, for example, Committee on the Global Financial System (2006); Bank for International Settlement (2004, Chapter I).
64. Greenspan, 2007.
65. Bernanke, 2005*b*.
66. Farlow, 2004*a*.
67. See Muellbauer (2007) and Aron and Muellbauer (2006).
68. Farlow, 2004*a*.
69. On the last point, see Himmelberg, Mayer, and Sinai (2005).
70. Farlow, 2004*b*.
71. Ibid.
72. Brunnermeier and Julliard, 2007; Farlow, 2004*a*, Section 3.
73. Notice how money illusion can look very similar to the relaxation of a credit constraint caused by lower nominal interest rates.
74. In the early days of money illusion those who tank up on debt *do* get more housing services; it is the later arrivers who lose out.
75. This is a delayed 'externality' effect imposed by lots of individual lenders on all other lenders (and indeed on sellers of all other, non-housing, goods and services).
76. For a model with a house-price bubble builder and a bubble burster, see Abraham and Hendershott (1996).
77. In noise-trader models some of the traders in a market are not rational, in that they adopt momentum trading strategies. It is not rational for the rational non-noise traders to carry on as if the noise traders are not there. DeLong, Shleifer, Summers, and Waldmann, 1990.
78. Case and Shiller, 1988.
79. As quoted in Lowenstein (2000, p. 123).

80. Calverley (2004) quotes a survey of appraisers (p. 101) that shows the heavy pressure they come under from mortgage brokers and loan officers to make sales targets and generate a target level of business, or risk having their custom withdrawn.

81. And there is always the risk of having to wait out the market for a long time as prices get ever more out of line, and being forced to enter anyway at a very much higher price.

82. Harrison and Kreps, 1978.

83. This, of course, is an example of moral hazard in action. Pozsar, Z., T. Adrian, A. Ashcraft, and H. Boesky, 2010. 'Shadow Banking'. Federal Reserve Bank of New York Staff Report, no. 458 (Revised February 2012).

84. I am applying the logic of Allen and Gale (2007). See Section 9.1.

Chapter 3

1. Greenspan, 2005*a*. It is always worth reading the Greenspan speeches from which such quotes are taken, since they are often a great deal more balanced than the quote. In this case there was a subtle awareness of the ways in which the use of credit derivatives could lead to hidden concentrations of risk outside the banking system and of what happens when there are problems with counterparties. Yet Greenspan also reassures his listeners that the market will discipline these non-bank entities.

2. Brown, 2007.

3. A comment much reported in the media at the time, based on a round-table discussion for *Prospect* magazine. See *Prospect* (2009).

4. Financial Services Authority, 2009*a*.

5. Diamond and Dybvig, 1983.

6. Of course, supply and demand are both at work here. If the wholesale market expands dramatically, this may drive the cost of capital lower for any given credit-rating counterfactual.

7. The commercial paper was 'asset-backed' because the owners of the paper had the right to the assets in the case of a default of the seller of the paper.

8. According to net shadow banking liabilities. See Pozsar, Adrian, Ashcraft, and Boesky (2010).

9. See Section 5.3 ('"Deeper" Mortgage Markets?') and Section 5.4 ('US Lender of Last Resort') of Farlow (2005).

10. For a good introduction see Coval, Jurek, and Stafford (2009). See also Blundell-Wignall, (2007).

11. Shin, 2009*b*.

12. International Monetary Fund, 2006.

13. Kuttner, 2009.

14. Krugman, 2009.

15. Bernanke, 2009*a*.

16. Duffie, 2008.

17. Quoted in *The Love of Money*, BBC documentary broadcast in September 2009.

18. 'DNA, you know, is Midas' gold. Everyone who touches it goes mad.' Judson, 1979, p. 714.

19. There are some caveats to this, or so I am told, such as if there is accounting arbitrage or something similar going on, but I leave that to the experts.

20. Greenspan, 2002*a*.
21. International Monetary Fund, 2001, Chapter 3, p. 44.
22. They were triggered, for example, in the case of Enron, which flagged that there was a problem. Various IMF reports were quite erudite on the dangers. Such warnings were ignored.
23. People who like this sort of thing will find this the sort of thing they like. "Abraham Lincoln (1809–1865), U.S. president. Quoted in Russell (1898).
24. Shakespeare, *Macbeth*, Act 1, Scene 7.
25. Greenspan, 2005*a*.
26. Haldane, 2009*b*.
27. This distinction between 'market liquidity' and 'funding liquidity' is made by Crockett (2008) and Brunnermeier and Pedersen (2009).
28. Brunnermeier, 2009.
29. Allen and Gale, 2007.
30. *Financial Times*, 2007*a*.
31. Lowenstein, 2000.
32. See Shiller (2000). pp. 149–153.
33. See Rajan (2005).
34. Keynes, 1931.
35. Part of the burden of 'equity injection' would come via governments allowing bank mergers and newly created pricing power to help banks recapitalize at the expense of their customers. The cost of this would not show on the government's books. Ex ante, banks would price this in as much as the government's direct equity injections.
36. For literature on capital adequacy, see Kim and Santomero (1988), Furlong and Keeley (1989), Gennotte and Pyle (1991), Rochet (1992), and Besanko and Kanatas (1996).
37. Alessandri and Haldane (2009) enumerate the first five.
38. Volatility in returns has also risen to a similar degree.
39. Modigliani and Miller, 1958; Miller, 1988.
40. Tobias and Shin, 2009.
41. Ibid.
42. Technically, the banking book has a beta of zero while the trading book has a beta of one, so this shift increases the equity beta of the bank, which, in less technical language, is a polite way of saying that in good times banks make an even bigger killing and rely on the state to take more loss.
43. Alessandri and Haldane, 2009.
44. Allen and Gale, 2007. See p. 241.
45. Actually, this had bubble-like properties, because those who pumped tail risk early got good returns for sure, while those who pumped tail risk later were taking bigger risks of losing and relying heavily on being bailed out.
46. Danielsson, 2002; Danielsson and Shin, 2003.
47. Coval, Jurek, and Stafford, 2009.
48. Quoted in *Financial Times* (2007*b*).
49. Alice laughed: "There's no use trying", she said; "one can't believe impossible things". "I daresay you haven't had much practice," said the Queen. "When I was younger, I always did it for half an hour a day. Why, sometimes I've believed as many as six impossible things before breakfast". See Dodgson, C.L. (Lewis Carroll) 1865.

50. Especially as used in banking, insurance, and asset management, and less so in derivatives markets where some adjustments were made to try to mitigate the damage of tail events.
51. See, for example, Mandelbrot and Hudson (2004) and Taleb (2007).
52. Candidates (or mixes of candidates for suitable frameworks) for explaining fat-tail distributions include the role of 'network externalities', disaster myopia (non-rational decision heuristics), and various models of misaligned incentives. For network externalities, see Haldane (2009*a*).
53. Greenspan, 2008.
54. Mishkin with Herbertson, 2006.
55. Geithner, 2009*b*.
56. Madoff in his plea allocution stated that his Ponzi scheme started in 1991, but the trial judge accepted the prosecutor's argument that it started at some point in the 1980s.
57. *Financial Times*, 2009*b*.

Chapter 4

1. The OIS is considered stable because both counterparties only swap the floating rate of interest for the fixed rate of interest.
2. Based on S&P/Case-Shiller Home Price Indices.
3. Federal Deposit Insurance Corporation, 2006; International Monetary Fund, 2006.
4. Bernanke, 2007*a*.
5. Brown, 2007.
6. Gorton, 2008.
7. Brunnermeier and Pedersen, 2009.
8. Brunnermeier and Oehmke, 2012.
9. Brunnermeier, 2009.
10. Akerlof, 1970; Stiglitzand Weiss, 1981.
11. Holmstrom and Tirole, 1997, 1998.
12. Caballero and Krishnamurthy, 2008.
13. See, for example, Bank of England (2007).
14. Appearing on the BBC's *Politics Show* on Sunday 23 November 2008. (Brown failed to respond when asked if he, as 'Mr Prudent chancellor', thought that when he saw that Northern Rock was offering 125% mortgages it was unsustainable.)
15. Two key reports on the collapse of the Northern Rock are HM Treasury (2008*a*) and HM Treasury, Financial Services Authority, and the Bank of England (2008).
16. Bagehot, 1908, p. 19.
17. Shin, 2009*a*.
18. For a good detailed account, see Milne and Wood (2009).
19. *Fortune*, 2007.
20. Allen and Gale (2007, p. 282) show how 'contagion depends on the endogenous pattern of financial claims' with the interesting result that '[a]n incomplete network structure . . . may preclude a complete pattern of financial connectedness and thus encourage financial contagion; but a complete network structure does not imply the opposite: even in a complete network there may be an endogenous choice of overlapping claims that causes contagion'.

21. Bebchuk, Cohen, and Spamann, 2010.
22. In so doing, they provided a contemporary twist in answer to Bertolt Brecht's question: 'What is robbing a bank compared with founding a bank?' See Brecht, B. (1928).
23. US Treasury, 2007.
24. Brown, 2010*a*.
25. Bebchuk, Cohen, and Spamann, 2010.
26. Fahlenbrach and Stulz, 2010.
27. Chapman, 2010.
28. *Newsweek*, 2008.
29. Brunnermeier, Crocket, Goodhart, Persaud, and Shin, 2009.
30. Geithner, 2009*a*.
31. See Gorton (2008).
32. Veronesi and Zingales, 2009.
33. RPF had the misfortune to hold some $800 million of Lehman's commercial paper.
34. *The Guardian*, 2009.
35. *The Economist*, 2009*a*.

Chapter 5

1. Heiskanen, 1993; Drees and Pazarbasioglu, 1995; Englund and Vihriälä, 2006.
2. Paulson briefing reporters at the White House on the afternoon of 15 September 2008.
3. Buiter, 2008.
4. Gale and Vives, 2002.
5. Bernanke, 2011.
6. Claessens, Dell'Ariccia, Igan, and Laeven, 2010.
7. International Monetary Fund, 2008.
8. BIS data. The Netherlands was next at 80%, then the UK at 45%. France and Germany were at about 28% and 25% respectively.
9. *Financial Times*, 2008.
10. Swagel, 2009.
11. In his testimony to the FDIC.
12. King, 2008, pp. 4–5.
13. Quoted in *The Love of Money*, BBC documentary broadcast in September 2009.
14. Davidoff and Zaring, 2008.
15. Posner, 2009.
16. Testimony of Calomiris in Congressional Oversight Panel (2009*c*).
17. King, 2010.
18. Financial Crisis Inquiry Commission, 2011.
19. Taylor, 2008.
20. Ibid., p. 25.
21. Financial Crisis Inquiry Commission, 2010.
22. Transcript of Paulson briefing, 15 September 2008.
23. Financial Crisis Inquiry Commission, 2008.
24. Reuters, 2008.

25. Actually no US law firm would agree to these being deemed genuine sales, so Lehman shopped around and found a British law firm, Linklaters, that found a way to exploit the difference between English and New York law that would deem them genuine sales so long as the transactions moved through London.
26. Lehman Brothers, 2007.
27. A portion of this was available but not used, and a large chunk would be repaid.
28. Bernanke, 2009*b*.
29. Congressional Oversight Panel, 2010*a*, pp. 94–5.
30. *Wall Street Journal*, 2009*a*.
31. *New York Times*, 2009*b*.
32. Over the life of the US liquidity programmes about a tenth of US support was to non-US banks.
33. Bernanke, 2009*b*.
34. Bloomberg, 2011*b*.
35. Bernanke, 2011.
36. From a speech made on the lawn of the White House on 19 September 2008. Taken from a website of 'Bushisms' ('updated frequently', which says it all really).
37. 'They misunderestimated me.' Bentonville, Arkansas, 6 November 2000.
38. In reading the following account, one must not get the impression that policymakers were consistently thinking through these issues at the time.
39. See Klemperer (2004), especially Chapter 3, 'What Really Matters in Auction Design'.
40. Diamond and Rajan, 2009.
41. International Monetary Fund, 2009*a*, Figure 1.28.
42. IMF 2009*c*.
43. It read, '. . . to ensure there's a coordinated effort to possibly recapitalize the global banking system . . . King suggested that the U.S., UK, Switzerland, and perhaps Japan might form a temporary new group to jointly develop an effort to bring together sources of capital to recapitalize all major banks.'
44. Brown, 2010*a*.
45. HM Treasury, 2008*b*.
46. This was reduced to 41% in February 2010 after LBG issued 3.14 billion new shares.
47. Sheikh Mansour bin Zayed al-Nahyan booked a £1.5 billion profit on about £2 billion of his investment in under a year and a further £800 million profit from the other £1.5 billion within two years.
48. Prime Minister's Questions, 10 December 2008: 'And we not only saved the world . . . er . . . saved the banks . . . saved . . . saved . . . the banks and led the way.'
49. Ten, if we consider Wachovia still independent.
50. Myers, 1977.
51. We see how moral hazard gets in everywhere; even injecting new private capital risks moral hazard!
52. This is an application of the financial accelerator in a crash. See Kiyotaki and Moore (1997).
53. See in particular Veronesi and Zingales (2009) and Zingales (2008).
54. US Treasury, 2008*c*.
55. Congressional Oversight Panel, 2009*a*.

56. These include the following: limitations on dividends and bonuses; pressure on banks to lend at less than commercial terms, to keep jobs of bank workers in the home country, to invest with an emphasis on the domestic economy, to replace managers, to give government a say in restructuring decisions; challenging tax-haven behaviour.
57. *Financial Times*, 2009a.

Chapter 6

1. Until December 2009.
2. More precisely: Australia (all deposits and those over a million if maturity less than five years); Austria (all deposits); Germany (household deposits); Hungary (deposits of small banks); Iceland (domestic deposits); Ireland (all deposits); Mongolia (all deposits); Slovenia (individuals and small enterprises).
3. According to New York Federal Reserve Bank figures.
4. Bernanke, 2011.
5. *The Times*, 2009.
6. i.e. financial institutions are insolvent even with the efficiently priced, self-fulfilling, public-good properties of guarantees in place.
7. See the 'Chief Executive's Foreword' of Asset Protection Agency (2010).
8. As UK's then City minister Lord Myners put it in September 2009. See BBC (2009b).
9. Assets should not already be backed by the GSEs, and must be secured directly by mortgages, leases, or other assets (i.e. not be synthetic), and have started life as AAA before 2009.
10. *Wall Street Journal*, 2009b.
11. *The Economist*, 2009d.
12. *New York Times*, 2009c.
13. Buiter, 2009a.
14. See Congressional Oversight Panel (2010b).
15. Bulow and Klemperer, 2009.
16. Ibid.; Hall and Woodward, 2009; Buiter, 2009b.
17. Congressional Oversight Panel, 2009b.
18. Congressional Oversight Panel, 2009d.
19. Bordo, Eichengreen, Klingebiel, and Martinez-Peria, 2001; Hoggarth, Ries, and Saporta, 2002; Roubini and Setser, 2004; Boyd, Kwak, and Smith, 2005; Honohan and Laeven, 2005.
20. It should be adjusted downwards to exclude any prior real-estate bubble that may have exaggerated the trend upwards.
21. Laeven and Valencia, 2008.
22. Laeven and Valencia, 2010.
23. Zingales, 2011. See also Veronesi and Zingales (2009).
24. Figures from Moneyfacts website.
25. US Treasury, 2009c.
26. Congressional Oversight Panel, 2010b.
27. Congressional Budget Office, 2010.
28. White House, 2009.

29. Indeed, money is fungible, so just the freeing up of funds via GSE-guaranteed MBS sales would do the trick. I don't believe Obama understood this, so his was an honest mistake.
30. Laeven and Valencia, 2008.
31. Ibid.
32. International Monetary Fund, 2009c.
33. International Monetary Fund, 2010b.
34. Laeven and Valencia, 2010.
35. Congressional Oversight Panel, 2010b, p. 4.
36. Haldane, 2010.
37. Moody's Investor Service, 2009.
38. Haldane, 2010. The figures are derived from a sample of 26 banks in 2007 and 28 banks in 2008 and 2009. All are year-end figures, ignoring subsidies on retail deposits, and so are 'no more than illustrative'.
39. Ibid.
40. Kotlikoff, 2010.
41. Haldane, 2010, p. 5.
42. *The Economist*, 2009b.
43. Hoshi and Kashyap, 2008.
44. Ibid.
45. Yorulmazer, 2009.
46. Plutarch *Life of Pyrrhus* 21: ἂν ἔτι μίαν μάχην Ῥωμσίομς νικήσωμεν, ἀπολούμεθα παντελῶς.

Chapter 7

1. *Financial Times*, 2011b.
2. Marco Annunziata, chief economist at UniCredit Group in a note regarding EU leaders' handling of the euro crisis.
3. *The Guardian*, 2008.
4. Reinhart and Reinhart, 2010.
5. Eichengreen and O'Rourke, 2010. It should be noted that they date the start of the current global recession to April 2008 and that of the Great Depression to June 1929.
6. Auboin, 2009.
7. Amiti and Weinstein, 2009a, 2009b; Chor and Manova, 2009; Iacovone and Zavacka, 2009.
8. Eichengreen and O'Rourke, 2010.
9. Auboin, 2009.
10. Eichengreen and O'Rourke, 2010.
11. Reinhart and Rogoff, 2009a, 2009b.
12. International Monetary Fund, 2009a, pp. 103–38.
13. The analysis covered various country and crisis characteristics including the depth and length of impact, degree of prior boom, macroeconomic vulnerabilities, policy responses, and external conditions after a crisis began.
14. Cecchetti, Kohler, and Upper, 2009.
15. Hoover (1952, p. 30), reflecting on the advice of his Treasury Secretary, Andrew Mellon.

16. These have to be removed to work out the real economic activity in which government is engaging.
17. Aizenman and Pasricha, 2011*a*, 2011*b*.
18. Bernanke, 2007*b*.
19. King, 2009*a*.
20. Speech in Phoenix, Arizona, 1 November 2010.
21. These are financial instruments issued by banks and backed by mortgages or public-sector loans.
22. Bank for International Settlement, 2011.
23. Ibid. The study looked at the average impact on gilts with outstanding maturities of five to 25 years.
24. King was speaking at the Treasury Select Committee Meeting of 25 October 2011.
25. Alessandri and Haldane, 2009.
26. Keynes, 1930.
27. Romer, 2009; Freidman and Schwartz, 1963.
28. Romer, 2009.
29 See, for example, Bernanke (1983) and Bernanke (2000).
30. For a developed economy, the US has a sizable rate of population growth, such that taking raw country-level figures without adjusting for population growth is misleading.
31. I base this on the US government's own revision, as of November 2011, of the peak-to-trough fall in US national output from 4.1% to 5.1%, a 24% revision upwards. The figures for the other countries may well also in time be adjusted, such is the challenge of trying to measure national output at a time of severe economic turmoil.
32. Reinhart and Rogoff, 2009*a*.
33. Ibid. (all at purchasing power parity).
34. Eichengreen and O'Rourke, 2010.
35. The VAT reduction would go also on goods and services being bought already, which would add to the deficit without adding to economic output (i.e. there would be a deadweight cost). If it applied to household durables, a chunk would go abroad. Less benefit would go to the poor (because necessities are not VAT-rated and the poor consume less), making it regressive at least within a range.
36. Why encourage the relatively more vulnerable and those with low asset holdings to take on debt and enter housing markets when prices are still falling, and levy a charge on other taxpayers for the pleasure of it all? Such schemes were asset price support mechanisms dressed up as social policy. Attached to new-build homes, as they were in the UK, they were a transfer from the average taxpayer to large home-builders, and heaped risk on buyers in the process. It was sadly fascinating to watch politicians brazenly present such schemes as somehow to the advantage of poor house-buyers. In the US anyone who took advantage of such schemes quickly lost out.
37. Eichengreen and O'Rourke, 2010.
38. Chor and Manova, 2009.
39. International Monetary Fund, 2011.
40. Speaking on *Meet the Press* on Sunday 1 August 2010.
41. Hayashi and Prescott, 2002.
42. Haugh, Ollivaud, and Turner, 2009.

43. Cerra and Saxena, 2008.
44. Furceri and Mourougane, 2009.
45. Speech to Joint Session of Congress, 8 September 2011.
46. The other case, of course, was the 1930s when banks also played a key role in feeding the initial boom. Japan too had experienced a huge swing of its private sector towards savings after its bubble had burst in the early 1990s.
47. OECD, 2010.
48. Summers, 2009.
49. McKinsey Global Institute, 2010*a*.
50. Farlow, 2005, p. 49.
51. Reinhart and Rogoff, 2009*b*. This covers the 'big five' developed-economy crises (Spain 1977, Norway 1987, Finland 1991, Sweden 1991, and Japan 1992) and three well-known emerging-market crises (the 1997–1998 Asian crisis (affecting Hong Kong, Indonesia, Malaysia, the Philippines, and Thailand), Colombia 1998, and Argentina 2001). In comparisons they also used two earlier crises (Norway 1899 and the United States 1929) for which housing data is available.
52. Wolf, 2010.
53. McKinsey Global Institute, 2010*b*.
54. International Monetary Fund, 2010*b*.
55. King was speaking at the Commons Treasury Committee on 1 March 2011.

Chapter 8

1. Well, the book goes to press before the process is fully through.
2. Congressional Oversight Panel, 2010*b*. Early foreclosure figures are given in Mayer, Pence, and Sherlund (2009).
3. All figures are from the S&P/Case-Shiller House Price Index and real (i.e. adjusted for inflation).
4. Yellen, 2009.
5. By December 2011, 50% of all subprime mortgages taken out in 2006 had defaulted.
6. According to IMF figures.
7. We must note, however, that average figures were being heavily distorted by price gyrations in London.
8. Remember that most of the stock of housing does not change hands in any given year, so a 10% price rise is caused by the few, 'at the margin', active over the year.
9. Broadbench, 2012.
10. Standard and Poor's, 2008.
11. In the spring of 2011 UK net new mortgage lending was less than a tenth what it had been in October 2006.
12. All figures are from the Council for Mortgage Lending.
13. Farlow, 2004*a*.
14. Prices also rose sharply in the high-end markets of places such as London (Knightsbridge, Belgravia, Mayfair), where property had become a global reserve currency of sorts for the elite of capital-rich economies.

15. See Mishkin (2007*b*) for a review of the role of housing and credit in the monetary transmission mechanism. See also Goodhart and Hofmann (2008) and Duca, Muellbauer, and Murphy (2010). Empirical work on the housing–consumption macroeconomic link include Catte, Girouard, Price, and André (2004), Case, Quigley, and Shiller (2005), Carroll, Otsuka, and Slacalek (2006), and Slacalek (2006).

16. Reinhart and Rogoff, 2008. These comprised (where the starting year is in parenthesis) the 'big five' crises in Spain (1977), Norway (1987), Finland (1991), Sweden (1991), and Japan (1992) and other banking and financial crises in Australia (1989), Canada (1983), Denmark (1987), France (1994), Germany (1977), Greece (1991), Iceland (1985), Italy (1990), New Zealand (1987), the United Kingdom (1973, 1991, 1995), and United States (1984).

17. Kaminsky and Reinhart, 1999.

18. Reinhart and Rogoff, 2009*a*, Section 10.8.

19. Stijn, Kose, and Terrones, 2008.

20. Leamer, 2007*a*, 2007*b*.

21. Reinhart and Rogoff, 2009*a*.

22. Kohn, 2009.

23. Bank of England Housing Equity Withdrawal (HEW) statistics.

24. Reinold, 2011.

25. Ibid., Chart 1.

26. According to the Office of the Comptroller of the Currency.

27. HAMP was part of an even bigger three-part package of measures totalling $275 billion, including to support the GSEs.

28. Figures that follow are from the Center for Public Integrity.

29. Foote, Gerardi, Goette, and Willen, 2009.

30. Cordell, Dynan, Lehnert, Liang, and Mauskopf, 2008.

31. Gerardi, Shapiro, and Willen, 2007; Hunt, 2009.

32. Foote, Gerardi, and Willen, 2008.

33. So as not to distort the figures, we presume that all pay 'rent', even if it means some pay rent to themselves.

34. I am not going to complicate the logic in the main text for the general reader by discussing the implications for securitized mortgages. When the mortgages are packaged up and securitized into residential MBSs, the mortgages remain the liabilities of homeowners. The MBSs are a liability of the Special Purpose Vehicle (SPV) that issues them, backed by the assets of the mortgages bought from the originator of the mortgages. The MBSs end up as assets of those who hold them, such as SIVs owned by other banks. A similar pattern of redistribution to that discussed in the main text goes on between those who hold and those who issue MBSs.

35. Again, if loans are securitized, banks lose consequent on the rise in expected defaults.

36. 'Lost' since this only measures equity as measured by market prices multiplied by the number of properties, and excludes gains to those low in housing assets.

37. Defaulters do, however, face an offsetting loss if their default affects their future creditworthiness and hence their future costs of borrowing. If house prices have fallen a long way and there is safety in numbers from bailing out of a collectively-induced crash, at some level of price fall homeowners regard this offsetting cost as being worth it.

38. Incidentally, if one tries to evaluate the impact on the real economy of the collapse in the value of assets held by banks and shadow banks, one also needs to factor in the fall in the burden of the liabilities on households and not just the financial hit on the banks.
39. Farlow, 2005.
40. Bernanke, 2009a.
41. They might find they lose flexibility, but some market would arise for trading in these instruments.
42. Shiller, 1993.
43. Farlow, 2005.
44. Her actual language is not clear. See *Wall Street Journal* (2010).
45. Bernanke, 2008.
46. Ibid.
47. Mishkin, 2007a.
48. *Wall Street Journal*, 2011a.
49. See Crockett (2000a) and Kiyotaki and Moore (1997).
50. Borio and White, 2003; Bank for International Settlement, 2003, Chapter VIII.
51. Bank for International Settlement, 2005, p. 141.
52. Blanchard, Dell'Ariccia, and Mauro, 2010.
53. Mishkin, 2007a.
54. Galbraith, 1954. p. 70.
55. Lawrence, 1929, p. 179.
56. Farlow, 2004a.
57. Blanchflower, 2009.
58. See Bernanke and Gertler (2001), Greenspan (2002a), Bean (2003, 2004), and Mishkin (2007a).
59. Bordo and Jeanne, 2002; Borio and Lowe, 2002; Cecchetti, Genberg, Lipsky, and Wadhwani, 2000.
60. The arguments are in Cecchetti et al. (2000).
61. Goodhart and Hofmann, 2008. See also Goodhart and Hofmann (2007, Chapters 9 and 10).
62. Solow, 2008.
63. Miller and Stiglitz, 2009.

Chapter 9

1. Farlow, 2005.
2. Quoted in the *Wall Street Journal*, 25 February 1993.
3. The infinite regress argument based on turtles, as a way to explain the existence of the universe, was popularised by Stephen Hawking in his classic 1988 book 'A Brief History of Time'. The argument has its economic counterpart. See Hawking (1988).
4. See Morris and Shin (1999).
5. Backwards induction is a process of backwards reasoning. Facing a decision problem taking place over time, the optimal response at the last time a decision has to be made is used to work out the optimal response at the penultimate time a decision has to be made, and so on back to the first time a decision has to be made.
6. US Treasury, 2010.

7. US Treasury, 2011.
8. *The Economist*, 2009c.
9. Romer, 2009.
10. Dickens, 1849. The words are spoken by Wilkins Micawber (the line is to be found on p. 253 of the 1863 edition).
11. Farlow, 2003.
12. US Treasury, 2008a. See Chart 1: OASDI Beneficiaries per 100 Covered Workers 1970–2082, p. 122.
13. Ibid.
14. Meeker, 2011.
15. Washington Post, 2004, p. A11.
16. OECD, 2011a. See Table A.
17. International Monetary Fund, 2010a, p. 24, Table 5a.
18. *Washington Examiner*, 2011.
19. This first appeared in a *National Journal* magazine interview in late October 2010, and was subsequently repeatedly defended in television interviews.
20. BBC, 2011.
21. The non-partisan Committee for Responsible Budget argued the plan would cut nearer to $2.5 trillion, and other estimates put it at $3 trillion.
22. Standard and Poor's, 2011.
23. *Financial Times*, 2011d.
24. Office for Budget Responsibility, 2010.
25. Interviewed on the BBC's *Politics Show* on 30 January 2011.
26. Actually, it might better be called the 'Barro equivalence theorem'. See Barro (1974, 1979, 1989).
27. Announcing his spending review in Parliament on 20 October 2010.
28. BBC, 2011.
29. Guajardo, Leigh, and Pescatori, 2011.
30. Ball, Leigh, and Loungani, 2011.
31. Keynes, 1930.
32. Fitch, 2011.
33. This was extensively quoted. See Bloomberg News (2011a).
34. Krugman and Wells, 2010.
35. International Monetary Fund, 2012.

Chapter 10

1. See, for example, CNBC (2012).
2. *Sunday Times*, 2009.
3. Subsequently, attempts were made to pull the date forward. The ESM finally settled on a start date of 8 October 2012, and there was a period of overlap with the EFSF. However, at the end of 2012 it was still unclear as to when, and on what terms, the ESM would perform key functions, such as the recapitalization of banks. In the main text I stick to 2013 because that was the understanding at the time.

4. *Daily Telegraph*, 2010c.
5. Cottarelli, Forni, Gottschalk, and Mauro, 2010.
6. Chamley and Pinto, 2011.
7. Even then, a doubling or trebling in size would not have the same power as a central bank, able to guarantee that sovereign debt obligations would always be met.
8. See Corsetti, Guimarães, and Roubini (2006) and Morris and Shin (2006).
9. Taken from OECD Statistical Extracts.
10. Based on OECD figures.
11. Calvo, Izquierdo, and Mejia, 2004.
12. Based on Bank of England figures.
13. Although export and private-sector investment response was nevertheless still very weak.
14. *Financial Times*, 2011c.
15. Eurostat figures, 26 April 2011.
16. *Financial Times*, 2011f.
17. Roubini, 2010.
18. Borensztein and Mauro, 2002.
19. *Wall Street Journal*, 2011b.
20. Peterson Institute for International Economics, 2011.
21. At a Town Hall meeting in Mountain View, California, 26 September 2011.
22. Senior banking figures quickly made it clear that they had not been consulted and argued that Cameron's intervention was likely to backfire. They wished to be in and shaping a core financial union, and Cameron, in a case of ill-thought through diplomacy, had just thrown away their seat at the negotiation table.
23. Standard & Poor's, 2012.
24. Reuters, 2011.
25. Fitch Ratings, 'Fitch Downgrades Spain to "BBB"; Outlook Negative', 7 June 2012.
26. Or as Tacitus put it: 'solitudinem faciunt, pacem appellant'. Tacitus *Agricola* 30.
27. Commission of the European Communities, 1993.
28. De Grauwe, 2011.
29. Actually, sometimes Merkel hinted that she understood that eurobonds might have a role in the long run but that they were not a solution to the crisis.
30. Spiegel Online, 2011.

Chapter 11

1. Japan was a persistent balance of payments surplus country but was an exception because it was working off its past problems.
2. Farlow, 2005.
3. Ibid. 'If eventual adjustment to a more stable world balance sheet is too rapid or disorganized, the risk is that [China] will be too dependent on tradables, and unable to switch smoothly and rapidly enough to domestically-generated demand (and, observe that this would be taking place at the same time as the US would be reorientating itself away from consumption towards export).'

4. Even if a country is more efficient at producing everything than another country (i.e. it has an absolute advantage), the other country will still have a comparative advantage in something. It is relative, and not absolute efficiencies, that drive countries' comparative advantages. Both countries will benefit from trading with each other.
5. See Krugman (1994).
6. This, of course, might have good side effects if the recipients are deflating.
7. Trimmed to 20% in December 2011 as worries shifted to growth and not inflation.
8. Reuters, 2010 (quoting Jeffrey Bader, senior National Security Council official for Asia, describing the discussion between Obama and Chinese premier Wen Jiabao).
9. *Financial Times*, 2010a.
10. Ostry, Ghosh, Habermeier, Chamon, Qureshi, and Reinhardt, 2010.
11. Quoted in the *Financial Times* (2011a).
12. Magud, Reinhart, and Rogoff, 2011.
13. Eichengreen, 2009.
14. Eichengreen, Park, and Shin, 2011.
15. Remember that this uses a PPP measure and is also the average figure for a whole country.
16. Farlow, 2005.
17. Hannoun, 2009.
18. As I discovered on one of my trips back to the UK while writing this book.
19. Which may of course be owned by domestic residents such that this is a redistribution issue.
20. Of course, if voters understand that their pension funds hold foreign sovereign debt that might suffer the same fate, they will be less sympathetic to inflation.
21. *Financial Times*, 2009c.
22. Gross, 2009.

Chapter 12

1. *New York Times*, 1999.
2. Kane, 2000; Wilmarth, 2002.
3. Shull and Hanweck, 2002.
4. Barth et al., 2000.
5. Based on the value of the instruments underlying the contracts.
6. *Financial Times*, 1998.
7. The US is not the only country where politics shapes regulation. A good treatment of this phenomenon can be found in Barth, Caprio, and Levine (2008).
8. Schmitt, 2009.
9. Ibid.
10. *New York Times*, 2009a.
11. Citigroup, 2009.
12. Hirsh, 2009.
13. Ibid.
14. Ibid.
15. John F. Kennedy Presidential Library and Museum, 2009.
16. Speaking on *The Greenspan Years*, BBC Radio 4 programme broadcast 2 January 2006.

17. Brown, 2005.
18. HM Treasury, 2005.
19. BBC, 2009*a*.
20. HM Treasury, 2007.
21. King, 2009*a*.
22. McKinsey and Company, 2007; US Chamber of Commerce, 2007.
23. *New York Times*, 2008.
24. Brown, 2010*a*.
25. Ibid.
26. According to Simon & Schuster's promotional material for *Beyond the Crash*.
27. White House Office of the Press Secretary, 2010.
28. To name just a few: Acharya and Richardson, 2009; Financial Services Authority, 2009*a*; International Monetary Fund, 2009*a* (especially regarding early warning systems); Group of Thirty, 2009; Brunnermeier, Crocket, Goodhart, Persaud, and Shin, 2009; HM Treasury, 2009*b*; US Treasury, 2008*b*; US Treasury, 2009*a*; de Larosière, Balcerowicz, Issing, Masera, McCarthy, Nyberg, Pérez, and Ruding, 2009; Warwick Commission, 2009.
29. Persaud, 2010.
30. *New York Times*, 2009*d*.
31. Via the 'principal investments' get-out clause, that allowed banks to spin off their prop desks but retain most 'principal investments' (longer-term investments in property or companies).
32. Independent Commission on Banking, 2011.
33. Herring and Santomero, 2000; Santos, 2001; Freixas and Santomero, 2004.
34. For the regulation as a substitute for monitoring, see Dewatripont and Tirole (1994).
35. Allen and Gale, 2007, p. 191.
36. Basel Committee on Banking Supervision, 2010*b*.
37. Given the unequal impact of a crash, some extra weighting might be put on the welfare harm to the unemployed and savers.
38. Mehra and Prescott, 1985.
39. Barro, 2006.
40. See Modigliani and Miller (1958) for the underlying logic.
41. *Financial Times*, 2010*b*.
42. All of these were based on 'stricter criteria' and had 'stricter adjustments'.
43. Kashyap, Raghuram, and Stein, 2008; Tucker, 2009; Coval, Jurek, and Stafford, 2008.
44. Acharya, Pedersen, Philippon, and Richardson, 2009.
45. There might be ways around this, such as giving shareholders pre-emptive rights at a conversion price.
46. To avert this, perhaps some sort of hybrid system might be developed, with a small private-insurance component to achieve price discovery of the state of systemic risk, topped up by public capital.
47. Bank for International Settlement, 2010*c*. This followed on from the earlier BIS statement of principles for sound liquidity (Bank for International Settlement, 2008*b*).
48. The FSA and others were working on various stress tests too.
49. Bank of England, 2008.
50. Financial Services Authority, 2009*b*.
51. Kotlikoff, Mehrling, and Milne, 2008.

52. Ranked by tier-one capital. See Haldane (2010).
53. Alessandri and Haldane, 2009.
54. Wilmarth, 2009.
55. Schumpeter, 1942.
56. Saunders, 1996; Berger and Mester, 1997; Amel, Barnes, Panetta, and Salleo, 2004.
57. Berger and Humphrey, 1997.
58. DeLong, 2001.
59. Stiroh and Rumble, 2006.
60. Laeven and Levine, 2007; Schmid and Walter, 2009.
61. Stiglitz, 2009.
62. House Financial Services Committee, 2009.
63. King, 2009*b*.
64. According to the company's 2008 SEC filings.
65. Alessandri and Haldane, 2009.
66. As if to prove the point, when J.P. Morgan confessed in May 2012 to a \$2 billion loss caused by its London traders, it took weeks for the bank's managers to understand the complex trade and quantify the loss, and regulators could not work out whether the loss was the result of trading that would be allowed by the Volcker rule or not.
67. Or rather, it would trade an ongoing extra cost of £3–4 billion per year against an occasional large cost that averaged £3–4 billion per year.
68. Financial Services Authority, 2011.
69. Bank for International Settlement, 1986.
70. Crockett, 2000*b*.
71. Borio, Furfine, and Lowe, 2001; Borio, 2003; White, 2006; Borio and Drehmann, 2008.
72. Knight, 2006; Mayes, Pringle, and Taylor, 2009.
73. Bank for International Settlement, 2008*a*.
74. An early paper would be Evans, Leone, Gill, and Hilbers (2000).
75. Two notable early examples are Cecchetti, Genberg, Lipsky, and Wadhwani (2000) and Danielson, Ermbrechts, Goodhart, Keating, Muenich, Renault, and Shin (2001). And from a few years later, see also Goodhart, Hofmann, and Segovino (2004), Goodhart and Segovino (2004), Goodhart and Taylor (2007), and Goodhart and Schoenmaker (2006).
76. King, 2009*a*.
77. Bank for International Settlement, 2009, Section I, p. 12.
78. Adrian and Brunnermeier, 2008.
79. International Monetary Fund, 2009*b*, Executive Summary, p. xxiii.
80. This is nicely explained in Blanchflower (2009).
81. Ibid.
82. US Treasury, 2009*b*.
83. Bank for International Settlement, 2010*a*.
84. Turner, 2009.
85. Beltratti and Stulz, 2009. This analysis is made possible by the fact that there was significant variation in the cross-section of stock returns of large banks across the world during this period.

86. In the UK, the Walker Review (HM Treasury, 2009*a*) into the governance of banks recommended that chief risk officers have board-level positions. Some companies have moved in this direction.

87. Such as in mark-to-market valuation of assets, price volatility in market-risk models, credit spreads in credit-risk models, credit ratings, and so forth.

88. This has long been known. The Cross Report found that new financial instruments seemed to be underpriced because of lack of history and understanding of systemic risk. See Eurocurrency Standing Committee (2006).

89. However, this might also help banks arrange their credit structures to maximize ratings.

90. Centre for Responsive Politics.

91. Since announcements of sales can move market prices in instances when the trade in instruments is large relative to the market for those instruments, transparency should not be pre-trade.

92. Fitzgerald and Harper, 2009 (quoting Tony Fratto, a spokesman for President George W. Bush and former Treasury Secretary Henry M. Paulson).

93. HM Treasury, 2005.

94. Benediktsdottir, Danielsson, and Zoega, 2011.

95. As Goodhart (2009) has put it.

96. The Warwick Commission (2009) is good on this point. For example, the new Basel III 'liquidity coverage ratio' requires countries to hold high-quality corporate and government bonds, assets that are easy to sell in a market crisis but in short supply in poor countries. Western banks can buy CDSs to reduce the Basel III measurement of counterparty risk, an option that is not available in poor countries.

97. Goodhart and Schoenmaker, 2009.

98. For an early treatment of the issue, see International Monetary Fund (2002, especially Chapter 4). See also de Larosière et al. (2009).

99. Schneider, 2010.

100. *Financial Times*, 2011*e*.

101. White, 1997.

102. Quoted in University of Rochester (2008).

Closing Thoughts

1. *Daily Telegraph*, 2008.

2. *The Observer*, 2009.

3. International Monetary Fund, 2002.

4. All the quotes below are from International Monetary Fund (2002).

5. Greenspan, 2002*b*.

6. OECD, 2011*b*.

BIBLIOGRAPHY

Abraham, J. and P. Hendershott. 1996. 'Bubbles in Metropolitan Housing Markets'. *Journal of Housing Research* 7(2): 191–207.

Acharya, V., L. Pedersen, T. Philippon, and M. Richardson. 2009. 'Regulating Systemic Risk'. NYU-Stern Report, Chapter 13.

—— and M. Richardson (eds.). 2009. *Restoring Financial Stability: How to Repair a Failed System*. New York: Wiley Finance.

Adrian, T. and M. K. Brunnermeier. 2008. 'CoVaR'. Federal Reserve Bank of New York Staff Reports 348 (revised September 2011).

Ahearne, A., J. Gagnon, J. Haltmaier, S. Kamin, et al. 2002. 'Preventing Deflation: Lessons from Japan's Experience in the 1990s'. International Finance Discussion Papers 72. Washington: Board of Governors of the Federal Reserve System.

Aizenman, J. and G. K. Pasricha. 2011a. 'The Net Fiscal Expenditure Stimulus in the U.S. 2008–2009: Less than What You Might think, and Less than the Fiscal Stimuli of Most OECD Countries'. *The Economists' Voice*, June.

—— —— 2011b. 'Net Fiscal Stimulus During the Great Recession'. NBER Working paper 16779.

Akerlof, G. A. 1970. 'The Market for "Lemons": Quality Uncertainty and the Market Mechanism'. *Quarterly Journal of Economics* 84(3): 488–500.

Alessandri, P. and A. G. Haldane. 2009. 'Banking on the State'. Federal Reserve Bank of Chicago twelfth annual International Banking Conference on 'The International Financial Crisis: Have the Rules of Finance Changed?' 25 September.

Allen, F. and D. Gale. 2007. *Understanding Financial Crises (Clarendon Lectures in Finance)*. Oxford: Oxford University Press.

Amel, D., C. Barnes, F. Panetta, and C. Salleo. 2004. 'Consolidation and Efficiency in the Financial Sector: A Review of the International Evidence'. *Journal of Banking & Finance* 28(10): 2493–519.

Amiti, M. and D. Weinstein. 2009a. 'Exports and Financial Shocks'. Columbia University mimeo.

—— —— 2009b. 'Exports and Financial Shocks: New Evidence from Japan'. *Vox*, 23 December.

Aron, J., J. V. Duca, J. Muellbauer, K. Murata, and A. Anthony. 2012. 'Credit, Housing Collateral, and Consumption: Evidence from Japan, the UK, and the US'. *Review of Income and Wealth* 58(3): 397–423.

—— and J. Muellbauer. 2006. 'Housing Wealth, Credit Conditions and Consumption'. CSAE Working Paper 2006–08.

Ashcraft, A. B. and Y. Schuermann. 2008. 'The Seven Deadly Frictions of Subprime Mortgage Credit Securitization'. *The Investment Professional*, Fall issue: 2–11.

Asset Protection Agency. 2010. 'Annual Report and Accounts 2009–10 of the Asset Protection Agency'.

Atkinson, A. B. and S. Morelli. 2011. 'Economic Crises and Inequality'. Human Development Research Paper, Nuffield College, Oxford.

Attanasio, O., G. Weber, L. Blow, R. Hamilton, and A. Leicester. 2005. 'Booms and Busts: Consumption, House Prices and Expectations'. Institute for Fiscal Studies, Working Paper 05/24, London.

Auboin, M. 2009. 'Boosting the Availability of Trade Finance in the Current Crisis: Background Analysis for a Substantial G20 Package'. Centre for Economic Policy Research, Policy Insight, No. 35.

Avery, R. B., K. P. Brevoort, and G. B. Canner. 2007. 'The 2006 HMDA Data'. *Federal Reserve Bulletin* 93(December): 73–109.

Bagehot, W. [1873] 1908. *Lombard Street: A Description of the Money Market*. London: Kegan Paul, Trench, Trubner.

Ball, L., D. Leigh, and P. Loungani. 2011. 'Painful Medicine'. IMF. Finance & Development, Vol. 48, No. 3. September.

The Banker. 2003. 'Sir John Bond Lays Bare HSBC's Strategy for Gaining Ground'. 6 October.

Bank for International Settlement. 1986. 'Recent Innovations in International Banking'. Report prepared by a study group established by the central banks of the Group of Ten countries. April.

—— 2003. 73rd Annual Report.

—— 2004. 74th Annual Report.

—— 2005. 75th Annual Report.

—— 2008a. 'Addressing Financial System Procyclicality: A Possible Framework'. Note for the FSF Working Group on Market and Institutional Resilience, 1 September.

—— 2008b. 'Principles for Sound Liquidity Risk Management and Supervision', September.

—— 2009. 79th Annual Report.

—— 2010a. 'Basel III: A Global Regulatory Framework for More Resilient Banks and Banking Systems'. Report of Basel Committee on Banking Supervision (revised June 2011).

—— 2010b. 'An Assessment of the Long-Term Economic Impact of the New Regulatory Framework'. Report of Basel Committee on Banking Supervision.

—— 2010c. 'Basel III: International Framework for Liquidity Risk Measurement, Standards and Monitoring', December.

—— 2011. Quarterly Review, December.

Bank of England. 2007. 'Markets and Operations'. *Bank of England Quarterly Bulletin* 47(3): 346–61.

—— 2008. 'The Development of the Bank of England's Market Operations: A Consultative Paper by the Bank of England'.

Barker, K. 2004. 'Review of Housing Supply'. HM Treasury.

Barrett, W. 2008. 'How Andrew Cuomo Gave Birth to the Crisis at Fannie Mae and Freddie Mac'. *Village Voice*, 5 August.

Barro, R. J. 1974. 'Are Government Bonds Net Wealth?' *Journal of Political Economy* 82(6): 1095–1117.

—— 1979. 'On the Determination of the Public Debt'. *Journal of Political Economy* 87(5): 940–71.

—— 1989. 'The Ricardian Approach to Budget Deficits'. *Journal of Economic Perspectives* 3(2): 37–54.

—— 2006. 'Rare Disasters and Asset Markets in the Twentieth Century'. *Quarterly Journal of Economics* 121(3): 823–66.

Barth, J. R., R. D. Brumbaugh Jr, and J. A. Wilcox. 2000. 'Policy Watch: The Repeal of Glass-Steagall and the Advent of Broad Banking'. *Journal of Economic Perspectives* 14(2): 191–204.

—— G. Caprio, and R. Levine. 2008. *Rethinking Bank Regulation: Till Angels Govern.* Cambridge, New York, and Sydney: Cambridge University Press.

BBC. 2009*a*. 'Huge Crisis, Huge Causes', 17 September.

—— 2009*b*. 'Head of Toxic Asset Team Named', 25 September.

—— 2010. 'Ghost Estates Testify to Irish Boom and Bust', 30 April.

—— 2011. 'Obama Visit to UK: Leaders Admit Deficit Differences'. 25 May.

Bean, C. 2003. 'Asset Prices, Financial Imbalances and Monetary Policy: Are Inflation Targets Enough?' In A. Richards and T. Robinson (eds.) *Asset Prices and Monetary Policy*. Reserve Bank of Australia, Conference Proceedings.

—— 2004. 'Asset Prices, Financial Instability, and Monetary Policy'. *American Economic Review* 94(2): 14–18.

—— 2008. 'Some Lessons for Monetary Policy from the Recent Financial Turmoil'. Remarks at Conference on Globalisation, Inflation and Monetary Policy, Istanbul, 22 November.

Bebchuk, L. A., A. Cohen, and H. Spamann. 2010. 'The Wages of Failure: Executive Compensation at Bear Stearns and Lehman 2000–2008'. *Yale Journal on Regulation* 27: 257–82.

Beltratti, A. and R. M. Stulz. 2009. 'Why Did Some Banks Perform Better during the Credit Crisis? A Cross-Country Study of the Impact of Governance and Regulation'. NBER Working Paper 15180.

Benediktsdottir, S., J. Danielsson, and G. Zoega. 2011. 'Lessons for a Collapse of a Financial System'. *Economic Policy* 66(April): 183–231.

Benito A., J. Thompson, M. Waldron, and R. Wood. 2006. 'House Prices and Consumer Spending'. *Bank of England Quarterly Bulletin* 46(2): 142–54.

Berger, A. N. and D. Humphrey. 1997. 'Efficiency of Financial Institutions: International Survey and Directions for Future Research'. *European Journal of Operational Research* 98: 175–212.

—— and L. J. Mester. 1997. 'Inside the Black Box: What Explains Differences in the Efficiencies of Financial Institutions?' *Journal of Banking & Finance* 21(7): 895–947.

Bernanke, B. S. 1983. 'Nonmonetary Effects of the Financial Crisis in the Propagation of the Great Depression'. *American Economic Review* 73(3): 257–76.

—— 2000. *Essays on the Great Depression*. Princeton, NJ: Princeton University Press.

—— 2004. 'The Great Moderation'. Remarks by Governor Ben S. Bernanke at the meeting of the Eastern Economic Association, Washington, DC, 20 February.

—— 2005a. 'The Global Saving Glut and the US Current Account Deficit'. Homer Jones Lecture, St Louis, 14 April.

—— 2005b. 'The Economic Outlook'. Testimony before the Joint Economic Committee, 20 October.

—— 2007a. 'The Subprime Mortgage Market'. Speech at the Federal Reserve Bank of Chicago's 43rd Annual Conference on Bank Structure and Competition, Chicago, 17 May.

—— 2007b. 'The Recent Financial Turmoil and its Economic and Policy Consequences'. Speech at the Economic Club of New York, 15 October.

—— 2008. Speech at the UC Berkeley/UCLA symposium 'The Mortgage Meltdown, the Economy, and Public Policy', Berkeley, CA, 31 October.

—— 2009a. 'The Future of Mortgage Finance in the United States'. *The B.E. Journal of Economic Analysis & Policy* 9(3), Article 2.

—— 2009b. Testimony to House Ways and Means Committee, 3 March.

—— 2011. Letter to the Committee on Banking, Housing and Urban Affairs, 6 December.

—— and M. Gertler M. 2001. 'Should Central Banks Respond to Movements in Asset Prices?' *American Economic Review* 91(2): 253–7.

—— V. R. Reinhart, and B. P. Sack. 2004. 'Monetary Policy Alternatives at the Zero Bound: An Empirical Assessment'. *Brookings Papers on Economic Activity* 2004(2): 1–78.

Besanko, D. and G. Kanatas. 1996. 'The Regulation of Bank Capital: Do Capital Standards Promote Bank Safety?' *Journal of Financial Intermediation* 5: 160–83.

Blanchard, O., G. Dell'Ariccia, and P. Mauro. 2010. 'Rethinking Macroeconomic Policy'. IMF Research Department.

—— and J. Simon. 2001. 'The Long and Large Decline in U.S. Output Volatility'. *Brookings Papers on Economic Activity* 2001(1): 135–64.

Blanchflower, D. 2009. 'The Future of Monetary Policy'. Open Lecture, Cardiff University, 24 March.

Bloomberg News. 2011a. 'Cameron Says Reducing Debt Is Proving Harder Than Envisaged', 21 November.

—— 2011b. 'Secret Fed Loans Gave Banks $13bn Undisclosed to Congress', 28 November.

Blundell-Wignall A. 2007. 'Structured Products: Implications for Financial Markets'. *OECD Financial Market Trends* 93(2): 27–57.

—— and P. Atkinson. 2008. 'The Subprime Crisis: Causal Distortions and Regulatory Reform'. In *Lessons from the Financial Turmoil of 2007 and 2008*. Reserve Bank of Australia Conference, July.

Bordo, M., B. Eichengreen, D. Klingebiel, and M. Martinez-Peria. 2001. 'Is the Crisis Problem Growing More Severe?' *Economic Policy* 16: 53–82.

—— and O. Jeanne. 2002. 'Monetary Policy and Asset Prices: Does Benign Neglect Make Sense?' *International Finance* 5(2): 139–64.

Borensztein, B. and P. Mauro. 2002. 'Reviving the Case for GDP-Indexed Bonds'. IMF Policy Discussion Paper 02/10.

Borio, C. 2003. 'Towards a Macroprudential Framework for Financial Supervision and Regulation?' *CESifo Economic Studies* 49(2): 181–216.

—— and M. Drehmann. 2008. 'Towards an Operational Framework for Financial Stability "Fuzzy" Measurement and its Consequences'. 12th Annual Conference of the Banco Central de Chile, 'Financial Stability, Monetary Policy and Central Banking', Santiago, 6–7 November.

—— C. Furfine, and P. Lowe. 2001. 'Procyclicality of the Financial System and Financial Stability Issues and Policy Options'. In *Marrying the Macro- and Micro-prudential Dimensions of Financial Stability*', BIS Papers, No. 1, pp. 1–57.

—— and P. Lowe. 2002. 'Asset Prices, Financial and Monetary Stability: Exploring the Nexus'. BIS, Working Paper, No. 114.

—— and W. White. 2003. 'Whither Monetary and Financial Stability? The Implications of Evolving Policy Regimes'. Paper presented to the symposium 'Monetary policy and uncertainty: adapting to a changing economy', Jackson Hole, WY, 28–30 August.

Boston Globe. 2009. 'HSBC Ends US Subpime Lending'. 3 March.

Boyd, J., S. Kwak, and B. Smith. 2005. 'The Real Output Losses Associated with Modern Banking Crises'. *Journal of Money, Credit, and Banking* 37: 977–99.

Brecht, B. 1928. *The Threepenny Opera*. Penguin Classics.

Brenner, R. 2006. *The Economics of Global Turbulence; the Advanced Capitalist Economies from Long Boom to Long Downturn, 1945–2005*. New York: Verso.

Broadbent, B. 2012. 'Deleveraging'. Bank of England. Speech at Market News International, London, 15 March.

Brown, G. 2005. Budget speech to Parliament, 16 March.

—— 2007. Speech to Mansion House, 20 June.

—— 2010a. *Beyond the Crash: Overcoming the First Crisis of Global Capitalism*. Simon & Schuster UK Ltd.

—— 2010b. 'Chronic Recklessness Powered by Unchecked Greed'. Book extract published in *The Guardian*, 7 December.

Brunnermeier, M. K. 2009. 'Deciphering the Liquidity and Credit Crunch 2007–2008'. *Journal of Economic Perspectives* 23(1): 77–100.

—— A. Crocket, C. Goodhart, A. Persaud, and H. S. Shin. 2009. *The Fundamental Principles of Financial Regulation*. Geneva Report on the World Economy, 11. Geneva: CEPR.

—— and C. Julliard. 2007. 'Money Illusion and Housing Frenzies'. *Review of Financial Studies* 21(1): 135–80.

—— and M. Oehmke. 2012. 'The Maturity Rat Race'. *Journal of Finance* (forthcoming).

—— and L. H. Pedersen. 2009. 'Market Liquidity and Funding Liquidity'. *Review of Financial Studies* 22(6): 2201–38.

Bucks, B. K., A. B. Kennickell, and K. B. Moore. 2006. 'Recent Changes in U.S. Family Finances: Evidence from the 2001 and 2004 Survey of Consumer Finances'. *Federal Reserve Bulletin* 92(1): A1–A38.

Buiter, W. 2008. 'Lessons from Northern Rock: Banking and Shadow Banking'. *Vox*, 4 March.

—— 2009a. 'The New Toxic and Bad Legacy Assets Programs of the US Treasury: Surreptitiously Squeezing the Tax-Payer until the PPIPS Squeak'. FT blog posting, 4 March.

—— 2009b. 'Good Bank vs Bad Bank: Don't Touch the Unsecured Creditors! Clobber the Tax Payer Instead. Not.' *Vox*, 14 March.

Bulow, J. and P. Klemperer. 2009. 'Reorganising the Banks: Focus on the Liabilities, Not the Assets'. *Vox*, 21 March.

Business Insider. 2009. 'Don't Just Blame The Bankers', 7 April.

Caballero, R. J., E. Farhi, and P. Gourinchas. 2008. 'An Equilibrium Model of "Global Imbalances" and Low Interest Rates'. *American Economic Review* 98(1): 358–93.

—— and A. Krishnamurthy. 2008. 'Collective Risk Management in a Flight to Quality Episode'. *Journal of Finance* 63(5): 2195–230.

Cagan, C. L. 2007. 'Mortgage Payment Reset: The Issue and the Impact'. First American Core Logic White Paper. March.

Calverley, J. 2004. *Bubbles and How to Survive Them*. London: Nicholas Brealey Publishing.

Calvo, G. A., A. Izquierdo, and L-F. Mejia. 2004. 'On the Empirics of Sudden Stops: The Relevance of Balance-Sheet Effects'. NBER Working Paper 10520.

Carroll C. D., M. Otsuka, and J. Slacalek. 2006. 'How Large Is the Housing Wealth Effect? A New Approach'. Economics Working Paper 535, Johns Hopkins University.

Case, K. E., J. M. Quigley, and R. J. Shiller. 2005. 'Comparing Wealth Effects: The Stock Market versus the Housing Market'. *Advances in Macroeconomics* 5(1). Article 1.

—— R. J. Shiller. 1988. 'The Behaviour of Home Buyers in Boom and Post-Boom Markets'. *New England Economic Review* (November/December): 29–46.

Catte, P., N. Girouard, R. Price, and C. André. 2004. 'Housing Markets, Wealth and the Business Cycle'. Working Paper 394, Economics Department, Paris, Organization for Economic Cooperation and Development.

Cecchetti, S. G., H. Genberg, J. Lipsky, and S. Wadhwani. 2000. *Asset Prices and Central Bank Policy*, Geneva Reports on the World Economy 2. Geneva: International Centre for Monetary and Banking Studies and Centre for Economic Policy Research.

—— M. Kohler, and C. Upper. 2009. 'Financial Crises and Economic Activity'. Paper presented at the symposium on financial stability and macroeconomic policy organized by the Federal Reserve Bank of Kansas City, Jackson Hole, WY, 20–21 August.

The Center for Public Integrity. 2009. 'Who's Behind the Financial Metldown, the Top Ten Subprime Lenders and Their Wall Street Backers.'

Cerra, V. and S. Saxena. 2008. 'Growth Dynamics: the Myth of Economic Recovery'. *American Economic Review* 98(1): 439–57.

Chamley, C. P. and B. Pinto. 2011. 'Why Official Bailouts Tend Not To Work: An Example Motivated by Greece 2010'. *The Economists' Voice* 8(1).

Chapman, P. 2010. *The Last of the Imperious Rich: Lehman Brothers, 1844–2008*. New York: Portfolio/Penguin.

Chor, D. and K. Manova. 2009. 'Off the Cliff and Back? Credit Conditions and International Trade during the Global Financial Crisis'. Stanford University mimeo.

Citigroup. 2009. 'Robert E. Rubin Announces His Retirement from Citi'. Press release, 9 February.

Claessens, S., G. Dell'Ariccia, D. Igan, and L. Laeven. 2010. 'Cross-Country Experiences and Policy Implications from the Global Financial Crisis'. *Economic Policy* 62: 267–93.

CNBC. 2012. 'Europe's Core Begins to Look Like the Periphery', 14 August.

Collins, S. M. and B. P. Bosworth. 1996. 'Economic Growth in East Asia: Accumulation Versus Assimilation'. *Brookings Papers on Economic Activity* 1996(2): 135–91.

Commission of the European Communities. 1993. 'Stable Money—Sound Finances'. Eurozone Economy, No. 53, Report of an independent group of economists.

Committee on the Global Financial System. 2006. 'Housing Finance in the Global Financial Market'. CGFS Publications, No. 26.

Congleton, R. 2009. 'On the Political Economy of the Financial Crisis and Bailout of 2008–2009'. *Public Choice* 140: 287–317.

Congressional Budget Office. 2010. 'Budgetary Treatment of Fannie Mae and Freddie Mac'. Background paper, 14 January.

Congressional Oversight Panel. 2009*a*. February Oversight Report: Valuing Treasury's Acquisitions.

—— 2009*b*. Congressional Oversight Report, April.

—— 2009*c*. 'Taking Stock: Independent Views on TARP's Effectiveness'. Transcript of hearing, 19 November.

—— 2009*d*. Congressional Oversight Report, December.

—— 2010*a*. Congressional Oversight Report, June Report.

—— 2010*b*. 'Assessing the TARP on the Eve of Its Expiration'. Congressional Oversight Report, September.

Cordell, L., K. Dynan, O. A. Lehnert, N. Liang, and E. Mauskopf. 2008. 'The Incentives of Mortgage Servicers: Myths and Realities'. Finance and Economics Discussion Series, Federal Reserve Board No. 46.

Corsetti, G., B. Guimarães, and N. Roubini. 2006. 'International Lending of Last Resort and Moral Hazard: A Model of the IMF's Catalytic Finance'. *Journal of Monetary Economics* 53(3): 441–71.

Cottarelli, C., L. Forni, J. Gottschalk, and P. Mauro. 2010. 'Default in Today's Advanced Economies: Unnecessary, Undesirable, and Unlikely'. IMF, Fiscal Affairs Department.

Coval, J. D., J. W. Jurek, and E. Stafford. 2008. 'Economic Catastrophe Bonds'. Harvard University mimeo.

—— —— —— 2009. 'The Economics of Structured Finance'. *Journal of Economic Perspectives* 23(1): 3–25.

Crafts, N. 1999. 'East Asian Growth Before and After the Crisis'. *IMF Staff Papers* 46(2): 139–66.

Crockett, A. 2000*a*. 'In Search of Anchors for Financial and Monetary Stability'. Speech delivered at the SUERF Colloquium, Vienna, April.

—— 2000*b*. 'Marrying the Micro- and Macroprudential Dimensions of Financial Stability'. BIS Speeches, 21 September.

—— 2008. 'Market Liquidity and Financial Stability'. *Financial Stability Review* 11: 13–17.

Daily Telegraph. 2008. 'The Queen Asks Why No One Saw the Credit Crunch Coming', 5 November.

—— 2010*a*. 'A Prime Minister Who Knows Something about the Economy?', 9 April.

—— 2010*b*. 'Tony Blair: My Deep Misgivings about Gordon Brown', 31 August.

—— 2010*c*. 'Angela Merkel Consigns Ireland, Portugal and Spain to their Fate', 31 October.

Danielsson, J. 2002. 'The Emperor Has No Clothes: Limits to Risk Modelling'. *Journal of Banking and Finance* 26(7): 1273–96.

—— P. Ermbrechts, C. Goodhart, C. Keating, F. Muenich, O. Renault, and H. S. Shin. 2001. 'An Academic Response to Basel II'. LSE Financial Markets Group Special Report, No. 130. London School of Economics, London.

—— and H. S. Shin. 2003. 'Endogenous Risk'. In *Modern Risk Management—A History*. London: Risk Books.

Davidoff, S. M. and D. T. Zaring. 2008. 'Regulation by Deal: The Government's Response to the Financial Crisis'. Working Paper, 24 November.

De Grauwe, P. 2011. 'The Governance of a Fragile Eurozone'. Mimeo.

de Larosière, J., L. Balcerowicz, O. Issing, R. Masera, C. McCarthy, L. Nyberg, J. Pérez, and O. Ruding. 2009. 'The High-level Group on Financial Supervision in the EU' (the de Larosière Report). European Union report, February.

DeLong, G. L. 2001. 'Stockholder Gains from Focusing Versus Diversifying Bank Mergers'. *Journal of Financial Economics* 59: 221–52.

DeLong, J. B., A. Shleifer, L. H. Summers, and R. J. Waldmann. 1990. 'Noise Trader Risk in Financial Markets'. *Journal of Political Economy* 98: 703–38.

Demyanyk, Y. and O. Van Hemert. 2008. 'Understanding the Subprime Mortgage Crisis'. Federal Reserve Bank of St. Louis Supervisory Policy Analysis Working Papers 2007–05.

Dewatripont, M. and J. Tirole. 1994. *The Prudential Regulation of Banks*. Cambridge, MA: MIT Press.

Diamond, D. W. and P. H. Dybvig. 1983. 'Bank Runs, Deposit Insurance, and Liquidity'. *Journal of Political Economy* 91(3): 401–19.

—— and R. G. Rajan. 2009. 'Fear of Fire Sales and the Credit Freeze'. University of Chicago Booth School of Business mimeo.

Dickens, C. 1849. *David Copperfield*.

Dodgson, C. L. (Lewis Carroll). 1865. *Alice's Adventures in Wonderland*.

Drees, B. and C. Pazarbasioglu. 1995. 'The Nordic Banking Crises: Pitfalls in Financial Liberalization?' Working Paper 95/61, International Monetary Fund, Washington, DC.

Duca, J., J. Muellbauer, and A. Murphy. 2010. 'Housing Markets and the Financial Crisis of 2007–2009: Lessons for the Future'. *Journal of Financial Stability* 6(4): 203–17.

Duffie, D. 2008. 'Innovations in Credit Risk Transfer: Implications for Financial Stability'. BIS Working Paper 255.

The Economist. 2004. 'The Dragon and the Eagle', 2 October.

The Economist. 2005. 'In Come the Waves', 16 June.

——— 2009*a*. 'Scapegoat Millionaire', 5 March.

——— 2009*b*. 'Three Trillion Dollars Later . . .', 14 May.

——— 2009*c*. Economics Focus: 'The Lessons of 1937', 18 June.

——— 2009*d*. 'Heads I Win, Tails You Lose', 20 October.

Eggertsson, G. and W. Woodford. 2003. 'The Zero Bound on Interest-Rates and Optimal Monetary Policy'. *Brookings Papers on Economic Activity* 2003(1): 139–211.

Eichengreen, B. 2009. 'The Irresistible Rise of the Renminbi'. Project Syndicate, 23 November.

——— 2011. *Exorbitant Privilege: The Rise and Fall of the Dollar and the Future of the International Monetary System.* New York: Oxford University Press.

——— and K. H. O'Rourke. 2010. 'What do the New Data Tell Us?' *Vox*, 8 March.

——— D. Park, and K. Shin. 2011 'When Fast Growing Economies Slow Down: International Evidence and Implications for China'. NBER Working Paper 16919.

Ellis, L. 2008. 'The Housing Meltdown: Why Did It Happen in the United States?' BIS Working Paper 259.

Englund, P. and V. Vihriälä. 2006. 'Financial Crisis in Developed Economies: The Cases of Finland and Sweden'. Chapter 3 in L. Jonung (ed.), *Crises, Macroeconomic Performance and Economic Policies in Finland and Sweden in the 1990s: A Comparative Approach.*

Eurocurrency Standing Committee. 2006. 'Recent Innovations in International Banking' (The Cross Report).

European Central Bank. 2009. 'Housing Wealth and Private Consumption in the Euro Area'. *ECB Monthly Bulletin*, January: 59–71.

Evans, O., Alfredo M. Leone, M. Gill, and P. Hilbers. 2000. 'Macroprudential Indicators of Financial System Soundness'. IMF Occasional Paper 192, April.

Fahlenbrach, R. and R. M. Stulz. 2010. 'Bank CEO Incentives and the Credit Crisis'. *Journal of Financial Economics* 99(1): 11–26.

Farlow, A. W. K. 2003. 'Is the US Heading for a Fiscal Crisis', November.

——— 2004*a*. 'UK House Prices: A Critical Assessment', January.

——— 2004*b*. 'The UK Housing Market: Bubbles and Buyers', January.

——— 2005. 'UK House Prices, Consumption and GDP in a Global Context'.

Federal Deposit Insurance Corporation. 2006. 'Quarterly Banking Profile: Second Quarter 2006', June.

Financial Crisis Inquiry Commission. 2008. Congressional hearing, 23 September.

——— 2010. 'Chronology of Selected Events Related to Lehman Brothers and the Possibility of Government Assistance'.

——— 2011. 'Final Report', January.

Financial Services Authority.2009a. 'The Turner Review: A Regulatory Response to the Global Banking Crisis', March.

────── 2009b. 'Strengthening Liquidity Standards—Including Feedback on CP08/22, CP09/13, CP09/14'. Policy Statement, 16 September.

────── 2011. 'The Failure of the Royal Bank of Scotland'. December.

Financial Times. 1998. 'Man of the Year Alan Greenspan: Guardian Angel of the Financial Markets', 24 December.

────── 2004. 'A Housing Collapse Draws Nearer', 16 April.

────── 2007a. 'Citigroup Chief Stays Bullish on Buy-Outs', 9 July.

────── 2007b. 'Goldman Pays the Price of Being Big', 13 August.

────── 2008. 'Wall St Banks Seek to Ring-Fence Bad Assets', 2 April.

────── 2009a. 'Greenspan Backs Bank Nationalisation', 18 February.

────── 2009b. 'A Boom Based on Little More than a Bezzle', 6 May.

────── 2009c. 'Merkel Mauls Central Banks', 2 June.

────── 2010a. 'Wen Warns against Renminbi Pressure', 6 October.

────── 2010b. 'Healthy Banking System Is the Goal, Not Profitable Banks'. Letters, 9 November.

────── 2011a. 'Tensions Rise in Currency Wars', 9 January.

────── 2011b. INSIGHT column, 13 January.

────── 2011c. 'Merkel Warned on Greek Bail-Out Standoff', 14 July.

────── 2011d. 'Strained Debate Tests Boehner's Ability to Cut Historic Deal', 15 July.

────── 2011e. 'Regulatory Reform: A Disappearing Act', 20 July.

────── 2011f. 'Ireland's Unexpected Economic Comeback', 16 August.

Fitch, 2011. 'Fitch Comments on UK Autumn Statement', 29 November.

Fisher, I. 1933. 'The Debt-Deflation Theory of Great Depressions'. Econometrica 1(4): 337–57.

Fitzgerald, A. and C. Harper. 2009. 'Lehman Monday Morning Lesson Lost With Obama Regulator-in-Chief'. Bloomberg Special Report, 10 September.

Fleckenstein, B. 2005. 'Contrarian Chronicles: Lessons from Japan's bubble—for ours'. Moneycentral.com. 9 May.

Foote, C., K. Gerardi, L. Goette, and P. S. Willen. 2008. 'Just the Facts: An Initial Analysis of Subprime's Role in the Housing Crisis'. Journal of Housing Economics 17(4): 291–305.

────── ────── ────── ────── 2009. 'Reducing Foreclosures: No Easy Answers'. NBER Working Paper 15063.

────── ────── and P. S. Willen. 2008. 'Negative Equity and Foreclosure: Theory and Evidence'. Journal of Urban Economics 6(2): 234–45.

Fortune. 2007. 'America's Most Admired Companies 2007.'

Freidman, M. and A. J. Schwartz. 1963. A Monetary History of the United States, 1867–1960. Princeton, NJ: Princeton University Press.

Freixas, X. and A. Santomero. 2004. 'Regulation of Financial Intermediaries: A Discussion'. In S. Bhattacharya, A. Boot, and A. Thakor (eds.) Credit, Intermediation, and the Macroeconomy: Models and Perspectives. Oxford and New York: Oxford University Press.

Fuhrer, J. C. and B. F. Madigan. 1997. 'Monetary Policy When Interest Rates Are Bounded at Zero'. *The Review of Economics and Statistics* 79(November): 573–85.

Furceri, D. and D. Mourougane. 2009. 'The Effect of Financial Crises on Potential Output: New Empirical Evidence from OECD Countries'. OECD, Economics Department Working Papers, No. 699. May.

Furlong, F. T. and M. C. Keeley. 1989. 'Capital Regulation and Bank Risk-taking: A Note'. *Journal of Banking and Finance* 13: 883–91.

Galbraith, J. K. 1954. *The Great Crash 1929*. New York: Penguin Business.

Gale, D. and X. Vives. 2002. 'Dollarization, Bailouts, and the Stability of the Banking System'. *Quarterly Journal of Economics* 117(2): 467–502.

Geithner, T. 2009a. Testimony to House Ways and Means Committee, 3 March.

——— 2009b. Written Testimony to House Financial Services Committee Hearing, 26 March.

Gennotte, G. and D. Pyle. 1991. 'Capital Controls and Bank Risk'. *Journal of Banking and Finance* 15: 805–24.

Gerardi, K., A. Lehnert, S. Sherlund, and P. Willen. 2008. 'Making Sense of the Subprime Crisis'. *Brooking Papers on Economic Activity* (Fall): 69–145.

——— A. Shapiro, and P. Willen. 2007. 'Subprime Outcomes: Risky Mortgages, Home-ownership Experiences, and Foreclosures'. Federal Reserve Bank of Boston Working Paper 07-15.

Goodhart, C. A. E. 2009. 'Procyclicality and Financial Regulation'. *Banco de España, Estabilidad Financiera* 16: 9–20.

——— and B. Hofmann. 2007. *House Prices and the Macroeconomy: Implications for Banking and Price Stability*. Oxford: Oxford University Press.

——— ——— 2008. 'House Prices, Money, Credit, and the Macroeconomy'. *Oxford Review of Economic Policy* 24(1): 180–205.

——— ——— and M. Segovino. 2004. 'Bank Regulation and Macroeconomic Fluctuations'. *Oxford Review of Economic Policy* 20(4): 1–25.

——— and D. Schoenmaker. 2006. 'Burden Sharing in a Banking Crisis in Europe'. *Sveriges Riksbank Economic Review* 2: 34–57.

——— ——— 2009. 'Fiscal Burden Sharing in Cross-Border Banking Crises'. *International Journal of Central Banking* 5(1): 141–65.

——— and M. Segovino. 2004. 'Basel and Procyclicality: A Comparison of the Standard-ised and IRB Approaches to an Improved Credit Risk Method'. Financial Markets Group Discussion Paper, No. 524. London School of Economics.

——— and A. Taylor. 2007. 'Procyclicality and Volatility in the Financial System: The Implementation of Basel II and IAS 39W'. In S. Gerlach and P. Gruenwald (eds.) *Procyclicality of Financial Systems in Asia*. London: Palgrave Macmillan.

Gorton, G. B. 2008. 'The Panic of 2007'. NBER Working Paper 14358.

Greenspan, A. 1996. 'The Challenge of Central Banking in a Democratic Society'. Speech, American Enterprise Institute, 5 December.

——— 2002a. 'Opening Remarks, in Rethinking Stabilization Policy'. Symposium sponsored by the Federal Reserve Bank of Kansas City, Jackson Hole, WY.

——— 2002b. Speech on 'World Finance and Risk Management' at Lancaster House, London, 25 September.

—— 2005*a*. 'Risk Transfer and Financial Stability'. Remarks (via satellite) by Chairman Alan Greenspan to the Federal Reserve Bank of Chicago's Forty-first Annual Conference on Bank Structure, Chicago, IL, 5 May.

—— 2005*b*. Remarks (via satellite) by Chairman Alan Greenspan to the National Association for Business Economics Annual Meeting, Chicago, IL, 27 September.

—— 2007. *The Age of Turbulence: Adventures in a New World*. New York: Penguin Press.

—— 2008. Testimony to the House of Representatives, 23 October.

—— and J. Kennedy. 2008. 'Sources and Uses of Equity Extracted from Homes'. *Oxford Review of Economic Policy* 24(1): 120–44.

Gross, Bill. 2009. 'Andrew Mellon vs. Bailout Nation'. PIMCO Investment Outlook Podcast, 9 January.

Group of Thirty. 2009. 'Financial Reform: A Framework for Financial Stability' (the G30 Report'), chaired by Paul Volcker.

Guajardo, J., D. Leigh, and A. Pescatori. 2011. 'Expansionary Austerity: New International Evidence'. IMF Working Paper 11/158.

The Guardian. 2008. 'Economy at 60-year Low, Says Darling. And It Will Get Worse', 30 August.

—— 2009. 'Twenty-Five People at the Heart of the Meltdown . . . ' 26 January.

—— 2010. 'Gordon Brown Predicts a Decade of Decline for the West', 6 December.

Haldane, A. G. 2009*a*. 'Why Banks Failed the Stress Test'. Speech at the Marcus-Evans Conference on Stress-Testing, 13 February.

—— 2009*b*. 'Rethinking the Financial Network'. Bank of England speech, April.

—— 2010. 'Regulation or Prohibition: The $100bn Question'. *Journal of Regulation & Risk North Asia* 2010(March): 101–19.

Hall, R. E. and Susan Woodward. 2009. 'The Right Way to Create a Good Bank and a Bad Bank'. *Vox*, 24 February.

Hannoun, H. 2009. 'Long-Term Sustainability Versus Short-Term Stimulus: Is There a Trade-Off?' Speech at the 44th SEACEN Governors' Conference, Kuala Lumpur, 7 February.

Harrison J. M. and D. M. Kreps. 1978. 'Speculative Investor Behavior in a Stock Market with Heterogeneous Expectations'. *Quarterly Journal of Economics* 92: 323–36.

Hart, O. 1995. *Firms, Contracts, and Financial Structure: Clarendon Lectures in Economics*. Oxford: Oxford University Press.

—— and J. Moore. 1994. 'A Theory of Debt Based on the Inalienability of Human Capital'. *Quarterly Journal of Economics* 109(4): 841–79.

—— —— 1995. 'Debt and Seniority: An Analysis of the Role of Hard Claims in Constraining Management'. *American Economic Review* 85(3): 567–85.

—— —— 1998. 'Default and Renegotiation: A Dynamic Model of Debt'. *Quarterly Journal of Economics* 113(1): 1–41.

—— —— 1999 'Foundations of Incomplete Contracts'. *Review of Economic Studies* 66(1): 115–38.

—— —— 2007. 'Incomplete Contracts and Ownership: Some New Thoughts'. *American Economic Review* 97(2): 182–6.

Haugh, D., P. Ollivaud, and D. Turner. 2009. 'The Macroeconomic Consequences of Banking Crises in OECD Countries'. OECD, Economics Department Working Papers 683.

Hawking, S. 1988. *A Brief History of Time*. Bantom Books.

Hayashi, F. and E. C. Prescott. 2002. 'The 1990s in Japan: A Lost Decade'. *Review of Economic Dynamics* 5(1): 206–35.

Heiskanen, R. 1993. 'The Banking Crisis in the Nordic Countries'. *Kansallis Economic Review* 2: 13–19.

Herring, R. and A. Santomero. 2000. 'What is Optimal Financial Regulation?' In B. Gup (ed.) *The New Financial Architecture, Banking Regulation in the 21st Century*. Westport, CT: Quorum Books.

Himmelberg, C., C. Mayer, and T. Sinai. 2005. 'Assessing High House Prices: Bubbles, Fundamentals and Misperceptions' *Journal of Economic Perspectives* 19(4): 67–92.

Hirsh, M. 2009. 'The Reeducation of Larry Summers'. *Newsweek Magazine*, 20 February.

HM Treasury. 2005. 'Chancellor Launches Better Regulation Action Plan'. Press release, 24 May.

—— 2007. Speech by the Chancellor of the Exchequer, the Rt Hon Gordon Brown MP, Mansion House, 20 June.

—— 2008*a*. 'The Run on the Rock'. Treasury Committee report, January.

—— 2008*b*. Statement by the Chancellor on Financial Stability, 8 October.

—— 2009*a*. 'A Review of Corporate Governance in UK Banks and Other Financial Industry Entities: Final Recommendations' (The Walker Review).

—— 2009*b*. 'Reforming Financial Markets'. Banking White Paper.

—— Financial Services Authority, and the Bank of England. 2008. 'Financial Stability and Depositor Protection: Strengthening the Framework'. Consultation document.

Hoggarth, G., R. Ries, and V. Saporta. 2002. 'Costs of Banking System Instability: Some Empirical Evidence'. *Journal of Banking and Finance* 26: 825–55.

Holmstrom, B. and J. Tirole. 1997. 'Financial Intermediation, Loanable Funds and the Real Sector'. *Quarterly Journal of Economics* 112(3): 663–91.

—— —— 1998. 'Private and Public Supply of Liquidity'. *Journal of Political Economy* 106(1): 1–40.

Honohan, P. 2008. 'Discussion of *Financial Innovation and European Housing and Mortgage Markets*, by David Miles and Vladimir Pillonca'. *Oxford Review of Economic Policy* 24(1): 176–9.

—— and L. Laeven. 2005. *'Systemic Financial Crises: Containment and Resolution*. Cambridge: Cambridge University Press.

Hoover, H. 1952. *Memoirs*. London: Hollis and Carter.

Hoshi, T. and A. K. Kashyap. 2008. 'Will the US Bank Recapitalization Be a Success? Eight Lessons from Japan'. NBER Working Paper 14401.

House Financial Services Committee. 2009. Geithner's 'Testimony on Financial Regulatory Reform' to House Financial Services Committee, 23 September.

Hunt, J. 2009. 'What Do Subprime Securitization Contracts Actually Say about Loan Modification?' Working Paper, Berkeley Center for Law, Business and the Economy.

Iacovone, L. and V. Zavacka. 2009. 'Banking Crises and Exports: Lessons from the Past for the Recent Trade Collapse'. In R. Baldwin (ed.) *The Great Trade Collapse: Causes, Consequences and Prospects. Vox.*

Independent Commission on Banking. 2011. 'Final Report: Recommendations'.

International Monetary Fund. 2001. 'Global Financial Stability Report', March.

—— 2002. 'Global Financial Stability Report', March.

—— 2006. 'Global Financial Stability Report', April.

—— 2008. 'Global Financial Stability Report', April.

—— 2009a. 'World Economic Outlook'.

—— 2009b. 'Global Financial Stability Report', April.

—— 2009c. 'Global Financial Stability Report', October.

—— 2010a. 'Strategies for Fiscal Consolidation in the Post-Crisis World'. February.

—— 2010b. 'Global Financial Stability Report', April.

—— 2011. 'World Economic Outlook'.

—— 2012. 'World Economic Outlook'.

Jaffee, D. et al. 2009. 'Mortgage Origination and Securitization in the Financial Crisis'. In V. Acharya and M. Richardson (eds.) *Restoring Financial Stability: How to Repair a Failed System*. New York: John Wiley & Sons.

John F. Kennedy Presidential Library and Museum. 2009. '2009 Profile in Courage Award Recipients Announced'. News release, 25 March.

Joint Centre for Housing Studies at Harvard University. 2006. 'The State of the Nation's Housing'. Report.

Judson, H. F. 1979. *The Eighth Day of Creation*. New York: Simon & Schuster.

Kaminsky, G. L. and C. M. Reinhart. 1999. 'The Twin Crises: The Causes of Banking and Balance of Payments Problems'. *American Economic Review* 89: 473–500.

Kane, E. J. 2000. 'Incentives for Banking Megamergers: What Motives Might Regulators Infer from Event-Study Evidence?' *Journal of Money, Credit, and Banking* 32(2): 671–701.

Kashyap, A. K., R. G. Raghuram, and J. C. Stein. 2008. 'Rethinking Capital Regulation', Paper presented to symposium 'Maintaining Stability in a Changing Financial System'. Jackson Hole, WY, 21–3 August.

Keynes, J. M. 1930. *A Treatise on Money*. London: Macmillan (2 volumes).

—— 1931. 'The Consequences to the Banks of the Collapse of Money Values'. In *Essays in Persuasion*. London: Macmillan.

Kiff, J. and P. Mills. 2007. 'Money for Nothing and Checks for Free: Recent Developments in U.S. Subprime Mortgage Markets'. IMF Working Paper 07/188.

Kim, C-J. and C. Nelson. 1999. 'Has the U.S. Economy Become More Stable? A Bayesian Approach Based on a Markov-Switching Model of the Business Cycle'. *Review of Economics and Statistics* 81: 608–16.

Kim, D. and A. M. Santomero. 1988. 'Risk in Banking and Capital Regulation'. *The Journal of Finance* 43(5): 1219–33.

King, M. 2008. Speech to the CBI, Institute of Directors, Leeds Chamber of Commerce and Yorkshire Forward, Leeds, October.

—— 2009a. 'Finance: A Return from Risk'. Speech to the Worshipful Company of International Bankers at the Mansion House, 17 March.

King, M. 2009*b*. House of Commons, Minutes of Evidence, Treasury Committee, Regarding November 2009 Inflation Report, 24 November.

—— 2010. Speech to the UK's Trades Union Congress, Manchester, UK, 15 September.

Kiyotaki, N. and J. Moore. 1997. 'Credit Cycles'. *Journal of Political Economy* 105(2): 211–48.

Klemperer, P. 2004. *Auctions: Theory and Practice*. Princeton, NJ: Princeton University Press.

Knight, M. 2006. 'Marrying the Micro and Macroprudential Dimensions of Financial Stability: Six Years On'. Speech delivered at the 14th International Conference of Banking Supervisors, BIS Speeches, October.

Kohn, D. L. 2009. 'Monetary Policy and Asset Prices Revisited'. *Cato Journal* 29(1): 31–44.

Kotlikoff, L. 2010. *Jimmy Stewart is Dead: Ending the World's Ongoing Financial Plague with Limited Purpose Banking*. London and New York: John Wiley and Sons.

—— P. Mehrling, and A. Milne. 2008. 'Recapitalising the Banks Is Not Enough'. *Financial Times*, 26 October.

Krugman, P. 1994. 'Competitiveness: A Dangerous Obsession'. *Foreign Affairs* 73(2): 28–44.

—— 2009. 'The Market Mystique'. *New York Times*, 26 March.

—— and R. Wells. 2010. 'The Way Out of the Slump'. *The New York Review of Books*, 14 October.

Kuttner, R. 2009. 'Slouching Towards Solvency'. *American Prospect*, 23 March.

Laeven, L. and R. Levine. 2007. 'Is There a Diversification Discount in Financial Conglomerates?' *Journal of Financial Economics* 85(2): 331–67.

—— and F. Valencia. 2008. 'Systemic Banking Crises: A New Database'. IMF, Working Paper 08/224.

—— —— 2010. 'Resolution of Banking Crises: The Good, the Bad, and the Ugly'. IMF Working Paper, 10/146.

Lawrence, J. S. 1929. *Wall Street and Washington*. Princeton, NJ: Princeton University Press.

Leamer, E. 2007*a*. 'Housing and the Business Cycle'. Paper presented at symposium 'Housing, Housing Finance, and Monetary Policy', Jackson Hole, WY, 30 August–1 September.

—— 2007*b*. 'Housing Is the Business Cycle'. NBER Working Paper 13428.

Lehman Brothers. 2007. Annual Report.

Leonnig, C. 2008. 'How HUD Mortgage Policy Fed the Crisis'. *Washington Post*, 10 June.

Lowenstein, R. 2000. *When Genius Failed: The Rise and Fall of Long-Term Capital Management'*. New York: Random House.

Magud, N., C. M. Reinhart, and K. Rogoff. 2011. 'Capital Controls: Myth and Reality—A Portfolio Balance Approach'. NBER Working Paper 16805.

Mandelbrot, B. B. and R. L. Hudson. 2004. *The (Mis)behaviour of Markets: A Fractal View of Risk, Ruin and Reward*. New York: Basic Books.

Mayer, C. and K. Pence. 2008. 'Subprime Mortgages: What, Where, and to Whom?' Finance and Economics Discussion Series, Federal Reserve Board, Washington, DC.

—————— and S. M. Sherlund. 2009. 'The Rise in Mortgage Defaults'. *Journal of Economic Perspectives* 23(Winter): 27–50.

Mayes, D., R. Pringle, and M. Taylor. (eds.). 2009. *Towards a New Framework for Financial Stability*. London: Central Banking Publications.

McConnell, M. and G. Perez-Quiros. 2000. 'Output Fluctuations in the United States: What Has Changed since the Early 1980s?' *American Economic Review* 90: 1464–76.

McKinsey and Company. 2007. 'Sustaining New York's and the US' Global Financial Services Leadership'. Report commissioned by Mayor Michael R. Bloomberg and Charles E. Schumer.

McKinsey Global Institute. 2010a. 'Debt and Deleveraging: The Global Credit Bubble and Its Economic Consequences'.

McKinsey Global Institute. 2010b. 'From Austerity to Prosperity: Seven Priorities for the Long Term in the United Kingdom'.

Meckling, W. H. and M. C. Jensen. 1976. 'Theory of the Firm: Managerial Behavior, Agency Costs and Ownership Structure'. *Journal of Financial Economics* 3(4): 305–60.

Meeker, M. 2011. 'USA Inc.: A Basic Summary of America's Financial Statements'.

Mehra, R. and E. C. Prescott. 1985. 'The Equity Premium: A Puzzle'. *Journal of Monetary Economics* 15: 145–61.

Mian, Atif R. and Amir Sufi. 2009. 'The Consequences of Mortgage Credit Expansion: Evidence from the U.S. Mortgage Default Crisis'. *Quarterly Journal of Economics* 124(4): 1449–96.

Miles D. and V. Pillonca. 2008. 'Financial Innovation and European Housing and Mortgage Markets'. *Oxford Review of Economic Policy* 24(1): 145–75.

Miller, M. H. 1988. 'The Modigliani-Miller Propositions after Thirty Years'. *Journal of Economic Perspectives* 2(4): 99–120.

—————— and J. Stiglitz. 2009. 'Leverage and Asset Price Bubbles: Averting Armageddon with Chapter 11?' Working Paper, University of Warwick.

Milne, A. and G. Wood. 2009. 'Shattered on the Rock? British Financial Stability from 1866 to 2007'. *Journal of Banking Regulation* 10: 89–127.

Minsky, H. 1986. *Stabilizing an Unstable Economy*. New York: McGraw-Hill.

Mishkin, F. S. with T. Herbertson. 2006. 'Financial Stability in Iceland'. Icelandic Chamber of Commerce.

—————— 2007a. *Monetary Policy Strategy*. Cambridge, MA and London: MIT Press.

—————— 2007b. 'Housing and the Monetary Transmission Mechanism'. Paper presented at the symposium 'Housing, Housing Finance, and Monetary Policy', Jackson Hole, WY, 30 August–1 September.

Modigliani, F. and M. H. Miller. 1958. 'The Cost of Capital, Corporation Finance and the Theory of Investment'. *American Economic Review* 48(3): 261–97.

Moody's Investor Service. 2008. 'Measuring Deviation and Stressing Prices', 24 July.

—————— 2009. 'Calibrating Bank Ratings in the Context of the Global Financial Crisis'. February.

Morris, S. and H. S. Shin. 2006. 'Catalytic Finance: When Does It Work?' *Journal of International Economics* 70(1): 161–77.

Morris, S. and H. S. Shin. 1999. 'A Theory of the Onset of Currency Attacks'. In Agenor, P-R, M. Miller, D. Vines and A. Weber (eds) *Asian Financial Crisis: Causes, Contagion and Consequences*. Cambridge University Press.

Muellbauer J. 2007. 'Housing, Credit and Consumer Expenditure'. Paper presented at the symposium 'Housing, Housing Finance, and Monetary Policy', Jackson Hole, WY, 30 August–1 September.

—— and N. Blake. 2009. 'Imbalances in EU Housing Markets'. *Economic Outlook* 33(4): 19–25.

—— and K. Murata. 2008. 'Consumption, Land Prices and the Monetary Transmission Mechanism in Japan'. Paper presented at ESRI and the Center on Japanese Economy and Business at Columbia Business School workshop on 'Japan's Bubble, Deflation and Long-Term Stagnation', 21 March.

—— and A. Murphy. 2008. 'Housing Markets and the Economy: The Assessment'. *Oxford Review of Eonomic Policy* 24(1): 1–33.

Myers, S. 1977. 'Determinants of Corporate Borrowing'. *Journal of Financial Economics* 5: 147–75.

New York Times. 1999. 'Congress Passes Wide Ranging Law Repealing Bank Laws', 5 November.

—— 2003. 'New Agency Proposed to Oversee Freddie Mac and Fannie Mae', 11 September.

—— 2008. 'Greenspan Concedes Error on Regulation', 23 October.

—— 2009*a*. 'Rubin Leaving Citigroup; Smith Barney for Sale', 9 January.

—— 2009*b*. 'Obama's Statement on AIG', 16 March.

—— 2009*c*. 'US Expands Plan to Buy Banks' Troubled Assets', 23 March.

—— 2009*d*. 'White House Pares Its Financial Reform Plan', 23 September.

Newsweek. 2008. 'Depression Economics', 2 December.

The Observer. 2009. 'This Is How We Let the Credit Crunch Happen, Ma'am', 26 July.

Obstfeld, M. 2005. 'America's Deficit, the World's Problem'. *Monetary and Economic Studies (Bank of Japan)* 23(October): 25–35.

—— and K. Rogoff. 2001. 'Perspectives on OECD Capital Market Integration: Implications for U.S. Current Account Adjustment'. In *Global Economic Integration: Opportunities and Challenges*. Kansas City, MO: Federal Reserve Bank of Kansas City.

—— —— 2005. 'Global Current Account Imbalances and Exchange Rate Adjustments'. *Brookings Papers on Economic Activity* 2005(1): 67–146.

—— —— 2007. 'The Unsustainable U.S. Current Account Position Revisited'. In Richard H. Clarida (ed.) *G7 Current Account Imbalances: Sustainability and Adjustment*. Chicago: University of Chicago Press.

OECD. 2010. 'Economic Outlook', May.

—— 2011*a*. OECD Tax Database.

—— 2011*b*. 'Divided We Stand: Why Inequality Keeps Rising'.

Office for Budget Responsibility. 2010. 'Economic and fiscal outlook-November 2010'.

Ostry, J. D., A. R. Ghosh, K. F. Habermeier, M. Chamon, M. S. Qureshi, and D. B. S. Reinhardt. 2010. 'Capital Inflows: The Role of Controls'. IMF Staff Position Note, IMF Research Department.

Persaud, A. 2010. 'The Empire Strikes Back' *Vox*, 14 September.

Peterson Institute for International Economics. 2011. 'Europe on the Brink', July.

Posner, R. A. 2009. *A Failure of Capitalism: The Crisis of '08 and the Descent Into Depression*. Cambridge, MA: Harvard University Press.

Pozsar, Z., T. Adrian, A. Ashcraft, and H. Boesky. 2010. 'Shadow Banking'. Federal Reserve Bank of New York Staff Report, no. 458 (Revised February 2012).

Prospect. 2009. 'How to Tame Global Finance', 27 August.

Rajan, R. G. 2005. 'Has Financial Development Made the World Riskier?' Paper presented to symposium 'The Greenspan Era: Lessons For The Future'. Jackson Hole, WY, 25–7 August.

—— 2006. 'Monetary Policy and Incentives'. Remarks at the Bank of Spain conference 'Central Banks in the 21st Century', Madrid, 8 June.

Reifschneider, D. and J. C. Williams. 2000. 'Three Lessons for Monetary Policy in a Low-Inflation Era'. *Journal of Money, Credit and Banking* 32(November): 936–66.

Reinhart, C. M. and V. R. Reinhart. 2010. 'After the Fall'. NBER Working Paper 16334.

—— and K. S. Rogoff. 2008. 'Is the 2007 U.S. Sub-Prime Financial Crisis So Different? An International Historical Comparison'. NBER Working Paper 13761.

—— —— 2009a. *This Time Is Different: Eight Centuries of Financial Folly*. Princeton, NJ: Princeton University Press.

—— —— 2009b. 'The Aftermath of Financial Crises'. *American Economic Review* 99(2): 466–72.

Reinold, K. 2011. 'Housing Equity Withdrawal since the Financial Crisis'. *Bank of England Quarterly Bulletin* 51(2): 127–33.

Reuters. 2008. 'UPDATE 1-Payment on Lehman CDS Only Around $5.2 bn –DTCC', 22 October.

—— 2010. 'Obama Asks Wen for More Action on Yuan', 23 September.

—— 2011. 'Comprehensive Euro Zone Deal "Beyond Reach"—Fitch', 15 December.

Rochet, J. C. 1992. 'Capital Requirements and the Behavior of Commercial Banks'. *European Economic Review* 36: 1137–78.

Rodrik, D. 2008. 'The Real Exchange Rates and Economic Growth'. *Brookings Papers on Economic Activity* 2008: 365–412.

Romer, C. 2009. 'Lessons from the Great Depression for Economic Recovery in 2009'. Presented at the Brookings Institution, Washington, DC, 9 March.

Roubini, N. 2010. 'The Eurozone's Autumn Hangover'. Project Syndicate, 15 September.

—— and B. Setser. 2004. *Bailouts or Bail-Ins? Responding to Financial Crisis in Emerging Economies*. Washington, DC: Institute for International Economics.

Russell, G. W. E. 1898. *Collections and Recollections*, Chapter 30.

Santos, J. 2001. 'Bank Capital Regulation in Contemporary Banking Theory: A Review of the Literature'. *Financial Markets, Institutions and Instruments* 14: 289–328.

Saunders, A. 1996. *Financial Institutions Management: A Modern Perspective*. Burr Ridge, IL: Irwin Professional Publishing.

Schmid, M. M. and I. Walter. 2009. 'Do Financial Conglomerates Create or Destroy Economic Value?' *Journal of Financial Intermediation* 18(2): 193–216.

Schmitt, R. B. 2009. 'The Born Prophecy'. *American Bar Association Journal*, 1 May.

Schneider, H. 2010. 'Geithner Urges Swift "Global Agreement" on Financial Reforms to Support Recovery'. *Washington Post*, 3 June.

Schumpeter, J. A. 1942. *Capitalism, Socialism and Democracy*, New York: Harper and Brothers. 5th ed. London: George Allen and Unwin, 1976.

Sherlund, S. 2008. 'The Past, Present, and Future of Subprime Mortgages'. Federal Reserve Board, Finance and Economics Discussion Series 2008-63.

Shiller, R. J. 1993. *Macro Markets: Creating Institutions for Managing Society's Largest Economic Risks*. Oxford and New York: Oxford University Press.

—— 2000. *Irrational Exuberance*. Princeton University Press.

—— 2009. 'Unlearned Lessons from the Housing Bubble'. *The Economists' Voice* 6(7), Article 6.

Shin, H. S. 2009*a*. 'Reflections on Northern Rock: The Bank Run that Heralded the Global Financial Crisis'. *Journal of Economic Perspectives* 23: 101–19.

—— 2009*b*. 'Securitisation and Financial Stability'. *Economic Journal* 119(536): 309–32.

Shull, B. and G. A. Hanweck. 2002. 'Bank Merger Policy: Proposals for Change'. *Banking Law Journal*, March.

Slacalek, J. 2006. 'What Drives Personal Consumption? The Role of Housing and Financial Wealth'. DIW Berlin: German Institute for Economic Research, mimeo.

Solow, R. 2008. 'The State of Macroeconomics'. *Journal of Economic Perspectives* 22(1): 243–9.

Soros, G. 1988. *The Alchemy of Finance*. New York: Simon & Schuster.

Spiegel Online. 2011. 'Fateful Day for Europe: Four Ideas to Save the Common Currency', 7 December.

Standard & Poor's. 2008. 'Risk of Negative Equity for U.K. Mortgage Borrowers Returns', July.

—— 2011. 'United States of America "AAA/A-1 +" Ratings Placed on CreditWatch Negative on Rising Risk of Policy Stalemate', 14 July.

—— 2012. "Standard & Poor's Takes Various Rating Actions On 16 Eurozone Sovereign Governments', 13 January.

Stiglitz, J. E. 2006. 'The High Cost of the Iraq War'. *The Economists' Voice* 3(3).

—— 2009. 'America's Socialism for the Rich'. *The Economists' Voice* 6(5).

—— and A. Weiss. 1981. 'Credit Rationing in Markets with Imperfect Information'. *American Economic Review* 71(3): 393–410.

Stijn, C. M., A. Kose, and M. E. Terrones. 2008. 'What Happens During Recessions, Crunches and Busts?' Paper presented at the 9th Jacques Polak Annual Research Conference Hosted by the International Monetary Fund, Washington, DC, 13–14 November.

Stiroh, K. and A. Rumble. 2006. 'The Dark Side of Diversification: The Case of US Financial Holding Companies'. *Journal of Banking and Finance* 80: 2131–61.

Summers, L. 2009. Brookings Institution, speaking on the Economic Crisis and Recovery, 13 March.

Sunday Times. 2009. 'Take Control or Step Aside, Mr Cowen', 18 January.

Swagel, P. 2009. 'The Financial Crisis: An Inside View'. *Brookings Papers on Economic Activity* 2009: 1–63.

Taleb, N. N. 2007. *The Black Swan: the Impact of the Highly Improbable*. London: Allen Lane.

Taylor, J. B. 2008. 'The Financial Crisis and the Policy Responses: An Empirical Analysis of What Went Wrong'. NBER Working Paper 14631.

The Times. 2009. 'Banks in Wrangle over Share of Risk for Taxpayers', 25 February.

Tobias, A. and H. S. Shin. 2009. 'Liquidity and Leverage'. FRB of New York Staff Report 328.

Tucker, P. 2009. 'Regimes for Handling Bank Failures: Redrawing the Banking Social Contract'. Bank of England speech, 30 June.

Turner, A. 2009. Mansion House speech, 22 September.

University of Rochester. 2008. 'Resolution of Respect: Nelson George Hairston, Sr. 1917–2008', Obituary.

US Chamber of Commerce. 2007. 'Commission on the Regulation of U.S. Capital Markets in the 21st Century: Report and Recommendations'.

US Treasury. 2007. 'Treasury Senior Preferred Stock Purchase Agreement'. Department Office of Public Affairs, 7 September. Fact Sheet.

—— 2008a. '2008 Financial Report of the United States Government'.

—— 2008b. 'Blueprint for Modernized Financial Regulatory Structure', March.

—— 2008c. 'Statement by Secretary Henry M. Paulson, Jr on Capital Purchase Program', 20 October.

—— 2009a. 'Financial Regulatory Reform: A New Foundation: Rebuilding Financial Supervision and Regulation', June.

—— 2009b. 'Principles for Reforming the US and International Regulatory Capital Framework for Banking Firms', 3 September.

—— 2009c. 'Troubled Asset Relief Program Transactions Report for Period Ending 25 November'.

—— 2010. 'Monthly Statement of the Public Debt of the United States', 30 September.

—— 2011. 'Major Foreign Holders of Treasury Securities', November.

Veronesi, P. and L. Zingales. 2009. 'Paulson's Gift'. NBER Working Paper 15458.

Wall Street Journal. 2008. 'Blame Fannie Mae and Congress for the Credit Mess'. 23 September.

—— 2009a. 'Fed's Kohn Concedes Risk in AIG Rescue', 6 March.

—— 2009b. 'My Plan for Bad Bank Assets: The Private Sector Will Set Prices. Taxpayers Will Share in Any Upside'. 23 March.

—— 2010. 'Fed Economist: Housing Is a Lousy Investment', 5 January.

—— 2011a. 'UK Has No Inflation Problem, Former BOE Policy Maker Says', 16 February.

—— 2011b. 'Statement of Greek Finance Minister Evangelos Venizelos', 18 September.

Warwick Commission. 2009. 'The Warwick Commission on International Financial Reform: In Praise of Unlevel Playing Fields'.

Washington Examiner. 2011. 'Internal Memo: Romney Courting Kochs, Tea Party', 2 November.

Washington Post. 2004. 'Reagan Policies Gave Green Light to Red Ink', 9 June.

Weale M. 2007. 'Commentary: House Price Worries'. *National Institute Economic Review* 2007(April): 2–4.

White, E. N. 1997. 'Deposit Insurance'. In Gerard Caprio, Jr and Dimitri Vittas *Reforming Financial Systems: Historical Implications for Policy*. New York: Cambridge University Press.

White, W. 2006. 'Procyclicality in the Financial System: Do We Need a New Macro-financial Stabilisation Framework?'. BIS Working Papers 193.

White House. 2009. 'Remarks on Fiscal Responsibility and Pay-As-you-Go Legislation'. Speech given by President Obama in the East Room at the White House, 9 June.

White House Office of the Press Secretary. 2010. 'Remarks by the President on Financial Reform', 21 January.

Wilmarth, Jr, A. E. 2002. 'The Transformation of the U.S. Financial Services Industry, 1975–2000: Competition, Consolidation, and Increased Risks'. *University of Illinois Law Review* 2002(2): 215–476.

—— 2009. 'The Dark Side of Universal Banking: Financial Conglomerates and the Origins of the Subprime Lending Crisis'. *Connecticut Law Review* 41(3): 963–1050.

Wolf, M. 2010. 'Assets Matter Just as Much as Debt'. *Financial Times*, 26 November.

World Economic Forum. 2011. 'Global Risks Report', sixth edition.

—— 2012. 'Global Risks Report', seventh edition.

Yellen, J. 2009. 'The Mortgage Meltdown, Financial Markets, and the Economy'. *The B.E. Journal of Economic Analysis & Policy*, Berkeley Electronic Press, 9(3).

Yorulmazer, T. 2009. 'Lessons from the Resolution of the Swedish Crisis'. Federal Reserve Bank of New York mimeo.

Zingales, L. 2008. 'Why Paulson is Wrong'. *Vox*, 21 September.

—— 2011. 'Overall Impact of TARP on Financial Stability'. Oral testimony before the Congressional Oversight Panel, United States House of Representatives, 4 March.

INDEX